"Reading the Bible is a cross-cultural experience. *Grounded Theology in the Hebrew Bible* makes the ancient context accessible and understandable, helping students and adult learners understand what they are reading and why it matters. My own students will benefit from the book's clear organization and orientation to key aspects of culture on display in the Hebrew Bible. Backfish and Shafer-Elliott prove able guides to the ancient context and its implications for the Bible's message. Bravo!"

—**Carmen Joy Imes**, Talbot School of Theology

"*Grounded Theology in the Hebrew Bible* bridges the gap between cultural-historical context and theological reflection, showing how ancient Israel's everyday life shaped its theology—and how that theology can still shape modern faith. Backfish and Shafer-Elliott offer a work that is academically credible yet highly accessible. It is spiritually formative, blending thoughtful scholarship, engaging writing, and modern illustrations to bring the ancient world and its theological insights to life."

—**Roger S. Nam**, Emory University

"Reading the Old Testament can be confusing if we don't understand the various contexts in which the people in Israel lived, ate, married, worshiped, engaged in warfare, and viewed kingship, etc. This helpful volume by Dr. Elizabeth Backfish and Dr. Cynthia Shafer-Elliott examines how Israel's cultural contexts can enrich our understanding of Israel's theologies. The thoughtful trajectory of each chapter moves from an insightful archaeological discussion of Israel's cultural context to an exploration of how that understanding affects our theology of the Hebrew Bible. It is a valuable resource for those interested in a deeper understanding of the Old Testament."

—**May Young**, Taylor University

"Backfish and Shafer-Elliott offer readers a rare gift: the ability to see. They serve as interpretive optometrists, helping us to perceive how various aspects of Israel's cultural and material context illuminate the theology of the Hebrew Bible. From households and covenant to worship and warfare, they connect the ground to God. Prepare to look down and then to look up to discern the depths of divine accommodation through the interconnectedness of culture and theology."

—**Christopher Ansberry**, Grove City College

"Backfish and Shafer-Elliott bring their respective expertise in biblical theology and archaeology complemented by years of classroom teaching experience to this one-of-a-kind resource that, quite literally, 'grounds' theological inquiry in the Hebrew Bible. Cautioning against typical approaches that impose modern strictures on ancient texts, Backfish and Shafer-Elliott astutely derive their thematic categories from the cultural contexts of ancient Israel gleaned from archaeology and comparative explorations of ancient Near Eastern texts to engage relevant but oft-neglected topics including ancient conceptions of households, kingship, food, and hospitality, among others, in this eminently readable introduction that will serve students for years to come."

—**Jonathan S. Greer**, Grand Valley State University

GROUNDED THEOLOGY
IN THE HEBREW BIBLE

Exploring the Cultural Context
That Formed Ancient Israel

Elizabeth Backfish AND
Cynthia Shafer-Elliott

Baker Academic
a division of Baker Publishing Group
Grand Rapids, Michigan

© 2025 by Elizabeth Backfish and Cynthia Shafer-Elliott

Published by Baker Academic
a division of Baker Publishing Group
Grand Rapids, Michigan
BakerAcademic.com

Printed in the United States of America

All rights reserved. No part of this publication may be reproduced, stored in a retrieval system, or transmitted in any form or by any means—for example, electronic, photocopy, recording—without the prior written permission of the publisher. The only exception is brief quotations in printed reviews.

Library of Congress Cataloging-in-Publication Data
ISBN 9781540962539 (paper)
ISBN 9781540969538 (casebound)
ISBN 9781493451579 (ebook)
ISBN 9781493451586 (pdf)

Unless otherwise indicated, Scripture quotations are from the New Revised Standard Version of the Bible, copyright © 1989 National Council of the Churches of Christ in the United States of America. Used by permission. All rights reserved.

Scripture quotations labeled NIV are from the Holy Bible, New International Version®, NIV®. Copyright © 1973, 1978, 1984, 2011 by Biblica, Inc.® Used by permission of Zondervan. All rights reserved worldwide. www.zondervan.com. The "NIV" and "New International Version" are trademarks registered in the United States Patent and Trademark Office by Biblica, Inc.®

Baker Publishing Group publications use paper produced from sustainable forestry practices and postconsumer waste whenever possible.

25 26 27 28 29 30 31   7 6 5 4 3 2 1

For my parents, Dana and Steve Pruitt,
who have consistently shown me how to love God
with all my heart, mind, soul, and strength.
—EB

For my parents,
To my father, David Shafer, whose memory I carry
with every step forward—your wisdom, love,
and quiet strength continue to guide me.
And to my mother, Christine Shafer, whose unwavering support
and encouragement made this journey possible.

"Let your father and mother be glad;
let her who bore you rejoice."
(Prov. 23:25)

With deepest gratitude and love.
—CSE

CONTENTS

Acknowledgments ix
Introduction: *Planning the Dig* xiii

1. Households: *The Relationship of God* 1
2. Covenant: *The Loyalty of God* 23
3. Land: *The Presence of God* 49
4. Holiness and Purity: *The Sanctity of God* 71
5. Worship: *The Grace of God* 93
6. Images of God: *The Reflection of God in Humanity* 119
7. Kingship and Politics: *The Sovereignty of God* 137
8. Law and Wisdom: *The Guidance of God* 157
9. Warfare and Peace: *The Shalom of God* 179
10. Food, Feasting, and Hospitality: *The Generosity of God* 199

Conclusion: *Sifting the Data* 219
Bibliography 229
Scripture Index 251
Subject Index 257

ACKNOWLEDGMENTS

I (Elizabeth, or "Libby" as most people know me) have always loved the acknowledgment sections of books. They feel like a backstage tour and a diary entry wrapped into one concise (too concise!) summary of gratitude. My gratitude begins with my brilliant coauthor, Cynthia, who has been a mentor and friend, always ready to celebrate my triumphs, lament my struggles, and think through the hard issues with me.

We had the privilege of working with the best publishing team at Baker Academic, most notably Brandy Scritchfield, whose wise feedback and patience is unparalleled.

My colleagues at Jessup University have offered continued support and reminded me of the value of this project. In particular, my department dean, David Timms, has advocated for the resources and time needed to finish this project. The university library staff, particularly those who tracked down countless interlibrary loan resources for me, are some of my favorite heroes at the university.

I am also grateful for the students in my Theology of the Hebrew Bible class, who read through earlier versions of each chapter as ~~Guinea pigs~~ test readers. Two of my favorite New Testament scholars, Paul Owen and Max Botner, were kind enough to read several chapters of the manuscript, providing valuable feedback and encouragement. Our blind peer reviewers offered critiques and suggestions that have served to improve the final version of this book. Any remaining errors or faults are solely our own responsibility.

My pastors at Granite Springs Church—Kevin Adams, Matt Timms, and Kyu Hahn—have been huge encouragements to my work and my faith, offering a space for spiritual rest, worship, and formation. They are infinitely wise and as genuine as they come.

Two people who have offered the most enduring support are my parents, Steve and Dana Pruitt. They were my first and most influential theology teachers, modeling faithfulness in every aspect of their lives. There are not enough years in my life or breath in my lungs to adequately thank them.

My children, Dana and Drew, keep me on my toes, and more importantly keep me grounded in what matters most. Our dog, Watson, has overtaken my personal space with his persistent cuddles and attention, which has been exactly what I've needed in this stage of life. Finally, I am most grateful for my best friend and husband, Michael. He has loved me at my worst, and pushed me to be my best. He makes me laugh hard and think even harder. Loving him has been easy and joyous, and I hope to do it for the rest of my life.

—EB

The journey of writing this book has been one of collaboration, inspiration, and intellectual discovery. It is with gratitude that I (Cynthia) acknowledge the many individuals and institutions that have supported and contributed to this work.

This book would not exist without the creativity and insight of my coauthor, Libby, who first conceived the idea and whose collaboration has been both enriching and inspiring. Working together has been one of the most rewarding experiences of my academic career.

I would like to express my heartfelt thanks to Baker Academic for their support in bringing this book to life. A special thanks to our editor, Brandy Scritchfield, whose keen insights and meticulous attention to detail have greatly enhanced the final product. I am also deeply appreciative of the two anonymous peer reviewers, whose thoughtful feedback and constructive critiques have been invaluable in refining this work. While this book has benefited greatly from the insights and contributions of many, any errors or shortcomings are ours alone.

My academic path has been shaped by the profound influence of both past and present institutions. I am deeply thankful to Jessup University, where my career as a scholar first took root, and to Dr. David Timms, my chair during that time, whose guidance and encouragement were instrumental in my early development as a scholar.

At Baylor University, my current academic home, I have found a community that fosters rigorous scholarship and creative exploration. I am especially grateful to Dr. Doug Weaver, my chair, for his unwavering support and leadership. Baylor's commitment to excellence has provided the ideal environment in which to bring this project to fruition.

Acknowledgments

I would like to extend my sincere thanks to my colleagues at both Jessup University and Baylor University. Your intellectual contributions, encouragement, and camaraderie have been invaluable throughout this journey. Working alongside such dedicated and insightful scholars has greatly enriched my work.

I want to express my deep appreciation to my students, past and present. Your curiosity, questions, and enthusiasm for the subject matter have continually inspired me to dig deeper and think more critically. This book is as much a product of our shared inquiry as it is of my own research.

I am deeply grateful to be part of the archaeological excavations at Tel Halif and Tel Abel Beth Maacah (Israel). The hands-on experience of uncovering the past has profoundly informed my understanding of the ancient world. Additionally, my research at the Albright Institute of Archaeological Research in Jerusalem has provided invaluable resources and insights, allowing me to connect the material culture with the biblical texts in ways that have greatly deepened this book.

To my husband, Rob, who has been my partner in all things—your love, patience, and steadfast belief in my work have been a constant source of strength. Your support has allowed me to pursue my passion with confidence and clarity.

Finally, I am also profoundly grateful to my parents, Dave and Chris Shafer, whose love and guidance have shaped every step of my life. My father's memory continues to inspire me, and my mother's unwavering support has been a source of endless encouragement. Their influence is present in every page of this book.

As this book goes out into the world, I hope it serves as a testament to the power of collaboration, the importance of community, and the enduring value of scholarly exploration.

—CSE

INTRODUCTION

Planning the Dig

Reading the Bible is a little bit like traveling in a time machine. It takes us back to an ancient place and time, with ancient people who seem at times similar and at other times quite dissimilar to ourselves. It might be easy to relate to Ruth's desire to marry the kind and generous Boaz, but her unique "marriage proposal" of uncovering his feet in the middle of the night (not to mention that another man had "dibs" on her!) is much more difficult to wrap our heads around.

Some of these cultural norms were recorded in Scripture, but many were not. They were taken for granted by the ancient authors, because these customs were second nature to their readers. Similarly, we would never expect a modern author to explain things like social media, jury duty, or Netflix. One of my (Libby's) favorite classroom mantras is that the Bible was written *for* us but not *to* us. Because the Bible is God's Word written for all people in all contexts, we sometimes lose sight of the fact that it was first written to very specific people, in very specific historical and cultural contexts.

We say "contexts" (plural) because we are talking about centuries of times and conditions that changed radically throughout Israel's history, especially with the transition to the monarchy and then the exile and the return from exile. Additionally, books went through years of editing and transmission, so even the original audience of a book lived in a very different context than those who would read it in its final form.[1]

---

1. It is often impossible and even speculative to dissect these "layers" of compositional history and context, but it is important to keep in mind so that we do not treat all of the Hebrew Bible as a flat, simplistic text.

God made himself known in these various contexts in ways that Israel would understand, by working in and through systems and customs known in the ancient Near Eastern world. Theologians often call this "divine accommodation." John Calvin called it the "lisping" of God,[2] and far from being an embarrassing aspect of divine revelation, it is actually God's gracious way of being Immanuel, "God with us." By gaining an understanding of these practices and customs, we begin to understand how Israel might have thought about them, which in turn sheds light on how those aspects of their lives functioned theologically.

For example, we learn from the material culture that Israelite households included not just the immediate family but also the extended family and anyone living and working together on the property, including servants and sojourners. We know from these living arrangements, and from laws in the Hebrew Bible and in other ancient law codes, that people in the ancient Near East thought much more communally than many modern Westerners, who tend to be more individualistic. This communal focus is central in the theology of the Hebrew Bible as well. God often revealed himself to individuals, but in the larger scheme of things, his promises were made to an entire household, and later to an entire nation. Similarly, his judgments and mighty acts of salvation were directed toward the community, who worshiped him in community. It is our hope that by digging into the cultural contexts of ancient Israel, readers will gain a more accurate and fuller understanding of their theology. This is what we mean by a "grounded theology"—an understanding of Israel's theology that is inextricably rooted in the contexts in which it originated and blossomed.

EXCAVATING THE SITE: How Will We Do It?

Each chapter in this book explores a different aspect of Israel's cultural context and how that aspect informs our understanding of the theology of the Hebrew Bible. For example, chapter 2 looks at the types of treaties and contracts made in the ancient Near East. Discussing ancient "paperwork" might seem tedious, but it actually helps us to understand one of the most important theological concepts in the Hebrew Bible: covenant. By understanding the various types of treaties and how they functioned, we gain a much richer understanding of what it meant for God to enter into a covenant relationship with Israel.

A brief glance at the table of contents might suggest that several important theological themes are missing from this book. Where are the chapters on creation, prophecy, or eschatology, for example? Because we are focusing

---

2. Calvin, *Institutes of the Christian Religion* 1.13.1.

particularly on theology that is informed by the cultural contexts of Israel, it is the cultural context, and not the standard categories of theology, that have set the agenda and structure for this book. That said, it has been our goal to include all of the major themes of theology in this book, even if some might be found in unexpected chapters.

The order in which each topic is discussed is also intentional, with each chapter dovetailing into the next in some way. The household was foundational to an Israelite's everyday life, so we naturally begin there. The concept of covenant uses household ideology and is the topic of chapter 2. Land, the topic of chapter 3, was a gift of the covenant and the "barometer" of the health of the covenant. The physical location of the land, and the tabernacle and temple in particular, are tied to God's holiness, the topic of chapter 4. How Israel could worship and commune with a holy God is then the topic of chapter 5. Images of the deity, which were typically housed in these holy sanctuaries, take on different meaning in the theology of the Hebrew Bible when they are applied to humanity, which is the topic of chapter 6. Kings, who were also God's images and represented God in distinct ways, are covered in chapter 7. Naturally tied to kingship and politics are the ideas of law and wisdom, which are the topics of chapter 8. Warfare (and peace) was also within the purview of the human king and ultimately the divine King, and that is the topic of chapter 9. Finally, we conclude with food, feasting, and hospitality because those themes punctuate some of the most pivotal moments in Scripture, and they often provide a glimpse of an eschatological restoration, a hope connecting present and future and showcasing the generous and gracious character of God.

As for organization, Cynthia has written the first section of each chapter ("Looking Down"). As a specialist in archaeology and the cultural context of ancient Israel, she brings to the discussion years of experience as a field archaeologist and biblical scholar. In the second section of each chapter ("Looking Up"), Libby explores how this understanding of Israel's cultural context enhances our understanding of the theology of the Hebrew Bible. The third section of each chapter ("Looking Back") engages the readers with review and reflection questions that can be used by individuals or in a group or classroom setting. The final section ("Looking Beyond") offers a short list of resources for further study. Because we both bring different, complementary perspectives and tools to our respective tasks, we will each outline our respective methodologies below.

Cultural Contexts: Definitions and Methodology

The word "archaeology" is a composite of two Greek words—*archaios*, meaning "ancient or old," and *logia*, which means "learning or study." Thus in its simplest form, the word "archaeology" refers to the study of ancient things. Archaeology is fundamentally the study of humanity and its past. This is done through excavating sites and analyzing material culture from those sites. Material culture is the physical evidence of a culture reflected in the architecture and objects it left behind. Objects could include cooking pots, storage jars, oil lamps, ovens, water cisterns, houses, and temples. Material culture reflects the social reality of the people who lived at that time. In other words, we learn not only about the objects left behind but also about the behaviors, norms, and rituals for which people used those objects.

Studying ancient societies is easier said than done, for it is much more complex than we might imagine. One major issue has to do with the types of sites that are being studied. Ancient Israel was part of the geographical region known as the Southern Levant, which is located along the eastern Mediterranean shores. The modern-day countries that make up the Southern Levant include Israel, the West Bank, Gaza, Jordan, southern Lebanon, and southwestern Syria. Archaeologists who work in the Southern Levant have historically focused on large, urban settlements—sort of like our cities—which are called "tells." A "tell" is "a mound, especially in the Middle East, made up of the stratified remains of a succession of settlements. When structures of a later period of occupation are built directly on top of an earlier layer, over time a settlement becomes raised above the landscape due to the buildup of layers."[3] However, most ancient Israelites lived not in cities but rather in rural villages and farmsteads. These rural types of settlements rarely get the attention they deserve, especially since they more adequately reflect the daily lives of most Israelites.

A second issue is what I refer to as the "monumental versus the mundane" issue. Historically, biblical scholars and archaeologists have been primarily interested in the *monumental* or what Carol Meyers refers to as the people, places, and events of prestige—that is, the kings, priests, and prophets (who are typically male); their official kingly, priestly, and military activities; and the locations where these official activities took place, such as the temple, palace, and battlefields.[4] The authors of the Hebrew Bible were likewise more concerned with the monumental. This is typical of most ancient texts, which provide accounts of monumental events such as military conquests, the anointing of a new king, the development of law codes, and religious rituals—usually through the interpretative lens of their relationship with their deity. Opposite of the monumental is the mundane, or the ordinary people, places, and performances of the everyday. The mundane is typically overlooked in the

---

3. Archaeological Institute of America, "Tell or Tel." "Tell" is the English spelling for the Hebrew "Tel."
4. Meyers, "Having Their Space and Eating There Too," 15.

Hebrew Bible unless it plays a role in narrating the monumental. For example, in the succession narrative in 2 Samuel 13, the narrator includes what Tamar was cooking, not because the author had a particular interest in documenting cooking but because of the role the meal plays in the narrative itself.

These complexities are why an interdisciplinary approach to studying ancient Israel is helpful. Like skilled artisans in any craft or any archaeologist working in the field, we want to use every tool at our disposal to understand ancient Israel and its world.[5] For the purposes of our study here, the tools that will be most useful are archaeology, the Hebrew Bible, and other ancient Near Eastern texts. These tools will help us in our journey to understand Israel's theology from the ground up.

Theology: Definitions and Methodology

What is "theology" anyway, and what kind of theology is the focus of this book? Simply put, theology denotes the reflections and articulations humans have about God. Unlike systematic theology, which attempts to summarize what all of Scripture says about "x," this book is interested in biblical theology, which looks at the individual theological currents that develop throughout the course of Scripture as redemptive history unfolds.

According to John H. Sailhamer, theology is informed by both revelation (which is an act of God) and religion (which is a human act). He explains, "The relationship between the two terms can be demonstrated by saying humanity accepts God's revelation and acts in accordance with it and that is called religion."[6] As a divine act, revelation presupposes certain faith commitments about the God of the Hebrew Bible, which means that doing theology is, at least at its fullest, a spiritual task. As a human act, religion is always embedded in layers of social and cultural contexts, which means that careful attention to these contexts is essential for doing theology.

Theology must also consider the theological contexts of its practitioners because no scholar approaches the material or textual worlds of ancient Israel in a vacuum, or even from a place of neutrality. Both Jewish and Christian theologians do theology in light of their respective canons and traditions. Where their studies overlap, there is room for fruitful collaboration, and

---

5. There are many tools, but some are more helpful than others. Some of the tools I find most helpful include the Hebrew Bible, other ancient Near Eastern texts, archaeology and its various subtypes, iconography (representational art), ethnography (the study of contemporary cultures through direct observation), and ethnoarchaeology (the observation of contemporary cultures in order to understand the behaviors and relationships that underlie the production and use of material culture). See especially Shafer-Elliott, "Gender Archaeology"; Ebeling, "Ethnoarchaeology."

6. Sailhamer, *Introduction to Old Testament Theology*, 12.

where they diverge, there is room for increased appreciation for the other's perspective. Amy-Jill Levine and Marc Zvi Brettler model this beautifully in their coauthored book, *The Bible With and Without Jesus: How Jews and Christians Read the Same Stories Differently*.

The methodological approach I take in the "Looking Up" sections comes from my Christian tradition, but it has been shaped by many different perspectives and people, both Jewish and Christian (most of whom you will soon meet in the coming chapters). One such scholar is Benjamin Sommer, who advocates for a "dialogical biblical theology." Dialogical refers to conversation or dialogue, which means dialogical biblical theology places the fruits of historical-critical scholarship into conversation with the concerns of a scholar's context. Such a theology brings biblical texts to bear on postbiblical theological concerns—specifically, on modern Jewish or Protestant or Catholic or Orthodox or post-Christian theological concerns.[7] Similarly, John Monson describes his "context-canonical" approach as a "dialectic" between the "web" of Israel's historical contexts and the "web" of the canon.[8] He explains, "At first glance it might appear that there is an uncomfortable tension between eternal, theological truths of the normative Word of God and the temporal, spatial corporeality of the Bible's original context. To the contrary, we have found there is a synergy between original context and canonical intertextuality."[9] The theological explorations within this book will explore that same synergy, albeit with a few preliminary words of caution.

The first word of caution pertains to our direction of reading. Scholars differ over this point, but the strategy modeled in this book will be one that tries to follow the theological development in the Hebrew Bible chronologically, moving from earlier texts and stages in Israel's history to later ones and finally (though briefly) seeing how those themes are picked up in the New Testament. Of course, from that vantage point, we may look back at the Hebrew Bible, seeing in it fresh insights, but such reflections will be outside the scope of this book.

A second word of caution pertains to supersessionism—the view that Israel was merely "preparatory or figurative in nature" and has now been replaced by the church.[10] R. Kendell Soulen argues that "a canonical narrative establishes the hermeneutical foundation of Christian theology and doctrine," but we must ensure that we have a right understanding of this canonical narrative and the consummation (or end goal) of the story.[11] He explains, "God's history

---

7. Sommer, "Dialogical Biblical Theology," 21.
8. Monson, "Original Context and Canon," 32.
9. Monson, "Original Context and Canon," 41–42.
10. Soulen, *The God of Israel and Christian Theology*, 110.
11. Soulen, *The God of Israel and Christian Theology*, 14.

with Israel and the nations is the enduring form of God's gracious work as Consummator, apart from which the realization of the final end of human life is inconceivable."[12] Every effort will be made in this book to guard against a canonical narrative or theology that would diminish the value or place of Israel within the redemptive story of God's love and good news, which, according to a certain Jewish Christian, is to "the Jew first and also the Greek" (Rom. 2:9–10; see also 1:16).[13]

It is my hope that the methodology employed here might serve as a helpful model for readers who wish to bring their exploration of Israel's cultural context into dialogue with their own faith commitments.

Terminology

There are a few terms that we have chosen to use that may be unfamiliar to some of our readers. For this reason, it will be helpful for us to take a moment to explain those terms and why we have chosen to use them. The first has to do with the divine name. Most English translations render the divine name, or the tetragrammaton, as LORD, which suggests a title rather than a personal name. Throughout this book, we will refer to the divine name as Yhwh. Readers will also notice that we sometimes use gendered pronouns to refer to God (especially in the "Looking Up" sections). We try to do this sparingly, recognizing that God is beyond gender, and yet also very personal, a quality that alternative references ("it," "Godself," etc.) can sometimes obscure.[14]

We must also discuss what term to use when referring to Israel's scriptures. While there are various options for describing Israel's scriptures (and none of them are without limitations or weaknesses), we have chosen to use the terminology "Hebrew Bible." Reasons for this largely depend on the context of the person speaking or writing. The term "Hebrew Bible" is regularly used by scholars, often in more academic settings. One reason for this is because these scholars are approaching the biblical texts from various perspectives, including historical, linguistic, or cultural, rather than only theological. The term "Hebrew Bible" allows us to highlight the languages and contexts of the text; furthermore, it encourages us to include those of our readers who are not coming from a particular (Protestant) Christian context. One final set of terms pertains to the historical time periods.

Today, scholars generally prefer to use BCE and CE when dating historical events instead of BC and AD. BCE stands for "before the Common Era" and

---

12. Soulen, *The God of Israel and Christian Theology*, 112 (see also p. 110).
13. All Scripture citations are from the NRSV unless otherwise noted.
14. Jones, *Practicing Christian Doctrine*, 173–75; Peeler, *Women and the Gender of God*.

CE for "Common Era." Contrary to popular belief, the BCE/CE system does not alter any historical dates; rather, it is only a change in label that (while still technically anchored in the birth of Jesus) uses more neutral and inclusive terminology. Consequently, this book will use the terms BCE and CE.[15] One further point of clarification has to do with chronology. We recognize that most of our readers will be unfamiliar with the names and dates of the various time periods under discussion. Consequently, a (very!) simplified chronology of ancient Israel is provided below. Please note, however, that the links between periods and dates are always under considerable discussion between historians and archaeologists.

Neolithic: 8500–4500 BCE
Chalcolithic: 4500–3500 BCE
Bronze Age: 3500–1200 BCE
Iron Age: 1200–586 BCE
Neo-Babylonian Period: 586–539 BCE
Persian Period: 539–332 BCE
Hellenistic Period: 332–53 BCE
Roman Period: 53 BCE–337 CE[16]

INTERPRETING THE FINDINGS: What Are Our Goals?

This book was born out of a deep desire to fill what we consider to be a gap in written resources. There is no shortage of books on the cultural context of ancient Israel or on the theology of the Hebrew Bible (many of these resources are listed near the end of each chapter). However, we have yet to encounter any books to help connect the dots between these two fields.

Our goals are twofold: First, we hope that readers will gain a better understanding of how the cultural background of ancient Israel informs the theology of the Hebrew Bible. Second, we hope to provide some interpretive tools for moving from the material culture of ancient Israel to the theological world of Scripture, so that as readers continue to explore Israel's cultural world, they can make their own connections to the theology that flows like milk and honey from its scriptures.

---

15. For more on this topic, see Cook, "BCE and CE versus BC and AD"; Cargill, "Why Christians Should Adopt the BCE/CE Dating System."

16. Master, "Chronology of the Southern Levant," 455–61.

1

HOUSEHOLDS
The Relationship of God

When we imagine ancient Israelite families, most of us would assume that they resembled our own families. However, if we could travel back in time, we would see that the ancient Israelite family did not resemble what we would describe as a traditional Western family; that is, "traditional" consisting of a nuclear family living within their own home. In fact, a more fitting term to describe this community in ancient Israel would be "household," instead of "family." The ancient Israelite household was a multigenerational community living and working together for their survival. This chapter explores the cultural context of the ancient Israelite household and how that context sheds important light on our understanding of how God related to Israel in household terms and how they thought, lived, and worshiped together in community.

LOOKING DOWN

You may have heard it said that we can learn a lot about people by observing how they live. How they spend their time and money on a daily basis can provide clues to what that person sees as a necessity and what they value. For instance, if you are invited to someone's home, you will observe any number of things. If the host likes to cook, you will likely see a lot of cookbooks and cooking ware; hence, you would rightly assume that this person values food and preparing meals. The same is true regarding ancient Israel—we can learn much about them by shifting our attention away from the monumental places (like the palace or the temple) to the stage where the mundane moments of daily life occurred—the home. Focusing on the home provides insight into the physical reality of the daily lives of ancient cultures. There are at least three aspects to consider when studying households: material, social, and behavioral.[1]

The Material Aspect of Households

The first aspect to consider when studying households is the material, which consists of the physical features of the household. This includes the land, the main dwelling, secondary buildings (like a storeroom or a family tomb), features (such as a well or an oven), areas where household activities took place (like a kitchen or a courtyard), and the household's possessions (such as cooking pots and oil lamps). The household's possessions (artifacts to us) are seen as important, but we often overlook the significance of the household's land and animals, which were vital to their survival.

Houses excavated from Israel's Iron Age (ca. 1200–586 BCE) have a similar floorplan and common features. The typical house had two floors and a flat roof. The first floor had a room in the back running the width of the house (often called the "broad room") with one to three rooms running perpendicular to it (often called "long rooms"). Pillars made of stone or wood were used to segregate space on the first floor and to support the second floor. Some scholars debate whether or not the central long room was roofed or whether it served as a courtyard. It is also thought that houses had a shared open work space in front of the house, also referred to as a courtyard or, more appropriately, a forecourt. Houses were small and space was limited for average Israelites, but the typical house size was about thirty to thirty-five feet long and thirty-five to forty feet wide, depending on the needs of the household and the location of the house.[2] Some houses located in a walled city were built using the city wall as the back wall of the broad room, and they also usually shared walls with the houses on either side. In an unwalled village, houses were built close to each other and in a semicircle to create an informal boundary. Regardless of the size and environment, houses in Iron Age Israel were multifunctional with several household activities taking place in the limited space available (see figs. 1.1 and 1.2).

Historically, many scholars interpreted these houses as having four rooms (three long rooms and one broad room), and thus referred to them as the

---

1. Wilk and Rathje, "Household Archaeology," 618.
2. Meyers, *Rediscovering Eve*, 106.

Figure 1.1. Depiction of an Iron Age house in ancient Israel (Harvard Museum of the Ancient Near East)

"Israelite Four-Room House." However, many scholars have rightfully noticed that many houses had two long rooms, and some had just one, so labeling them as four-room houses is technically inaccurate. The variety in room numbers is likely because the layout of the house could change with the needs of the household. For example, if the household determined that a smaller room dedicated to store liquids was needed, then a wall could be erected within one of the side long rooms to create a separate room. Furthermore, it is impossible to determine unequivocally if the Israelites were the only people who used this style of house. For this reason, many scholars refer to this house style as the "pillar house" because of the pillars used in the first floor of the house or as the "Iron Age house" because of its popularity throughout the Iron Age.

The main function of a house was to provide shelter for the household members

Figure 1.2. Artist's rendition of an Iron Age house in ancient Israel (Israel Museum)

Chamberi / CC BY-SA 3.0 / Wikimedia Commons

and animals, but houses were much more than that—they were just as much of a workplace as a dwelling place. Houses were multifunctional with several activities performed throughout. The bottom floor was used for a variety of daily domestic chores, storage, and the housing of small livestock. The top floor was where the household members slept and also engaged in some light household chores. The flat roof of the house was also used as a place for certain household activities (such as the drying of flax; see Josh. 2:6) and a cool place to sleep in the hot and dry summer months (2 Kings 4:10).

The Social Aspect of Households

The social aspect includes the members of the household and their relationship to each other. A common misconception is that "household" is synonymous with "family." The terms are related but do contain important distinctions. A family is a group of people who are related to each other either biologically or through marriage, but they may or may not live or work together. A household, however, is defined by co-residence and/or the sharing of domestic activities. In other words, a household is a group of people who typically live and/or work together but who may or may not be related. The average ancient Israelite household was multigenerational and usually included immediate and extended family members, such as grandparents, parents, children, married sons and their families, and any unmarried or widowed women. The household also included nonrelated members, such as slaves, guests, concubines, or hired workers. Some members of the household lived together in the same house or compound, while others (like hired workers) lived elsewhere but came to the household land to work. Some contemporary examples of the extensive nature of a household would be, for example, if you have roommates. You live together but aren't related. Or if you have someone who comes to your house to work, like a home health-care aide or a nanny. You work together in the dwelling, but you aren't related.

Being an individual and living an individual life like many of us do today was a foreign concept to the Israelites. In their world, everything was centered on community, especially the community of family or kinship. People were known by who their family or kin were. For instance, sons and daughters were known by their name and who their father (and sometimes mother) was, like Jacob son of Isaac or Rachel daughter of Laban. Several terms within the Hebrew Bible refer to the various degrees of kinship and highlight its importance. The smallest kinship group and the nucleus of ancient Israelite society was the household. The terms used to illustrate the household include *bet 'ab* (Gen. 46:31) and occasionally *bet 'em* (24:28), translated as "the father's household" or "the mother's household," respectively. The middle kinship

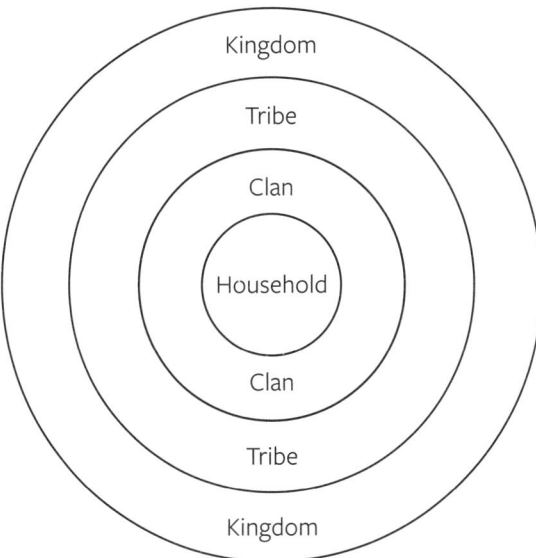

Figure 1.3. Kinship social structures of ancient Israel

group is called the *mishpahah*, and the term is often used in the Hebrew Bible to indicate a clan or an extended family, which could be quite large at times (Exod. 6:14, 25; Num. 1:2). The *mishpahah* forms a major unit of the tribe (*shebet* or *matteh*), which was the larger social group (Gen. 49:28; Num. 1:16). Israelite tribes claimed common, unilineal descent from a founding ancestor and occupied a particular geographic region. Once the monarchy was established and stabilized, the kingdom (*mamlakah*) could be considered as the next and largest kinship social group (1 Sam. 24:20). However, the *bet 'ab* (household) and *mishpahah* (clan) were the most important kinship groups for the average ancient Israelite. As was mentioned earlier, in the ancient Near Eastern world, of which Israel was a part, a person was rarely seen as an individual; rather, a person was considered in light of those to whom he or she was connected: the person's *bet 'ab* (immediate household), *mishpahah* (clan), *shebet* (tribe), and *mamlakah* (kingdom) (see fig. 1.3).

Having a social structure centered on kinship highlights not only the familial, communal nature of ancient Israelite society but also the importance of marriage in this world. Like those of its ancient Near Eastern neighbors, Israel's marriage customs were largely based on endogamy, or marrying only within the limits of a local community, clan, or tribe.[3] Marriage in ancient Israel was different from marriage today. When a young woman reached

---

3. *Oxford English Dictionary*, "endogamy," accessed August 9, 2024, https://www.oed.com/dictionary/endogamy_n.

puberty, her parents would arrange a marriage between her and a man within her clan or tribe. She would then leave her *bet 'ab* and merge into her husband's *bet 'ab* (what we call patrilocal or living with the male side). Marriage was not usually founded on love but was more of a contract between two households; however, that is not to say that love did not manifest itself in these marriages.

Even though every member of the Israelite household was vital to its survival, certain household members had more specific roles to perform. The patriarch and matriarch (the male and female heads of a household) possessed the most power and authority within their *bet 'ab* and would have required great wisdom, skill, expertise, and diplomacy.

The responsibility of protecting the household belonged to the patriarch. The patriarch also had the power over life and death within the household, which seems like a massive amount of power. However, the patriarch's authority was not absolute; rather, his authority was primarily over his wives, sons, and daughters. In cases of household disobedience and dishonor, it was the patriarch who decided the outcome. For example, the commandment to "honor your father and your mother" (Exod. 20:12) is regularly used today to teach children to obey their parents. In reality, however, the commandment held much more weight for adult children living within their household.

Similar to the patriarch, the matriarch also possessed a great deal of authority and power within the household. Women's reproductive roles made it more necessary for them to work close to the house. Because of this, women in general and the matriarch in particular managed and controlled some of the most important household activities that occurred—textile production and preparation, storage, distribution, and consumption of food, just to name a few. Essentially, it was the matriarch who decided who ate, when, what, and how much. Proverbs 31 sings the praises of the matriarch as the manager of the household and its foodways:

> She is like the ships of the merchant,
>   she brings her food from far away.
> She rises while it is still night
>   and provides food for her household
>   and tasks for her servant-girls. . . .
> She looks well to the ways of her household,
>   and does not eat the bread of idleness. (vv. 14–15, 27)

It is not surprising that, as the manager of the household, the matriarch held much authority and earned the praise of her household.

The Behavioral Aspect of Households

If the social aspect is interested in the "who" and the material aspect the "where and how," then the behavioral aspect is concerned with the "what" or, for our purposes, "What did the Israelites do all day?" The behavioral aspect suggests what activities the ancient Israelite household performed. Since neither the social or behavioral aspects leave any physical traces, we depend on the material aspect to help us determine what activities the household performed. Archaeology is essential in this task. The physical remains excavated from dwelling places reflect the shape and activities, and thus the behavior, of the household. In order to determine what activities members of a household performed, archaeologists use spatial analysis to recognize and understand patterns and regularities. For instance, if the remains of a house are being excavated and a cluster of cooking pots is found near an oven that contains carbonized grain, then it is quite plausible that this area was used for cooking food.

Ancient Israel was predominantly a kinship-based society with a household-dominant mode of production. The household economy ranged in levels of subsistence but was always agrarian/pastoral in nature.[4] Whether they lived in rural villages or farmsteads or in urban fortified settlements, Israelites were agrarians concerned with living off the land. The activities a household engaged in can be classified into either daily occurrences or special occasions.

Daily Functions in Everyday Life

In our daily lives today, there are many day-to-day functions that households must do to continue their existence, such as grocery shopping or cooking. But imagine if you had to do this without grocery stores, electricity, or indoor plumbing. Ancient Israelite households were responsible for everything: They were the farmer, distributor, retailer, and cook all in one. The numerous daily functions that the average Israelite household engaged in on a daily basis can be divided into six categories:[5]

1. Production. This refers to the securing of resources or increasing their value. Production would include farming, herd maintenance, and the making of tools or fabric, for example.
2. Preparation. This is an element of production that focuses on transforming ingredients and foodstuffs into edible food.
3. Distribution. This refers to the sharing of resources with others. This could include storage and trade.

---

4. Boer, *Sacred Economy*, 80.
5. Wilk and Rathje discuss four of these six: production, distribution, transmission, and reproduction. See Wilk and Rathje, "Household Archaeology," 622, 624, 627, 630.

4. Transmission. This refers to transferring "rights, roles, land, and property" from one generation to the next.[6]
5. Reproduction. This involves "the rearing and socializing of children."[7]
6. Cultic or religious ritual. This is often included as a category, since everything in the ancient Near Eastern world was spiritual, and these rituals, along with the agricultural calendar, dominated the functions an ancient household performed.

The excavation of Iron Age houses in Israel indicates that households were engaged in the expected domestic activities of production, preparation, distribution, storage, reproduction, and religious ritual.

We can narrow our focus a bit more when we consider the essential elements for survival in the ancient Near Eastern world. Subsistence-level domestic economies were concerned with survival, which was so imperative that each member was expected to participate regardless of sex, age, or other differentials. Out of the six categories of daily functions listed above, two were the most imperative to the survival of the household: production and reproduction. However, one further function, protection, must be examined for us to gain a fuller perspective of daily survival. In other words, the survival of the Israelite household was dependent on three main factors: protection, procreation, and production.[8]

As noted earlier, the protection factor was managed by the household males, most often the patriarch of the household, whose role it was to protect the other members of the household, especially females and children.[9] Protection of the household was conducted in a variety of ways, including war and making decisions regarding the farming and care of the household's land and herds. Another form of protection can be seen through the concept of the *go'el* or kinsman-redeemer. When a member of the household (or clan and tribe) was in crisis, a close male relative could intervene to help. For instance, in Genesis 14:12–16 Abraham's nephew, Lot, was kidnapped by a coalition of foreign kings. Abraham stepped in as a *go'el* and rescued him. A second example of a man fulfilling his kinsman-redeemer obligation is within the role of a levirate marriage. This law is found in Deuteronomy 25:5–10, and it assigns a man the duty of marrying the sonless widow of his deceased brother.[10] The dual importance of land and inheritance is evident in the role of the *go'el*, in particular if they take on the responsibility of a levirate marriage. Inheritance,

---

6. Wilk and Rathje, "Household Archaeology," 627.
7. Wilk and Rathje, "Household Archaeology," 630.
8. Meyers, "Procreation, Production, and Protection," 574–76.
9. Matthews and Benjamin, *Social World of Ancient Israel*, 8.
10. Kilchör, "Levirate Obligation."

Figure 1.4. A tannur clay oven from Tel Halif. It is open on top to show hot embers inside and two round flatbreads cooking on the side wall.

especially land, was passed down from father to son. If a couple was childless and the husband died, then the wife and the rest of the household would likely have lost that inheritance, putting them and their survival into jeopardy.

In order for a household to survive, the fertility of its land, animals, and members was of utmost importance. Procreation was part of the female domain because it involved women's larger role in reproduction and concerns relating to menstruation, conception, birth, lactation, and weaning. The nature of the reproductive role dictated that female daily household activities oftentimes occurred within or near the dwelling.[11]

If protection was facilitated by the men of the household and reproduction was facilitated by the women, production was the essential element in which the entire household participated. Production tasks were dominated by industry related to agriculture, animal husbandry, and the making of various goods, such as pottery and fabric. Certain times of year, such as planting and harvest, required all able members of the household to contribute. During times of war, however, household women were required to bear the full burden of production.[12]

One crucial aspect of production was food preparation. When houses from ancient Israel are excavated, the remains of ovens or hearths are found both inside the house and in the courtyard (see fig. 1.4). Both of these spaces served

---

11. Meyers, "Procreation, Production, and Protection," 574.
12. Meyers, "Procreation, Production, and Protection," 574.

as seasonal "living rooms." They were centrally located, and the majority of household activities were carried out there. This encouraged social relationships and cohesion among the group (Lev. 26:26).[13] Ancient Israelite women spent at least ten hours a day engaged in domestic labor, two hours of which were spent processing grain.[14] Consequently, the seasonal living rooms were dominated by the household women and the activities in which they engaged. The main task that monopolized the daily activities of the women in the household was the production and preparation of food.[15]

Special Occasions and Feasting

It is important to distinguish between a household's ordinary, daily life and more extraordinary times, or special events. Daily life for an average household, as explored above, illustrates that ancient Israel was predominantly a kinship-based society with a household-dominant mode of production. The average household often functioned at a subsistence level. However, even subsistence-level societies like to party!

Extraordinary events usually centered around a special meal or feast. Feasts occupied an important place in the behavioral aspect of the household since meals, especially special occasion meals, contained diverse and powerful meanings that bind groups together. Sacrifices were a significant part of the feast. Once the sacrifice was offered and the superior portion of meat burned, depending on the type of sacrifice, what remained became part of the household feast (Lev. 7:15). Sacrifices offered by the household were also highly symbolic in that they could be seen as the household sharing a meal with the household ancestors and deities (Deut. 26:14; Ps. 106:28; Jer. 16:5–9).[16] Thus, the festive meal was not just about the household members, but it also included the household ancestors and deities playing their perceived role within the household. The Hebrew Bible supports the notion that

---

13. Archaeological excavations of Iron Age houses always uncover features and artifacts related to food preparation within the house and the courtyard: ovens, grinding installations and stones, cooking pots, bowls, and storage jars—just to name a few. The central locations of ovens would have enabled women to keep an eye on the children while conducting other household chores and would have allowed for sharing of resources, such as the oven itself and dung used for fuel.

14. Meyers, "Family in Early Israel," 25–27.

15. For more on food and feasting, see chapter 10.

16. Douglas, "Deciphering a Meal," 71. In the ancient Near Eastern world, of which Israel was a part, it was widely assumed that it was the duty of the living to care for dead ancestors through food offerings, especially at the place of burial or at the family tomb. Archaeological evidence supports this assumption as do other ancient Near Eastern texts (like the Ugaritic Aqhat Epic). Biblical scholars argue that the western Semitic word *mrzh*, often pronounced *marzeah* in its Hebrew form, is a meal associated with the dead, either at burial or in later remembrance ceremonies (Jer. 16:5–9). See Johnston, *Shades of Sheol*, 181.

religious feasts occurred within the home (Exod. 12:3–4a, 7–9; Deut. 14:26; Job 1:4); furthermore, archaeological evidence of religious domestic feasting can be found in numerous dwellings from Israel's Iron Age. For example, artifacts relating to religious rituals and the serving and consumption of food were found in an eighth century BCE house at Tel Halif in Israel, and these finds plausibly indicate that religious domestic feasting was a primary household activity.[17]

Summary

Although "the household" is not explicitly the focus in most biblical texts, it is foundational to how we understand much of Israelite life, so to gain a good understanding of Scripture (or Israelite life as a whole), we must understand its basis for existence. Archaeology helps us visualize the form and function of the Israelite household. The study of the material, social, and behavioral aspects of an ancient Israelite household clarify what the daily lives of the average man, woman, and child would have looked like during Israel's Iron Age. What we can be certain of is that every member of the Israelite household was imperative to its survival and thus highly valued.

LOOKING UP

This understanding of ancient Israelite households can help us imagine how the original audience lived and thought and how they might have interpreted the household imagery of the Hebrew Bible that is so fundamental to its theology. As Leo G. Perdue explains, "The household was the theological lens, the ethical paradigm, and the human context for understanding the character and activity of God and for living out moral responsibilities to others."[18] In fact, the concept of a covenant (which will be covered in the next chapter), comes from the realm of the household.[19] Having a better understanding of how the Israelites thought about their own households sheds invaluable light on how they thought about their relationship to God and to one another.

The influence of the household on Israel's theology is seen in two primary areas. First, the Israelites understood their relationship to God through metaphors of household roles. For example, God is sometimes described as a father or a mother and Israel as God's son or daughter. Other times God is depicted as a husband, and his people are either his faithful bride or (more

---

17. Shafer-Elliott, "Role of the Household."
18. Perdue, "Household," 253 (cf. 225).
19. Smith, "'Your People Shall Be My People.'" In this article, Smith builds on the work of Cross, *From Epic to Canon*, 11.

often!) his adulterous bride. Even the two most prominent terms for Israel as a nation are taken from the household: *bet Yisrael* ("the household of Israel") and *bene Yisrael* ("the sons/children of Israel").[20] Moreover, the very use of the name "Israel" to refer to God's people denotes a kinship relationship, and it is a constant reminder that God's people descended from one man, Jacob, whose name was changed to Israel (Gen. 32:28).[21]

The second way that our understanding of ancient Israelite households helps to inform the theology of the Hebrew Bible is by its emphasis on the communal nature of the household and, by extension, the larger community. We have seen that it took the entire household to accomplish the community's protection, procreation, and production. Every member of the household was essential to the survival of the whole, and no member could survive without the whole. Ancient Israelites thought in terms of solidarity rather than individualism and in terms of "we" more than "I." They lived as an interdependent community, and they related to their God in community.

Theology of Household Roles and Metaphors

One of my favorite Christmas movies has always been *It's a Wonderful Life*. It is also one of those movies that can appeal to just about everybody, which comes in handy when three or more generations are trying to decide on a movie! One reason it might have such a wide appeal is that the main character, George Bailey, has many roles throughout the film. We first meet him as a playful and protective big brother and as a son who honors his father's reputation. We watch him make sacrifices as he grows to be a man, then a husband and father. In fact, the climax of the film is when his roles as protector and provider for his family are threatened by his uncle Billy's foolish mistake, and George considers committing suicide to protect his family and escape his predicament. George's multiple roles make him relatable, even to audiences decades removed from 1940s America, and they draw us into George's character.

In a similar way, God makes himself known to his people in language they can understand and relate to, specifically using language from the household. How Israel understood these household roles has important implications for how we should understand their theological importance. John Goldingay explains, "Both the household and the extended family are key providers of theological imagery. People's experience of God shapes

---

20. While the masculine "sons" is most common in referring to God's people collectively, daughter imagery is also used, specifically with reference to Jerusalem, as in the phrase "daughter Zion" (e.g., Ps. 9:14; Isa. 1:8; Lam. 2:1).

21. Goldingay, *Israel's Faith*, 173.

their experience of family, and their experience of family shapes their experience of God."[22] So when God reveals himself as a "father," for example, we should be careful not to impose expectations on that metaphor from our own experience. We must consider how these roles were understood in their ancient cultural context.

The portrayal of God as father is a fine place to begin. Theophoric names, such as Abijah ("Yah[weh] is my father") and Eliab ("my God is father") show that the fatherhood of God was a prominent idea.[23] God occasionally relates as a father to individuals, most notably to the Davidic king (2 Sam. 7:14; Ps. 2:7), but he most often relates as a father to Israel as a nation. As their father and ultimate patriarch, God created them (Deut. 32:6[24]; Isa. 64:8), delivered them (Hos. 11:1–4), and protected them (Ps. 91:14). In response, Israel was to honor God as children honor their earthly fathers (Mal. 1:6).

Israel's status as God's child also precedes the exodus and their establishment as a nation at Sinai (as Exod. 4:22–23 makes clear), which, according to Christopher Wright, has significant theological implications: "The father-son relationship between God and Israel contained within itself an element of permanence, which injected hope into an otherwise hopeless situation. Wrath, exile, and loss of land would not be permanent. Yahweh would not abandon his people. The father could not ultimately disown his son."[25] God chose the Israelites to be his children before delivering them from Egypt and before giving them the law at Sinai. Their status as God's children was never dependent on their status as a nation. They would be punished for disobedience (Lev. 26; Deut. 28), just as earthly children are punished by their earthly parents, but their status as God's children was unconditional and indissoluble.

Isaiah 49:15 offers moving words about God never abandoning his children, likening God to a nursing mother:

> Can a woman forget her nursing child,
> or show no compassion for the child of her womb?
> Even these may forget,
> yet I will not forget you.

Most people can probably remember a time when they were lost from their parents. However, I doubt if many of us can say that we were lost or forgotten while we were nursing! By using this intimate image of compassion and

---

22. Goldingay, *Israel's Faith*, 538.
23. C. Wright, "אב," 222.
24. Just a few verses later in this chapter, God is compared with a nurturing and protective mother eagle (Deut. 32:11–13).
25. C. Wright, "אב," 222.

steadfastness, God is affirming that his love is even more unfaltering than that of a nursing mother.²⁶

Similarly, God likens himself to a midwife in passages like Psalm 22:9–10, Job 10:18, and Isaiah 66:9. Infant and mother mortality rates in the ancient Near East were staggeringly high compared to today's Western standards. According to Jennie R. Ebeling, infant mortality was greater than 50 percent. The average lifespan of a woman was thirty years, due in large part to high maternal mortality.²⁷ It is easy to imagine, then, how midwives were viewed as essential and life-giving. Thus, when God likens himself to a midwife, he likens himself to one of the most important and life-giving roles in Israelite culture.²⁸

In addition to relating vertically to Israel as a parent or midwife, God also related horizontally to Israel as a husband to his beloved wife. As such, they were to be one flesh (Gen. 2:22–24) and loyal to each other. The exclusivity of (traditional) marriage also makes it an apt metaphor for the exclusivity of Israel's relationship to God.²⁹ This is a central image in the prophetic books. The book of Jeremiah describes the (brief) honeymoon period after the exodus, when Israel was a faithful bride:

> I remember the devotion of your youth,
>   your love as a bride,
> how you followed me in the wilderness,
>   in a land not sown. (2:2)

Unfortunately, spiritual adultery plagued Israel's history, eventually warranting a divine divorce for both the northern and southern kingdoms (Jer. 3:8). However, divorce and judgment did not have the last word. When God restored Judah from exile, it would be a "remarriage" of covenant partners:

> You shall no more be termed Forsaken,
>   and your land shall no more be termed Desolate;
> but you shall be called My Delight Is in Her,
>   and your land Married;
> for the LORD delights in you,
>   and your land shall be married.
> For as a young man marries a young woman,
>   so shall your builder marry you,

---

26. In Deut. 32:13, God is not only compared to a nursing mother but described as a mother nursing Israel in the wilderness: "[God] set [Israel] atop the heights of the land, / and fed him with produce of the field; / [God] nursed him with honey from the crags, / with oil from flinty rock."
27. Ebeling, *Women's Lives in Biblical Times*, 101.
28. Matthews, *Cultural World of the Bible*, 77.
29. Longman, *Genesis*, 57.

> and as the bridegroom rejoices over the bride,
> so shall your God rejoice over you. (Isa. 62:4–5)

Perhaps no book paints the picture of Israel's marriage, infidelity, and restoration more vividly than Hosea. The prophet Hosea's message to adulterous Israel mirrors his own marriage to an adulterous woman, which served as a living object lesson. In Hosea 2, God claims that Israel is no longer his wife (v. 2) because she has failed to serve him exclusively as a wife must do (v. 5), and she will be punished for her spiritual adultery (vv. 6–13). However, immediately after this indictment, God promises that he will woo her back:

> Therefore, I will now allure her,
> and bring her into the wilderness,
> and speak tenderly to her.
> From there I will give her her vineyards,
> and make the Valley of Achor a door of hope.
> There she shall respond as in the days of her youth,
> as at the time when she came out of the land of Egypt. (vv. 14–15)

After God woos Israel back to himself, she will respond with love, once again calling God "my husband" (v. 16) and knowing him intimately (v. 20).[30]

In this passage from Hosea, God's role as a husband has a restorative effect: He will restore his bride and reunite their bond. Another household term used for Yhwh has even stronger connotations of restoration and salvation. When the Israelite household was threatened, the *go'el* (translated variously as "avenger of blood" or "kinsman-redeemer") was a close relative who could help in various ways. For example, if someone in the household was murdered, it was the responsibility of the *go'el* to avenge the murder (Num. 35:19–27). If property or family members were sold to pay debts, the *go'el* could buy back those assets and family members for the sake of his kinsmen (Lev. 25:25–33, 48–49).[31] In this way, the *go'el* served as both an instrument of justice and a redeemer for the vulnerable. How fitting, then, that the verbal root of *go'el* is used thirty-six times to refer to God: seventeen times as a verb, referring to the redemption that God has or will achieve, and nineteen times as a noun, referring to God as Israel's

---

30. To "know" (from the Hebrew *yada*) someone in Hebrew can be a euphemism for sexual intimacy. That is clearly not the case when God is the subject or the object of the knowing, but an intimate bond is clear: to know the Lord is not merely to know about him or to acknowledge him (as the NIV translation mistakenly translates) but to know him in relationship. According to Jeremiah, this relational "knowledge" of the Lord is one of the promises of the new covenant (24:7; 31:34).

31. Hess, "Family in the Old Testament," 272.

"redeemer."³² Indeed, God was Israel's first and great *go'el*, and any later Israelite *go'el* was to perpetuate that great redemption.

In the New Testament, Jesus steps into all of these metaphors, though in different ways. As fully God, he is the husband of his covenant people (Luke 5:33–35; Rev. 19:7–9). As the perfect representative of humanity, he fulfills perfectly Israel's role as God's "son" (Matt. 3:17; Luke 9:35). As Israel's *go'el*, Jesus's divinity and humanity are both emphasized, fulfilling the redemption initiated in the Hebrew Bible and fulfilling Israel's role to perpetuate that redemption.

Theology of Communal Solidarity

When George Bailey is contemplating suicide in the movie *It's a Wonderful Life*, an angel named Clarence shows him what life would be like if he had never been born (by the way, please do not take your theology of angels from this film!). By this point in the movie, audiences have already been drawn into the multifaceted character of George Bailey, but their heart strings are pulled to a breaking point when Clarence shows George the impact that his life has had on his immediate family, his extended family, and his entire community. Even in our highly individualistic society, we can see how our lives are intertwined and work together for the greater good of the community.

What was an "aha" moment for George Bailey, in which he recognized that his worth was tied to the entire community and theirs to him, was embedded in the thought world of ancient Israel. Their very living arrangements encouraged communal identity and solidarity, as Victor Matthews explains: "With living space at a minimum, there was no room for luxuries or privacy."³³ Children did not have their own bedrooms, to say nothing of their own social media accounts or cell phones. Everyone in the household had to do their part for the survival of the household.

Not only was this communal attitude a result of living arrangements or the household economics, but it was the basis for Israel's well-being as a whole, well beyond the household. According to Deuteronomy 15:7–9, Israelites were to be generous to fellow Israelites in need, treating them as they would the brothers and sisters within their households. The household was also intended to be a vehicle for generosity to those outside the bounds of the larger family ties of clan and even nation.³⁴ John Rogerson describes this extension of responsibility as a "structure of grace" and "a social arrangement designed

---

32. The vast majority of these references occur in Psalms (nine times) and Isaiah (twenty times), but the foundational uses are probably Exod. 6:6 and 15:13, both of which refer to the exodus as the paradigmatic event of redemption.
33. Matthews, *Cultural World of the Bible*, 56.
34. Goldingay, *Israel's Life*, 398.

to mitigate hardship and misfortune, [one] grounded in God's mercy."[35] This extension of grace beyond the household is not a minor or peripheral element of Israel's ethics, as Perdue argues: "The high point of Israelite social ethics comes in the commandment to love the resident alien (Deut. 10:19) as oneself (Lev. 19:34), for in so doing, one actualizes God's own love and care for the stranger, that is, the other, who lives outside the immediate protection and support of his or her own family household."[36] God showed mercy to his people when they were enslaved, immigrants, and poor, and they were to extend that same mercy to their neighbors.

One of the best illustrations of how these structures of grace worked for the restoration of both native and immigrant Israelites is in the book of Ruth. The story begins with Naomi and her family moving to the neighboring country of Moab because of a famine in their hometown of Bethlehem.

Figure 1.5. *Naomi and Ruth* by Evelyn De Mogan, 1887

When Naomi's husband and two sons die, she is left with one daughter-in-law who is willing to return with her to Bethlehem. This daughter-in-law, Ruth, is not just along for the ride because she has no better options. Her vow shows us that by identifying with Naomi's household, Ruth will also be identifying with Israel as a whole, including their customs and even their God (1:16). Ruth's loyalty and love are met by God's provision, through Boaz, who serves as the family's *go'el*, redeeming the family property. A similar "structure of grace" known as "levirate marriage" (Deut. 25:5–6) was also at play, for by redeeming the land, Boaz also redeemed the widows of the land and perpetuated their family line through marriage and an heir who would be the great-grandfather of King David (Ruth 4:5, 13–22).[37]

---

35. Rogerson, "Family," 36.
36. Perdue, "Household," 234 (cf. Deut. 24:17–22).
37. Scholars disagree on the exact relationship between the role of the *go'el* and levirate marriage, whether they are one and the same or whether they are overlapping means of restoring a broken household situation. See Longman, "Kinsman-Redeemer and Levirate."

The levirate system was also known in other ancient Near Eastern cultures, so is there anything expressly theological about it?[38] What we see in the Hebrew Bible with levirate marriages is what we see in many other cases: God takes a standard cultural custom and fills it with theological meaning. Specifically, levirate marriage was an extension of God's protection and grace. God was the ultimate protector of widows and other vulnerable groups (Pss. 68:5–6; 146:9), but he often worked indirectly through social structures. Walter Brueggemann explains, "The social requirement commanded in Israel [i.e., levirate marriage] is linked to and grounded in a theological claim."[39] Through the levirate "structure of grace," God is able to protect some of the most vulnerable members of his household.

In addition to being a vehicle for generosity and restoration, the household was also a conduit of God's promises. The household was the context for receiving God's blessings, including fertility, life, prosperity, security, health, and wholeness. It was also the means through which God's plan for all creation would be achieved: God's people were to be fruitful and fill the earth (Gen. 1:28; 9:1, 7; 35:11), they were to be a blessing and light to the nations (Gen. 12:3; Isa. 42:6), and through the promised "offspring" of Eve a savior would one day come to defeat evil (Gen. 3:15). If the household was threatened, either by forces beyond their control (e.g., famine, death, infertility) or by forces within their control (such as dysfunction, laziness, or foolishness), then God's promises were also threatened.[40] Much of the history of the Hebrew Bible is a testimony to God's ability to surmount any kind of obstacle to his covenant promises. Just think of all of the obstacles that were apparently no match for God's sovereignty: infertility, famine, wives passed off as sisters and taken by foreign kings, nearly fatal sibling disputes, and so on.

As the conduits of covenant promises, households were naturally the center of religious devotion, which is clear from both the archaeological evidence mentioned above and the Hebrew Bible. When we think of "worship" in the Hebrew Bible, we might first envision the temple and sacrifices and priests adorned in their festal robes, but most worship and spiritual devotion took place within the household. Passover, arguably the most important feast day on Israel's calendar, was celebrated first and foremost within the household. Central to this festival was the yearly dialogue between parents and children, wherein the children inquire of the meaning of the feast and the parents

---

38. See, for example, the Middle Assyrian Law Code A.33, A.45; and the Code of Hammurabi 172 (cited in Matthews, *Cultural World of the Bible*, 76).

39. Brueggemann, *Reverberations of Faith*, 230.

40. According to Goldingay, "The relationship of parents and children is of crucial significance for the fulfillment of God's purpose. Dishonoring parents and abusing children imperils the one structure upon which the fulfillment of that purpose depends." Goldingay, *Israel's Gospel*, 185.

explain that it commemorates how God spared and then delivered the Israelites (Exod. 12:26–27; 13:8). Even pilgrimages to Jerusalem and to the temple were family, household affairs (Luke 2:41–51). Worship was primarily a communal affair, and the bedrock of that community was the household.

Israel's collectivism is also reflected in genealogies. As a professor who struggles to communicate to my undergraduate students the importance of the biblical genealogies, I was surprised to find out that most people are actually quite fascinated with their own genealogies. It is often said that genealogy is the second most popular hobby in the US (right after gardening).[41] Mapping our own genealogies reminds us that we are part of something bigger than what we currently see and experience. It helps us to understand our histories, and from where and whom we came. Biblical genealogies did the same thing for Israel, and they were expressly theological. They connected individuals to a common identity and to the original promises of God.[42] Stephen G. Dempster describes the genealogies as a means to provide "a sense of movement within history towards a divine goal."[43] For example, Genesis 5 traces the ancestry of Noah all the way back to Adam, which suggests to the reader that the same Creator God who made humanity in his own image is the same God who re-created through Noah, a new Adam for a new starting point. The short genealogy in Ruth 4:18–22 looks back six generations to Perez and looks forward three generations to David, showing how David's ancestry is traced to a rare exemplar of faithfulness and *hesed* ("steadfast love") during the otherwise dark period of the judges.[44] When introducing his account of Israel's history, the Chronicler uses extensive genealogies to offer hope to God's people upon returning from Babylonian exile.[45] The genealogies reminded the Israelites that the God who made and fulfilled promises to Abraham and David is the same God who will make good on his promises to their descendants.

Israel's communal attitude, reflected in structures of grace, genealogies, and worship, is no mere artifact. Perdue considers the element of corporate solidarity to be "the most significant feature of the Israelite and early Jewish family that may serve as a social basis for contemporary ethical action."[46] What that might look like will vary from faith community to faith community,

---

41. Jasanoff, "Ancestor Worship."
42. Plum, "Genealogy as Theology," 79, 85.
43. Dempster, *Dominion and Dynasty*, 76.
44. It should not be missed that two of the ten men mentioned in this genealogy would not have been alive were it not for the structures of grace in the customs of levirate marriage and the role of the *go'el*. Perez was the child born of Tamar and her father-in-law Judah (Gen. 38), and Obed was the child born of Ruth and her *go'el*, Boaz.
45. Plum, "Genealogy as Theology," 86.
46. Perdue, "Household," 253.

but at the very least it should encourage God's people as individuals to look beyond themselves to their immediate community, and then beyond their immediate community to the entire world.

CONCLUSION

In summary, the cultural context of the ancient Israelite household helps us understand the various household metaphors for Israel's relationship with God and the communal way in which the Israelites thought, lived, and worshiped.

LOOKING BACK

1. What do you consider to be some of the most significant differences between an Israelite household and your own cultural understanding of a household?
2. Can you think of a modern "structure of grace" that you might be able to contribute to or invest in?
3. Which household metaphor for God (father, mother, midwife, husband, go'el, master) or Israel (child, wife, servant, sojourner) most interests you? How was Israel's conception of that role similar to or dissimilar from your own conception of the role?
4. How might household language for God and his people help us reframe our own family and household experiences? Are there broken parts of our households that can be mended or soothed when we think of God in these relationships with us?
5. How might thinking more communally and less individualistically affect how you think and act?

LOOKING BEYOND

Hess, Richard S. "The Family in the Old Testament as a Theological Model for Covenant Community." In *Interpreting the Old Testament Theologically: Essays in Honor of Willem VanGemeren*, edited by Andrew Abernethy , 270–79. Zondervan, 2018.

King, Philip J., and Lawrence E. Stager. *Life in Biblical Israel*. Westminster John Knox, 2001.

Matthews, Victor H., and Don C. Benjamin. *Social World of Ancient Israel: 1250–587 BCE*. Baker Academic, 2005.

Perdue, Leo G., Joseph Blenkinsopp, John J. Collins, and Carol Meyers, eds. *Families in Ancient Israel*. The Family, Religion, and Culture Series. Westminster John Knox, 1997.

Rogerson, John. "The Family and Structures of Grace in the Old Testament." In *The Family in Theological Perspective*, edited by Stephen Barton, 25–42. T&T Clark, 1996.

Wilk, Richard R., and William L. Rathje. "Household Archaeology." *American Behavioral Scientist* 25, no. 6 (1982): 617–39.

Yasur-Landau, Assaf, Jennie R. Ebeling, and Laura B. Mazow, eds. *Household Archaeology in Ancient Israel and Beyond*. Culture and History of the Ancient Near East 50. Brill, 2011.

2

COVENANT
The Loyalty of God

One of the most important concepts within the Hebrew Bible is "covenant." Covenant has long been the subject of extensive research within the fields of biblical studies and theology, and within the last hundred years, archaeological discoveries have broadened and deepened our understanding of covenants in the ancient Near Eastern world, including in ancient Israel. This chapter will briefly discuss the terminology of covenant, examples from the wider ancient Near Eastern world, and the three main categories of covenant in the Hebrew Bible: kinship and secular covenants, covenant treaties, and royal grant covenants. Furthermore, we will discuss how the biblical covenants compare to their ancient Near Eastern counterparts and how they relate to one another theologically.

LOOKING DOWN

Terminology

The Hebrew word *berit* is often translated in English as "covenant"; however, as with most words, there are shades of meaning. *Berit* can also be translated as "agreement," "treaty," "alliance," "contract," and "pact"—all of which demonstrate the political nature of *berit*. *Berit* comes from the root *barah*, which generally means "a cutting." This definition alludes to the custom of cutting or dividing animals in two for the parties of the covenant to pass between as a symbol of ratifying the covenant (Gen. 15; Jer. 34:18, 19).[1] A corresponding term, *'edut*, meaning "testimony" is occasionally used (Exod. 30:6). The word *berit* occurs in the Hebrew Bible some four hundred times, while *'edut* occurs just over forty times. Both terms convey the essential biblical understanding of a pledge or a formal agreement between two or more parties that is usually accompanied by an oath.[2] While this basic understanding of covenant is generally accepted within the scholarly community, the exact nature of covenant, including its social and legal framework, is still up for discussion.

Ancient Near Eastern Treaties

Hittite Treaties

Treaties and loyalty oaths seem to be as ancient as time itself. Examples of treaties in the ancient Near East range from the third millennium BCE to the Hellenistic and Roman periods.[3] One of the oldest collections of treaties is the Hittite treaties. The Hittites were located in the broad lands of Anatolia (modern-day Turkey) and were one of the superpowers of the ancient Near East during the Late Bronze Age (1500–1200 BCE). While the Hittite treaties are the most well-known from this time period, we must keep in mind that they did not invent the treaty form but borrowed it from others, primarily in Mesopotamia.[4]

There were two types of Hittite treaties: The first is known as the "suzerain treaty," which is a treaty between two parties of unequal power. The suzerain is the more powerful of the participants and the actual giver of the treaty. The vassal, or lesser power, is the only party to take an oath of obedience and must submit to the suzerain's demands; hence why it is called a suzerain treaty. The treaty may include promises of protection by the suzerain; however, the suzerain is not obligated to honor those promises due, in part, to the suzerain's privilege of self-determination and sovereignty. A suzerain treaty is unilateral, meaning that the treaty was done or undertaken by one party, the suzerain, and thus it benefits the suzerain only. For example, the Hittite king Muršili II was the first Hittite king to expand his kingdom far to the west. Consequently, the suzerain treaties that he created not only forced his new vassals into submission but also created a new identifiable political entity in the western part of his empire, whether the new vassals liked it or not.[5]

---

1. Koehler et al., *Hebrew and Aramaic Lexicon of the Old Testament*, 1:157–59.
2. Viviano, "Covenant."
3. Hays, *Hidden Riches*, 179.
4. Mendenhall, *Law and Covenant*, 28. See also Kitchen and Lawrence, *Treaty, Law and Covenant*.
5. Mendenhall, *Law and Covenant*, 30; Hays, *Hidden Riches*, 180.

The second treaty is the "parity treaty," which is a treaty between two parties that are equally powerful and who agree on the stipulations of the treaty. Parity treaties are bilateral, meaning the treaty affects the two parties reciprocally. In a parity treaty both parties are obligated to honor identical stipulations. The most well-known parity treaty is between the Hittite king Hattusili III and Ramses II of Egypt. In this treaty both kings are acknowledged as "Great King"; however, Ramses is mentioned first, which may indicate his superiority over Hattusili.[6]

Both the suzerain and parity treaties had several basic elements. While these basic elements are consistently found in all Hittite treaties, it must be noted that the form is a flexible one. There is considerable variation in the order, length, and wording of the elements, and, periodically, a treaty may be missing one or another of the elements; however, it is difficult to determine if this is accidental or deliberate and, if so, why that element was left out. The basic elements are briefly outlined below.

1. A *preamble* identifying the giver of the treaty.
2. A *historical prologue* that offered a detailed account of the relationship between the two parties. In a suzerain treaty, the historical prologue can be quite lengthy, emphasizing the benevolent deeds that the suzerain has bestowed upon the vassal, which was meant to motivate the vassal to remain loyal to the suzerain.
3. *Stipulations* of the treaty are provided in great detail and are nonnegotiable. The stipulations generally consisted of the vassal's unwavering loyalty to the suzerain and an offering of annual tribute.
4. A list of *divine witnesses*. Treaties were legal contracts and, as such, required witnesses. But treaties were also seen as sacred law; thus, the most fitting witnesses would be the sacred kind—the gods of the parties involved.
5. *Blessings and curses*. In a suzerain treaty, if the vassal obeyed the treaty, then there were benefits or blessings. However, if the vassal disobeyed the treaty, there were consequences, or curses. Within the text of the treaties, the blessings and curses are viewed as the actions of the gods, not the suzerain.
6. Provision for the *reading of the treaty and its deposit* in an official location. It was necessary to periodically hold a public reading of the treaty.
7. It is quite possible that some sort of *formal oath ceremony* finalized the making of the treaty.[7]

---

6. Hays, *Hidden Riches*, 180.
7. Hays, *Hidden Riches*, 183–84; Mendenhall, *Law and Covenant*, 34–35; Mendenhall, "Covenant Forms in Israelite Tradition," 58–61.

To summarize: The basic form of the suzerain treaty is consistent, with some elements receiving more or less attention than others, depending on the circumstances. The suzerain treaty form was considered the standard for treaties and was adapted throughout the next several centuries.

Assyrian Treaty-Oaths

One of the more famous adaptations of the Hittite treaty form are the Assyrian treaty-oaths. The Neo-Assyrian Empire (911–605 BCE) dominated the ancient Near Eastern world and initiated an imperialistic system that depleted their vassal states of their wealth, redirecting it to Assyria.[8] The Assyrians imposed treaty-oaths that functioned like a suzerain treaty, a unilateral treaty designed to benefit the Assyrian king. The Akkadian word *adê* is commonly translated as "treaty" or "loyalty oath," and in many instances the text functions as such; however, in other texts the terms "treaty" or "loyalty oath" seem to restrict our understanding of the character of these texts. The term "treaty" restricts *adê* to the realm of international relations, when in reality an *adê* was imposed not only on client kings but also on members of the royal family, the palace administration, and the populace of Assyrian cities, just to name a few. Furthermore, the translation of *adê* as "loyalty oath" focuses on one important component of the *adê*, the oath that was sworn by the vassal at its establishment and possible ceremony. Not only was the *adê* an obligatory behavior that was imposed on an individual or group of individuals, but the *adê* is transformed from a legal tool into what Assyriologist J. Lauinger calls a "supernatural loyalty oath" or "destiny." He argues that *adê* are projected into the divine realm by incorporating the name or image (like on a seal) of the divine and through the giving of the oath by the subordinate party or vassal.[9] As was mentioned earlier, in the ancient Near Eastern world, most things were seen as spiritual, and in today's world it is too easy for the spiritual nature of some of these treaties to be overlooked.

An Assyrian treaty-oath had seven elements.[10] These elements are similar to those of the Hittite suzerain treaty, with a couple minor adaptations. The elements also appear in an altered order, which further demonstrates that treaties had a basic form that each society or person altered to meet their needs. These elements, in order of their typical appearance, are described below.

1. The *preamble*, which identifies the Assyrian king and the vassal who is taking the oath.

---

8. Vitalis Hoffman and Mullins, *Atlas of the Biblical World*, 94.
9. Lauinger, "Neo-Assyrian Scribes," 286; Lauinger, "Neo-Assyrian *adê*," 114–15.
10. See Hays, *Hidden Riches*, 232–35.

2. The *designation* of the Assyrian ruler (or successor) to whom the vassal was swearing loyalty.
3. *Divine witnesses* to the treaty.
4. A *historical introduction*.
5. *Stipulations* of the treaty.
6. *Curses* for failing to fulfill the stipulations.
7. A *vow* of loyalty.

The most well-known example of an Assyrian treaty-oath is the Vassal Treaties of Esarhaddon (VTE; see fig. 2.1). In this treaty the Assyrian king, Esarhaddon (680–669 BCE), is concerned with his succession. Esarhaddon chose his son, Assurbanipal (668–627 BCE), as his successor. The transfer of power rarely went smoothly in the ancient Near East. The disruption of leadership brought with it battles for succession, instability, and uprisings by both the locals and the vassal states. The purpose of the VTE was to guarantee Assurbanipal's smooth transition to power by protecting him from threats, both abroad and from within Assyria—especially his brothers who may have wanted power for themselves. The vow of the treaty obligates the oath-taker to be faithful and loyal to Assurbanipal. This included foreign nations, who were required to provide aid and take military action against any person or group who conspired against Assurbanipal.[11] In this instance, a ceremony ratified the treaty with the local Assyrian population. The treaty itself mentions the ceremony where the people swore their loyalty to Assurbanipal:

Figure 2.1. Copy of the Vassal Treaties of Esarhaddon found at Tayinat

> Esarhaddon, king of Assyria, my father and begetter, heeded the command of Assur and Mullissu, the gods in whom he trusted, who told him that I was to exercise kingship. On the 12th of Iyyar,

---

11. Arnold and Strawn, *World Around the Old Testament*, 95; Hays, *Hidden Riches*, 182.

at the noble command of Ashur, Mullissu, Sin, Shamash, Adad, Bel, Nabu, Ishtar of Nineveh, Ishtar of Arbela, Ninurta, Nergal and Nusku, he convened the people of Assyria, great and small, from coast to coast, made them swear a treaty-oath by the gods and established a binding agreement to protect my crown-princeship and future kingship over Assyria.[12]

Alongside the treaty that the local population agreed to at the ceremony, eight copies of the VTE have been recovered, each with the name of a vassal ruler listed as the oath-taker. This indicates that this Assyrian treaty-oath was not just a local treaty but also functioned as a sort of form letter that could be addressed to individual rulers.

Royal Land Grants

Royal land grants were given by the suzerain to a vassal, and there are several reasons why a suzerain might do this: (1) To recognize a vassal who remained loyal. The purpose of the royal grant is to both reward the vassal for their past behavior and encourage their continued loyalty.[13] (2) Land grants were also allocated to a group of state craftsmen to provide them with sustenance.[14] (3) Royal land grants were seen as a way to expand the suzerain's territory. These privately owned agricultural estates attempted to link the central Assyrian cities with networks of communication and trade and to expand the vassal's territory.[15] One example comes from the land grant that the Neo-Assyrian king Adad-nerari III (811–783 BCE) allocated to a state governor. The inscription concludes that "[he shall not give these] towns, fields, houses and orchards [to any other governor], he shall give them (only) [to] the governor of the temple of Aššur. [The king will punish] the one who giv[es] them to another governor."[16] To expand one's territory with people who are obligated to be loyal to you in one way or another is a win-win.

Hebrew Bible Treaties

As we can see, the treaty genre has a long history in the ancient Near East. While the form and elements of the treaty genre were preserved over time, it is not unusual to see various people groups in the ancient Near East adapting its form to suit their specific needs. The covenant genre of ancient Israel is an adaptation of the treaty form, with impressive and unquestionable similarities between covenants found in the Bible and those of the Hittite

---

12. Parpola and Watanabe, *Neo-Assyrian Treaties*, xixx.
13. Viviano, "Covenant."
14. Baker, "Urban Craftsmen."
15. Harmanşah, "Beyond Aššur."
16. Kataja and Whiting, *Grants, Decrees and Gifts*, 79.

and Neo-Assyrian groups. The biblical covenants contain numerous concepts and worldviews that are common within the ancient Near East, as well as including the same elements as the Hittite treaties and Neo-Assyrian treaty-oaths. Within biblical covenants, the order and the weight of treaty elements can differ; however, this type of modification also happened in Hittite and Neo-Assyrian treaties, as we discussed above.[17] As a genre, treaties seemed to have a general blueprint that could be modified and adapted to suit the needs of particular societies.

The book of Deuteronomy gives us a particularly good example of the Bible using the same ancient Near Eastern treaty elements. A fuller description of Deuteronomy's role as a covenant will be addressed later on; however, the basic comparison between the treaty genre and Deuteronomy is as follows:

1. Identification of the giver of the covenant (Deut. 5:6).
2. Historical prologue (5:6b; 1:1–4:14).
3. Divine witnesses (4:26).
4. Stipulations (4:44–27:8).
5. Blessings (28:1–14).
6. Curses (28:15–68).
7. Oath taking (27:9–26).
8. Deposit/recital (10:1–2; 31:10–13, 24–29).[18]

As you can see, the similarities with the treaty genre (both Hittite and Neo-Assyrian treaty-oaths) are striking. In the Hebrew Bible there are three main categories of covenants or occasions that would necessitate such a treaty: kinship and secular covenants, covenant treaties, and royal grant covenants.

Kinship or "Secular" Covenants

The first type of biblical covenant is a kinship covenant, which is an agreement between related households, clans, and tribes. Ancient Israelite society was based on these kinship social groups, which would often need to make a covenant where each party agreed to abide by particular guidelines or to accept responsibilities that were seen as beneficial to the group.[19] One example of a kinship covenant is marriage, which was viewed as a treaty between two households, usually within the same clan or tribe. Marriage is quite possibly the oldest form of a kinship covenant. The Hebrew Bible views marriage

---

17. Hays, *Hidden Riches*, 183.
18. Arnold and Strawn, *World Around the Old Testament*, 96; Hays, *Hidden Riches*, 179.
19. Viviano, "Covenant."

as a covenant (Prov. 2:17; Mal. 2:14), and the metaphor of marriage is used throughout the Hebrew Bible to describe the covenant relationship between Israel and God (see Hosea).

The Hebrew Bible also mentions numerous covenants between individuals and/or groups. Some of the covenants between individuals within the Hebrew Bible include Abraham and Abimelech (Gen. 21:25–34), Isaac and Abimelech (26:26–33), Jacob and Laban (31:44–50), David and Jonathan (1 Sam. 18:3; 20:8; 23:18), David and Abner (2 Sam. 3:12–13), Solomon and Hiram (1 Kings 5:12), Asa and Ben-hadad (15:18–19), and Ahab and Ben-hadad (20:34). Covenants between an individual and a group include Abraham and the Amorites (Gen. 14:13), Joshua with the Gibeonites (Josh. 9), Joshua and the people of Shechem (24:25), Jehoiada the priest with the guards (2 Kings 11:4, 12), and Zedekiah with the people (Jer. 34:8–9). These types of covenants are also sometimes called "secular" covenants because the two parties involved are individuals or nations and the little information available on these covenants resembles other ancient Near Eastern treaties. For instance, in the Hebrew Bible the taking of an oath is only mentioned some of the time, but it can be assumed that it was always part of the making of a covenant, even if not specifically mentioned. Furthermore, the covenant terms or stipulations vary depending on the covenant, which further demonstrates that the treaty/oath/covenant was hardly a form set in stone; rather, it varied depending on the circumstances and needs or desires of the parties involved. Some of the more regular stipulations in biblical covenants include to "not deal falsely" (Gen. 21:23), to "do . . . no harm" (26:29), to gain protection (Josh. 9), to reap economic benefits (1 Kings 5:12), to gain military support (15:18–19), and to establish peace (20:34).[20]

Covenant Treaties Between Israel and God

Covenant is important to our understanding of the Hebrew Bible not just because of its use within the wider ancient Near East but also because "covenant" became the fundamental way Israel spoke of its special relationship with God. One of the major covenants in the Hebrew Bible that illustrates the covenantal relationship between Israel and God is the Sinai/Horeb covenant in Deuteronomy 5–8 (which is also related in Exod. 20–24).

The treaty form of the book of Deuteronomy was outlined earlier, so a few brief observations will be addressed here. Four interesting points of comparison are worth noting: (1) Deuteronomy not only adapted the suzerain treaty form but also adopted some of its typical terminology. For instance, the words "love," "know," and "fear" are typically found in suzerain

---

20. Viviano, "Covenant."

treaties and are used to describe the relationship between the suzerain and its vassal(s) (Deut. 5:29; 6:4–5; 7:7–10; 28:65–67). Similarly, the phrases "walk after," "obey [God's] voice," and "serve" are used to establish the expected conduct of the vassal (13:4 NKJV). A common reward for such good behavior is prosperity (4:40; 5:29; 6:3, 18, 24; 10:13–14; 30:9). (2) The covenant is not just with their ancestors but also for them in that day (5:2–3; 29:10–12). (3) God will remain faithful to the covenant, but Israel may or may not (and indeed does not) remain faithful to the covenant. God's end of the treaty is to provide land, protection, and descendants (or sometimes dynasty) (28:1–11; 30:9). Israel's obligation is to obey the laws that are attached to the covenant, especially remaining loyal to God alone (by not worshiping other gods) (6:14; 28:14; 29:18). (4) Deuteronomy stresses that Israel's experiences of the covenant blessings are conditional. Both parties in the "special relationship" are bound by an oath to keep the terms of the covenant.[21] The prophets later use this point to try to persuade the Israelites, who have disobeyed by worshiping other gods (i.e., not loving God) *and* by taking advantage of the less fortunate (i.e., not loving others), to return to their covenant relationship with God or suffer the consequences. Once Israel is taken into exile, they attempt to make sense of their current circumstances by viewing the exile as a punishment for their breaking of the covenant treaty with God (28:20, 25, 36–37; 29:26–28; 30:1). The conditional nature of the covenant is also reconsidered during this time—that is, if they return to the covenant treaty, then God will restore them and bless them with a return to the land, with descendants, and with God's protection (30:1–8). In other words, God is punishing them, but God has not abandoned them. It is interesting to note that the Sinai/Horeb covenant in Exodus 20–24 also views the covenant as conditional, but only for individuals, not for the community of Israel. Rather, the covenant made with Israel's ancestors (Abraham, Isaac, and Jacob) will be honored as an everlasting or perpetual covenant with the collective Israel (Exod. 31:16).[22]

Royal Grant Covenants

The final type of biblical covenant to be addressed is royal grants. This type of covenant is given by the king to a vassal who has remained loyal. It includes a gift that usually consists of land. Whereas the purpose of a treaty is to reinforce future behavior, the purpose of the royal grant is to both reward the vassal for their past behavior and to encourage their continued loyalty.[23] In

---

21. Viviano, "Covenant."
22. The Priestly authors/redactors appear to be interested in the everlasting covenant between God and the community of Israel. See also Gen. 9:12, 16; 17:7, 13, 19; Num. 25:13.
23. Viviano, "Covenant."

the Hebrew Bible, several covenants resemble royal grants more than secular covenants or basic treaties. The following covenants would fit in the royal grant category: Noah, Abraham, Phinehas, and David.

In Genesis 9, Yhwh makes an everlasting covenant with Noah, his sons, their descendants, and all living creatures. Yhwh vows to never again flood the earth and in return requires that humanity "not eat flesh with its life, that is, its blood" (9:4).

In the covenant with Abraham, Yhwh bestows on Abraham descendants (Gen. 17:5–6) and land (17:8) (which will be passed on to his descendants). This covenant is also portrayed as an everlasting covenant (17:7) that requires Abraham and every male in his household to be circumcised as a sign of the covenant (17:11).

A brief mention of a "covenant of peace" with Phinehas, the grandson of Aaron, and his descendants is found in Numbers 25:10–13. Here Phinehas is rewarded for punishing a couple who, along with the rest of Israel, committed idolatry by attaching themselves to the Moabite god, Baal of Peor.

The covenant with David is more complicated. The establishment of the dynasty of David (2 Sam. 7) does not use the term "covenant"; however, "covenant" is used elsewhere in the Hebrew Bible to describe the special relationship between David/David's dynasty and Yhwh (2 Sam. 23:5; 1 Kings 8:24; 2 Chron. 21:7; Ps. 89:3–4, 29, 35–36; Isa. 55:3; Jer. 33:12–26). The agreement between Yhwh and David does reflect the land grant covenant: David is gifted with a dynasty due to his past behavior (1 Kings 3:6; 9:4–5; Ps. 132:5, 13–18). The Davidic covenant is referred to as an everlasting covenant (2 Sam. 7:13–16; 23:5), but it can be lost (and indeed is) by David's descendants (1 Kings 11:11; Pss. 89:39; 132:12). The view that the Davidic covenant was conditional is likely due to the destruction of the kingdom of Judah in 586 BCE and, as such, the Davidic covenant was reinterpreted in two main ways: (1) The Davidic covenant was universalized to be for all of Israel, not just David, with the perpetual blessings of land, protection, and descendants (2 Sam. 7:10), or (2) the covenant's fulfillment was going to occur in the future, thus laying the groundwork for messianic expectations.[24]

Summary

As we can see, the treaty genre is clearly visible in the covenants of the Hebrew Bible. The three main types of covenants—kinship and secular covenants, covenant treaties, and royal grant covenants—only further illustrate that the treaty genre was adapted to suit the needs of the ancient Israelites.

---

24. Viviano, "Covenant."

LOOKING UP

Having surveyed the various types of covenants in the ancient Near East and in the Hebrew Bible, we now turn to explore how Israel's theological understanding of covenant was informed by their cultural climate. First, we will consider the theological significance of kinship and secular covenants, and then we will turn specifically to the covenants between God and his people, which reflect various aspects of the treaties and land grants discussed above. Next, we will use the Sinai covenant (and especially Exod. 19:4–6) as an entry point for teasing out some of the theological distinctions of a biblical covenant vis-à-vis ancient Near Eastern conceptions of covenant. We will conclude by examining how the biblical covenants relate together theologically.

Kinship and Secular Covenants

Since kinship and secular covenants were between human partners, they may not seem like fertile ground for exploring theology. However, as noted in chapter 1, the concept of covenant was actually built on household commitments (and not vice versa), so that covenants are often referred to as "fictive kinships."[25] The order of influence matters because it is the difference between describing families in political terms or describing political relationships in family terms. In the Hebrew Bible, we have the latter.

The various kinship and secular covenants in the Hebrew Bible bear out the elements of strong commitment seen in similar covenants in the ancient Near East. One of the strongest examples of this is in Malachi. The book opens with an affirmation of divine love: "I have loved you, says the LORD" (Mal. 1:2), and then moves into an indictment of Judah's unrequited love, using analogies from social relationships: "A son honors his father, and servants their master. If then I am a father, where is the honor due me? And if I am a master, where is the respect due me?" (1:6). Using the analogies of kinship and secular covenants, God makes an argument from lesser to greater: If my people can be loyal to each other in these types of covenants, why are they not being loyal to me?

Or, consider the many times that God likens himself to the estranged partner in an adulterous marriage (the entire book of Hosea is a case in point). There is a reason why God uses family metaphors to describe his relationship to Israel: These are the relationships that are most binding, most important in our lives. As Don Vito Corleone said in *The Godfather*, "You can do anything, but never go against family." It is no surprise that covenant readily employs language of kinship, even in divine-human covenants.

---

25. Richter, *Epic of Eden*, 70–72.

A Brief Overview of Treaty and Grant Covenants in the Hebrew Bible

We now turn to the covenants specifically made between God and his people. God's covenantal relationship with his people can be described in terms of one overarching covenant, with individual covenants also contributing to make up that big-picture covenant. Just as we can analyze both the scenes within a play and the overarching plot of the entire play, so also our focus will be on both the individual covenanting acts between God and his people and the overarching covenantal relationship to which each "scene" contributes.

As we saw above, the concept of covenant is broader than the term itself and arguably permeates the whole of Scripture, even where the term "covenant" is not expressly mentioned.[26] The first mention of *berit* ("covenant") in the Hebrew Bible is in Genesis 6:18 when God tells Noah, "But I will establish my covenant with you; and you shall come into the ark, you, your sons, your wife, and your sons' wives with you." Scholars like William Dumbrell and Daniel Block argue that this mention of covenant refers back to a unilateral covenant that God had already made with creation in Genesis 1–2 but that is now being established specifically with Noah.[27] After the flood, we read that God's covenant was not just with Noah but with the entire world, including the animals and the earth itself (9:9–17).

A few chapters later, God seems to narrow his focus to one man and one family: Abraham. However, it is clear from the beginning that this relationship is ultimately for the sake of the whole world. In Genesis 12, God commands Abraham to leave his homeland for a new land (v. 1) that he will give to him (v. 7). God promises to make Abraham a "great nation" and that he will make his "name great" (v. 2). He promises to bless Abraham, as well as those who bless him (vv. 2–3), and he promises Abraham that "in you all the families of the earth shall be blessed" (v. 3). All of creation is clearly still in view, as it was with the Noahic covenant and implicitly in Genesis 1–2. These promises made to Abraham in Genesis 12 are then reaffirmed and officially ratified with a covenant ceremony in Genesis 15. Abraham's responsibility in the covenant is made clear in Genesis 17, when God commands him to do two things: "Walk before me, and be blameless" (v. 1), and "Every male among you shall be circumcised" (v. 10).

---

26. Several theologians have argued that "covenant" is the theological "center" of the Old Testament, most famously Eichrodt, *Theology of the Old Testament*, 1:17.

27. Dumbrell, *Covenant and Creation*, 1–18; Block, *Covenant*, 16; Robin Routledge is a bit more cautious but states, "It may be more appropriate to talk about a covenant implicit within the act of creation itself, a 'covenant with creation,' which is then *confirmed* in the Noahic covenant." Routledge, *Old Testament Theology*, 164.

As God fulfilled his promises to Abraham, making Abraham's descendants into a great nation and delivering them into their own land, the covenant was recontextualized to accommodate Israel's changing context. The covenant made at Mount Sinai reaffirmed God's commitment to Israel once they had become a nation, and it detailed (with 613 laws!) *how* the Israelites (like Abraham before them) were to "walk before [God], and be blameless" (Gen. 17:1).

Once the Israelites inherited the land and God gave them a human king to represent his own kingship, God established a covenant with David. As recounted in 2 Samuel 7, God affirmed his promises to Abraham of a "great name" (v. 9), land (v. 10), and descendants (v. 12), and he added that those descendants would have an everlasting dynasty (vv. 13–16).

After the kingdoms of Israel and Judah were destroyed by the Assyrians and Babylonians, God's people questioned whether or not they had forfeited God's covenant forever (Ps. 89:38–51; Lam. 5:20–22). God assured them through prophets like Jeremiah and Ezekiel that he had not abandoned them, and that he would make a new covenant with them that would never be threatened because he would write his law on their hearts (Jer. 31:33) and give them new hearts of flesh to replace their hearts of stone (Ezek. 11:19; 36:26). In short, God would transform Israel so that their covenant with God would never again be threatened by unfaithfulness.

Israelite Covenants Compared to Ancient Near Eastern Covenants

What do we learn about these biblical covenants by comparing them with their ancient Near Eastern neighbors? And what kind of "suzerain" was Israel's God? Exodus 19:4–6 serves essentially as the thesis statement, as it were, of the Sinai covenant. It also covers in a succinct way three distinctives of biblical covenants, each of which correspond to one element of the suzerain-vassal treaty structure. These three verses will serve as the outline for this section, showing how the covenants of the Hebrew Bible were (1) grounded in a historical relationship (Exod. 19:4), (2) uniquely gracious (19:5), and (3) universal in scope (19:6). Because the suzerain covenant is the point of comparison in this section, most of our focus will remain on the Sinai covenant, though (as we will see in the next section) there is much continuity between all of the covenants.

The Historical Prologue of the Covenant Reveals Yhwh as a Relational, Saving God

You have seen what I did to the Egyptians, and how I bore you on eagles' wings and brought you to myself. (Exod. 19:4)

The first unique feature of covenant in the Hebrew Bible is the fact that Israel's God himself entered into the history and story of his people to become their covenant partner.[28] Within the ancient Near Eastern worldview, all things were considered "spiritual." We saw this with the Assyrian "loyalty oath" (*adê*), which elevated human treaties to the divine realm. Despite the spiritual nature of treaties and covenants, they were typically made between kings or families. Nowhere else (with one possible exception[29]) does a god make a covenant with an entire people. The "I-You" style of the suzerain-vassal treaty highlights the relational quality of the treaty, but in the biblical covenants, that relational bond was uniquely between Israel and their God.

The historical prologue of most biblical covenants recounts the historical relationship between covenant members (as in the Exod. 19:4 quotation above), and it finds its clearest expression in the Sinai covenant, especially in Exodus 20:2, Deuteronomy 1–4, and Joshua 24:2–13.[30] These statements recount what God has done for Israel as reminders of his commitment and as motivation for Israel's obedience to their part of the covenant. As Jon Levenson explains, "Awareness of divine grace sets the stage for the stipulations."[31] Exodus 20:2 opens the Decalogue by saying, "I am the LORD your God, who brought you out of the land of Egypt, out of the house of slavery." God's faithfulness is made clear in the history and story of Israel's experience. Exodus 20:2 is not a proposition that *tells* us "God has been faithful." Rather, it is part of the story that *shows* us God's faithfulness. And that faithfulness, to rescue and protect his people, must be met by Israel's faithfulness to the stipulations of the covenant.[32]

Another important implication of the historical prologue is that biblical covenants were made within existing relationships. Covenants rarely established new relationships but, rather, built on existing ones.[33] Israel was not

---

28. McConville, "בְּרִית," 1:753.

29. Zevit, "Phoenician Inscription."

30. Traces of a historical prologue are also seen in the Abrahamic covenant (Gen. 15:7: "I am the LORD who brought you from Ur of the Chaldeans"), the Davidic covenant (2 Sam. 7:6: "Since the day I brought up the people of Israel from Egypt to this day . . ."; and 2 Sam. 7:9: "I have been with you wherever you went, and have cut off all your enemies from before you"), and the new covenant (Ezek. 11:16: "Yet I have been a sanctuary to them for a little while in the countries where they have gone").

31. Levenson, *Sinai and Zion*, 32. Similarly, Sandra Richter notes how the inclusion of the historical prologue in the Hittite treaties serves to motivate the vassal with gratitude, unlike the later Assyrian treaties, where such a prologue was "conspicuously absent." Richter, *Epic of Eden*, 80.

32. In other words, this covenant relationship is not static but based on obligation and commitment, which is why covenants are said to be "remembered," "kept," and "commanded." Hugenberger, *Marriage as a Covenant*, 169.

33. Hugenberger, *Marriage as a Covenant*, 169.

coming into relationship with Yhwh for the first time at Mount Sinai, nor were biblical writers fabricating a glamorous past to muster faith in their contemporaries.[34] Moreover, covenants were not made within natural, family relationships because the commitment is inherent in those relationships. That is why covenants use the language of household roles, because the relationship "father" and "son" is inherently one of deep commitment. Covenants establish commitments in relationships where commitment is not inherent, such as between kings or between marriage partners or between parents and adopted children. Goldingay explains, "Covenant comes to be involved when people extend a commitment beyond such natural groupings."[35] The implication is that there is something unnatural about the relationship between God and humanity. That is why it involves grace.[36]

The historical prologue also enabled subsequent generations to identify—historically—with the original covenant community. Levenson explains:

> A major function of the historical prologue is to narrow the gap between generations, to mold all Israel, of whatever era, into one personality that can give an assent to the divine initiative.... What your ancestors saw is what you saw. God's rescue of them implicates you, obliges you, for you, by hearing this story and responding affirmatively, become Israel, and it was Israel whom he rescued. Telling the story brings it alive. The historical prologue brings the past to bear pointedly on the present. In the words of the rabbinic Passover liturgy (Haggadah), "Each man is obligated to see himself as if he came out of Egypt."[37]

Indeed, that is the very purpose of this book: Instead of trying to relate to Scripture by rashly pulling it into our own conceptual worlds and immediately trying to apply it to our own needs, we need first to experience Scripture in its own world. The historical prologue of these covenant passages invites us to become original witnesses and recipients of its message. What a privilege and adventure!

---

34. Contrast, for example, Mendenhall, who argues that the covenant necessitated a fabricated history of the covenant partners ("Covenant Forms in Israelite Tradition," 70), and Levenson, who argues that their history gave rise to something sacred and binding—namely, a covenant (*Sinai and Zion*, 41).

35. Goldingay, *Israel's Faith*, 182.

36. Von Rad describes this commitment by saying, "The covenant is therefore a legal relationship, and comprises the firmest guarantee of a relationship of human communion," which is why it often involved a solemn ceremony (sometimes with blood) (von Rad, *Old Testament Theology*, 1:130). Note the parallel relationship between the promise to Abraham in Gen. 12:1–3 and the sealing of that promise in a covenant with blood (Gen. 15:10) with the promise to Israel as a nation in Exod. 19:4–6 and the sealing of that covenant with blood in Exod. 24:8. Goldingay, *Israel's Gospel*, 474.

37. Levenson, *Sinai and Zion*, 37.

The Stipulations and Consequences of the Covenant Reveal God's Grace

> Now therefore, if you obey my voice and keep my covenant, you shall be my treasured possession out of all the peoples. (Exod. 19:5)

The second unique aspect of God's covenant with Israel is the amount of patience and grace God showed to Israel, his vassal. Consider this analogy: Landlords and tenants sign a lease that obligates the tenants to certain stipulations in return for living in the landlord's property. These stipulations include paying the rent on time and keeping the property clean and maintained. If the tenants violate the stipulations of their "renting covenant," the landlord has the right to terminate the covenant (in other words, evict them!). Few landlords would allow their tenants to continually break the terms of their lease, and yet this is precisely what we see God doing with Israel.

The stipulations of the covenant, which are summarized in the Ten Commandments (or, more accurately, the "Ten Words"), are the conditions that Israel had to meet in order to experience the blessings of the covenant. As noted above, a typical suzerain-vassal treaty was unilateral, privileging the sovereignty of the suzerain, who was under no obligation to keep any covenant promises given. Yhwh not only keeps his promises but does so even after Israel's repeated violations of the covenant stipulations. Again and again God chooses to forgive, restore, and rescue his people. Even when he finally allows them to experience tastes of the covenant curses, and even when he finally allows them to experience the covenant curses in full through the destruction of the temple and the exile, it is only after years—centuries!—of patiently enduring their sinful waywardness.

This is illustrated in Exodus 32–34. Nearly as soon as Israel confirms their allegiance to the covenant (19:8; 24:3), they violate that covenant by worshiping Yhwh as a graven image, a golden calf. Moses intercedes on their behalf, and God forgives his covenant-breaking people, revealing his character in what becomes a creedal formula that will be repeated throughout Scripture:

> The LORD, the LORD,
> a God merciful and gracious,
> slow to anger,
> and abounding in steadfast love and faithfulness,
> keeping steadfast love for the thousandth generation,
> forgiving iniquity and transgression and sin,
> yet by no means clearing the guilty,
> but visiting the iniquity of the parents
> upon the children
> and the children's children,
> to the third and the fourth generation. (34:6–7)

Hosea 11:8–9 offers another beautiful picture of Yhwh's radical compassion for his undeserving people:

> How can I give you up, Ephraim?
> > How can I hand you over, O Israel?
> How can I make you like Admah?
> > How can I treat you like Zeboiim?
> My heart recoils within me;
> > my compassion grows warm and tender.
> I will not execute my fierce anger;
> > I will not again destroy Ephraim;
> *for I am God and no mortal,*
> > the Holy One in your midst,
> > and I will not come in wrath.

God is Israel's king and suzerain, but he is unlike any ancient Near Eastern king. He is "God and no mortal," and his compassion outruns that of any woman or man.[38] Even when God finally does bring the judgment of the covenant curses, restoration is always in view and his compassion is never far off. Thus, the prophets who speak of Judah's judgment also promise restoration.[39]

Finally, Exodus 19:5 also showcases God's great love for his chosen people, who are said to be his "treasured possession out of all the peoples." God's election of Israel is based first and foremost on his great love for them: "Because he loved your ancestors, he chose their descendants after them. He brought you out of Egypt with his own presence, by his great power" (Deut. 4:37). God's love for his covenant people, Israel, is the basis for their election, their deliverance, and their blessing.

The Blessings of the Covenant Reveal the Universal Scope of God's Revelation and Redemption

But you shall be for me a priestly kingdom and a holy nation. (Exod. 19:6)

God's love for his covenant children was never isolated from his love for the rest of creation. As Soulen explains, "The path to new creation leads through

---

38. McConville, "בְּרִית," 1:753.
39. For example, Isa. 40:10–11; 43:16–21; 49:1–26; Jer. 30:1–3; 32:36–41; Ezek. 34:11–24; 36:24; 37:11–14. A rabbinic tractate from the Talmud (fifth century CE) describes Abraham walking through the temple on the eve of its destruction (586 BCE). The famous intercessor and patriarch tells God that he should have spared the temple and his people for the sake of his covenant of circumcision, but God tells Abraham that sparing them the covenant curses of exile will not lead to repentance but only enable them to sin more. God then assures a mourning Abraham saying, "With regard to the Jewish people, their final purpose will be fulfilled at their end, i.e., they will ultimately repent and return to Me." Babylonian Talmud, Menahot 53b, trans. William Davidson, Sefaria, https://www.sefaria.org/Menachot.53b.8?lang=bi.

God's fidelity toward the tribes of Israel, yet in such a way that God's fidelity toward Israel is simultaneously an act of healing judgment and reconciliation between the Lord, the whole human family, and all creation."[40] The function of covenant as a creation-wide blessing was also unique in the ancient Near East. As a "priestly kingdom" Israel was to mediate God's blessing and *shalom* to those around them.[41] The official priesthood was limited to the tribe of Levi, but according to Exodus 19:6, all of Israel was called to be holy mediators between God and the world. This echoes the promise given to Abraham in Genesis 12:3 ("in you all the families of the earth shall be blessed"), and it is affirmed throughout the Sinai covenant. The instrumental aspect of God's election in the Hebrew Bible echoes the cosmic tones of his covenant at creation (Gen. 1–2) and the Noahic covenant (Gen. 9).

T. F. Torrance describes the instrumentality of election this way: "This movement was paradoxical in character—the more particular it became, the more universal it also became; the deeper the bond between God and man was driven into the human existence of Israel, the closer redemption made contact with creation; the more intimately Israel was tied to the one and only God, the God of all, the more the activity of grace broke through the limitations of national Israel and reached out to all the world."[42] Election was a means whereby God could reach the world with his covenant grace.[43]

The prophets also highlighted the universal scope of God's covenant love in passages like Isaiah 19:16–25, which depicts Israel's prime enemies of the time, Egypt and Assyria, enfolded in the covenant and worshiping Yhwh within their own nations. This eschatological vision of blessing is not one in which Israel is replaced by the nations, nor is it one that erases Israelite-gentile distinctions, as Soulen explains: "God's history with Israel and the nations is ordered from the outset towards a final reign of *shalom* in which the distinction between Israel and the nations is not abrogated and overcome but affirmed within a single economy of mutual blessing."[44]

---

40. Soulen, *The God of Israel and Christian Theology*, 176.

41. According to Routledge, election is always tied to Israel being an instrument of blessing to the world, *Old Testament Theology*, 171–73; cf. C. Wright, *Mission of God*.

42. Torrance, "Israel of God," 311–12. This view of the instrumentality of election is widespread among Old Testament theologians and has been taken by some as the primary purpose of election (von Rad, Block, C. Wright). Viewing election primarily in terms of instrumentality to the nations (rather than as divine love) can lead to the faulty conclusion that Israel's election was merely a means to an end. Such views are helpfully critiqued by Soulen (*The God of Israel and Christian Theology*, 5–12) and Moberly (*Old Testament Theology*, esp. 46–48).

43. This instrumentality, of course, works in both directions, with the nations also functioning as instruments to bring Israel back into right relationship with Yhwh. Cornell, "Israel's Priority," 349.

44. Soulen, *The God of Israel and Christian Theology*, 132 (emphasis removed).

In summary, God's covenant with Israel underscores his relationship with them, his grace, and their mission to extend that blessing to the rest of creation.

How Are the Biblical Covenants Related?

There are points of continuity and discontinuity between the covenants in the Hebrew Bible. Deuteronomy illustrates both with respect to the Abrahamic and Sinai covenants. Deuteronomy 4:31 emphasizes continuity: "Because the Lord your God is a merciful God, he will neither abandon you nor destroy you; he will not forget the covenant with your ancestors that he swore to them." Deuteronomy 5:2–3 emphasizes discontinuity: "The Lord our God made a covenant with us at Horeb [Sinai]. Not with our ancestors did the Lord make this covenant, but with us, who are all of us here alive today."[45]

At least three additional observations can help tease out the relationship between the covenants in the Hebrew Bible: (1) They are a dynamic unity, (2) they are bolstered by God's accommodating grace, and (3) they are never fully abrogated.

First, the covenants are a dynamic unity, bound together by God's faithful pattern of fulfilling his promises. By "dynamic," we refer to the ability to stretch and accommodate. God's relationship with his people grew and changed according to Israel's changing circumstances, but at its core it remained the same. This is clear, for example, in the reaffirmations of covenants long after their original establishment (e.g., Josh. 24, Ps. 81). Moreover, each covenant "renegotiation"[46] built on themes from previous covenants: The Sinai covenant was necessitated by God's fulfilled promises to Abraham that his descendants would become a great nation and be given the land, and the Davidic covenant was built on prior covenant promises that God's people would eventually become a kingdom (Gen. 17:6; 35:11; Deut. 17:14–20).

This could be illustrated in the way that a tree grows and changes, but it remains the same organism. Many trees send a strong taproot down deep into the soil, with smaller roots branching out from it. If the roots of the tree are likened to God's covenant promises and the terms of the covenant, then the tap root would be that central promise of relationship from which the others flow: "I will be their God, and they shall be my people" (Jer. 31:33; see also Exod. 6:7; Ezek. 37:23). The smaller roots are other promises common to all covenants including land, fruitfulness, and blessing for his people and for the

---

45. McConville, "בְּרִית," 1:749–50.
46. I am borrowing this term from Goldingay (*Israel's Gospel*, 371), who likewise stresses the continuity of covenant.

nations. Everything above ground, the tree and branches and leaves and fruit, all represent Israel's response to God and experience in the covenant. The tree adds roots and branches and grows in various ways throughout time, but it remains the same tree. Similarly, God's covenant relationship with his people grew and changed with his people's changing experiences, but it remained the same covenant.

Second, covenants are bolstered by God's accommodating grace. Israel's wandering from God's will did not permanently destroy their relationship with God. When Israel was faithful to the covenant, they were like a tree that flourished, produced fruit, and even drew the attention of onlookers. Even when they were unfaithful to the covenant, and they experienced the covenant curses (Lev. 26; Deut. 28), the covenant itself was not discarded.

Similarly, a tree can suffer broken branches, lack of fruit, withered leaves, and even disease without dying. In my (Libby's) backyard is a beautiful and towering blue oak tree. It bends over into my neighbor's yard at a 45° angle. It looks like it is literally trying to leave our yard, just like Israel often tried to leave her covenant partner. The tree seems precarious, but if we could look underground, we would see that the roots are also reaching far into my neighbor's yard, underground, to compensate for the tree's irregular growth. In the same way, God's covenant relationship with Israel was able to change and compensate for Israel's changing situations and even for their periods of waywardness.

Third, the covenant was never fully abrogated. Even when Israel was destroyed as a nation and exiled to a foreign land, God had not abandoned his covenant with them. He knew that Israel's unfaithfulness had gotten to the point where nothing but full judgment of the covenant curses would turn her heart back to the covenant. He also promised to restore Israel to life, as Ezekiel's vision of the dry bones being restored to life so powerfully illustrates (Ezek. 37:1–14). This is like an olive tree that has been chopped down to a stump. On the surface, it looks hopelessly destroyed, but the roots of the tree are able to regenerate the tree completely, and often are far more productive as a result (this is called coppicing). In the words of Jeremiah, when God "pull[s] down" his people, he knows exactly how to "build them up" again (Jer. 1:10; 24:6).[47]

In summary, the covenants in the Hebrew Bible relate together like a tree that develops, adapts, suffers, and flourishes, with complex root systems and

---

47. Similarly, in the words of the prophet Hosea, God had the right to name his people "not my people" (Hosea 1:9–10), and then show his radical compassion to restore them and to call them once more "you are my people" (2:23). Or, in the book of Isaiah, God can cut his people down to a stump (Isa. 6:13), from which a "shoot" can sprout renewed life and hope (11:1).

branches that are all one organism grounded in one taproot: God's grace in sustaining a relationship with his people and fulfilling his promises to them.

The New Covenant

But what about the new covenant? Again, there are points of continuity and discontinuity. The central promises, or "taproot," remain the same. The people with whom God covenants even remain the same. Jeremiah and Ezekiel proclaim a new covenant that will be for both Judah and Israel (Jer. 31:31; Ezek. 37:16–22). The substance of the covenant is also the same, as Jeremiah 31:33 highlights: "I will put my law within them, and I will write it on their hearts." Even the Hebrew word for "new" (*hadash*) does not carry the sense of something that is "brand new" in essence but, rather, something that is renewed or made new.[48]

If the promises, people, and substance remain the same, what exactly is different in the new covenant? Israel's ability to keep it. It was always the goal of the old covenant for Israel to internalize God's will (e.g., Deut. 30:6), and some Hebrew Bible saints were able to do so in part (e.g., Ps. 40:8; Isa. 51:7), but in the new covenant age, Israel will finally be enabled to do so in full. With renewed hearts and spirits (Ezek. 36:26) and the law written on their hearts and minds, they will all know Yhwh (Jer. 31:33–34).

Looking back from the vantage point of the New Testament, this promise is fulfilled through the indwelling, sanctifying work of the Holy Spirit, made possible through the life-giving love of Jesus. Notice how Jesus's language at the Last Supper in Matthew 26:28 ("for this is my blood of the covenant, which is poured out for many for the forgiveness of sins") directly echoes Moses's words in Exodus 24:8: "Moses took the blood and dashed it on the people, and said, 'See the blood of the covenant that the LORD has made with you in accordance with all these words.'"[49] As the mediator of the new covenant, Jesus is also portrayed as the new Adam, who is faithful to the covenant where the original Adam was not (Rom. 5:14–19; 1 Cor. 15:12–22); the new Moses, who offers an enduring rest (Heb. 3–4); and a new and final David, whose kingdom and throne will truly "be established forever" (2 Sam. 7:16; cf. Rev. 11:15).[50]

---

48. The Greek translation of the Hebrew Bible (the Septuagint) renders the Hebrew word for "new" (*hadash*) with the Greek word *kainos*, which Dumbrell describes as "a new dimension being added to the covenant experience and not merely or necessarily to a totally new divine initiative having no temporal reference to the past" (*Covenant and Creation*, 256). There is, in fact, so much continuity between the old and new covenants that some scholars consider the new covenant a "confirmation" of the old covenant (e.g., Goldingay, *Israel's Gospel*, 201).

49. Richter, *Epic of Eden*, 89.

50. Block, *Covenant*, 621.

Are God's Covenants Conditional or Unconditional?

One final theological issue that brings us back to the cultural context of covenant is the question of whether or not God's covenant relationship with and promises to Israel were conditional or unconditional. Some scholars argue that the Noahic, Abrahamic, and Davidic covenants most resemble grant treaties, and should therefore be considered unconditional, whereas the Sinai covenant most resembles suzerain-vassal treaties and should therefore be considered conditional.[51] Even the wording of Exodus 19:5 seems to indicate a conditional nature to the covenant (e.g., "if you obey . . . you shall be"). However, upon a closer reading, there appear to be both conditional and unconditional elements within each covenant. The instigation of the covenant is an unconditional, unilateral work of God alone, which the covenant ceremony in Genesis 15:12–21 illustrates so well, with God doing everything while Abraham sleeps (see fig. 2.2)! Yet Israel's experience within the covenant is conditioned on their faithfulness, which is emphasized in Genesis 22 after Abraham offers his son Isaac to God.

As we saw in the first section of this chapter, grant treaties were often "conditioned" on previous acts of loyalty, and the Noahic, Abrahamic, and Davidic covenants seem to follow suit. Noah had to build a boat to be spared (Gen. 6:14, 22). God promises Abraham great things, but Abraham will not receive them unless he first obeys God's initial command to "go from your country and your kindred and your father's house to the land that I will show you" (12:1).[52] Later, the conditional elements of that covenant are made even clearer, when Abraham is told to "walk before [God], and be blameless" (17:1) and to circumcise every male in the household (17:10). When God gave Abraham the ultimate test of sacrificing

Figure 2.2. Illustration from the 1728 *Figures de la Bible* by Gerard Hoet

---

51. Brueggemann sees the Noahic, Abrahamic, and Davidic covenants as unconditional, but calls the Sinai covenant "harshly conditional" (Brueggemann, *Reverberations of Faith*, 38). Levenson finds continuity between the Davidic and Sinai covenant in the fact that Jerusalem did not become the capital until David brought the ark of the covenant (a central symbol of the Sinai covenant) there. Levenson, *Sinai and Zion*, 216.

52. Goldingay describes the unconditional and conditional aspects of the Abrahamic covenant this way: "Yhwh gives gifts on the basis of trust, but trust has to open its hands to receive, or even to empty them to receive." Goldingay, *Israel's Gospel*, 198.

his son Isaac, God reaffirmed his previous promises "because you have done this" (22:16) and "because you have obeyed my voice" (22:18).

Similarly, the Davidic covenant, which may seem like an unconditional promise in 2 Samuel 7, had conditions that are made explicit in other texts (1 Kings 6:12; 8:25; 9:1–7). On his deathbed, David charges Solomon to keep the Torah: "*Then* the LORD will establish his word that he spoke concerning me: '*If* your heirs take heed to their way, to walk before me in faithfulness with all their heart and with all their soul, there shall not fail you a successor on the throne of Israel'" (1 Kings 2:4; cf. Ps. 132:11–12).[53] Even the promise that David's throne will be established "forever" does not mean that the promise of David's dynasty could never be revoked (we know that it was, starting in 586 BCE!) but that it was an *open-ended* promise, as the Hebrew term generally translated "forever" (*olam*) is better understood.[54]

Nor was the Sinai covenant completely conditional upon Israel's obedience to the law. It too was based on God's grace. Von Rad explains, "The law became visible alongside, indeed even within, the very offer of grace itself."[55] Thus there are both unconditional and conditional aspects within each phase of the covenant. The unconditional aspects always involve the initiation of the covenant, its promises, and their ultimate fulfillment. God's promises are not a response to Israel's obedience, and their ultimate fulfillment is not thwarted by the faithlessness of individuals. However, some people exclude themselves from the covenant either by choice or by disobedience.[56] In other words, the Israelites could not earn their place within the covenant, but they could forfeit their place by not living in accordance with the terms of the covenant.[57]

CONCLUSION

Covenant-making was widespread in various contexts of the ancient Near East, and its function in the Hebrew Bible is likewise pervasive, if not central. Henrich Bullinger was a Swiss theologian and reformer in the sixteenth century, and he described covenant as "both one and everlasting,"[58] likening covenant to a "target" to which the law, prophets, and apostles continually

---

53. McConville, "בְּרִית," 1:750.
54. Koehler et al., *Hebrew and Aramaic Lexicon of the Old Testament*, 1:798; Tomasino, "עוֹלָם," 3:349.
55. Von Rad, *Old Testament Theology*, 1:131.
56. Von Rad, *Old Testament Theology*, 1:171.
57. The unconditional and conditional aspects of covenant are likened to a marriage by some of the prophets (e.g., Hosea; Mal. 2:14). For an excellent and more extended treatment of this topic, see Hugenberger, *Marriage as a Covenant*.
58. Bullinger, "Brief Exposition," 117.

return.[59] If God's covenant is so central to the whole of Scripture, then surely it should be central to our lives as well. How so? It is the way that vassal-sinners can live in intimate relationship with a gracious God. It is also the way that God's people can look beyond themselves to a world deeply beloved by God. As John Walton says, covenant is "the opportunity and privilege to participate in bringing about the purposes of God."[60] Let us be faithful covenant partners to that end!

LOOKING BACK

1. What types of ancient Near Eastern treaties were there?
2. How are ancient Near Eastern treaties similar to or different from the covenants in the Hebrew Bible?
3. In what way has this chapter added to your understanding of covenant?
4. What would we miss, theologically, if the historical prologue of the covenant were missing?
5. How is the biblical idea of covenant similar to and different from contracts or agreements that you have made?
6. Identify at least one attribute of God that is highlighted in each of the following covenants: Noahic, Abrahamic, Sinai, Davidic, and new.
7. Do you think it is more accurate to think of Scripture as describing one covenant with multiple phases or multiple covenants with commonalities?

LOOKING BEYOND

Arnold, Bill T., and Brent A. Strawn, eds. *The World Around the Old Testament: The People and Places of the Ancient Near East*. Baker Academic, 2016.

Block, Daniel I. *Covenant: The Framework of God's Grand Plan of Redemption*. Baker Academic, 2021.

Eichrodt, Walther. *Theology of the Old Testament*. 2 vols. Translated by John A. Baker. SCM, 1961; Westminster, 1967.

Hays, Christopher B. *Hidden Riches: A Sourcebook for the Comparative Study of the Hebrew Bible and Ancient Near East*. Westminster John Knox, 2014.

Kitchen, Kenneth A., and Paul J. N. Lawrence. *Treaty, Law and Covenant in the Ancient Near East*. 3 vols. Harrassowitz Verlag, 2012.

---

59. Bullinger, "Brief Exposition," 112–13.
60. Walton, *Old Testament Theology for Christians*, 107. See also Walton's earlier work, *Covenant*, especially pp. 24–45.

Levenson, Jon D. *Sinai and Zion: An Entry into the Jewish Bible*. Harper & Row, 1985.

Mendenhall, George. *Law and Covenant in Israel and the Ancient Near East*. The Biblical Colloquium, 1955.

Richter, Sandra L. *The Epic of Eden: A Christian Entry into the Old Testament*. IVP Academic, 2008.

Strawn, Brent, ed. *The Oxford Encyclopedia of the Bible and Law*. Oxford University Press, 2015.

3

LAND

The Presence of God

"We are the land," writes Paula Gunn Allen of the Laguna Pueblo.[1] This central tenet for many Native Americans is probably closer to ancient Israel's understanding of land than that of many modern Westerners. For Israel, humanity finds its origin in the dust of the ground (Gen. 2:7; Job 10:9; Ps. 90:3), and the Promised Land in particular was so closely tied to Israel's fate that the prophet Isaiah nearly conflates the two:

> *You* shall no more be termed Forsaken,
>   and your *land* shall no more be termed Desolate;
> but *you* shall be called My Delight Is in Her,
>   and your land Married;
> for the LORD delights in *you*,
>   and your *land* shall be married. (Isa. 62:4)

In addition to representing Israel's covenant relationship (their "marriage") to God, the land also represented God's presence through fulfilled promises, and it provided opportunities for Israel to mediate God's presence through care for creation and care for the needy and marginalized people among them. Like Eden, it represented a place where God's special presence would dwell with his people, and a place where they would be tempted to distrust God's

---

1. Allen, "Psychological Landscape of Ceremony," 7.

provision. Their relationship to the land allowed Israel to demonstrate how ardently they believed God's presence dwelt among them.

LOOKING DOWN

One could say that two of the most important things in the ancient Near East were water and land. Of course, these two items are interrelated: The goodness of the land greatly depends on the amount of water it receives. Whether through rainfall (either too much or too little) or naturally occurring bodies of water (such as rivers, streams, lakes, and wetlands), water and land have a symbiotic relationship. The term "symbiosis" comes from the Greek words *sym* (meaning "together") and *bios* (meaning "life"). Biologists and ecologists use the term "symbiosis" to refer to "life working together" and employ it to define "relationship types . . . occurring between living entities."[2] The relationship between the land and the people/animals who live off of the land is also symbiotic in that they can affect each other both positively and negatively. The first part of this chapter will focus on the symbiotic relationship of the land to ancient Israel. More specifically, the following land-related relationships will be considered: geography and topography, economy, fertility, inheritance, how the development of the monarchy changed land ownership, the restoration of land in the stipulations of the sabbatical and Jubilee years, and land and social welfare.

Geography and Topography

The geographical region where ancient Israel was located is called the Southern Levant. Israel, like many places in the Southern Levant, has two main seasons: the dry season from May/June through September, and the wet season from October through March/April, with more rain falling in the north than in the south.[3] The land that we know today as ancient Israel was roughly the size of the state of New Jersey or the nation of Belgium; however, as small as it was, this little strip of land has amazingly diverse topography.[4] The topography of ancient Israel can be divided into five longitudinal zones, with two major latitudinal zones that cut through the longitudinal zones (see fig. 3.1). From west to east, the longitudinal zones include the Coastal Plain, the Shephelah, the Cis-Jordan hill country (the hill country in the north is called Galilee, in the middle Samaria or Ephraim, and Judah in the south),

---

2. Brenner, "What Is a Symbiotic Relationship?"
3. King and Stager, *Life in Biblical Israel*, 86.
4. Vitalis Hoffman and Mullins, *Atlas of the Biblical World*, 15. Topography can be defined, in part, as the natural and artificial physical features of an area.

Land

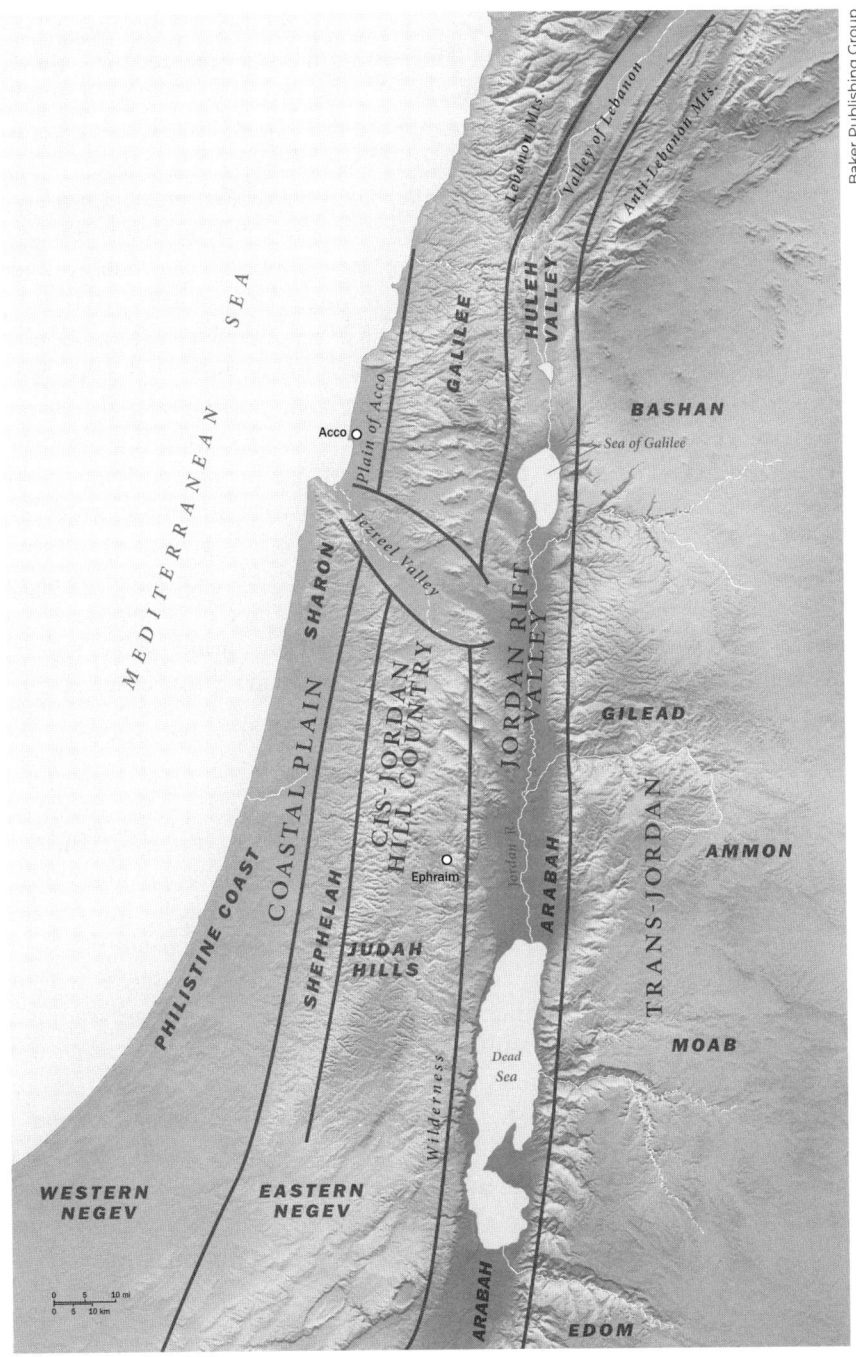

Fig. 3.1. Map of ancient Israel's topographical zones

the Jordan-Rift Valley, and the Trans-Jordan (including the regions of Gilead, Ammon, Moab, and Edom). The latitudinal zones include two valleys: the Jezreel/Esdraelon Valley (in the north) and the Negev of Judah (in the south).[5] The majority of the events that the Hebrew Bible reflects are set in the Shephelah and the hill country of the Cis-Jordan.

Even though ancient Israel was a small entity, its geographical importance was massive. The land of Canaan/Israel was a land bridge that connected Mesopotamia to the east with Egypt to the southwest. One could not get from Egypt to Babylon without traveling through the land of Israel. In fact, the main trade routes went through this strip of land: the International Trunk Road (sometimes referred to as the Via Maris or the Way of the Sea) was located in the Cis-Jordan, and the King's Highway was located in the Trans-Jordan.[6] These major routes facilitated trade and diplomacy. If a kingdom had grand plans to become the superpower of the day in the ancient Near East, it was imperative for them to gain power through controlling trade. In order to control the trade, one had to control the trade routes; and in order to control the trade routes, one had to control the land bridge where the main trade routes were located—that land bridge was the land of Israel. Israel was attractive to the superpowers of the ancient Near East primarily because of the importance of their geographical location as a land bridge between Egypt and Mesopotamia.

Land-Based Economy

Like most societies, both ancient and modern, the economy of ancient Israel was dependent on the land. Ancient Israelite society was predominantly based on kinship, with production mainly occurring within the household. Households existed on a subsistence level, which generally meant they had just enough to stay alive. More specifically, a subsistence economy is an economic system "in which communities rely primarily on the self-provisioning of their basic needs through hunting, agriculture, and the use of local natural resources. Wealth is not accumulated but measured in terms of access to renewable resources necessary for survival, such as food, water, and shelter."[7]

Ancient economies were socially determined and were usually in a state of "crisis" on one level or another; but ultimately, the household subsistence economy was the most resilient of all the regimes simply because kingdoms and empires collapse, but the average people are always working the land.[8] As

---

5. Vitalis Hoffman and Mullins, *Atlas of the Biblical World*, 15.
6. Vitalis Hoffman and Mullins, *Atlas of the Biblical World*, 16. See also Rasmussen, *Essential Atlas of the Bible*, 16–17.
7. Hunt, *Beyond Relativism*, 85.
8. Boer, *Sacred Economy*, 1–8.

we mentioned in chapter 1, the land was considered an important contributing member of the household; hence the fertility of the land was not only important but imperative.

Fertility of the Land

The household's dependency on their land, animals, and each other meant that the fertility of all of these was of utmost importance. This could be one possible reason the Israelites worshiped other deities besides Yhwh. According to the covenant, Israel was supposed to worship Yhwh alone (see Exod. 20:3; Deut. 6:13–14; 2 Kings 17:35–36); however, anyone who has read the Hebrew Bible can attest that the ancient Israelites did not follow through with this commandment well at all (Judg. 2:17; 1 Kings 9:9; Jer. 11:10). The local Canaanite deities of Baal (Num. 25:3; Judg. 6:25; 1 Sam. 12:10; 1 Kings 18:19) and Asherah (Judg. 6:25; 1 Sam. 12:10; 1 Kings 18:19) were particularly attractive to the Israelites. Baal was a fertility and agricultural god, especially associated with storms that would seasonally water the land and make it fertile, thus sustaining the household members and animals. Alongside Baal is the Canaanite goddess Asherah, the mother goddess who is associated with lions, serpents, and sacred trees.[9] The Israelites, like their Canaanite neighbors, were willing to worship any deity that may help their land and crops be fertile. Consequently, the authors and redactors of the Hebrew Bible labor to show that, unlike other gods, Yhwh is not trapped in one geographical location or limited to one or two spheres of influence; rather, they portray Yhwh as transcendent and universal, not limited to the inconsistencies of nature (1 Kings 18; 2 Kings 21:7; Pss. 29; 68:4, 9; 104:3; Jer. 11:17).[10]

Land as Inheritance

In the biblical world, land ownership and children were equal to economic security, with both viewed as economic assets to the household. Land and property belonged not to an individual but to the household. As such, land and property were significant factors in the household inheritance that was passed on to each succeeding generation. Victor Matthews writes that "having children and establishing clear patterns of inheritance functioned as a means to tie generations together."[11] In the Hebrew Bible, fruitful land and women (and subsequently their children) are used as images of a blessed life of covenant obedience, and the lack thereof as images of the consequences of covenant disobedience (Deut. 28:1–5; 15–18).

---

9. A fuller discussion of Baal and Asherah can be found in chapter 5.
10. Browning, "Baal"; Burke, "Baal," 70.
11. Matthews, "Family, Children, and Inheritance," 406.

Inheritance laws in the Hebrew Bible suggest a few typical scenarios, which will be addressed in chapter 8; suffice it to say, the most common inheritance pattern found in the ancient Near East is one according to birth order. Primogeniture—where the first born, surviving son was granted certain privileges—was practiced in ancient Israel. These privileges included preferential status through inheriting a double portion of his father's estate, receiving a special blessing from his father, and succeeding his father as the patriarch of the household (Gen. 27; 49).[12]

The terms used for inheritance appear over two hundred times in the Hebrew Bible, mostly within the books of Numbers, Deuteronomy, Joshua, and Psalms.[13] The crucial role of the land to the survival of the household can be seen in the laws of inheritance, but the concept of inheritance is also used by the biblical authors as a metaphor for the special, almost parental relationship between Yhwh and Israel, and it can be seen as an extension of or facet of the household metaphor used in their covenant. The land of Canaan is part of the covenantal blessings of land, protection, and descendants promised as an inheritance to Abraham and his offspring (Gen. 12:7); however, the prophets warn that if the Israelites break the covenant, they will lose that inherited land (Jer. 3:18; 16:13, 15).

The Monarchy and Its Influence on the Land

Pre-monarchic Israelite society was based primarily on the small, farming villages, hamlets, and farmsteads that survived in a subsistence and kinship mode and was mostly free of the extraction of surplus goods by a king or ruling elite.[14] Fortified settlements, or walled cities, also functioned at this level but had more access to trade networks than their rural counterparts. While villages were decentralized and more "egalitarian," and power was assumed by some of the patrons and elders of the village, cities were more centralized and had a single ruler who supervised the city and its land. However, the increase in population, the depletion of natural resources, and the continued threat of war contributed to the view that a "strongman" rule, or "one who leads or controls by force of will and character or by military methods,"[15] was necessary. In order for a singular leader to protect the town or village, the elders of the village ceded part of their authority to the new leader.[16] C. Carter writes that "the shift from a simple to a

---

12. King and Stager, *Life in Biblical Israel*, 47.
13. W. E. Brown, "Inheritance."
14. Boer, *Sacred Economy*, 1–2; Shafer-Elliott, "Economics—Hebrew Bible," 119; Yee, "Ideological Criticism," 153.
15. Matthews and Benjamin, *Social World of Ancient Israel*, 155, 157; *Merriam-Webster Dictionary*, "strongman," https://www.merriam-webster.com/dictionary/strongman.
16. Matthews and Benjamin, *Social World of Ancient Israel*, 157.

complex agrarian society roughly parallels the rise of the State. This is predictable as technological improvements in both tools and weapons allow for an increase in surplus, which generally leads to increased stratification and specialization."[17] This evolution is not only the beginning of the monarchy but also the beginning of Israel's shift from a kinship mode into a native tributary mode.[18]

A native tributary mode extracts surplus from the working class—in ancient Israel's case, the households. The monarchy extracted surplus from their subjects in four ways: taxes, drafting into corvée (i.e., forced labor), debt cycle, and foreign tributary mode. These types of extraction will be addressed more fully in chapter 7; however, the basic idea is that households were taxed primarily in the form of produce from the land (e.g., olive oil, wine, grain) and the herds who grazed on the land. If this was not possible, the monarchy employed other forms of extraction, such as conscripting people into corvée or extending credit (i.e., the debt cycle) to the household who worked land, which ultimately belonged to the monarchy. The tenant was expected to give over one-third to one-half of what they produced to the monarchy, leaving them to survive on what was left. The rise of the monarchy paralleled Israel's shift from a simple agrarian economy to a complex one, which included the Israelites having better tools and a better economic administration, but, as we will see, this wasn't always a good thing.

Land Cultivation and Rest

Over time, ancient Israel's population increased, resulting in scarcity of agricultural land; consequently, the land suffered from "over-cultivation" or the "excessive use of farmland to the point where productivity falls due to soil exhaustion or land degradation."[19] A system that allowed the land to recover was necessary; consequently, a cycle of sowing and fallowing developed.[20] To allow land to fallow means to let cultivated land lie idle during the growing season or to alter what is usually planted in that field. What type of fallowing system and when it was implemented is a complicated question to answer since our level of resources on the subject, at least related to ancient Canaan and Israel, is lacking.[21] In all likelihood, they used a fallowing system that consisted of a combination of strategies, including a biennial fallow, green fallow, crop rotation, and the sabbatical year.[22]

---

17. Carter, "Discipline in Transition," 10.
18. For more on the economies of ancient Israel, see Nam, *Portrayals of Economic Exchange*; and Boer, *Sacred Economy*.
19. Barcelona Field Studies Centre, "Over-Cultivation," https://geographyfieldwork.com/GeographyVocabularyGCSEFarming.htm.
20. Borowski, *Agriculture in Iron Age Israel*, 144.
21. Hopkins, *Highlands of Canaan*, 195.
22. Hopkins, *Highlands of Canaan*, 192–202.

The first system is the biennial fallow or short-term fallowing, which consists of allowing a field to rest after a year of cultivation. In this system, farmers would need to divide their land to follow this rotation. For instance, one field would lie fallow while the other was cultivated.[23] The second possible system is the green fallow system, which is when the field is planted with a different crop. For example, a common practice in the Mediterranean is rotating a field between cereals and legumes because the bacterium *rhizobium radicicola*, which grows on the root nodules of the legume plant, enriches the soil with nitrogen, thus maintaining higher levels of soil fertility.[24] The third fallow system is crop rotation, which includes alternating a field between a summer and a winter cultivation with periods of fallowing in between.[25]

The fourth possible land fallowing system is the sabbatical year. The command regarding the sabbatical year can be found in Exodus 23:10–11, which states, "For six years you shall sow your land and gather in its yield; but the seventh year you shall let it rest and lie fallow, so that the poor of your people may eat; and what they leave the wild animals may eat. You shall do the same with your vineyard, and with your olive orchard."[26] In other words, after seven years of cultivation, the land was to rest for one year. We often read this passage and conclude that this stipulation fully encompasses Israel's agricultural practice. If the sabbatical year was the only fallow system implemented, then we would have to describe ancient Israel's agricultural system as "one of extremely high intensity, bordering on continuous or permanent cultivation"[27]—in other words, the system would be highly unsustainable; rather, the sabbatical year, in terms of agricultural practice, should be seen as part of a larger agricultural system. The Hebrew Bible, however, views the sabbatical year as more than just a part of an agricultural system; it is also part of ancient Israel's social welfare system—as we will see below.

Land and Social Welfare

One of the main aspects of Israel's symbiotic relationship with the land is not only to care for the land but also to use the land to help care for those in their community who were unable to care for themselves. Those who owned or worked the land were required to pay taxes and firstfruits. They were also strongly encouraged to participate in specific social welfare measures related

---

23. Hopkins, *Highlands of Canaan*, 195.
24. Zohary et al., *Domestication of Plants*, 75; Shafer-Elliott, "Fruits, Nuts, Vegetables, and Legumes," 150.
25. For a fuller discussion on the rotation between summer and winter cultivation in ancient Israel, see Hopkins, *Highlands of Canaan*, 195–200.
26. See also Lev. 25:1–7; Deut. 15:1.
27. Hopkins, *Highlands of Canaan*, 194.

to the land, such as gleaning, the *go'el* (i.e., kinsman-redeemer), the sabbatical year, and the Jubilee year.

We noted in our discussion of ancient households that Israel implemented certain "structures of grace" as a means of caring for the most vulnerable inside and outside of the household. The gleaning laws are one such structure of grace that directly pertains to land. "Gleaning" means to gather grain or other produce left by reapers.[28] At harvest time, the household was to leave some of the produce behind so that the poor could come through and gather it. This was considered to be one way to help the poor and less fortunate in the Israelite community. The laws regarding gleaning are found in Leviticus 19:9–10; 23:22; and Deuteronomy 24:19–21. Gleaning also plays a small but significant role in the story of Ruth (Ruth 2:2–9).

A second form of land-related social welfare found in the Hebrew Bible is the kinship concept of a *go'el*, which comes from the Hebrew verb *ga'al* and is usually translated as "redeemer" or "near relative." A *go'el* is the nearest male relative who is customarily obligated with the responsibility to restore certain family rights and duties (Lev. 25:48–49; Num. 35:9–30; Deut. 25:5–6). With regard to the *go'el* and land, as discussed in chapter 1, land was just as much part of the household as any person was. Land was the inheritance that was passed on from father to son and was considered a living connection to one's ancestors. Land was intended to be kept within the household; however, if the household could not hold on to their ancestral land, it was the duty of the next of kin to redeem it so that it would stay within the clan (Lev. 27:9–25).

The sabbatical year is a third form of social welfare related to land within the Hebrew Bible. As was discussed above, the sabbatical year stipulates that after seven years of cultivation the land was to rest for one year; furthermore, depending on the passage, the law expands on who would also benefit from the land's rest: the poor and wild animals (Exod. 23:11), slaves, hired and bound laborers, livestock, and wild animals (Lev. 25:6–7).[29] During its rest, the land would still produce, and the people and animals may still eat from it. The land, people, and animals benefit from the rest; but it is interesting to note that the rest is also for the Lord. The sabbatical year stipulation in Leviticus 25:4 says, "But in the seventh year there shall be a sabbath of complete rest for the land, *a sabbath for the* Lord." Ellen Davis expands on this concept when she writes, "In the conception of Leviticus, arable land is not for a moment private. It could more accurately be said that the seventh year simply clarifies what the land always is: God's domain. This passage includes

---

28. *Merriam-Webster Dictionary*, "gleaning," https://www.merriam-webster.com/dictionary/gleaning.

29. The origin, date, and character of the various laws regarding the sabbatical and Jubilee years are beyond the scope of this book.

the most strident assertion [Lev. 25:23] in the whole Bible that the fertile land of Canaan belongs to God."[30]

The version of the sabbatical year stipulation found in Deuteronomy 15 expands on the social welfare aspect significantly in that it requires the remission of debt (v. 1) and the release of those Hebrews who were enslaved (v. 12).[31] If a household was unable to pay their taxes, the household had two options: (1) a member (or members) of the household were drafted into forced labor or slavery; (2) they sold their ancestral land and became tenants of a new landowner. If, as tenants, they could not pay their taxes, then debt slavery was enforced. Any of these options resulted in the significant loss of income for a household, if not loss of the household itself. The sabbatical year was a year of rest for the land but also a restoration of those who were forced into slavery.

The fourth and final biblical social welfare measure to be mentioned here is the year of Jubilee. The law regarding the year of Jubilee is found in Leviticus 25:8, 10–12, which stipulates:

> You shall count off seven weeks of years, seven times seven years, so that the period of seven weeks of years gives forty-nine years. . . . And you shall hallow the fiftieth year and you shall proclaim liberty throughout the land to all its inhabitants. It shall be a jubilee for you: you shall return, every one of you, to your property and every one of you to your family. That fiftieth year shall be a jubilee for you: you shall not sow, or reap the aftergrowth, or harvest the unpruned vines. For it is a jubilee; it shall be holy to you: you shall eat only what the field itself produces.

According to Leviticus 25, every seventh year was to be a sabbatical year and after seven sabbatical years (or forty-nine years), the fiftieth year was to be a year of Jubilee. The year of Jubilee included the restoration of land to its rightful owners and all Israelite slaves were to be released. Land and slaves could not be sold for more than fifty years, with the redemption price calculated by how many crop years were left until the next year of Jubilee.[32] In other words, all sales of land and people were to be considered leases, not final sales.[33] Land was an inheritance that was of utmost importance to the welfare of the household who lived and worked it. Without land, the household would not survive.

The significance of such land-related social welfare practices would have been immense, in that the welfare of the land and the people are connected.

---

30. E. Davis, *Scripture, Culture, and Agriculture*, 109.
31. For ancient Near Eastern parallels in the Law Code of Hammurabi, see Pritchard, *Ancient Near East*, 165.
32. Westbrook and Wells, *Everyday Law in Biblical Israel*, 124; Levine, *Leviticus*, 169.
33. Levine, *Leviticus*, 169.

Throughout the Hebrew Bible both the land and the people continue to be seen as sacred: They belong to Yhwh and as such cannot be permanently alienated from Yhwh. Redemption as a "socio-economic institution" comes from Yhwh alone; however, for it to be carried out, it is necessary for the household or clan to participate.[34]

Summary

This section focused on the symbiotic relationship between the land and the people of ancient Israel. Considering the land's geography and topography (and how that impacted Israel's economy), their understanding of the land's fertility, how household land was passed onto future generations, and the need for laws related to the restoration of land gives us a glimpse into this symbiotic relationship. Furthermore, how the development of the monarchy changed land ownership illustrates that the relationship between Israel and the land wasn't static. What can be said for certain is that the Hebrew Bible viewed the land as belonging to Yhwh and that Israel was its tenant and caretaker. Taking care of the land also meant taking care of each other.

LOOKING UP

The theological importance of land in the Hebrew Bible can hardly be overstated. According to Walter Brueggemann, "Land is a central, if not *the central theme* of biblical faith."[35] Land was one of the fundamental promises and blessings of the covenant, integrally tied to what we described in the previous chapter as the "taproot" of the Hebrew Bible covenant: God's relationship with his people ("I will be their God, and they shall be my people," Jer. 31:33).[36] God chose to dwell with his people in a particular place: first in Eden, then in Canaan (the Promised Land), and ultimately beyond any political boundary to the entire world. Because the land is God's creation, and because it is where God chooses to be in relationship with his people, land is fundamentally theological. The land represents God's order within a broken world of chaos, rest from war, and, above all, God's presence.

While the land represented something spiritual (God's presence), it was always a physical reality as well—real land, with dirt and worms and rocks,

---

34. E. Davis, *Scripture, Culture, and Agriculture*, 92–93.

35. Brueggemann, *Land*, 3; Gerhard von Rad's sentiments ("Promised Land," 79) about the Hexateuch could be extended to the whole of the Hebrew Bible: "In the whole of the Hexateuch there is probably no more important idea than that expressed in terms of the land promised and later granted by Yahweh."

36. Similarly, Gen. 17:8; Exod. 6:7; Lev. 26:12; Jer. 24:7; 32:38; Ezek. 11:20; 14:11; 37:23, 27; Zech. 8:8.

with a real potential to sustain life. Separations between the physical and the spiritual would have seemed nonsensical in the ancient Near East. Everything was quite spiritual and quite physical.[37] What we do see happening in the Hebrew Bible, and into the New Testament, is a universalizing of the land. Eden, and Canaan afterward, were only microcosms of what "land" really meant. If God is Creator of all the earth, then his rule and presence must likewise be over all the earth, and any smaller manifestation of his kingdom can be only a snapshot of the fuller reality.

In the previous chapter, we noted how the concept of covenant developed from a universal scope (with creation and the Noahic covenants) to a particular scope (with the Abrahamic, Sinaitic, and Davidic covenants), with the end goal again being universal. As one of the covenant blessings, land follows this same pattern, as figure 3.2 shows.

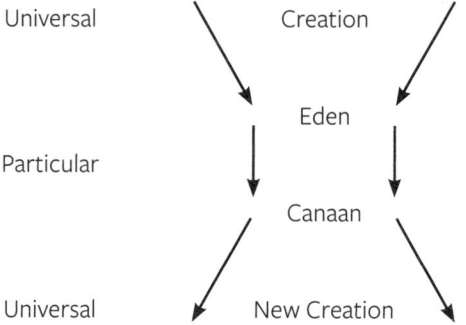

Figure 3.2. The theological focus of land in the Hebrew Bible (like that of covenant) moves from the universal to the particular and back to the universal.

While the Hebrew Bible has much to say about creation (e.g., Gen. 1–2; Ps. 104) and looks forward to a new creation (or, better, *re*newed creation; esp. Isa. 65–66),[38] the main focus of land theology is on the Promised Land, and that will be the focus of this section. In the Hebrew Bible, the Promised Land is presented as a representation of God's presence, and Israel's experience with the land can be divided into three eras: the land promised, the land possessed, and the land purged.

---

37. Brueggemann, *Land*, 2.
38. I prefer to use the term "renewed" to guard against the misunderstanding that God would abandon his prior creation and start from scratch. The essence of creation is not discarded with the "newness" of the new creation any more than our own essence is disregarded in our new rebirths. For a cogent discussion, see N. T. Wright, *Surprised by Hope*, esp. 103–6.

The Land Promised

The story of the land is a story of God's promise. When God made the first human, he "rested" him in a land (Eden) where God would personally dwell with his new image bearers (Gen. 3:8). God commanded the man to take care of the garden, and to guard it from harm (2:15), and in return he would be blessed with the bounty of the garden and the special presence of God. This is the "symbiotic relationship" mentioned in the section above. God's people were to take care of and bless the land, and the land would in turn provide for and bless God's people. When Adam and Eve disobeyed God, they were cast out—exiled—from that land and thus out of God's special presence (3:23–24). The rest of the biblical story can be seen as a struggle between God's people and the land God gives them—their struggle to enter the land, to take possession of the land, to remain in the land, and later to return to the land of God's presence.

When God exiled Adam and Eve from the garden of Eden, He did not give up on his original plan of dwelling with his people. He promised his people again and again that he would give them their own land where they could be with God. In Genesis through Joshua, God's promise of land is mentioned no less than sixty times, especially in Genesis and Deuteronomy.[39] It marked a transition from a disordered, wandering, homeless existence to an ordered, situated, and secure existence (Josh. 11:23; 21:43–45). Christopher Wright explains, "The land, in short, for an Israelite, meant security, inclusion, blessing, sharing and practical responsibility."[40] Living in the land was a physical, tangible reminder of God's faithfulness to the people. It would also be a reminder of God's grace, because the land was promised to them as a free gift. It would not be because of their size (Deut. 7:7–8) or because of their own righteousness (9:4–6) that God would give them the land. It was a free gift, manifest grace, from a God who keeps his promises.

However, this land would not *technically* be theirs. God expressly told Moses, "For the land is mine; with me you are but aliens and tenants" (Lev. 25:23). The Israelites likewise referred to themselves as sojourners, even when living in the land (Pss. 39:12; 119:19). As readers, we might wonder, how could the land be promised to Israel, given to Israel, and yet not fully belong to them? Israel's conception of "inheritance" (*nachalah*), discussed above, offers some clarity. Even when land was passed from father to son, it never belonged solely to the son but belonged to the entire household. Likewise, though Israel, as God's "son," inherited the Promised Land, this did not mean that ownership

---

39. For example, Gen. 12:7; 13:15, 17; 15:7, 18; 28:4, 13; 48:4; Exod. 6:4, 8; Lev. 14:34; Num. 11:12; Deut. 1:8, 35–36; 31:7, 20–21, 23; Josh. 1:6, 13.
40. C. Wright, *Old Testament Ethics*, 190.

of the land transferred entirely to Israel. Just as modern inheritances can be given with conditions attached, or with the original owner still in view, so also Israel inherited the land with the acknowledgement that the land and all that it produced ultimately belonged to God.

A certain farmer named Naboth, whose story is recounted in 1 Kings 21, fully understood the divine ownership of the land and its implications. Naboth owned a beautiful vineyard adjacent to the property of the wicked King Ahab of the northern kingdom of Israel. Naboth knew that his land was not really his to sell or Ahab's to buy. It was the "inheritance" of his fathers, given to his family by Yhwh. Brueggemann explains, "Naboth is responsible for the land, but is not in control over it. It is the case not that the land belongs to him but that he belongs to the land."[41] Ahab, however, did not share Naboth's theology of land, and he and his equally wicked wife, Jezebel, conspired to kill Naboth and to steal his vineyard.

The Land Possessed

God keeps his covenant promises. The possession of the Promised Land, as recounted in the book of Joshua, marked the fulfillment of God's covenant promises to Abraham and his descendants. It also marked a restoration—at least in part—of the relationship that God shared with Adam and Eve in the garden of Eden, when his holy presence could dwell with them in a physical place. Even some of the language used for the Promised Land harks back to the language of the creation account in Genesis 1–2. The book of Deuteronomy reflects Moses's parting words to a new generation of Israelites who were moments away from entering the Promised Land. It describes the land as "good" no less than twelve times, recalling the creation refrain in Genesis 1 of all things being created "good."[42] Moreover, the Israelites are told that they will "multiply" in the land, just as the animals and Adam and Eve were told to multiply in Eden.[43] Finally, the language of "subdue" used of Adam and Eve with respect to creation in Genesis 1:28 is echoed in Numbers 32:22, 29; Deuteronomy 9:3; and Joshua 18:1 to describe the subduing of the Promised Land.[44] The possession of the Promised Land marked the fulfillment of God's covenant promises, as well as a partial, if imperfect, restoration of the creation order, a return to Eden.

---

41. Brueggemann, *Land*, 88.

42. Compare Gen. 1:4, 10, 12, 18, 21, 25, 31 with Deut. 1:25, 35; 3:25 (2×); 4:21–22; 6:10, 18; 8:7, 10; 9:6; 11:17; see also Num. 14:7; Josh. 23:13, 15–16.

43. Compare Gen. 1:22, 28 with Deut. 6:3; 7:13; 8:1; 13:17; 30:16.

44. Martin, *Bound for the Promised Land*, 83–84. Additionally, Israel's "rest" in the land mirrors God's "rest" on the seventh day of creation, and just as God's rest in Gen. 2:2–3 marks his rule over his newly made creation, so also Israel's "rest" in the land represents their dominion over the land God has given them (87).

In addition to embodying the fulfilled promises and blessings of the covenant, the land also embodied the demands of the covenant. Just as Adam and Eve's enjoyment of Eden was dependent on their obedience to God's will, so also was Israel's enjoyment of the Promised Land dependent on their obedience to the terms of covenant. Their faithfulness was necessary for two reasons: the land belongs to God, and God is holy. If a perfect God is going to dwell with his people in a physical space, then that space also needs to be holy, and sin defiles space like dirty shoes defile white carpet. Numbers 35:34 explains, "You shall not defile the land in which you live, in which I also dwell; for I the Lord dwell among the Israelites." When we visit a friend's house, we take note of the cleanliness and expectations of the host. If the hosts remove their shoes before entering, we do likewise. If we splatter water on the bathroom counter, we are mindful to wipe it up. How much more so should God's people keep the place of his special presence clean by taking care not to defile it with disobedience? In a sense, the entire Hebrew Bible law served as the "lease agreement" of the covenant and secured Israel's blessing of remaining in the land. Some of these laws, particularly the ones protecting the social welfare of the community mentioned above, are directly tied to Israel's theology of land.

The laws of tithing, gleaning, and inheritance all illustrate how Israel's love for their neighbors was connected to their theology of land. The tithing laws are based on God's role as king (Isa. 43:15), who thus warrants a tithe from the land of his subjects (Lev. 27:30). Deuteronomy 14:28–29 explains how this tithe would be used to support the Levites (who had no land allotment), resident aliens, orphans, and widows. Similarly, the gleaning laws in Leviticus 19:9–10 (and Deut. 24:21) command the Israelites to leave portions of their harvest for those in need. Ruth and Naomi were beneficiaries of this law, grounded in Israel's theology of land. The land belonged to God, and as his tenant, Israel was to extend God's compassion to the most vulnerable in the land. Finally, Israel's inheritance laws that kept ancestral land within a household were a way to maintain equity and preserve household livelihood. As Wendell Berry explains, "It is a contradiction to love your neighbor and despise the great inheritance on which his life depends."[45] Viewing other people's land and livelihood as something available to the highest bidder or the shrewdest buyer is nothing short of covetousness.

So, the land was a blessing for Israel, but it also served as a barometer for Israel's faithfulness to God. And just as there was temptation in the garden of Eden, so also there was temptation in the Promised Land. In both cases, the people distrusted Yhwh to provide what they needed. In Eden, temptation

---

45. Berry, "Gift of the Good Land," 273.

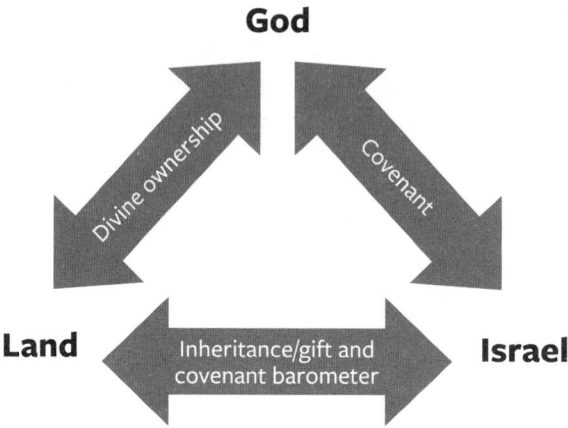

Figure 3.3. The symbiotic relationship between God, Israel, and the land

took the form of a serpent who seemed to offer them something that God did not (namely, to be "like God, knowing good and evil," Gen. 3:5). In the Promised Land, temptation took the form of Canaanite deities, which, as we've seen, appeared to promise rain and harvest when it seemed that Yhwh was not providing for them. Brueggemann states, "The gift of the land provides secured people with dangerous alternatives."[46] If they drove out the Canaanite practices and remained faithful to Yhwh, they could enjoy the land (Lev. 26:3–6), but if they chose to break their covenant obligations by worshiping other gods and failing to care for their neighbors, then God would purge them from the land (26:31–33).

At this point, we can expand our metaphor of symbiosis to illustrate how God fits into the land-people nexus (see fig. 3.3). God is not dependent on Israel or the land, but as the divine landowner, he graciously reaches out to Israel through the covenant to give them the inheritance of the land, which they need to flourish in life and in God's special presence. Israel's retention of this gift is conditioned on their faithfulness to the covenant stipulations, which includes faithful treatment of the land (Gen. 2:15; Lev. 25:3–5) and avoidance of moral sin that would "defile" the land (Lev. 18:28; Num. 35:34; Jer. 3:1–2).

The Land Purged

The land reflected God's presence and blessing, but it did not guarantee it. Ezekiel describes the presence of the Lord leaving the temple (Ezek. 10:18–19), probably in 592 BCE, five years before its destruction. Jeremiah had just recently delivered his famous "temple sermon" against those who hypocritically

---

46. Brueggemann, *Land*, 50.

Figure 3.4. Lachish relief depicting the Assyrian conquest and exile of the people of Lachish (southwest of Jerusalem)

worshiped at the temple while committing idolatry and disregarding the needs of immigrants, widows, and orphans (Jer. 7:4–6). The sins that led Israel into exile can, in part, be understood as their failure to understand their relationship to the land: failure to serve God as the sole landlord, failure to care for the land according to the Sabbath laws, and failure to care for others who were dependent on the land.

However, just as God did not abandon Adam and Eve in their exile from Eden, he would not abandon his people now, even in exile. The books of Daniel and Esther illustrate how God remained with his people, sometimes in miraculous ways (such as delivering them from fiery furnaces or lions' dens) and sometimes in subtler, "behind the scenes" ways (such as working through a young Jewish woman in the Persian court with a secret identity and great courage). The prophets also assured Israel and Judah that God would restore them after the punishment of exile. He would restore their relationship with him, forgiving their covenant violations, and he would also restore them to the land. God would deliver them from exile just as he had delivered their ancestors from Egypt. The return to the Promised Land after exile would be nothing less than a "new exodus," a new act of salvation, in which God's people were delivered back into the Promised Land and back into God's favor.

No prophet proclaimed and lived the story of the land more than Jeremiah.[47] Ministering in Judah before and during its final demise (roughly 628–586 BCE), Jeremiah knew what the land meant for Israel, and he knew how deeply its loss would grieve Israel. However, he also knew that losing the land was (paradoxically) necessary for regaining God's presence and favor because it was necessary for Israel's transformation to a genuinely repentant and believing people. In this way, according to Brueggemann, Jeremiah "transforms the evaluation of exile."[48] This is clear in Jeremiah's vision of the two baskets of figs in Jeremiah 24:1–10. The basket of good figs represents those who accept the punishment of exile; God promises to "build them up" when they "return to [him] with their whole heart" (Jer. 24:6–7). The bad figs, on the other hand, are those who remain in the land and do not accept God's punishment (24:8).

In addition to being transformative for Israel, the exile was also a key point of development in Israel's theology of the nations and their relationship to the land. It was during Judah's exile that the global scope of God's covenant and the universalizing of the land, from a small region of 10,000 square miles to the entire world (nearly 200 million square miles, if anyone is counting) gained serious real estate (to use an appropriate metaphor) in Israel's theology.[49]

At the heart of this transformation from a localized to a universalized theology of land is Zion theology. In its early conception, Zion theology focused on the city of Jerusalem and the temple therein. Zion was Israel's new and permanent Mount Sinai, the chosen locale of God's presence in the midst of his people.[50] However, with the loss of the land and the destruction of the temple, Zion theology became a symbol of God's universal reign over a renewed creation, and it shifted its purview forward in time to when Zion would be expanded to include all people who call Yhwh Lord and King (e.g., Pss. 87; 98; Isa. 60:10–14). The physical, tangible reality of land would not be *spiritualized* away as unimportant but rather *universalized* so as to encompass the ends of the earth.

---

47. Brueggemann says of Jeremiah, "In the Old Testament he is the poet of the land par excellence." Brueggemann, *Land*, 101.

48. Brueggemann, *Land*, 115.

49. Of course, even before the exile, Scripture hints at the symbolic nature of the land in passages like Deut. 9:8–9, which explain that the Levites were not allotted any land because Yhwh himself was their inheritance. This is not to say that land was unimportant or that it ever meant less than the physical reality of dirt, stone, and worms but that it always meant more than that too.

50. This is the central premise in Jon D. Levenson's excellent book, *Sinai and Zion*.

Christopher Wright explains, "The theological themes of security, inclusion, sharing and responsibility, which were once linked to the land, remain valid; but they are loosened from their literal, territorial moorings, as the scope of salvation is widened to include non-Israelites."[51] Isaiah 56:3–8 promises that foreigners and eunuchs will be included in Yhwh's covenant. Not only will non-Israelites pour into Israel to call Yhwh their own, but they will worship within their own national boundaries with their own national and cultural distinctiveness. Israel's most famous enemies, Egypt and Assyria, will worship Yhwh within their own borders (19:18–22) and God will call them his own saying, "Blessed be Egypt my people, and Assyria the work of my hands, and Israel my heritage" (19:25). In the book of Acts, the gospel goes out from Jerusalem to "the ends of the earth" (1:8) to create what Willie James Jennings describes as "intimate life that transgresses boundaries and border."[52] God's love for all the families of the earth, made especially clear in Genesis 12:3, is being fulfilled in the universalized worship of Yhwh in all of creation.[53]

CONCLUSION

Israel's theology of land has several important implications for the way we live out our faith today. First, Israel's theology of land has sociological implications grounded in the claim that Yhwh was the true owner of the land. We have seen that this theology undergirded the Hebrew Bible laws commanding Israel to leave some of the produce of the land for the poor, and the laws requiring land to be returned to its ancestral owner every fifty years. Regardless of how consistently these laws were practiced, they illustrate an important ethic of equality, serving to safeguard against massive discrepancies between the very rich and the very poor. These laws continue to provide hope to modern victims of inequality and oppression.[54]

When these laws are ignored, or when land is "spiritualized" (rather than universalized), people suffer. Brueggemann's charge is sobering: "While the issues are complex, few things have contributed more to our wrong understandings of theology than our false spiritual interpretation of Scripture that has made landlessness a virtue instead of a condition for receiving land. And from that interpretation has come the notion of poverty (landlessness) as

---

51. C. Wright, *Old Testament Ethics*, 191.
52. Jennings, *Acts*, 255.
53. J. David Stark describes and traces this universalization, or what he calls the "outward reverberations," of the land promise from the book of Genesis through Second Temple literature. See Stark, "To Your Seed I Will Give . . ."
54. See, for example, Ndikho Mtshiselwa's analysis of Lev. 25 as a message of hope and practical guidance to the impoverished living in post-apartheid South Africa in *To Whom Belongs the Land?*

virtue.... Spiritual Christianity, by refusing to face the land question, has served to sanction existing inequities."[55] Israel's theology of land should support efforts to make land and resource use equitable and fair for all. That is one of the ways that we can love our neighbors.

Second, Israel's land theology has implications for how we treat God's creation. In Genesis 2:15, Adam was placed in Eden to serve it (*'avad*) and to guard it (*shamar*), with clear protective overtones of what we would now call environmental stewardship or servanthood.[56] Many years later, when Israel and Judah are exiled for their many transgressions against God and against their fellow humanity, we are told that they also sinned against the land itself by not adhering to the fallowing laws (2 Chron. 36:21), and as a result, the land "vomited [them] out" (Lev. 18:25, 28; cf. 20:22). Sandra Richter contrasts this key principle of land stewardship with the age-old temptation to exploit the land for the sake of short-term gain: "It is not acceptable for any populace to take from the land everything that it can. Rather, as the law of Israel teaches us, God's people are commanded to operate with the long-term well-being of the land as their ultimate goal."[57] The applications for our modern ecological crises should not be missed, but they so often *are* missed because we do not love creation in the way that our Creator does. Wendell Berry writes, "The Creator's love for the Creation is mysterious precisely because it does not conform to human purposes."[58] Our loves and desires do not always conform to God's loves and desires. Let us pray that they would.

Third, Israel's land theology has implications for how we understand our relationship with God and his redemptive plan. God created humanity to be a landed people. This is clear from the opening pages of Scripture in Genesis to the closing pages in Revelation. The popular conception of disembodied souls floating on clouds playing harps for all eternity is the creation of human folly. The ultimate destination of humanity is one grounded in a renewed creation (Isa. 65:17; 66:22). Rather than "going to heaven," our ultimate hope is of heaven coming to earth in a new Jerusalem that looks remarkably like Eden (Rev. 21), ruled by and made possible by a divine king who looks remarkably like a new Adam (1 Cor. 15).

LOOKING BACK

1. How is the view of land in the Hebrew Bible similar to and different from your own view of land?

---

55. Brueggemann, *Land*, 205.
56. C. Wright, "Biblical Reflections on Land," 157.
57. Richter, *Stewards of Eden*, 24.
58. Berry, "Gift of the Good Land," 274.

2. Discuss three stories in the Hebrew Bible in which "land" is a central theological focus. In what way is land a "barometer" of Israel's covenant relationship in these stories?
3. How does the theme of land underscore God's faithfulness and justice?
4. Should a "theology of land" inform how we view the resources of creation? Does a "theology of land" challenge us with any particular social implications?

LOOKING BEYOND

Bartholomew, Craig G. *Where Mortals Dwell: A Christian View of Place for Today*. Baker Academic, 2011.

Borowski, Oded. *Agriculture in Iron Age Israel*. Eisenbrauns, 1987. Reprint, American Schools of Oriental Research, 2002.

Brueggemann, Walter. *The Land: Place as Gift, Promise, and Challenge in Biblical Faith*. 2nd ed. Overtures to Biblical Theology. Fortress, 2002.

Hopkins, David C. *The Highlands of Canaan*. The Social World of Biblical Antiquity Series 3. Almond Press, 1985.

Martin, Oren R. *Bound for the Promised Land: The Land Promise in God's Redemptive Plan*. New Studies in Biblical Theology 34. InterVarsity, 2015.

Richter, Sandra L. *Stewards of Eden: What Scripture Says About the Environment and Why It Matters*. IVP Academic, 2020.

Vitalis Hoffman, Mark, and Robert A. Mullins. *Atlas of the Biblical World*. Fortress, 2019.

von Rad, Gerhard. "The Promised Land and Yahweh's Land in the Hexateuch." In *The Problem of the Hexateuch and Other Essays*. Translated by E. W. Trueman Dicken, 79–93. SCM, 1984.

Wright, Christopher. "Biblical Reflections on Land." *Evangelical Review of Theology* 17, no. 2 (1993): 153–67.

4

HOLINESS AND PURITY
The Sanctity of God

Holiness and purity are two of the most significant concepts of ancient Israelite society, yet they are also the most foreign to us in our contemporary world. What images come to mind when you think of holiness/purity and people today? We decided to ask an AI language model this question, and this is the answer it gave: "When I think of purity in people, I visualize someone with a genuine and untainted spirit, someone whose intentions are sincere and whose actions are guided by kindness and integrity. It's like seeing the innocence in a child's eyes, unspoiled by the complexities and impurities of the world. Purity in people reflects qualities such as honesty, compassion, and authenticity, shining through in their words and deeds."[1] I don't know how this strikes you, but to us it seems that even AI software has a standard of purity that no person can live up to. Thank goodness ancient Israel's concepts of holiness and purity are not what we (or even AI) imagine. It is highly problematic for us to read the Hebrew Bible and impose our concepts of holiness and purity onto the ancient society it documents. Things get even more complicated when we attempt to persuade others to our misguided interpretations. Consequently, it is imperative for us to try as best we can to understand ancient Israel's worldview of holiness and purity.

1. Response to "What comes to mind when you think of purity and people?," ChatGPT-3.5, Open AI, April 15, 2024, chat.openai.com/chat.

LOOKING DOWN

The cultural context of purity and holiness in ancient Israel can be described as complex, at best. Here, the realm of the sacred and the realm of the profane (or secular) intertwine in profound ways. In the first part of the chapter, we will first look broadly at the idea of purity and holiness in the cultic context within the wider ancient Near East. Then we will narrow in on the concept of purity/holiness in the social and cultural world of ancient Israel.

Terminology

In the Hebrew Bible, there are several overlapping, paired terms related to holiness and purity that can seem quite vague and that possess numerous possible implications.[2] The various Akkadian and Hebrew words typically translated as "purity" and "holiness" contain many shades of meaning and potential applications. However, one consistent notion is the dual-aspected nature of the terms, which is imperative to its interpretation.[3] The Hebrew root *qds* is the word that best denotes or stands for the concept of holiness within the Hebrew Bible, so much so that Karel van der Toorn writes that *qds* "is at least as important as the notion of purity."[4] Defining "purity" is complicated; however, one way to look at it is that purity is more easily defined by what is contrary to it.[5] Here is where the dual nature of purity terms can be helpful. For instance, the Akkadian word *ellu*, meaning "cleanliness," is understood in the negative (such as the absence of dirt) but also in the positive (such as brilliance and luminosity).[6] Van der Toorn writes, "In religious use the negative component consists in the absence of all elements conflicting with the divine nature. The positive connotation of radiance, joy, vitality and vigour can be subsumed in the idea of communion with the transcendent energy. It is vacancy as well as fulfilment. Everything visited by the gods must meet the requirements of purity and holiness, if the contact with the divine is to be a blessing instead of a curse."[7] The dual-aspected nature of "holiness" or "purity," and the negative and positive connotation of these terms, should be considered when attempting to understand these concepts within

---

2. Such as clean/unclean, pure/impure, and holy/profane. Lawrence, "Clean/Unclean, Pure/Impure, Holy/Profane," 301.

3. Van der Toorn, *Sin and Sanction*, 29.

4. Van der Toorn, *Sin and Sanction*, 28. Other Hebrew terms include the root *thr*, which indicates the basic sense of cleanliness. This term is often used in contrast to that which is unclean or drab, like clothes (Num. 8:7), head coverings (Zech. 3:4–5), or the luminosity of gold (Exod. 25:11), and its use is restricted to religious contexts.

5. Guichard and Marti, "Purity in Ancient Mesopotamia," 64.

6. Van der Toorn, *Sin and Sanction*, 27–28.

7. Van der Toorn, *Sin and Sanction*, 29.

their wider ancient Near Eastern context. With that said, one thing these terms have in common is that they are used in cultic contexts. Furthermore, they are primarily used in relation to the suitability of that which comes into contact with the divine, particularly in service to the deity at its abode (i.e., a temple or a sanctuary).[8]

Purity and the Sanctuary

In order to appreciate the role of purity in the official cultic rituals conducted in the temple and shrines, we must widen our view to include the typical ancient Near Eastern view of cosmology. Cosmology is the "conception of the world and universe, possibly thought of as a cognitive map of the Earth in relation to various celestial bodies and other features."[9] This should not be confused with cosmogony, which "usually refers to any account of the origins and creation of the universe."[10] Cosmogonies, usually in the form of mythological texts, preserve the cosmologies of a particular society.[11] For instance, Genesis 1 is a cosmogony of a particular cosmology of ancient Israel.

Within the cosmology of the wider ancient Near Eastern world (including the Egyptians, Mesopotamians, Canaanites, Hittites, and Israelites), the geography of the cosmos was viewed as a three-tiered system: The top tier was the heavens, the earth consisted of the middle tier (considered to be a flat disk),[12] and the last tier was the netherworld (see fig. 4.1). The greater cosmos were surrounded by the cosmic waters on which the earth floated; in some cases the earth was thought to be on pillars. These chaotic cosmic waters were held back by the sky and fell to earth as precipitation through openings or gates in the sky (Gen. 1:6–7; 7:10–11; 8:2; 2 Kings 7:2, 19; Prov. 8:24–29; Isa. 24:18; Mal. 3:10).[13] It was commonly thought that the deities resided in their "houses" (a.k.a. temples) in the heavens, while humanity resided on earth, with the sky functioning as a boundary between the two. Mountains (or natural "high places") intersected all three tiers: Their roots were in the netherworld, they supported the sky, and they reached into the heavens; consequently, it was popularly thought in Canaan that the gods also lived on mountain tops.[14] In Mesopotamia, ziggurats were built next to temples and were considered artificial mountains or "high places." It was

---

8. Lawrence, "Clean/Unclean, Pure/Impure, Holy/Profane," 301.
9. McGeough, "Cosmology, Near East."
10. McGeough, "Cosmology, Near East."
11. McGeough, "Cosmology, Near East."
12. For iconography of the structure of the earth, see the Babylonian map of the world and Egyptian sarcophagus in Cornelius, "Visual Representation," 196–98, see esp. fig. 2 (p. 212) and fig. 6 (p. 215). See also Keel, *Symbolism of the Biblical World*, 21.
13. Walton, *Ancient Near Eastern Thought*, 132–33, 137.
14. Walton, *Ancient Near Eastern Thought*, 134.

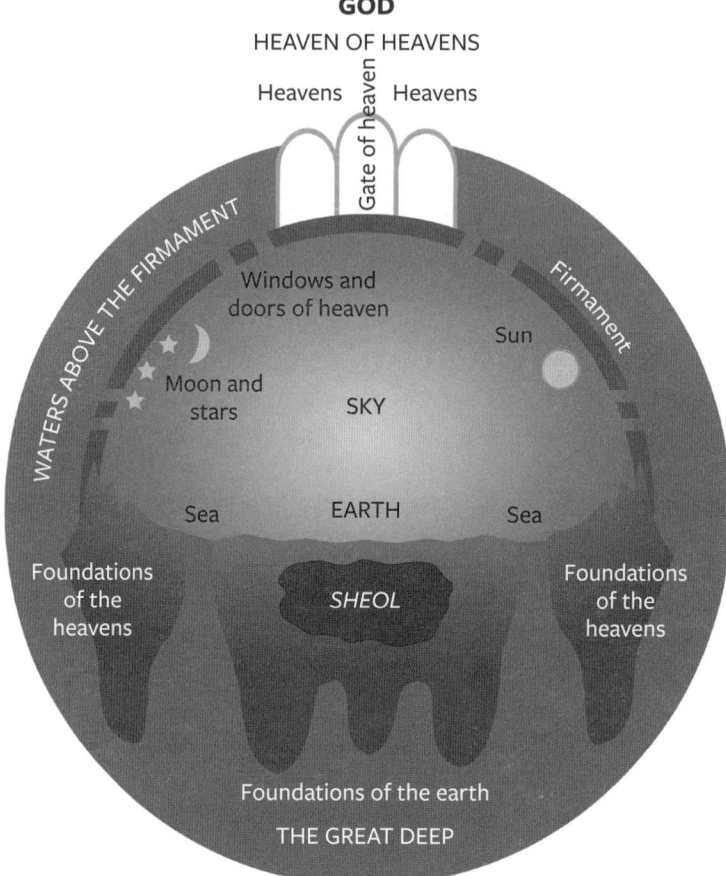

Figure 4.1. Cosmology of the ancient Near Eastern world
Based on a figure by Tom-L / Wikimedia Commons / CC-BY 4.0

thought that the gods would use the ziggurats to descend from their heavenly realm to take up residence within their earthly dwelling.[15] "Houses" (a.k.a. temples or sanctuaries) on earth were built in order to encourage the deities to descend from the heavens and dwell among their people. Various rituals were performed in the deity's house on earth as a way to serve the gods.

Maintenance of Order

The service rituals to the gods often represent and confirm the social order. The gods are holy, and their dwellings are sacred space and must remain holy. Consequently, there was a high standard for anything used in

---

15. Walton, *Ancient Near Eastern Thought*, 74.

the service of the deity. Ritual objects, practices, places, and personnel all had to conform to certain regulations and protocols to preserve the sanctity of the divine dwelling. Only that which meets the high standards of purity and holiness can come before the holy; and the only way to be pure and holy depends on the extent of conformity to the standards of the gods.[16] A closer look at what these standards consisted of will help us understand this concept.

Cultic personnel purified or washed themselves before they conducted the daily service rituals, in particular the parts of their body that were going to be in contact with the divine: the mouth (for speaking) and the hands (for conducting the rituals). They often anointed themselves with oil so that the state of purity would be maintained during the ritual. Clothing would also have to be purified before being worn in the presence of the divine.[17] In an Old Babylonian prayer found in Assurbanipal's library (ca. seventh century BCE),[18] we can see some of the purification process that a priest would go through.

> O Šamaš! I am placing in my mouth pure cedar (resin),
> I am wrapping it for you in the locks of my hair;
> I am placing for you in my lap compact cedar (resin).
> I washed my mouth and my hands,
> I wiped my mouth with compact cedar (resin);
> I wrapped pure cedar (resin) in the locks of my hair,
> I envelop for you compact cedar (resin).
> Being (now) clean to the assembly of the gods
> I shall draw near for judgment.[19]

Without the daily service rituals at the sanctuary, including purification offerings and cultic meals, the deity cannot dwell in its abode and thus becomes "hangry."[20] An unhappy deity is unlikely to want to control the chaos of the cosmos and thus the chaos of life on earth. Thus, the temple served as the chaos control center, with the purity service rituals to the gods playing a dual-aspected role: (1) The purity rituals kept the gods appeased. The gods, if kept happy, would use their energy to maintain order by keeping the cosmos in order and chaos at bay. (2) The purity rituals were dependent on the participation of humanity. If the personnel who conducted the temple purity rituals were pure, that helped maintain order within the cosmos and consequently

---

16. Van der Toorn, *Sin and Sanction*, 27.
17. Guichard and Marti, "Purity in Ancient Mesopotamia," 64.
18. Assurbanipal ruled the Neo-Assyrian Empire from 669–ca. 631 BCE. His library was found in the capital city of Nineveh and included a collection of over thirty thousand clay tablets and fragments inscribed in cuneiform.
19. Goetze, "Old Babylonian Prayer," 25.
20. "Hangry" means bad-tempered or irritable as a result of hunger.

society at large; for the temple rituals themselves would be ineffective without the required state of purity and cleanliness of those who attended to the gods.[21]

Purity Outside the Sanctuary

The sanctuary was regarded as sacred space, and any place outside of it was considered common. In the world of the common, impurity was more immediate, uncontrollable, and formidable. Risks of becoming impure were much greater than in the world of the sacred. Consequently, the purity/impurity of the common required just as much attention and precaution as the sacred domain, but people were always aware that strict and complete control over impurity was absolutely unattainable.[22] In the ancient Near East, impurity in the common world came in two major forms. The first type of impurity was a contamination of daily life, which was easy to rectify, and the person could become pure once again. The second was more acute and could be caused by sin, transgression, contact with something or someone impure, or an external attack by a deity or sorcerer.[23] Whatever the form, impurity aroused the rage of the gods who then subjected the victim to punishments or trials until the cause (if brought on by an unconscious act) was revealed (often with the help of a specialist) and rectified with an acceptable ritual. If the cause could not be revealed with certainty, the rituals increased in complexity and extensivity.[24]

How ancient Israel viewed purity and how a typical Israelite behaved on a daily basis regarding purity cannot easily be learned from the archaeological record; rather, our best source (however challenging) is the Hebrew Bible.[25] Like that of the wider ancient Near Eastern world, the views of impurity (or that which could pollute the sacred) in the Hebrew Bible can best be organized by the source of the pollution. Christophe Nihan argues that the Hebrew Bible establishes two main sources of pollution: physical (or biological) and moral.[26]

Impurity from Physical Pollution

The first type of pollution, physical,[27] is as the name suggests—it is concerned with "various physical or biological phenomena that affect especially the human body but also, by extension, materials such as houses, fabrics,

---

21. Walton, *Ancient Near Eastern Thought*, 90.
22. Guichard and Marti, "Purity in Ancient Mesopotamia," 106.
23. Guichard and Marti, "Purity in Ancient Mesopotamia," 106.
24. Guichard and Marti, "Purity in Ancient Mesopotamia," 106.
25. Of course, the compositional history is far beyond the scope of this chapter.
26. Nihan, "Forms and Functions," 321. Nihan's classification derives from the book of Leviticus, where purity and pollution play a significant role, possibly more so than in any other book of the Hebrew Bible (the book of Numbers being a close second), 311.
27. Some may refer to "physical pollution" as "ritual pollution."

or domestic utensils."²⁸ In these cases, a person comes into contact with a polluting substance, which causes them to be "unclean" or "impure" for a certain length of time. If it was a case of major pollution, the person would be impure for at least seven days. If it was a case of a minor pollution, the person would be impure until evening. There was no sense of blame, guilt, or wrongdoing associated with physical pollution, since most instances of this impurity were caused by outside phenomena or natural bodily functions. However, the impure person was considered "contagious" (some literally, but mostly figuratively) and was to avoid contact with other people, objects, and especially the sacred. While contagious, the person was not dangerous, other than if they were to come into contact with the sacred.²⁹

Physical pollution from external causes normally generated *minor* pollution and thus minor contamination; however, exceptions to this rule include two external causes that resulted in *major* pollution and contamination: death and leprosy. Corpse-related pollution occurred as a result of coming into contact with a corpse, being in the same tent/building during a person's death, or even just coming into contact with a grave or human bones (Num. 19:11, 14, 16). Furthermore, corpse-related pollution was extremely contagious, and anyone involved in the rituals to purify the pollution was considered contaminated, albeit minorly. Those polluted by coming into contact with a corpse were required to stay outside the community for seven days (31:19).³⁰

The second major pollution caused by an external source is that of *tsaraʿat*, which is some sort of infection that affects not only humans but also fabrics (Lev. 13:47–59) and houses (14:33–53).³¹ The etymology of *tsaraʿat* is unclear but, in relation to humans, it is consistently used in Leviticus as a generic term for various types of skin infections and is often wrongly translated as "leprosy." The skin conditions are wide ranging and include the appearance of shiny marks (13:2–8); discolorations (13:9–17); "boils" (13:18–23); burns (13:24–28); "scalls" (meaning scabs or scales, 13:29–37 KJV); tetters (like eczema, 13:38–39); and, finally, baldness (13:40–44).³² Those polluted with *tsaraʿat* are exiled alone outside the community and must subject themselves to a series of examinations and rituals in order to be declared free from the pollutant and allowed back into the community.³³

---

28. Nihan, "Forms and Functions," 321.
29. Frymer-Kensky, "Pollution, Purification, and Purgation," 399, 403.
30. Frymer-Kensky, "Pollution, Purification, and Purgation," 399.
31. For a detailed commentary on the *tsaraʿat* in Leviticus, see Milgrom, *Leviticus 1–16*, 768–826.
32. Nihan, "Forms and Functions," 324.
33. Frymer-Kensky, "Pollution, Purification, and Purgation," 399–400; Nihan, "Forms and Functions," 324–25.

There were other physical pollutants that were not caused by external agents but did generate major impurity. Interestingly, they all have to do with emissions from the human body, in particular those from the genital organs, which were the source of the pollution.[34] Leviticus 12 includes a series of regulations related to genital pollution, and Leviticus 15 addresses those for both males (vv. 2–17) and females (vv. 19–30).[35] Laws regarding male morbid genital discharges[36] that are highly contagious (such as gonorrhea) (15:2–15) include what to do with any objects that were touched by the contagious man and were thus also defiled: the bed (15:4–5), something he sat on (15:6), a saddle (15:9), or a vessel (15:12). The man had to wait seven days *after* the clearing of the pollution and then offer a sacrifice of two turtledoves or two pigeons (15:13–15). Non-morbid male genital discharges (such as the discharge of semen) were less severe; the man was considered unclean only until the end of the day, at which time he would bathe and wash anything that had come into contact with the discharge (15:16–17).[37] Before we discuss how these laws applied to women, we should note that there is a brief statement regarding pollution caused by sexual intercourse, which designated both partners as unclean until the end of the day, when they must bathe (15:18).

Laws regarding female pollution focused on two aspects: menstruation (Lev. 15:19–24) and abnormal discharges of blood outside of the menstrual cycle (15:25–30). The rules for abnormal female discharges are the same as those for normal menstruation, including that the objects of the polluted woman and those who come in contact with these items are also contaminated. However, the main difference between the two is that the woman with abnormal discharges must wait seven days *after* the clearing of the pollution and then offer a sacrifice of two turtledoves or two pigeons on the eighth day,

---

34. Frymer-Kensky, "Pollution, Purification, and Purgation," 399; Nihan, "Forms and Functions," 322.

35. For a detailed commentary on emissions from the human body in Leviticus, see Milgrom, *Leviticus 1–16*, 742–68, 902–1009.

36. In the context of male genital discharges, "morbid" refers to a discharge that is significantly abnormal, often accompanied by concerning symptoms like foul odor, thick pus-like consistency, noticeable discoloration, and significant discomfort or pain. It could potentially indicate a serious underlying medical condition. "Non-morbid" describes a discharge that is considered normal or relatively minor; it is usually clear or slightly milky, with minimal odor and no associated discomfort. Essentially, "morbid" discharge is a cause for immediate medical attention, while "non-morbid" typically is not. In the context of Lev. 15, male genital discharge is categorized into two types: morbid discharge (*zov*) and non-morbid discharge. Morbid discharge refers to pathological secretions, likely associated with infection or disease, such as gonorrhea or other sexually transmitted infections. Non-morbid discharge, on the other hand, refers to natural emissions such as seminal fluid, which are not symptomatic of illness (15:16–18). Milgrom, *Leviticus 1–16*, 932.

37. Nihan, "Forms and Functions," 322.

whereas a sacrifice is not required for normal menstruation.³⁸ Laws requiring impurity due to childbirth (Lev. 12), however, are more extensive. The mother is considered impure for the duration of seven days for a male child and fourteen days for a female child. After this initial time of impurity, the mother is still not completely pure and must go through an additional time of semi-impurity, known as the period of blood-purification (12:4). Again, the amount of time required for this semi-polluted state is based on whether the woman had a male child (thirty-three days) or a female child (sixty-six days).³⁹ The biblical text does not give a reason for these differences in time.

The reasons for the laws regarding physical impurity as found in Leviticus 12–15 are lost to us today. What can be observed, however, is that (excluding sexual intercourse) the sources of pollution are biological phenomena that invade the domestic realm, causing chaos and the loss of control over one's own body, the state of the objects it comes into contact with, and thus the order of the social world around them. Nihan argues that the purity laws in Leviticus 12–15 are attempting to reestablish a form of social control over these phenomena by exhibiting a consistent relationship between the degree of pollution and the rituals prescribed.⁴⁰ He writes, "The more a phenomenon identified as a source of pollution exemplifies the loss of social control over human bodies and domestic artifacts, the more severe the degree of contamination ascribed to it, and the more significant the ritual measures that need to be taken by the individual in order to eliminate that pollution and recover a state of purity."⁴¹ The purity laws, as Nihan sees it, maintain social order by ensuring standards of behavior that were seen as a divine mandate but enacted and enforced by the priests. Physical pollution (or impurity or uncleanliness) in the profane results in chaos of the domestic and social world, which then threatens the purity of the sacred (the sanctuary or temple), where Israel's patron deity, Yhwh, abides. The statutes (those discussed above and others like them) not only serve as rituals to purify those who are polluted but also as a boundary wall of sorts between the sacred and the profane.

Impurity from Moral Pollution

The second category of pollution (as deduced from the book of Leviticus) is moral pollution,⁴² which (unlike physical pollution) had a clear association with wrongdoing. Whether the pollutant was an individual or a group (or even the entire people of Israel), they have done something expressly forbidden and

---

38. Nihan, "Forms and Functions," 323.
39. Frymer-Kensky, "Pollution, Purification, and Purgation," 400.
40. Nihan, "Forms and Functions," 329.
41. Nihan, "Forms and Functions," 330.
42. Nihan, "Forms and Functions," 339.

have thus put themselves and the community in danger (such as worshiping other gods, committing adultery, or eating blood). This danger is viewed as a punishment from the deity for their actions. This is not the only way moral pollution diverts from physical pollution. In physical pollution, after a designated amount of time the polluted person can participate in purification rituals that would allow them to be readmitted to the community. Whereas in moral pollution, the danger from these serious moral offenses is permanent or lasts until a significant disaster occurs. While there are rituals for purification and reintegration for those who have physical pollutions, such remedies do not apply here. However, it is believed that sincere repentance and sacrifices might help reduce or prevent some of the impending consequences of moral pollution. Another way moral impurity differs from physical pollution is that moral pollution is not contagious; people cannot become impure simply by being near someone who has committed such acts. For instance, touching an adulterer or someone who has consumed blood does not pose an immediate risk to others, so there are no specific guidelines for how to interact with them. Allowing individuals who have committed these serious moral offenses to move freely poses no immediate threat to others, which is why there are no specific rules for avoiding them. However, if too many people engage in such wrongful acts, it could lead to a greater risk for the entire community, as society itself may become polluted and face the possibility of a collective disaster."[43]

Restrictions or rules pertaining to the category of moral impurity are often called "statutes" (*huqqot*) or "customs" (*mishpatim*) in the Hebrew Bible. This is the case in Leviticus 18 and 20, which begin with the rationale behind prohibiting certain behaviors that were not sanctioned by Yhwh but were practiced by the nations who used to inhabit the land (18:2–5). What follows is a list of behaviors, all related to sexual practices, which demonstrates that intercourse with the following is prohibited: with women who are related to the (assumed) male pollutant either by blood (mother, sister, granddaughter, etc.) or by marriage (sister-in-law, daughter-in-law, etc.) (18:6–18); with a menstruant (v. 19); with a neighbor's wife (v. 20); with another man (v. 22); and with a beast (v. 23). One final prohibition, not relating to sexual intercourse, is given—that is, offering sacrifices (possibly child sacrifice) to the Canaanite god Molech (v. 21).[44] The list of moral impurities ends with two imperative details (vv. 24–30): the reminder that these prohibitions are Yhwh's statutes and customs and that the purity of the land Yhwh gave to Israel is dependent

---

43. Frymer-Kensky, "Pollution, Purification, and Purgation," 404.
44. Frayne and Stuckey, *Handbook of Gods and Goddesses*, 213. There is some debate, however, about whether Molech is a deity or a type of sacrifice. See Smith, *Early History of God*, 171–81.

on Israel obeying these statutes. If Israel does not obey Yhwh's statutes, "the land will vomit [them] out for defiling it, as it vomited out the nation that was before [them]" (v. 28).[45] According to Leviticus, the previous inhabitants of the land defiled themselves and the land with these customs; as a result, the land was considered "unclean" and the inhabitants were "vomited out" of the land. Obedience to Yhwh's statutes would help Israel avoid the same fate while simultaneously singling them out from the other nations (20:24), transforming them into a "holy" (*qadash*) nation (v. 26).[46] Like the physical pollution laws, the moral pollution laws can be viewed as an even more extensive outermost boundary between the sacred and the common.

Summary

Taking part in these prohibitions is against the fundamental principles of Israelite cosmology—blurring the lines between the sacred and the common.[47] Like their ancient Near Eastern neighbors, the Israelites understood that the sanctuary was Yhwh's earthly dwelling place and, as such, protecting the sacred precinct, protocols, professionals, and objects was of utmost importance. Since the deity is holy and orderly, therefore their dwelling place on earth must be as well. In order for their dwelling place to remain sacred and free from pollution, anyone or anything that took part in the maintenance of order at the sanctuary must also be free from pollution. Keeping a sense of order in the sanctuary was thought to keep the chaos at bay in both the cosmological realm and the earthly realm.

But what is interesting to point out here is that many of these laws are set within a domestic context utilizing the framework of Israel's kinship groups: the household (Lev. 18:6–16), the clan (vv. 17–18), the tribe, and all of Israel (vv. 19–23).[48] In other words, the holiness or purity that could be acquired by following the laws of physical and moral purity (as seen in Leviticus) wasn't just for the priests, sacrifices, or the sanctuary—rather, holiness was for *all* of Israel. All of Israel was to be viewed as a holy nation and would be held accountable as such.

LOOKING UP

Recently, while my parents were visiting from Kentucky, we played the tourist game and visited a local attraction called Sutter's Mill, where the California

---

45. Nihan, "Forms and Functions," 339.
46. Nihan, "Forms and Functions," 341.
47. Frymer-Kensky, "Pollution, Purification, and Purgation," 404.
48. Nihan, "Forms and Functions," 341.

gold rush began in 1849. While the adults were busy reading the information placards and imagining lives of desperation and hope, my kids were mostly interested in panning for gold. Like the fortune-seekers of two centuries ago, they were *attracted* to its *value* and beauty, and they had a blast trying to *separate* the gold (or what they thought to be gold!) from the surrounding sand and pebbles. Real gold miners (which my kids are not, but don't tell them!) must also *refine*, or cleanse, the gold of its impurities.

These aspects of gold italicized above—its attractiveness, its value, and the separation and refinement processes—have direct parallels with the theological idea of holiness and the related idea of purity. There are also some key differences, which we will return to in the conclusion of this chapter.

A Theological View of Four Related Words

In the "Looking Down" section, we looked at the ideas of holiness and purity (and the opposites of each) as they were understood in the ancient Near East. In this section, we will consider how the concepts relate to each other theologically, according to the Hebrew Bible.

Holiness in the Hebrew Bible finds its source in God alone.[49] People, places, and objects can be holy only insofar as God deems them to be holy and allows them to share in or reflect his holiness.[50] In other words, God's holiness is independent, whereas all other holiness is *dependent* on God's holiness.[51] Throughout the book of Leviticus, God exhorts his people saying, "Be holy, for I am holy" (Lev. 11:44–45; 19:2; 20:7, 26; 21:8). God created humans to reflect his image (Gen. 1:26–28), so it naturally follows that they are also to reflect his holiness.[52] Indeed, Israel's holiness would in theory attract others to God's covenant presence (Deut. 4:6–8), like the attraction of a gold rush.

So, God is holy and his people are supposed to reflect his holiness. But what *is* holiness? Scholars have proposed different definitions. Some see holiness as God's power, whereas others think it has to do with his character. The most popular definition is the idea of separation: both separation *to* God

---

49. Jan Wilson goes so far as to say, "Although it is tempting to look to Mesopotamia for influences which might have been formative on Israelite religion, . . . where some very central religious concepts are concerned, there seems to be little likelihood of borrowing from Mesopotamia, for the Hebrew concepts of holiness are substantially different from the Sumerian concept and there simply is no corresponding Akkadian concept." Wilson, *"Holiness" and "Purity" in Mesopotamia*, 95.

50. Milgrom, *Leviticus 1–16*, 730; Jenson, "Holiness in the Priestly Writings," 107.

51. Sklar, *Leviticus*, 39.

52. Milgrom states, "The reason that Israel must aspire to holiness is *imitation dei*." Milgrom, *Leviticus 1–16*, 722.

and separation *from* everything else. Finally, others contend that holiness pertains foremost to God's presence or the realm of God.[53]

All of these aspects are supported by Scripture, but the one concept around which all the others revolve is the idea of God's presence.[54] Israel was to separate themselves and their food and their space from the world around them so that they could live in the presence of their holy God. Similarly, living holy lives that reflected God's good character was necessary if they were to live in the presence of a holy God of perfect character.

In fact, the idea of separation might be better understood as a consequence of holiness, rather than its primary meaning or purpose. Consider that objects dedicated to God became holy when they entered the realm of the divine (Lev. 27:28; Num. 7:1; Josh. 6:19). It was their contact with the divine sphere that caused them to be set apart from everything else. Moreover, priests were deemed holy when they ministered in the temple, but not when they went outside of that divine realm.[55] Israel's holiness was rooted primarily in their presence before God. Their separation from things like impure food or unbelieving nations was a secondary consequence, and one that would diminish as God's redemptive planned unfolded (as we will see below).[56]

That which is not holy is simply "common." Not everything "common" was necessarily sinful or bad.[57] You might have a favorite coffee mug or a favorite chair. There is nothing inherently wrong with those things, but they are not holy. When gold miners separate gold from the river pebble and sand, there is nothing wrong with the "common" river stones. In fact, they are quite beautiful! But they are not gold; they are "common" in comparison.

The next two words in this semantic field, "pure" and "impure," might further help to clarify the meaning of holiness. In the Hebrew Bible, something could be "pure" (or "clean" as some translations read) but not necessarily "holy." Trout and crickets, for example, would have been considered "pure" and admissible for eating, but they were not "holy" and admissible for sacrifice.

Leviticus 10:10 uses all four of these terms in chiastic (inverted) parallelism: "You are to distinguish between the **holy** and the **common**, and between the unclean [or **impure**] and the clean [or **pure**]." The opposing relationships between "holy" and "common," and between "impure" and "pure," seem clear enough, but the words in parallel (common in parallel with impure,

---

53. Philip Jenson describes these definitions and their supporters in detail in "Holiness in the Priestly Writings," 93–110.
54. Jenson, "Holiness in the Priestly Writings," 110.
55. Naudé, "קדש," 3:880–81.
56. Naudé, "קדש," 3:885.
57. Another possible misconception might be that God is here distinguishing between the "spiritual" and the "secular," as though some aspects of life come under the sovereignty of God and others do not. All things are "spiritual" in that sense, but not all things are holy.

and holy in parallel with pure) should *not* be seen as perfectly synonymous, as depicted in figure 4.2.

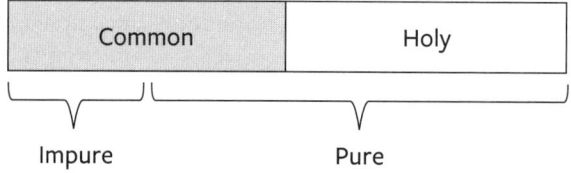

Figure 4.2.

Since not all that is common is impure (like your favorite coffee mug or trout), the relationship between these terms should be understood more like the depiction in figure 4.3.

Figure 4.3.

There are two types of impurities: sin impurities and physical impurities. Sin impurities resulted from breaking God's commands, whereas physical impurities (such as a bodily discharge) did not.[58] If the distinction between "pure" and "impure" was not necessarily a moral issue, then what purpose did such a distinction have? In other words, why would God deem lamb "pure" for eating, whereas shellfish was "impure"? Or why would the emission of menstrual blood or semen render a person temporarily "impure," but emissions of other bodily fluids did not?

Multiple rationales have been offered. With regard to the food purity laws (kosher laws), Mary Douglas argues that some animals were probably marked as impure as a means of protecting wild animals, much like modern conservation efforts.[59] Richard Averbeck offers another possible explanation for the distinction between edible and inedible animals: their connection to the organizational structures of creation. Much of the same terminology and taxonomy is evident

---

58. Ginsburskaya, "Purity and Impurity," 4.
59. In her earlier research, Douglas argued that the impure animals represented in-between classifications, but she later retracted that explanation in favor of the one above. Douglas, *Leviticus as Literature*, esp. 142–58.

in both the creation account in Genesis and the dietary laws in Leviticus.[60] A third reason, and one that seems quite likely, is that the physical purity laws were meant to be daily reminders of Israel's calling to be holy. Christopher Wright puts it well when he says, "Even for Old Testament Israel, ritual cleanness, from the kitchen to the sanctuary, was meant to *symbolize* God's greater requirement of moral integrity, social justice and covenant loyalty."[61] The food they ate and the clothes they wore were thus constant reminders that they lived in the presence of a holy God and were called to reflect his holiness in everything they did.[62]

Graded Holiness

Once gold miners separate the gold from the "common" river pebbles and sand, they then have it assessed to determine its value. After all, gold has various levels of purity, measured by carats, and the higher the number, the greater purity of the gold. Engagement and wedding rings are typically made from the higher levels of gold (unless, like me, you happen to have a homemade engagement ring made from clay and a pebble!).

Holiness and purity also have levels. Philip Jenson explains that "holiness is not an either/or concept, but one that admits gradations."[63] The gradations of ritual purity can be understood on a spectrum (see fig. 4.4).[64]

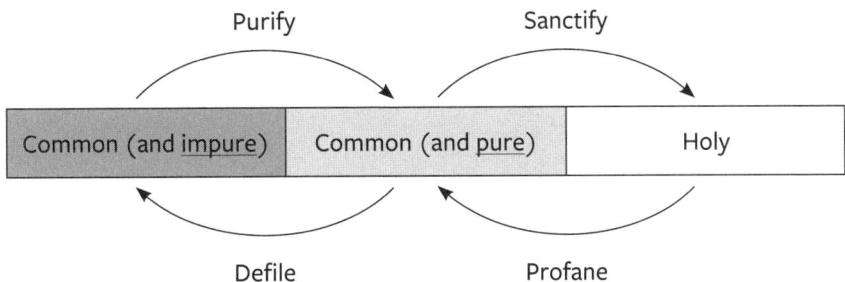

Figure 4.4. Graded holiness

---

60. Averbeck, "Clean and Unclean," 4:483.
61. C. Wright, "Leviticus," 139.
62. Several other rationales, from hygiene concerns to cultural taboos, have been proposed, but at this point, we might be wise to follow the counsel of the medieval Jewish philosopher Maimonides, who basically admitted that these purity laws are difficult to understand fully: "It is plain and manifest that the laws about uncleanness and cleanness are decrees laid down by Scripture and not matters about which human understanding is capable of forming a judgment; for behold, they are included among the arbitrary decrees." Maimonides, *Mishneh Torah (Code of Maimonides), Taharah* 8.11.12, p. 535.
63. Jenson, "Holiness in the Priestly Writings," 108.
64. This is a modified version of Jay Sklar's more detailed tables in *Leviticus*, 45–47.

It should be noted that this graded holiness is particularly true of *ritual* holiness, and not moral holiness. Just as there is a distinction between sin impurity and physical impurity, there is a related distinction between moral holiness and ritual holiness. Moral holiness was not restricted to a specific person or tribe, since all of Israel was to be holy in the moral sense of the word. Having a gradation of ritual holiness for the priesthood, however, meant that the priest was able to serve as a visible object lesson of God's holiness.

Places, objects, and people could all be categorized within this graded conception of ritual holiness. As the throne room of Yhwh, the most holy place (or the Holy of Holies) within the tabernacle and temple was naturally the holiest space on earth, whereas the Israelite camp was considered common (and pure) while certain places outside the camp were deemed impure. Movement between spheres was also possible in some circumstances, particularly with respect to objects and people. War plunder from pagan nations would be considered common and impure, but when it was devoted to Yhwh, it became purified. It even became sanctified once it was brought into the sanctuary (Josh. 6:19). If that plunder was taken out of the sanctuary (for example, the many times during Israel's history when unfaithful kings paid tribute with temple wealth), then those objects would become profane or even defiled. Similarly, when an Israelite incurred a wound that grew infected or experienced some other kind of bodily discharge, they would move from the "common and pure" category to the "common and impure" category because the discharge would render them "defiled." However, once the discharge cleared and they went through the appropriate priestly channels, they would return to the status of "common and pure."

This spectrum of graded holiness and its ritual states highlighted God's holiness and Israel's need to be holy in every aspect of life.[65] It also reminds us that holiness is integrally tied to God's presence. Its fluidity reminds us that the realm, or status, of holiness is not an open and closed gate but a process. For God's people, becoming holy—becoming sanctified people—is not a one-time event. It is a gradual journey into God's presence whereby we allow the great Refiner to purify us into greater and greater conformity to his goodness and grace.

Holiness and Purity Throughout the Bible

Much of the previous discussion is based on the theology of holiness and purity in Leviticus, but these themes are not limited to the book of Leviticus or the Torah, any more than the discovery of gold is limited to California. In this section, we'll see how holiness is understood in the creation accounts

---

65. Sklar, *Leviticus*, 48–49.

of Genesis, the prophets, the wisdom literature, and into the Second Temple and New Testament periods.

Creation Accounts

We noted above how the distinction between pure and impure animals might reflect the way in which God categorized and ordered his animal creation. Scholars such as John Walton have persuasively argued that the biblical creation account is concerned primarily with functional origins rather than material origins. In other words, what mattered most to the biblical authors and their readers was not whether the deity created everything they saw (that would have been a given) or how precisely that material came to be but, rather, how the deity organized and gave purpose to everything created.[66] In the six days of creation, God is separating (light from darkness, sky from water, and dry land from the waters) and giving purpose to everything he creates, including humans (Gen. 1:26–28).

If creation is largely about separating and ordering creation, then might we see holiness (especially as a graded system) as an outworking of that original creational ordering? Mila Ginsburskaya explains how Israel's holy living reflected not only God's own holiness but also his role as Creator: "It can be suggested that the ability to create an orderly world out of chaos is one of the main characteristics of the God of the Hebrew Bible. . . . When people of Israel live according to the divine commandments they imitate the creative and organizational activity of their God."[67] When people live within the creational norms and structures of their Creator, and when they seek to bring order (i.e., goodness, justice, equity, generosity, etc.) to the world around them, they reflect God's holiness.

Prophets

The prophets called the people of God back to the demands of the covenant. They reminded God's people that holiness is not passive. It is active and lived out. To be holy was primarily to separate oneself *for* or devote oneself *to* God, and only secondarily to separate oneself *from* the rest of the world. The "separation *for*" part of the equation was of particular interest for the prophets, who continually called out Israel for their failure to take seriously the social justice commands of Leviticus 19 in their identity as the holy people of God.

God's people could not feign service to God when their hearts and actions were in reality far from God. That was hypocrisy, empty ritualism, and it was

---

66. Walton, *Lost World of Genesis One*, 21–35.
67. Ginsburskaya, "Purity and Impurity," 23.

the exact opposite of true holiness. Isaiah, the prophet who had the glorious vision of "the Holy One of Israel" highly exalted in the temple (Isa. 6), repeatedly called out the people of Judah for attempting to worship a holy God while living unjust lives. They dared to approach God's holy presence and "trample" his courts while their hearts and actions were impure. How could they purify themselves so that they could enter God's holy presence? Isaiah 1:16–17 tells us:

> Wash yourselves; make yourselves clean;
>   remove the evil of your doings
>   from before my eyes;
> cease to do evil,
>   learn to do good;
> seek justice,
>   rescue the oppressed,
> defend the orphan,
>   plead for the widow.

Note in this passage how justice is still linked to cleanness. The prophets held both aspects together in their conception of holiness, as Walter Brueggemann explains: "The stress on cleanness prevents God's holiness from being reduced to moral requirement. Conversely, the urgency of justice precludes holiness from being generic, disinterested religion. This unresolvable tension in the very life of God shapes Israel's faith and evokes Israel as a community of both doxology and commandment, amazement and obedience."[68] Holiness pertained to God's majesty and the worship it required, as well as to how Israel lived their lives outside of the sanctuary. In modern Christian parlance, the prophets emphasized that the people's holiness needed to extend beyond Sunday morning.

Wisdom Literature

John G. Gammie has written a very helpful biblical theology on Israelite holiness in which he identifies cleanness as the unifying theme of holiness. For the priestly writers, holiness predominantly has to do with cleanness in the ritual sphere. For the prophetic writers, the emphasis is on the cleanness of social justice. For the wisdom writers, holiness pertains more to the cleanness of individual morality and integrity before God.[69]

In the book of Proverbs, holiness and purity must be sought but are not entirely attainable.

---

68. Brueggemann, foreword to Gammie, *Holiness in Israel*, xi.
69. Gammie, *Holiness in Israel*, 125.

> Who can say, "I have made my heart clean;
> I am pure from my sin"? (20:9)

Human means of measuring purity are also lacking.[70]

> All one's ways may be pure in one's own eyes,
> but the LORD weighs the spirit. (16:2)

Psalm 15, generally classified as a "wisdom psalm," identifies those who may approach God's holiness with moral integrity.

> O LORD, who may abide in your tent?
> Who may dwell on your holy hill?
>
> Those who walk blamelessly, and do what is right,
> and speak the truth from their heart. (vv. 1–2).

Job, in what Gammie calls the "high-water mark in Old Testament ethics," gives a detailed defense of his moral purity in chapter 31.[71] Job denies a range of sins, including lust (v. 1), falsehood (v. 5–6), injustice toward servants and the poor (vv. 13, 16), concealing sin (v. 33), and many more. The requirements of a holy God are many; Job denies violating them and thus sacrificing his moral purity. In all of these wisdom texts, holiness is tied to moral integrity, a cleanness of the heart.

Second Temple Judaism and the New Testament

If holiness has first and foremost to do with God's presence, then how could God's people be holy when the temple was destroyed or defiled, or when they lived far away from it? In the next chapter, we will consider more ways that Israel conceptualized God's presence apart from the temple, but here we will focus specifically on how Israel could be holy apart from the realm of God's holiness. Second Temple literature provides a clue, as well as a helpful link to the portrayal of holiness in the New Testament.

First Maccabees (considered canonical by many Christians) describes life for Israel under the Seleucid Empire in the second century BCE, when many Jews were scattered far from the temple and the temple itself was desecrated. In 1 Maccabees 12:9, the scriptures they hold in their hands are called "holy." The scriptures, and Torah in particular, in some ways were able to replace the temple and cult.[72] To approach the holy presence of God was to approach his holy presence in the Torah.

---

70. Gammie, *Holiness in Israel*, 127.
71. Gammie, *Holiness in Israel*, 146.
72. Naudé, "קדש," 3:887.

Similarly, in the New Testament, holiness is not confined to the temple but brought into the realm of humanity through the indwelling of the Holy Spirit.[73] Humanity then reflects that holiness outward, as we can see in 1 Peter 1:16, which echoes the charge given throughout Leviticus (11:44, 45; 19:2; 20:26): "You shall be holy, for I am holy."

In fact, if we are to see holiness primarily as separation *for* the presence of God and only secondarily as separation *from* anything antithetical to God, then might the eschatological hope for holiness be seen exclusively as the separation *for* God? Is this not the journey of sanctification, that God's people seek to grow closer and closer to God until all things are made right, at which point there will be nothing left from which we must separate ourselves because everything opposed to God will either be judged and removed or be turned toward God?

CONCLUSION

Just as gold is valuable and involves separation, so also holiness is a value for God's people to embody by entering into God's presence and thus separating themselves from impurities that are incompatible with the presence of a holy God. Just as gold must be refined, so also God refines us, removing our impurities. However, the superficial similarities end there because in many ways, God's holiness is the exact *opposite* of the California gold rush.

Whereas the gold rush provided wealth to a relatively small number who were lucky enough to find it and shrewd enough to keep it, God's holiness is infinitely more valuable and equally accessible to anyone willing to receive it and live faithfully in covenant with him. Whereas gold attracted people for the wrong reasons and repelled and scattered them after its pursuit, God's holiness attracts and sustains people. Finally, whereas the gold rush often brought disappointment and violence to those who sought it and to the native peoples from whose homeland it was taken, God's holiness is pure blessing, transforming people by God's grace to be their best selves, rather than their worst selves.

LOOKING BACK

1. How did purity regulations help keep social order? Why was this important?

---

73. Naudé explains, "The sacred no longer belongs to things, places, or rites, but to the manifestations of life produced by the Spirit." Naudé, "קדש‎," 3:887.

2. How do the themes of holiness and purity shed light on your view of God or on your relationship with God?
3. Can you think of a story or passage in Scripture (not mentioned in this chapter) that illustrates the theological concept of holiness?
4. What spiritual disciplines serve as formative reminders for you to "be holy" as "the LORD your God [is] holy" (Lev. 19:2)?

LOOKING BEYOND

Balentine, Samuel E., ed. *The Oxford Handbook of Ritual and Worship in the Hebrew Bible*. Oxford University Press, 2020.

Douglas, Mary. *Leviticus as Literature*. Oxford University Press, 2001.

Gammie, John G. *Holiness in Israel*. Fortress, 1989.

Jenson, Philip P. "Holiness in the Priestly Writings of the Old Testament." In *Holiness: Past and Present*, edited by Stephen Barton, 93–121. T&T Clark, 2002.

Milgrom, Jacob. *Leviticus 1–16: A New Translation with Introduction and Commentary*. Anchor Bible 3. Doubleday, 1991.

Sklar, Jay. *Sin, Impurity, Sacrifice, Atonement: The Priestly Conceptions*. Hebrew Bible Monographs 2. Sheffield Phoenix, 2015.

van der Toorn, Karel. *Sin and Sanction in Israel and Mesopotamia: A Comparative Study*. Van Gorcum, 1985.

5

WORSHIP
The Grace of God

When pop singers want to communicate a powerful feeling toward another (and let's face it—that's 99 percent of pop music), it should not surprise us that they sometimes use the metaphor of worship. One could think of Hozier's provocative 2013 lyrics, "Take me to church, I'll worship like a dog at the shrine of your lies." Or Taylor Swift's 2019 lyrics, "Even if it's a false god, we'd still worship this love." Though blatantly idolatrous (or, at least, irreverently metaphorical), these lyrics communicate something essential about worship, both ancient and modern: It involves intimacy and the deepest adoration. This chapter will explore the various facets of worship in ancient Israel and how they functioned theologically as a restorative means of grace within the covenant community.

LOOKING DOWN

Before we can dive into ancient Israel's worship practices, we first need to address an issue regarding so-called "official" and "unofficial" religious rituals. On the one hand, it is commonly thought that the Hebrew Bible solely reflects that the ancient Israelites worshiped one god (Yhwh) in one place (i.e., the tabernacle or the temple in Jerusalem) through certified rituals (offerings and sacrifices) led by a certain class of men (Levites). This is what may be called "official" or "centralized" religion—regulated religious rituals (often public) that were approved or endorsed by the priestly class and the authors/redactors of the biblical text. On the other hand, if one were to read the entire Hebrew Bible, one would see that the Israelites did not adhere to these sanctioned practices all too well—to put it mildly. Religious practices that did not conform to the endorsed ritual system, or those rituals that are considered "unofficial," are labeled as "popular" or "folk" religion.[1]

This either/or approach hardly reflects the complex world of religious rituals in ancient Israel; the reality is that *both* the Hebrew Bible and archaeology demonstrate that the ancient Israelites were engaged in diverse religious cultures and practices. Some were state sanctioned while others were not, and *both* were likely practiced in official and unofficial spaces.[2] Furthermore, we must acknowledge two additional factors: (1) It wasn't uncommon for different types of religious rituals to overlap; and (2) religious rituals changed over time—some rituals that were common at one period of time no longer were in another.[3] Israelite religious practices is a complicated subject and oversimplifying it can become a real danger; however, for the purposes of this chapter, I will attempt to illustrate the basic qualities of the religious rituals conducted in ancient Israel in both public (as reflected in the book of Leviticus)[4] and private environments.

Public, State Religion

As was mentioned in chapter 4, the intention behind "worship" in the wider ancient Near East was more as a service ritual to the gods, whether they be the deities of the official cult or others, particularly those in domestic contexts. These rituals were conducted to appease the deities so that they would maintain the social order; however, at the state level, the service rituals to the national or supreme deity or deities were a concern for all involved for a variety of reasons, including those that affect the wider population—like war and economics. These service rituals take care of the deity, who is considered orderly and holy, and are seeking the deity's orderliness in their own society; thus, everything used in those service rituals (including ritual objects, practices, places, and personnel) must also be orderly and holy.[5] In this section of the chapter, we will look at the public service rituals of ancient

---

1. Or what Patrick D. Miller refers to as "Orthodox Yahwism" and "Heterodox Yahwism." Miller, *Religion of Ancient Israel*, 48, 51.

2. Stavrakopoulou, "'Popular' Religion and 'Official' Religion," 37, 38, 50.

3. Miller, *Religion of Ancient Israel*, 47.

4. The discussion of the dating of the book of Leviticus and whether it reflects First or Second Temple practices is beyond the scope of this chapter. For more on this topic, please see any academic commentary, for example, Milgrom, *Leviticus 1–16*; Milgrom, *Leviticus 17–22*; Milgrom, *Leviticus 23–27*.

5. Van der Toorn, *Sin and Sanction*, 29.

Israel in their worship of their national deity, Yhwh, including where those rituals took place, when they occurred, in what manner were they conducted, and who conducted them.

Where Public Religious Rituals Took Place

If survival was the driving force of daily life, then it was to the gods that people turned to obtain some sort of control over the unpredictable chaos that made survival difficult. The hope was that by securing divine favor they would acquire their own security. In order to obtain this security, the gods needed to be constantly worshiped, influenced, even pacified, and the only way to accomplish this was through the embodiment of the gods as figurines (see chapter 6) and having continual access to them. To this end, divine houses (or temples, sanctuaries) were built in the middle tier (a.k.a. earth; see chap. 4) so that the resident deity would have a place to dwell on earth (1 Kings 8:27), all the while maintaining limited access to the common people. As long as the resident deity's needs were met, the deity would bestow their blessing and protection on the people. The purpose of a temple, therefore, is not for worshipers but for the worshiped.[6] The daily activities of the temple (or service rituals) centered on the care and feeding of the gods who, when appeased, maintained the cosmic order.

The temple was the abode of the residential deity and, as such, had to be made as attractive to the god as possible. Hence, temples and temple complexes were the most monumental and elaborate of architecture within a settlement.[7] As long as the gods were happy, they would continue to dwell among humanity in their earthly home and would respond with blessings. Temples in the ancient Near East often followed a similar blueprint (the Symmetric Syrian Temple Type[8]) that was full of symbolism (see figs. 5.1 and 5.2). Temples were perceived as a transitional space that served as a gateway from the divine realm to the human realm. While the temple opens access to the divine, it simultaneously restricts which humans have access to the divine abode. Each threshold is a boundary that restricts who can go further into the temple. Imagine a horizontal and vertical axis; the horizontal axis through thresholds of gates, courtyards, doors, and halls leads to the heart of the divine presence, the most holy place, where the embodied presence and the

---

6. Hundley, "Sacred Space and Common Space," 162.

7. Those familiar with the Hebrew Bible are aware of the term "temple" but perhaps not "temple complex." A temple is defined as "a (large) single-roomed or multi-roomed structure with adjacent or internal open spaces and courts used for cultic purposes," while a temple complex is "a combination of temples or temples and cult rooms (a room designed for cultic purposes)." Zevit, *Religions of Ancient Israel*, 123.

8. Mazar, "Temples"; Hurowitz, "Solomon's Temple."

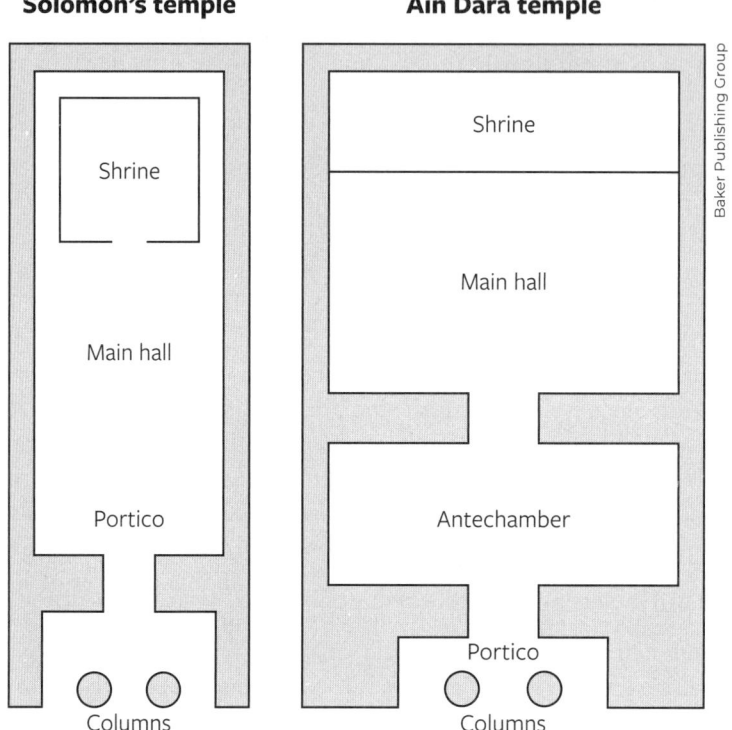

Figure 5.1. The plans of the temples at Ain Dara and the biblical temple of King Solomon

vertical axis to the divine can be found.⁹ Temples (as well as other cult sites or cult places¹⁰) were established because they were considered holy, and they were considered holy because it was thought that the deity was present there in some form or at some time (Gen. 28:10–22; Exod. 3:5).¹¹

While temples were important cult places, they were not the only locations where deities were worshiped. In addition to temples and temple complexes, official cult places included shrines, cult complexes, and cult centers.¹² Within

---

9. Hartenstein, "God, Gods, and Humankind (Worldview)," 151.

10. A "cult site" is a general designation for any type of cultic space, whether it was a cave, hill, city gate, corner, house, or temple, while a "cult place" is "a general designation for a place where cultic acts took place." See Zevit, *Religions of Ancient Israel*, 123–24.

11. Miller, *Religion of Ancient Israel*, 48, 137.

12. Zevit makes the distinction between a cult complex and a cult center in this way: "A cult complex is comprised of more than one structure, but does not contain within it any *dedicated* buildings. . . . A cult center is a large cult place comprised of more than one structure, that does contain a dedicated building. 'Shrines' are closet-sized, free-standing structures that housed images or symbols of a deity." Zevit, *Religions of Ancient Israel*, 123–24 (emphasis added).

Figure 5.2. The Ain Dara temple. This picture shows the front side entrance to the antechamber.

these were sanctuaries or holy places of various types, sizes, and locations that served as places where the enactment of worship to a deity occurred. The Hebrew Bible refers to several locations that served as official public cult places dedicated to the worship of Yhwh: Shiloh (1 Sam. 1:9; 3:3), Gilgal (1 Sam. 15:12–21, 33; Amos 4:4; 5:5), Mizpah (Judg. 20:1–3, 8–10; 21:1, 5, 8; 1 Sam. 7:5–11; 10:17–24), Mizpah in Gilead (Judg. 11:11, 29–31, 34, 39), Hebron (2 Sam. 5:3; 15:7), Bethlehem (Judg. 19:18), Nob (1 Sam. 21:1–10; 22:16–19), and Gibeah of Saul (2 Sam. 21:6).[13] The official, public temples, according to the Hebrew Bible, were located in Jerusalem (1 Kings 5–8; 1 Chron. 28; 2 Chron. 2–7:11), and after the kingdom split, they were located in Bethel (1 Kings 12:25–33; 2 Kings 23:19; Amos 7:13) and Dan (1 Kings 12:25–33; 2 Kings 10:29). Archaeological excavations have uncovered Iron Age temples or temple complexes in Philistia (e.g., Qasile, Miqne-Ekron, es-Safi/Gath) and Israel/Judah (Kuntillet 'Ajrud, Arad, Beer Sheba, Dan, Hazor, Kadesh, Megiddo, and Moẓa).[14]

13. Zevit, *Religions of Ancient Israel*, 255.
14. Zevit, *Religions of Ancient Israel*, 248–49. For a lengthy discussion of each site and sites listed in other categories, see pages 125–247. Zevit does not include (1) Tel es-Safi/Gath (see Maeir, "Gath"); and (2) Tel Moẓa (see Dospěl, "Rival to Solomon's Temple: The Place of Worship at Tel Moẓa Explained").

How Public Religious Rituals Took Place

Worship took on a variety of forms in the ancient Near East, including daily service rituals to the deity, celebrations on special occasions, sacrifices and non-sacrificial rituals, prayers, and hymns/music.[15] The Hebrew Bible identifies "sacrifice" and "offering" (*zebah* and *minhah*) as major parts of the formal religious rituals that were conducted at the public sanctuaries. Offerings and sacrifices are not unique to ancient Israel but were a major part of religious rituals throughout the ancient Near East; even still, a distinction between the terms "offering" and "sacrifice" will be helpful here. Patrick Miller defines "offering" as a "broad term that can refer to any sacred gift or donation brought to the altar or cult place to be given over to the deity and the deity's cultic personnel" and "sacrifice" as "those gifts that are totally or partially burned in the ritual of offering."[16] It is impractical to attempt to cover all the different types of offerings mentioned in the Hebrew Bible here; however, for our purposes, we will briefly identify some of the main types of offerings that are most conspicuous.

Types of Offerings

The most well-known type of sacrifice within the Hebrew Bible is that of the *'olah*, which is often translated as "burnt offering." It comes from the root word *'alah*, which means "to go up" or "to ascend" and is likely related to the smoke that comes from the offering and goes up to the deity who was thought to reside in the heavens.[17] The instructions for this type of sacrifice are found in Leviticus 1 and they make allowances for the presenter's economic status regarding what type animal to offer: fowl (turtledoves or pigeons) or an unblemished male from the herd (bull) or the flock (sheep or goat). Once the animal is slaughtered by the presenter or the priest, its blood is splashed or poured on the altar with the entire animal burnt and "consumed" by the deity. A burnt offering was conducted for a variety of reasons, including to express gratitude (Gen. 8:20–21), for expiation (Exod. 29:38–42; Lev. 16:24), to accompany a prayer of petition or entreat God's favor in time of need (1 Sam. 7:9), to fulfill a vow (1 Sam. 1:24–28), or to serve as a freewill offering (Lev. 22:18).[18] Burnt offerings were also offered in public celebrations/ceremonies, such as the ark's procession to Jerusalem (2 Sam. 6) or the founding of the temple (1 Kings 8).

Besides being used as a general term for offering, *minhah* (Lev. 2) can also refer to a specific offering of cereal or grain that can come in different forms

---

15. Gane, "Worship, Sacrifice, and Festivals," 362.
16. Miller, *Religion of Ancient Israel*, 107.
17. Miller, *Religion of Ancient Israel*, 107–8.
18. Gane, "Ritual and Religious Practices," 226.

(coarse grain in the ear, fine flour, or cakes; 2:1, 4, 14), cooked in several ways (oven, griddle, or pan; 2:4–5, 7), and mixed with oil, frankincense, and salt (2:1–2, 13, 15). According to Leviticus 2:8–10, a portion of the *minhah* is burned and the rest is consumed by the priests. This type of offering may have been a concession to those who could not afford to present an animal. In a subsistence household economy, this concession would have been absolutely necessary.

The offering of well-being (*shelem*, sometimes translated as "peace offering") differs from the *'olah* and the *minhah* in that only a portion of the animal (an unblemished male or female from the herd or flock) was offered to the deity (Lev. 3:3–4, 9–10, 14–15) and the rest was given to the presenter and other participants. The offering of well-being is associated with special occasions on both a communal and an individual level (Lev. 7:12–15; Num. 10:10; 1 Sam. 1:21; Prov. 7:14).

Two atonement offerings follow in Leviticus, the *hatta'ah* (often translated as "sin offering"; 4:1–5:13) and the *'asham* (often translated as "guilt offering"; 5:14–6:7). It is unclear how these two sacrifices differ from each other exactly: Both are to atone for an unintentional transgression of a prohibition or a violation of the sacred, which has brought guilt either on all of Israel or on the individual. The offerings are an attempt to use purification and atonement as a means to overcome the consequences of these transgressions.[19]

Who Oversaw the Official Public Religious Rituals?

According to the Priestly Code (P) in Leviticus (namely, chaps. 1–16), only men from a particular genealogy could serve as priests (singular *kohen*, plural *kohanim*) in any official capacity—that of the clan of Aaron (Aaronides) within the tribe of Levi.[20] A rite of passage marking them as leaving the realm of the ordinary and entering the service of the sacred is found in Leviticus 8–9. At the official sanctuary, priests would perform several functions where they serve both the deity and the people. They (1) perform the service rituals to the deity, (2) conduct the rites at the altar on behalf of the offeror or the people at large, (3) distinguish between "the holy and the common, and between the unclean and the clean" and teach this to the people of Israel (Lev. 10:10–11), and (4) bless the people (Num. 6:22–27; Deut. 10:8). In this way, priests serve as mediators between the people and Yhwh.[21]

---

19. For a fuller discussion on the difference of *hatta'ah* and *'asham*, see Miller, *Religion of Ancient Israel*, 113–18.

20. The term "Levites" has a few applications. Generally, it can refer to members of the tribe of Levi; more specifically, it can refer to servants (or ministers) that serve at the sanctuary (Jerusalem). "Levites" are also seen as ritual experts who perform different functions in various parts of the Hebrew Bible. See Hieke, "Ritual Experts," 185.

21. Hieke, "Ritual Experts," 183–84.

When Did Public Religious Rituals Take Place?

Daily temple service would include twice daily food offerings to the deity (burnt and grain offerings; Exod. 40:29), preparation of the bread on the table every Sabbath (or the bread of the presence; Exod. 40:23; Lev. 24:5–9), the sacrifice of olive oil for the lighting of the lamp (*menorah*) (Exod. 40:25; Lev. 24:1–4), and the burning of incense (Exod. 40:27).[22]

Yearly special occasions were also a cause for official religious rituals. According to the Hebrew Bible, there were three main annual festivals that began as agricultural feasts but adopted further significance for religious and group identity.[23] These include the Festivals of Passover (*Pesach*)[24] / Unleavened Bread (*Chag HaMatzot*),[25] celebrated side by side around March or April; seven weeks later is the Festival of Weeks (*Shavuot*);[26] and finally, the Festival of Booths (*Sukkot*), which takes place in September or October.[27] One further yearly occasion is that of the Day of Atonement (*Yom Kippur*), which purged the sanctuary from impurities that defiled it and whose rituals made atonement for the transgressions of all Israel.[28]

To Whom Were Public Religious Rituals Offered?

There is ample evidence from both archaeology and the Hebrew Bible that official temples and temple complexes were used to conduct religious rituals for both Yhwh and other deities throughout Israel's and Judah's histories. Both King Hezekiah (eighth century BCE) and King Josiah (seventh century BCE) attempted to reform state-sanctioned worship of the national deity, Yhwh. These regulations included the exclusive worship of Yhwh, taking away the *bamot*,[29] destroying *matstsebot*,[30] *asherim*,[31] and the Nehushtan serpent

---

22. Hieke, "Ritual Experts," 184; Hartenstein, "God, Gods, and Humankind (Worldview)," 153–54.

23. The significance for religious and group identity is this: "The festival of *Matzot* is related to the exodus event, *Shavuot* to the Sinai event (in postbiblical literature), and *Sukkot* to Israel's dwelling in booths in the wilderness, following the exodus." Frankel, "Integrating the Exodus Story."

24. Exod. 12:1–13, 21–27; Lev. 23:5; Num. 28:16; Deut. 16:1–2, 5–7.

25. Exod. 12:14–20; 13:3–10; 23:15; 34:18; Lev. 23:6–8; Num. 28:17–25; Deut. 16:3–4, 8.

26. Exod. 23:16; 34:22; Lev. 23:15–21; Num. 28:26–31; Deut. 16:9–12.

27. Exod. 23:16; Lev. 23:34–36, 39–43; Num. 29:12–34; Deut. 16:13–15; Neh. 8:14.

28. Exod. 30:10; Lev. 16; 23:26–32; 25:9.

29. A *bamah* (plural *bamot*) is an open-air altar or shrine that is often translated as "high place(s)" in the Hebrew Bible. It is thought that *bamot* usually consisted of some sort of human-made platform, were used for cultic purposes, and were often associated with buildings (2 Kings 17:29; 23:19). White, "High Places."

30. Or "standing stones," which William Dever defines as "any sort of deliberately erected stone—large or small, occurring singly or in multiples—that symbolizes the presence of a deity, thought to be particularly visible and efficacious in this particular place." Dever, *Did God Have a Wife?*, 99.

31. The cult symbol of the goddess Asherah was a living tree, which was often simplified as a consecrated wooden pole. These *asherah* (singular) or *asherim* (plural) were erected as part of the worship of the goddess Asherah.

(2 Kings 18:4). However, neither Hezekiah's nor Josiah's religious reforms became permanent since their sons and successors reversed their mandates (21:1–7, 19–22; 23:32, 37; 24:9, 19–20).

"Unofficial" Household Religion

In chapter 1, we looked at how the average ancient Israelite household lived. One important household aspect to include in that discussion is religious practices. Furthermore, as has been discussed, within the ancient Near East (including Israel), the world was viewed through a "spiritual" lens. Simply put, it was commonly thought that every aspect of life was governed by a deity or deities that were part of a larger collection or pantheon of deities, which were specific to a particular society. Appeasing and worshiping these deities was thought to be accomplished through performing various rituals with the hope that they would bring blessings and not chaos. These rituals, along with the agricultural calendar, dominated not only the rhythm of society at large, including state religion, but also the nucleus of society—the household.

We must remember that the average ancient Israelite household was part of an agropastoral society that lived at various levels of subsistence and was primarily concerned with survival—survival in the here and now, and survival into the future; consequently, the fertility of the household members, land, and animals was of utmost importance. Coupled with the urgency of the household members to reproduce are two factors: (1) the survival rate of newborns in ancient Israel is estimated to be about 50 percent[32] and (2) expected lifespans were short (admittedly by today's standards) with men living to around forty and women around thirty.[33] Not to mention that the reproductive role of women was risky at best, as mother and child regularly died in childbirth. Elizabeth Willett writes that "burial statistics show a high rate of infant mortality and short female life span."[34] Even supposing that the infant survived birth, its continuance was still precarious since 35 percent of all individuals died by the age five.[35] We can only imagine (and at that, probably not even very well) how crucial each stage of the life cycle was and how it acutely impacted the survival of the household.

---

32. Meyers, *Rediscovering Eve*, 99. Elizabeth Willett writes that "study results show very high infant mortality; of the average 4.1 births for each female, only 1.9 survived." Willett, "Women and Household Shrines," 201.

33. Willett, "Women and Household Shrines," 201.

34. Willett, "Infant Mortality," 97.

35. Willett, "Infant Mortality," 80; Alpert Nakhai, "When Considering Infants and Jar Burials," 109. Willett also writes that "data from the excavation of Roman Age Meiron indicate that 50% of individuals died before age 18, and 70% of those occurred within the first five years of life." Willett, "Women and Household Shrines," 201.

With this in mind, we can turn to the physical evidence of religious ritual conducted at the household level. Numerous houses in Iron Age Israel and Judah have been excavated, with many finds demonstrating that households were engaged in religious rituals on a regular, if not daily, basis. These finds include objects that are certainly related to cultic rituals, such as incense burners (like those used for burning incense in the temple), miniature altars and shrines (in which to place the offerings), anthropomorphic and zoomorphic vessels (often thought to be images of the deities themselves), and amulets (for protection)—just to name a few. Other more utilitarian objects were also used in religious rituals including juglets, lamps, and various utensils used for the making, serving, and consumption of food in religious domestic feasting. Other "special" objects include luxury and imported pottery, chalices and goblets, small and miniature vessels.[36]

As to where these activities took place within the dwelling, it is more than likely that households maintained their own shrines or shared one within the neighborhood. Archaeological excavations have identified both portable altars or shrines (often called "model shrines," see fig. 5.3)[37] and stationary shrines, such as benches or niches (sometimes called "cult corners")[38] or even a room (or part of one). One example of many can be found in a room in a dwelling at Tel Halif, where the broad room (labeled "Room 2") of the F7[39] house contained numerous objects used for domestic religious rituals: a polished triangular stone (possibly a *matstsebah*), two beveled and dressed standing stones (*matstsebot*), a fragmented pillar figurine, and a fenestrated stand.[40] Furthermore, the large amount of evidence for food preparation and feasting in this room indicates that religious domestic feasting occurred in this household.[41]

Figure 5.3. A four-horned altar from Tel Rehov

---

36. Albertz and Schmitt, *Family and Household Religion*, 59–75, see also appendix A; Shafer-Elliott, "Role of the Household," 205, 207, 210.

37. Mazar and Panitz-Cohen, "To What God?," 76.

38. Hitchcock, "Cult Corners," 321.

39. F7 is the location of the house on the Tel Halif archaeological excavations' grid; hence, archaeologists refer to the house as the F7 house.

40. Hardin, *Lahav II*, 133–43; Shafer-Elliott, "Role of the Household," 205, 207, 210.

41. Shafer-Elliott, "Role of the Household," 199–221.

The day-to-day survival of the household was of utmost concern; consequently, as we've discussed above, the fertility of the household's land, animals, and members was an immediate and ever present concern. As we can see throughout the Hebrew Bible, this concern is one possible reason that the Israelites worshiped gods other than Yhwh, in particular two local Canaanite deities, Baal and Asherah, who governed issues related to fertility. Baal was a fertility and agricultural god, and he was especially associated with storms that would seasonally water the land and make it fertile, thus sustaining the household members and animals. Baal's symbol was the bull, and he was also often depicted as the storm god, holding a thunderbolt in one hand and a mace in the other.[42] The Israelites, like their Canaanite neighbors, were willing to worship any deity that may help their land and crops be fertile. Worshiped alongside Baal was the Canaanite goddess Asherah, the mother goddess associated with lions, serpents, and sacred trees. In the Hebrew Bible the word "Asherah" most often refers to a stylized wooden tree, intended to represent and be used in the worship of the goddess Asherah.[43] The biblical authors and redactors clearly state that throughout their history the Israelites worshiped Asherah alongside their worship of Yhwh and Baal (Judg. 3:7; 2 Kings 21:7; 2 Chron. 33:3). Archaeological evidence seems to confirm that Asherah was even worshiped as a consort of Yhwh.[44] For example, at the site of Kuntillet 'Ajrud (ca. 801–786 BCE), located in the Northeast Sinai Desert, inscriptions that refer to "Yhwh and his Asherah" were found written in red ink on two large pithoi.[45]

The worship of Baal and Asherah became so popular in Israel that altars to Baal and Asherah poles were placed in official temples in Samaria (1 Kings 16:32) and Jerusalem (2 Kings 21:2–4). Furthermore, zoomorphic (animal) and anthropomorphic (human) figurines are regularly found in excavated Iron Age houses in Israel. Zoomorphic figurines in the form of a bull are thought to represent Baal or to have been used in the worship of Baal.[46] Female anthropomorphic figurines, which seem to have been particularly popular in Judah, are regularly theorized to represent Asherah or to have been used in

---

42. Browning, "Baal"; Burke, "Baal," 70; Snell, *Religions of the Ancient Near East*, 105.

43. Browning, "Asherah"; Meshel, "Kuntillet 'Ajrud." For more on Asherah, see Zevit, *Religions of Ancient Israel*; Dever, *Did God Have a Wife?*, 100–102; Snell, *Religions of the Ancient Near East*, 106.

44. Ackerman, "Asherah," 62.

45. Zevit, *Religions of Ancient Israel*, 650–51; Dever, *Did God Have a Wife?*, 160–67; Keel and Uehlinger, *Gods, Goddesses, and Images of God*, 210–48. Other inscriptions and drawings that illustrate the Israelite linkage of Yhwh and Asherah include those at El-Qôm (ca. 725 BCE) and Beit Lei (ca. 701 BCE) (see sources just mentioned). Others suggest that "his Asherah" refers to a sacred object, meaning that this is not proof that Asherah was worshiped as Yhwh's consort.

46. Hess, *Israelite Religions*, 156.

the worship of her.[47] Interestingly, female figurines are often found in houses, indicating that the average Israelite used them in a variety of ways, including as votives, cult images, and private objects of devotion. One such possible use is in fertility rituals devoted to a goddess (quite possibly Asherah), goddesses, or aspects of a goddess in the hope that they would help with the fertility of the women of the household.[48]

Since the fertility of the land and its relationship to the household was so crucial for the very existence and prolonging of the Israelite household, it shouldn't surprise us that the Israelites would turn to worshiping whichever deities they thought would assist them in their survival. Consequently, the authors and redactors of the Hebrew Bible labor to show that Yhwh is not trapped in one geographical location or limited in spheres of influence; rather, they portray Yhwh as transcendent and universal, not limited to the inconsistencies of nature (1 Kings 18; Pss. 29; 68:4, 9; 104:3).[49] As these few examples illustrate, "popular" religion on a household level was syncretic.

Summary

As I hope this section illustrates, the topic of Israelite religious practices is complicated at best. As is evident, both the Hebrew Bible and archaeology demonstrate that the ancient Israelites were engaged in diverse religious cultures and practices—some were state sanctioned while others were not, and *both* were likely practiced in official and unofficial spaces.

LOOKING UP

The fact that Israel's actual worship practices often directly contradicted the positions of the biblical authors and editors underscores some of the key theological themes discussed thus far. God had chosen to enter into a covenant with Israel, to be their metaphorical spouse and parent. This covenant was based on a historical relationship of promise (to the ancestors) and deliverance (from Egypt). A tangible promise of the covenant was the Promised Land, which served as a barometer for Israel's status within the covenant, and God's chosen locale for his holy presence. Israel's deviant worship demonstrates how sin and impurity endangered Israel's accessibility to their holy covenant partner. God, however, provided means of reconciliation through

---

47. For a full discussion on the topic of female figurines, see Kletter, *Judean Pillar-Figurines*; contra Darby, *Interpreting Judean Pillar Figurines*. See also Darby and de Hulster, *Iron Age Terracotta Figurines*.
48. Zevit, *Religions of Ancient Israel*, 273; Hess, *Israelite Religions*, 308, 311.
49. Snell, *Religions of the Ancient Near East*, 17.

repentance and the sacrificial system. Israel's worship also included praying, singing, feasting, and remembering and was arguably seen as a service that extended beyond the sanctuary and into the everyday lives of the Israelites, but the focus of this chapter will remain primarily on the facets of Israel's worship that might seem the most remote for readers: the sanctuary and the sacrificial system.

Building on the where, how, who, when, and to whom questions addressed above, we will now turn our attention to the theological implications of those aspects of worship. We will then conclude by addressing worship in light of the destruction of the temple and in light of the new covenant.

A Theology of the "Where"

At no point in Israel's history had their worship unequivocally been restricted to a central location. Prior to the Sinai covenant, sacrifice was not restricted to a central location. Prayer, song, and even the celebration of many feast days were likewise not confined to one place. Why, then, did God cap Israel's sanctuary status at one, and what did this sacred space mean for Israel?[50]

The focus on one central sanctuary could be tied to the very nature of God. Because Yhwh is one, he dwells in one sanctuary. Whereas other people typically worshiped local deities who dwelt in local sanctuaries, Israel's one sanctuary corresponds to the oneness of their God. Similarly, it could correspond to the oneness or unity they were to experience as a covenant community, thus guarding against division.[51] Centralized worship could also serve to highlight Yhwh's sovereignty in worship. Israel was to build the sanctuary according to *Yhwh's* specifications, and at the location that *he* chose.

The sanctuary was first and foremost sacred space and a means for a holy God to dwell with his people. The word translated "tabernacle" (*mishkan*) comes from the verb "to dwell," because it is God's special dwelling place with his people. The word for "temple" (*hekal*) also means "palace," which is fitting since the temple was the divine king's earthly footstool. Both sanctuaries were spatially located, but they also pointed beyond their spatial limitations. Indeed, the sanctuary was designed to be a microcosm of creation and a reflection of the heavenly sanctuary.[52] Jon Levenson notes the verbal parallels

---

50. Most scholars agree that Deuteronomy emphasizes the need for centralized worship (see, e.g., Deut. 12:11; 17:8; 18:6–8), though they disagree over when this centralization took place and how well it was honored in practice. See Wenham, "Deuteronomy and the Central Sanctuary."

51. The misunderstanding over the altar between the eastern and western tribes in Josh. 22 is an illustrative case in point.

52. Levenson, *Sinai and Zion*, 139–40.

between the first creation account in Genesis 1–2 and the construction of the tabernacle (see the following table).[53]

Creation of the Cosmos (Gen. 1–2)	Construction of the Tabernacle (Exod. 39–40)
"Thus the heavens and the earth were finished [*kalah*] . . . and God finished [*kalah*] on the seventh day the work that he had done ['*asah*], and he rested from all [*kal*] the work that he had done ['*asah*]." (2:1–2)	"In this way all the work of the tabernacle of the tent of meeting was finished [*kalah*], and the Israelites had done ['*asah*] everything [*kal*] just as the Lord had commanded Moses, thus they did ['*asah*]." (39:32)
"And God saw [*ra'ah*] all [*kal*] that he had made ['*asah*], and behold [*hinneh*], it was very good." (1:31)	"And Moses saw [*ra'ah*] all [*kal*] the work and, behold [*hinneh*], they made ['*asah*] it just as Yhwh had commanded they make ['*asah*] it, and Moses blessed [*barak*] them." (39:43)
"And God blessed [*barak*] the seventh day and he sanctified [*qadash*] it, for on it he rested from all his work which God had created to do ['*asah*]." (2:3)	"And you shall sanctify [*qadash*] it and all its vessels and it will be holy [*qadash*]." (40:9)

Levenson also notes other ways in which the sacred space of Israel's sanctuary echoed themes of creation: Solomon's temple was constructed in seven periods of time (years, 1 Kings 6:38), just as creation was brought forth in seven periods of time (days, Gen. 2:3); both accounts emphasize the kingly status of the creator/builder, and both emphasize "rest" as the climax of the event (Exod. 20:11; Ps. 132:13–14).[54] Even the liturgy of the temple, preserved in the psalms of its worshipers, depicts Yhwh as the divine King who is completely sovereign over the waters of chaos, reflecting the *chaoskampf* ("chaos battle") creational motif of Yhwh subduing and bringing to order the elements of chaos (Pss 24:2; 29:10; 46:3, 6).[55]

The physical space of the sanctuary also mirrored the cosmos. The water basin, also called "the sea" (1 Kings 7:23–26), represents the watery chaos that God brings to order in Genesis 1:2. The movement from less holy to most holy on the horizontal plane of the sanctuary mirrors the cosmic separation between the less holy space of earth and most holy space of heaven. The waters that flowed from the eschatological or idealized temple (Ps. 46:4; Ezek. 47:1–12; Zech. 14:8; Rev. 22:1–2) echo the waters that flowed from Eden

---

53. This table is adapted from Levenson, *Sinai and Zion*, 143.
54. Levenson, *Sinai and Zion*, 143.
55. Brueggemann, *Theology of the Old Testament*, 656.

(Gen. 2:10–14),⁵⁶ and the flora and fauna imagery decorating the vessels and instrument of the sanctuary likewise recall the garden. Moreover, just as the sanctuary imagery mirrored the cosmos, so also the creation account was crafted to depict creation as God's sanctuary. Lifsa Schachter notes how even the verbs used to describe Adam's charge to serve and protect the garden (*'avad* and *shamar*, Gen. 2:15) are the same used for the work of the Levites in the tabernacle (Num. 3:7–8), "suggesting a priest-like role for Adam"⁵⁷ (and, later, Eve). In short, the sanctuary was a tangible manifestation of God's presence and reign that also pointed beyond itself to the cosmic reality it represented.

A Theology of the "How"

Worship, especially the worship that centered around the sanctuary, involved quite a bit of detailed ritual. "Ritual" might seem foreign to some modern readers. Some people consider it cold or even meaningless, but whether we recognize it or not, ritual is an important part of our lives. Gordon Wenham claims that "people express in ritual what moves them most."⁵⁸ How true! Try telling a bride and groom that the wedding kiss ritual holds no meaning. Or tell a Latina that fifteen is just another year. In addition to marking importance, ritual also offers worshipers a tangible way of participating in a deep reality.

One of the most significant rituals in the Hebrew Bible was the sacrificial system. The various types of sacrifices were introduced above, and their theological significance is manifold, particularly when considered in light of purity and holiness. According to Wenham, the sacrificial system conveys two core theological concepts. First, it conveys the distinction between the elect (Israel) and the non-elect (everyone else) by identifying which animals are appropriate for Israel to sacrifice. Second, the sacrificial system conveys the opposition between life and death. Following the influence of Mary Douglas's earlier landmark work on purity laws,⁵⁹ Wenham explains that the things that make an animal or a human unclean are things linked in some way to mortality. Thus, blemished animals or people with disease, for example, represent death, rather than life, and cannot approach God's holy perfection.⁶⁰ According to this view, the clean/unclean distinction in worship also parallels the distinction

---

56. Walton, *Lost World of Genesis One*, 80–82.
57. Schachter, "Garden of Eden," 75.
58. Wenham, "Theology of Old Testament Sacrifice," 76.
59. Wenham is specifically building on and endorsing Douglas's earlier work, as reflected in her book *Purity and Danger* (1966), which argues for the difference in clean and unclean animals according to creational norms; Wenham's evaluation can be found in "Theology of Old Testament Sacrifice," 78, 85n7.
60. Wenham, "Theology of Old Testament Sacrifice," 77–78.

between Israel and the gentiles, thus underscoring Israel's election, a point supported by Peter's dream in Acts 10, when the unclean food is likened directly to the (previously) unclean gentiles.[61]

Another important aspect of sacrificial ritual was the restoration it symbolized between the worshiper and God. Scholars disagree whether the Hebrew word typically translated as "atonement" (*kipper*) specifically describes a ransoming, covering, or wiping away. Richard Averbeck argues that the underlying idea of the word has to do with cleansing, but because of the substitutionary nature of the sacrifice, ransom could be seen as a result of atonement.[62] Jay Sklar argues that *kipper* both ransoms and cleanses in cases of inadvertent sin and impurity because both endanger the worshiper before a holy God (and thus ransom is needed to avert death), and both taint the worshiper (and thus cleansing is required for purification).[63]

The blood of the sacrifice purified not only the worshiper but also—and according to some scholars, primarily—the sacred space of the sanctuary. The blood of the sin offering, for example, was applied to the horns of the incense altar and sprinkled on the curtain that separated the holy place from the most holy place (Lev. 4:6–7). On the Day of Atonement, the high priest would even sprinkle blood on the mercy seat of the ark of the covenant using the blood from the bull and goat sin offerings that were for himself and for Israel, respectively, thus cleansing the taint of sin from the entire sanctuary, including Yhwh's throne room.

This purification of sacred space was a prerequisite for maintaining God's presence,[64] which in turn was a prerequisite for the efficacy of the sacrificial system. Even though Israel brought the sacrifices to God, it was ultimately God who made them work. Leviticus 17:11 is a key passage in understanding God's sovereignty in the sacrificial system: "For the life of the flesh is in the blood; and *I have given it to you* for making atonement for your lives on the altar." Ritual sacrifice was not a begrudged obligation or a means of manipulating the deity in Israel's favor. Nor was it an effort at placating a wrathful God. It was a means of *receiving* purification from their Creator

---

61. Wenham, "Theology of Old Testament Sacrifice," 79.

62. For a detailed description and evaluation of these interpretative options in light of cognates and intertextual usage, see Averbeck, "כפר," 2:691–709.

63. Sklar, *Sin, Impurity, Sacrifice, Atonement*.

64. See Jonathan Klawans's extensive study, which highlights the importance of purity for the efficacy of sacrifice. Klawans also sees Israel's imitation of Yhwh as one of the two "organizing principles" of the sacrificial system, and this imitation of the divine is directly tied to purity. First, Israel had to raise and care for the pure, blemish-free animals that were to be sacrificed, thus mirroring Yhwh's role as shepherd. Second, Israel was to construct the sanctuary (and maintain it) according to the heavenly template, thus mirroring God's role as Creator. Klawans, *Purity, Sacrifice, and the Temple*, esp. pp. 53–62.

and King, which resulted in their ability to dwell in his presence. It was, in modern sacramental terms, a means of grace.

As such, ritual sacrifice was a context for gratitude and joy. As strange as it might seem to modern readers to imagine this bloody scene of death as a context for celebration, it represented the core of their covenant life together: their divine King being pleased to dwell with them and protect them because his holy space had been cleansed and honored, their own impurities being washed away so that they could fellowship with their God, and the community of worshipers coming together to worship and partake of sacrificial meals.

The well-being or peace offerings were one such occasion for community meals. They symbolized Israel's recognition that everything they had was first and foremost a gift from God and ultimately belonged to him. By offering God a portion of what he had given them, they were really giving back to him what was rightfully his.[65] The portion they received back to share in a sacrificial meal represented the renewed life God gave them through fellowship with him.[66]

The designations of "sin offering" and "guilt offering" can sometimes be misleading when considering the theology of Israel's sacrificial system. Sacrifices could atone for ritual impurity and *unintentional* sin (or the sin of the nation in general terms, on the Day of Atonement), but the Hebrew Bible is clear that *intentional* sin and guilt (that is, moral impurity) could only be forgiven through genuine repentance. John Goldingay suggests, rather, that these sacrifices removed the "shortcomings" (a more general rendering of *hatta'ah*) that would include unintentional sin as well as ritual impurity.[67]

The relationship between repentance and sacrifice can be understood in terms of sacred space and *hesed* (often translated "steadfast love" or "covenant faithfulness"). Deliberate sin "cuts off" the sinner from the covenant community. Repentance elicits God's *hesed*, which brings the sinner back into the covenant community, where they can then respond with gratitude by

---

65. Mira Balberg notes that in the rabbinic midrash Leviticus Rabbah, the offering of sacrifice was seen as the opposite of eating. Whereas eating was considered "animalistic" and immoral, the one who offered up their own nourishment was symbolically offering up their own soul. Balberg, "Animalistic Gullet."

66. Readers might wonder, in the case of well-being offerings, how the worshiper could identify with the sacrifice, offer it in part to God, and then receive it back to consume it? What exactly is being symbolized in this confusing scenario (which might sound like self-cannibalism)? The animal belongs to God and is a gift from God, just as the worshiper's life also belongs to God and is a gift from God. By identifying with the animal and then offering its lifeblood (and fat) to God, the worshiper is recognizing that she too belongs to God and is humbly dedicated to his service. When the edible part of the sacrifice is thus given back to her to consume, it represents the new life given to her due to God's grace. God is returning her life to her. Wenham, "Theology of Old Testament Sacrifice," 83.

67. Goldingay, *Israel's Life*, 143; cf. Walton, *Old Testament Theology for Christians*, 152.

offering right sacrifices to God. Robin Routledge explains, "Sacrifice, then, is limited within the boundaries of the covenant, and is unable to help those who step outside those boundaries. By contrast, God's *hesed*, which operates largely within the mutual relationship established by the covenant, is also able to reach out to those beyond its limits, and, by a miracle of grace, offer the forgiveness that allows them to be drawn back into a restored relationship with God."[68] Figure 5.4 highlights the spatial relationship between repentance and sacrifice, a sort of *ordo salutis* ("order of salvation") of Hebrew Bible theology.

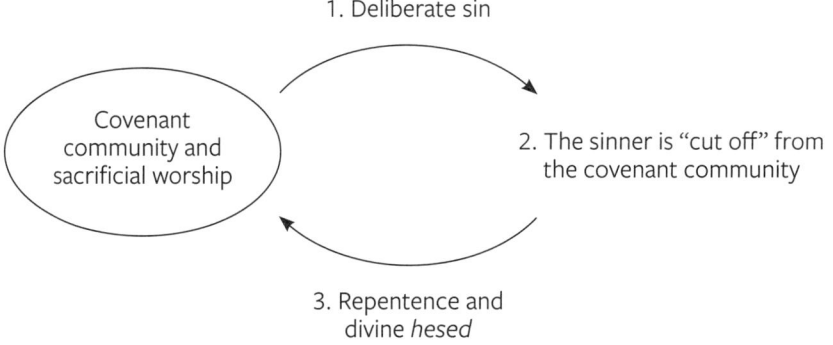

Figure 5.4. Repentance and sacrifice

Klawans explains, "It is not that the daily sacrifice undoes the damage done by grave transgression. Quite the contrary: grave transgression undoes what the daily sacrifice produces."[69] Deliberate sin removes the worshiper from the covenant community where sacrifice is even possible. King David's repentance in Psalm 51 illustrates this well. The first fifteen verses are heartfelt confessions of sin and pleas for forgiveness. David appeals to God's *hesed*, mercy, and compassion as the only means of restoration (v. 1). Verses 16–17 might seem to suggest that sacrifice has no part at all in genuine worship:

> For you have no delight in sacrifice;
>   if I were to give a burnt offering, you would not be pleased.
> The sacrifice acceptable to God is a broken spirit;
>   a broken and contrite heart, O God, you will not despise.

However, David is recognizing that sacrifice is ineffectual while the sinner is still cast out of the covenant community. Only when God restores the

---

68. Routledge, *Old Testament Theology*, 198.
69. Klawans, *Purity, Sacrifice, and the Temple*, 71.

repentant sinner can he then offer sacrifices acceptable to God, as verse 19 makes clear:

> Then you will delight in right sacrifices,
>   in burnt offerings and whole burnt offerings;
>   then bulls will be offered on your altar.

Perhaps no one emphasized the importance of genuine repentance as a prerequisite for temple worship more than the prophets.[70] In Jeremiah's famous "temple sermon," he rails against the hypocrisy of the people of Judah, who took for granted the security and blessings of temple worship while oppressing the poor and shedding innocent blood (Jer. 7:1–15). God is a holy God and a good God. His *hesed* and grace are abundant, but they cannot be taken advantage of or manipulated, and they cannot be divorced from the ethical expectations of a holy God or from one's genuine faithfulness.[71] The parallelism of Psalm 4:5 makes this connection clear:

> Offer right sacrifices,
>   and put your trust in the LORD.

The rightness of Israel's sacrifice was inextricably tied to the condition and orientation of their hearts.

A Theology of the "Who"

We saw above how priests functioned as mediators between God and Israel, serving in a multitude of ways, most notably bringing God's teaching to the people and overseeing the sacrifices on behalf of the people. This two-directional role is seen clearly in Moses's blessing of the tribe of Levi in Deuteronomy 33:10:[72]

> They [the Levites] teach Jacob your ordinances,
>   and Israel your law;
> they place incense before you,
>   and whole burnt offerings on your altar.

---

70. For an excellent discussion on the rhetoric of the prophetic passages that seem to suggest that sacrifice was not part of Israel's worship during the wilderness period, or that God does not desire sacrifice at all (e.g., Hosea 6:6; Amos 5:25), see Lucas, "Sacrifice in the Prophets."

71. As Levenson pointedly states, "Grace and law belong together. In separation, they become parodies of themselves." Levenson, *Sinai and Zion*, 168.

72. Routledge, *Old Testament Theology*, 172.

That Israel needed mediation underscores several important theological concepts, including the gravity of Israel's sin and impurity, the need for restoration in order to dwell with a holy God, and God's gracious desire to be present with his people.[73]

Before the establishment of the Levitical priesthood, God identifies all of Israel as a "priestly kingdom" in Exodus 19:5–6, saying, "Now therefore, if you obey my voice and keep my covenant, you shall be my treasured possession out of all the peoples. Indeed, the whole earth is mine, but you shall be for me a priestly kingdom and a holy nation." As we saw in chapter 2, God elects Israel out of all of the nations to be his "treasured possession" and "priestly kingdom." Israel, however, wastes no time in breaking the covenant by worshiping a golden calf in Exodus 32, and when Moses asks the Israelites, "Who is on the Lord's side?" (32:26), only the tribe of Levi comes forward to exact judgment on their fellow Israelites, thus "ordain[ing] [them]selves for the service of the Lord" (32:29). While this bloody scene may mark the time in which priestly duties were restricted from heads of all households to one tribe, it does not necessarily follow that Israel as a nation lost its metaphorical role as a "priestly kingdom."

What, then, does that priestly role entail for Israel as a whole? It speaks in part to Israel's privileged access to Yhwh, but the priestly metaphor also speaks to Israel's role as a mediator. Christopher Wright recognizes the echoes of Genesis 12:3 in Israel's priestly role.[74] Just as Abraham was promised "in you all of the families of the earth shall be blessed," so also Israel would bless all of the families of the earth by mediating God's law to them and by bringing them into right worship of Yhwh.

This two-directional mediation is seen throughout the Hebrew Bible, so a couple of examples should suffice. Deuteronomy 4:6–8 describes how Israel's law would attract the nations around them: "You must observe them diligently, for this will show your wisdom and discernment to the peoples, who, when they hear all these statutes, will say, 'Surely this great nation is a wise and discerning people!' For what other great nation has a god so near to it as the Lord our God is whenever we call to him? And what other great nation has statutes and ordinances as just as this entire law that I am setting before you today?" This "centripetal" attraction of the nations toward the center of the covenant was a key aspect of their election as God's special treasure and their priestly role.

---

73. Not all scholars agree that the priests were mediators. Brueggemann, for example, argues that the priests themselves do not mediate but officiate the rituals and practices that mediate (Brueggemann, *Theology of the Old Testament*, 664). I follow what I consider to be the majority opinion: that the priests were mediators, both in their ability to bring God's teaching to the people and in their ability to lead God's people to God in proper worship.

74. C. Wright, *Mission of God*, 331–32.

Israel's mediating role in bringing the nations into right worship of Yhwh is also seen in the many psalms that exhort the nations to praise Yhwh (Pss. 22:27; 47:1; 67:1–3; 138:4–5), as well as in prophetic oracles showing that the nations not only will bring offerings and worship to Yhwh but will be included within the identity of the covenant people (e.g., Isa. 19:24–25)— God will even choose some to be "priests" and "Levites" (66:21).[75] As we discussed in chapter 2, Israel's *particular* role as a priestly mediator was instrumental in God's *universal* redemptive goal to bless the world.

A Theology of the "When"

We saw above that Israel's liturgical calendar included festivals celebrating God's deliverance of his people (such as Passover), his forgiveness (such as Yom Kippur), and his generous provision for his people (such as the Festival of Weeks or the Festival of Firstfruits).[76] The regularity of this cycle of worship was formative for Israel in several ways. Naturally, it produced habits of faith and trust and praise. Just as humans are prone to desire the things for which they create habits in their everyday lives (think of brushing your teeth or checking the news or social media in the morning), so also the recurrent nature of religious celebration made Israel desire each season of worship. We see this in the psalmists' longing for the temple. Psalm 84 states:

> My soul longs, indeed it faints
>   for the courts of the Lord. . . .
>
> For a day in your courts is better
>   than a thousand elsewhere. (vv. 2, 10)

These repeated patterns of ritual also formed Israel's epistemology, or how they thought about their knowledge of God. Dru Johnson has convincingly shown the link between the two. He describes ritual (in summary) as "something scripted and something done," and when this carefully orchestrated event occurs regularly, as within the liturgical calendar, it shapes how people think about God and their relationship to him.[77]

We also saw that three of these festivals involved pilgrimage to the central sanctuary. Even if this were only an ideal and not possible for most ordinary people, it shows the importance of centralized worship. Conversely, it also illustrates that their spiritual life was not limited to the central sanctuary. The

---

75. Christopher Wright offers a lengthy discussion on Israel's role as a priestly mediator to the nation in *Mission of God*, 454–500.

76. See Lev. 23 for descriptions of most festivals, except for Purim, which is described in Esther 9:26–32.

77. Johnson, *Knowledge by Ritual*, 17. See pp. 33–56 for his fuller definition of "ritual."

sanctuary was holier than any other place on earth, and yet all of Israel's life was deemed spiritual. This is why the majority of feast days did not require pilgrimage.[78]

This non-dualistic sense of worship is also represented in the vocabulary of Israel's worship. Israel worshiped through the physical acts of bringing tribute (offerings) and "bowing down" to the divine King, as well as a commitment to "serve" him. Of course, faithful subjects of the king will not limit their service to when they are in the king's throne room; they will serve him in every aspect of their lives. Thus, worshipers "bow down" to Yhwh in the special presence of his sanctuary and then "serve" him throughout every aspect of their lives.[79] In this way, their entire lives were, to one degree or another, acts of worship, and no aspects of their lives fell outside the "spiritual" realm.

A Theology of the "To Whom"

The biblical and archaeological records are clear that Israel worshiped various deities. Of course, what Israel *did* was not always a reflection of what they were *supposed to do*. Biblical law is unique in the ancient Near East for its prohibition against worshiping other gods and against creating any images of Yhwh. These prohibitions are summarized in the first two of the Ten Commandments: "You shall have no other gods before me. You shall not make for yourself an idol" (Exod. 20:3–4).[80] Yhwh demands exclusive worship from his people because he alone is their Creator and their King. He forbids the worship of images because (as we will see in the next chapter) we *are* his images!

Scholars disagree about whether ancient Israel would have thought in the abstract terms of "monotheism" (the belief that only one god exists), or whether theirs was a more practical concern of "monolatry" (the practice of worshiping only one god, while acknowledging that other gods exist).[81] What is quite clear is that Israel was not to give praise and allegiance to any "god" other than their covenant suzerain, Yhwh. They were also not permitted to

---

78. It is also why there did not exist an order of priests who lived completely sequestered lives apart from the rest of "normal life." Levenson explains, "There did not develop an ideal of religious life that was demarcated from the daily concerns of the masses." Aside from the few Levites who lived at the temple to care for it, worshipers would come to the sanctuary and then return to their "ordinary lives" to continue worshiping in appropriate ways: by loving their neighbors and upholding justice and mercy and singular devotion to Yhwh (Lev. 19). Levenson, *Sinai and Zion*, 178.

79. Goldingay notes the contrast between this God-focused model of worship dripping in ritual and the human-focused worship that is often wary of ritual in many modern churches. Goldingay, *Israel's Life*, 116–17.

80. This is according to most Protestant numberings of the commandments. Judaism, Roman Catholicism, and others consider the two commands together.

81. See Routledge, *Old Testament Theology*, 94–110, for a discussion of the interpretative options.

worship Yhwh as an image, a point made clear after the Israelites tried to worship Yhwh, who "brought [them] up out of the land of Egypt" in the image of the golden calf at Mount Sinai (Exod. 32:4–5).

According to Scripture, language itself is incapable of fully describing God. Consider Ezekiel's carefully qualified descriptions of God's glorious presence: "And above the dome over their heads was something *like* a throne, in appearance *like* sapphire; and seated above the *likeness* of a throne was something that seemed *like* a human form. Upward from what appeared *like* the loins . . . *like* gleaming amber . . . *like* fire . . . ," and so on (Ezek. 1:26–28). If language cannot fully describe God, how much less could our physical depictions?[82]

Iain Provan explains that such idolatry is an offense to God, a perversion of the true nature of things, and also destructive to the worshiper. Whereas worship of the true God brings worshipers closer and closer into covenant relationship with Yhwh, forming them more and more into his own image so that they can reflect his holiness, idolatry brings worshipers further and further from God's presence, making them more and more like the false gods or the false image of God with which they supplant him.[83]

Worship Without the Temple, Then and Now

The impact of Israel's loss of temple and land in 586 BCE can hardly be overstated. It served as the much-needed wake-up call for God's people to reassess their understanding of God and their relationship to him. It also forced them to consider how God would be present with them in exile. At least four theological developments provide potential answers to this question. First, we saw in chapter 4 that God's presence and holiness were identified in the Torah. Second, "name theology" proposed that God put his "name" (a representation of his identity) in the temple, but his real presence remained in the heavenly temple. Thus, a destruction of the temple could not be a destruction of its deity.[84] Third, "*kabod* theology" emphasized the mobility of God's "glory" and presence, as seen in the imagery of the pillar of cloud that traveled with the Israelites during the period of the wilderness wanderings. This same imagery is later employed by Ezekiel to describe the glory of the Lord leaving the temple (10:3–4) and returning to the restored temple (43:2–5).[85] A fourth means of understanding God's presence apart from the temple was through

---

82. Provan, *Seriously Dangerous Religion*, 165.
83. Provan, *Seriously Dangerous Religion*, 167. Goldingay likewise asserts that idolatrous images are formative because they shape the way that we see God and reality, and as such they are destructive. Goldingay, *Israel's Life*, 127.
84. Terrien, *Elusive Presence*, 198–203.
85. Kutsko, *Between Heaven and Earth*, 77–99.

his spirit, which was associated with God's people more so than the temple, making it an apt means of conceptualizing God's presence even in exile.[86]

As for the sacrificial system itself, Israel's forgiveness and salvation were never tied exclusively to these rituals; they were tied to the grace of God to which they pointed and to which they directed God's people. Levenson explains, "The destruction of the Temple did not close the gates of heaven to those who walk the path of Sinai up to the world of which Zion is the symbol."[87] In other words, those who continue to follow God's will (as reflected in the covenant at Sinai) will continue to live in God's presence and progress toward their heavenly reward of enjoying the fuller presence of God in his heavenly temple.

For modern Christians, Brueggemann laments how the Hebrew Bible sacrificial system is too often disregarded as either obsolete, and thus irrelevant, or valuable only insofar as one can discern "types" that point to Christ.[88] Another mistake is to see the sacrificial system as having been "spiritualized" under the new covenant, which implies that it was never spiritual to begin with. The theological principles communicated by the worship system of the Hebrew Bible are the same theological principles fulfilled in the sacrifice of Christ and in the Christian response of worship. The sacrificial system teaches God's people of every generation that God is relational and desires to be present with his people, that sin is serious and destructive, that God is sovereign and holy and yet willing to forgive, and that forgiveness needs to be sought regularly and with gratitude.[89]

One question that I regularly ask my undergraduate students is "Did the Hebrew Bible sacrifices really atone for sin and impurity?" I enjoy seeing the mixed responses of heads bobbing up and down or shaking side to side because it seems to be a tension between the Hebrew Bible and the New Testament. According to the Hebrew Bible, of course they did (Leviticus alone claims as much at least forty-five times); but according to the book of Hebrews, of course they did not (e.g., Heb. 10:4, "For it is impossible for the blood of bulls and goats to take away sins."). I break the awkward silence and conflicted looks by telling my students that, in a sense, both groups are correct. The author of Hebrews is not denying the atoning effectiveness of the sacrifices but arguing that atonement under the old covenant was temporal, whereas the atonement offered in Christ under the new covenant is eternal

---

86. MacDonald, "Spirit of YHWH."
87. Levenson, *Sinai and Zion*, 184.
88. Brueggemann, *Theology of the Old Testament*, 655.
89. These are similar but not identical to the spiritual principles summarized by Routledge, *Old Testament Theology*, 204.

(9:13–14). What was good under the old covenant has been made permanent under the new covenant.

CONCLUSION

Israel's worship was spatially located but not spatially constrained. It included formal worship at the sanctuary, as well as a lived-out service in the Israelites' daily lives and even in exile. It was multifaceted in order to point to the multiple ways in which God blessed his people. It was temporally recurrent, which served to shape Israel's spiritual habits and enable them to enter into God's redemptive story of his people. It was restricted to the priesthood and to the covenant community, and yet it looked beyond Israel to the nations who would one day come to share in Israel's worship of Yhwh. It was restricted to one God, who alone deserved Israel's praise. It was a time to be serious and penitent, and it was a time for jubilance and thanksgiving. It was, in a very real sense, the heartbeat of Israel's covenant relationship with their divine King.

LOOKING BACK

1. What do you consider to be the most significant differences between worship in the ancient Near East and worship in Israel?
2. What are some points of continuity and discontinuity between Israel's worship and your own?
3. How did Israel understand the theological relationship between sacrifice and repentance? How does this relationship shed light on the life of faith and the character of God?
4. How does Israel's worship relate to other theological themes discussed so far (covenant, land, etc.)?

LOOKING BEYOND

Albertz, Rainer, and Rüdiger Schmitt. *Family and Household Religion in Ancient Israel and the Levant*. Eisenbrauns, 2012.

Balentine, Samuel E., ed. *The Oxford Handbook of Ritual and Worship in the Hebrew Bible*. Oxford University Press, 2020.

Beckwith, Roger T., and Martin J. Selman, eds. *Sacrifice in the Bible*. Wipf & Stock, 1995.

Brueggemann, Walter. *Worship in Israel: An Essential Guide*. Abingdon, 2005.

Klawans, Jonathan. *Purity, Sacrifice, and the Temple: Symbolism and Supersessionism in the Study of Ancient Judaism.* Oxford University Press, 2006.

Levenson, Jon D. *Sinai and Zion: An Entry into the Jewish Bible.* Harper & Row, 1985.

Schachter, Lifsa. "The Garden of Eden as God's First Sanctuary." *Jewish Bible Quarterly* 41, no. 2 (2013): 73–77.

Zevit, Ziony. *The Religions of Ancient Israel: A Synthesis of Parallactic Approaches.* Continuum, 2001.

6

IMAGES OF GOD

The Reflection of God in Humanity

In today's world, it seems like we are constantly inundated with the concept of "image." With the rise of social media and its culture takeover, we can't seem to get away from the image we are choosing to project to the world. From the various social media outlets, to developing your own "brand," to kids wanting to be "influencers" when they grow up, as a society we have become obsessed with "image"—even at the expense of our own well-being.

The concept of "image" in ancient Israel was, on the one hand, very different from what it is today. In the ancient world "image" usually had to do with physical divine representation. On the other hand, the underlying principle of "image" is similar—humanity is Yhwh's image bearer, and how we choose to project that image to the world matters a great deal. In this chapter, we will discover the ancient Near Eastern concept of the physical image of the deity and discuss whether humanity had a role in the physical representation of the deity and how that helps us better understand ancient Israel's theology of the image of God (often described by theologians with the Latin phrase *imago Dei*).

LOOKING DOWN

As was discussed in chapters 4 and 5, taking care of the local, national, and domestic deities was of utmost importance in the ancient Near Eastern world.

On a national level, houses[1] were built to encourage the deity to descend from the heavens to earth and dwell among the people. We also noted that the houses of the gods (temples) were often designed according to a similar floor plan, which eventually led to the most holy place where the embodied presence (or image) of the divine could be found.[2] On a domestic level, households also encouraged and appeased their local deities but likely in a less circumscribed manner. If the deity or deities had an official dwelling inside the house, it was likely a simple niche, bench, cult stand, or what archaeologists call an altar or a model shrine, which do not seem to have one typical style over another.

Religion in the ancient Near East was iconic, meaning that the deities were depicted as images. An image of a particular deity was seen as the representation of that deity.[3] Images of the divine could come in a variety of forms, some of which were authorized while others were not. While it is beyond the scope of this chapter to cover all of the different types of divine material media, we will focus on figurines as the form that is well attested in both the material culture and the biblical text; furthermore, we will address kingship and its function—namely, that the king was thought to be the image of the divine.

Figurines as Literal Images

The gods and goddesses of the various pantheons of the ancient Near East were visually conceptualized as symbolic images. Common visual images of the divine were in the shape of a statue or figurine, often in the form of a human (anthropomorphic), an animal (zoomorphic or theriomorphic), or a combination of the two (therianthropic[4]). Most statues/figurines are made of terracotta or clay, but some are made of metal, wood, faience, stone, ivory, gold, or silver; they could be overlaid with gold or silver (see fig. 6.1). They typically wore lavish garments. Figurines are small, ranging from approximately 5 to 25 cm (2 to 10 inches) in height, what could be called a "handy size," indicating that they are small enough to carry around in your hand.[5] In Neo-Assyrian reliefs, soldiers are pictured plundering cult statues/figurines, some of which appear to be almost life-sized.[6] With limited and varied evidence, it is difficult to know for certain if these images are accurate or intentional exaggerations; however, one could state that figurines were

---

1. "Houses" for the gods are more commonly known as temples or shrines, but they were in essence a house for the god to dwell in among the people. Van der Toorn, *Sin and Sanction*, 29.
2. Hartenstein, "God, Gods, and Humankind (Worldview)," 151.
3. Cornelius, "Many Faces of God," 21.
4. An example of a therianthropic visual image is a human body with the head of an animal, as often seen in Egypt. For instance, the divine statue of Sekhmet in the temple at Karnak is portrayed as a woman with the head of a lioness. See Cornelius, "Many Faces of God," 24, fig. 1.
5. De Hulster, "Iron Age Terracotta Figurines," 13.
6. Uehlinger, "Anthropomorphic Cult Statuary," 124, 127–28.

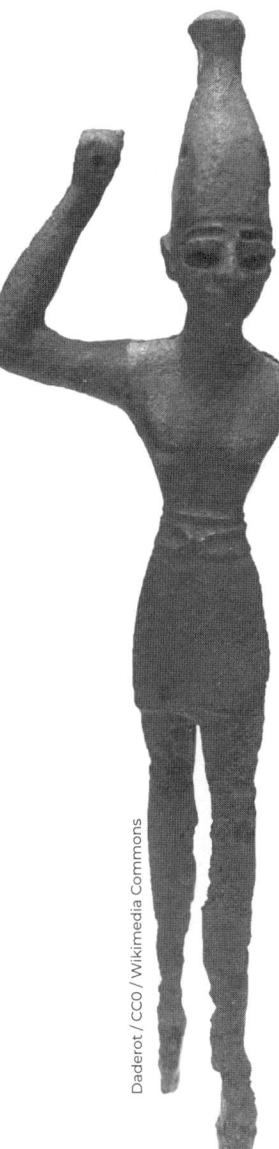

Figure 6.1. A bronze figurine of Baal as a smiting god. He stands with his left leg forward and his right arm raised. His left arm is missing, and he is wearing a crown-shaped hat.

likely at most three-quarters the size of a human, but they were typically much smaller.[7] The Hebrew Bible refers to these figurines as *teraphim*, a word often translated as "idols" or "household gods" (Gen. 31:19, 34–35; Judg. 17:5; 18:14–20; 1 Sam. 19:13, 16; 2 Kings 23:24).[8]

Regardless of what form they took, what they were made of, or their size, the prevailing view was that deities were distinguished from regular humans by their *imagined* "superhuman size, splendor, power, and opacity."[9] The gods were powerful but temperamental, so careful attention to their needs was imperative to keep them appeased.

The house of a particular deity was meant to encourage the presence of that god among their people. Within that house was the most holy place where the divine presence dwelled, which was thought to be embodied in the form of a figurine. However, no ordinary figurine could inhabit the most holy space. The figurine had to be specially made by the craftsman of the temple according to cultic regulations; furthermore, numerous rituals were conducted in order for the figurine to embody the presence or image of the divine. Tablets from first millennium Mesopotamian sites[10] provide detailed instructions on how to perform the rituals that would allow the figurine to become the embodied image of a particular deity. These rituals were known as the "mouth-washing" and "mouth-opening" rituals. The ritual itself consisted of several mouth washings, each combined with a mouth-opening rite. In general, the mouth-washing and mouth-opening rituals were to function as a transition of the figurine from its ordinary human aspect to its sacred aspect, "enabling it to become a pure and perfect god," seated in its most holy place.[11]

7. Hundley, *Gods in Dwellings*, 340–41.
8. The worship of these sacred images is referred to as "iconolatry." For further discussion on the use of *teraphim*, see van der Toorn, "Nature of the Biblical Teraphim."
9. Hartenstein, "God, Gods, and Humankind (Worldview)," 148.
10. Such as Ashur, Nineveh, Nimrud, Babylon, Sippar, Nippur, Uruk, Sultantepe, and Hama. Berlejung, "Washing the Mouth," 48.
11. Berlejung, "Washing the Mouth," 46, 68.

The ritual activated the vertical connection between the image and the deity (the vertical plane). As the embodied image of the deity, the statue guaranteed its presence and its participation with the king, priests, and worshipers (the horizontal plane).[12]

Once the god through its image "dwells in its house," its needs are also personified in that it eats, drinks, sleeps, washes, and gets dressed. It was the responsibility of the cultic personnel at the temple to take care of the deity's needs and its general well-being.[13] If the deity was pleased with its care, then it would continue to dwell in its house; but if it was displeased, it could leave. The divine image could also be forcibly removed; for example, if enemies plundered a city, it was commonplace for them to rob the temple of its divine image, which would cause the deity's presence to leave its image and house.[14]

Within Hebrew Bible studies, there is discussion about whether there was a figurine intended to serve as the image of Yhwh. We have all heard that Israel was supposed to worship Yhwh alone and that no image of Yhwh was supposed to be made (Exod. 20:4–5; Deut. 5:8–9). From an exilic and postexilic theological perspective, this is true; Yhwh's presence cannot be contained to one place since Yhwh's people are no longer in one place. However, in preexilic texts there are hints that within Yhwh's dwelling place in Jerusalem, there may have been some sort of divine image.[15] It has been argued that references to seeing the face of God or being in the presence of God could indicate a person being in the presence of the divine image of Yhwh in Yhwh's dwelling place (Pss. 11:7; 17:15; 27:4, 7–8; 42:2; 63:2; 84:9). For instance, Psalm 84 celebrates the embodied image of Yhwh in his dwelling place where "the God of gods will be seen in Zion" (v. 7).[16] Furthermore, the rituals to take care of the divine image can also be seen in various references from the Hebrew Bible. For example, the feeding ritual of the divine statue can be seen in the providing of the showbread (Exod. 25:30; 35:13; 39:36; 1 Sam. 21; 1 Kings 7:48; 2 Chron. 4:19); in libations as drinking rituals (Gen. 35:14; Exod. 25:29; 29:40–41; 37:16; Lev. 23:13, 18, 37; Num. 4:7; 6:15, 17; 15:24; 28–29; 1 Sam. 7:6; 2 Sam. 23:16); in descriptions of Yhwh being adorned with clothing (Pss. 60:10; 108:10; Isa. 6:1; 63:1–3; Ezek. 16:8; Dan. 7:9) and jewelry (Exod. 24:10; Ezek. 1:22, 26; 10:1); and in numerous metaphors of Yhwh being clothed with clouds, justice, strength, and light.[17]

---

12. Berlejung, "Washing the Mouth," 71–72.
13. Niehr, "In Search of YHWH's Cult Statue," 76.
14. Niehr, "In Search of YHWH's Cult Statue," 76–78.
15. For a fuller discussion of this topic, see Niehr, "In Search of YHWH's Cult Statue."
16. Other passages that have been argued to celebrate the image of Yhwh can be found in Pss. 24:7, 9; 47; 68:24–35; 93; 96–99; see also 1 Kings 22:19 and Isa. 6.
17. Niehr, "In Search of YHWH's Cult Statue," 76–78.

While there is no archaeological evidence of an image of Yhwh at the temple in Jerusalem,[18] there is evidence of images of Yhwh found in other temples. For instance, in Samaria (the capital city of the northern kingdom of Israel), there was a temple to Yhwh as the national deity. Hosea 13:2 indicates that the divine image placed in the temple was of a bovine (cow) made of silver with sacrifices being made to it and, as the text writes, "People are kissing calves!" Furthermore, the northern kingdom of Israel was condemned for placing zoomorphic images of Yhwh in the temples erected in Dan and Bethel (1 Kings 12:26–13:1). The Nimrud Prism of Sargon II recounts the Assyrian siege in 721 BCE that destroyed the house of Yhwh in Samaria and what plunder was taken, including "the gods, in which they trusted, as spoil I counted."[19]

Others point out that Yhwh's presence in the form of material media is more explicitly portrayed in the Hebrew Bible. For instance, the ark of the covenant can be seen as functioning as a model shrine that housed the divine presence, which could still be an object that Yhwh could choose to inhabit or abandon. A more flexible vehicle of divine presence is the *kabod* (or glory) of Yhwh. Its flexibility is a result of the glory not being a human-made object and thus not subject to the volatilities of other medias. Like other divine media, both the ark and the glory of Yhwh created space between Yhwh and the people.

A final example is the creation of humanity in Genesis 1:27. The text states that humanity is created as *betselem 'elohim* or "in the image of the deity."[20] Instead of the image of Yhwh being in the form of a figurine or another object, here humanity is created as an alternative image of the divine.[21] As we shall see next, the idea of a human as the image of the divine is nothing new.

The King as Image

Along with divine representations in the form of various types of figurines, there was also the concept of divine or sacral kingship in the ancient Near East.[22] In ancient Egypt, the Pharaoh was considered the son of a god and thus divine himself. Pharaoh was simultaneously the son of Re and the

---

18. The temple in Jerusalem was destroyed by the Neo-Babylonian Empire in 586 BCE, and archaeological excavations on the temple mount are unable to be carried out.

19. Niehr, "In Search of YHWH's Cult Statue," 79. Niehr uses the Akkadian text and its translation from Becking, *Fall of Samaria*, 28f.

20. McClellan, *YHWH's Divine Images*, 154.

21. McClellan, *YHWH's Divine Images*, 136, 146, 154–55.

22. Sacred (or sacral) kingship can be defined as the "religious and political concept by which a ruler is seen as an incarnation, manifestation, mediator, or agent of the sacred or holy (the transcendent or supernatural realm)." Westermann, "Sacred Kingship."

incarnation of Horus, and assimilated to Osiris postmortem.[23] In Mesopotamia, deification of the king only occurred in the Akkadian Period (ca. 2350–2150 BCE), after which the monarch was viewed as divinely appointed by the patron deity to rule.[24] In ancient Canaan, Israel, and Judah, the monarch was seen as the adoptive son of the patron deity. Whether the monarch was divine, the adopted son of the divine, or appointed by the divine, the wider ancient Near East shared a royal ideology where the monarch was seen as the image or representative of the divine on earth.[25]

Representation of a monarch can also be seen in texts and iconography (or representational art) of the region. Monarchs in the ancient Near East had statues of themselves created and erected in parts of their territory, possibly as boundary markers or so that when they were physically absent, the statue could serve as a symbol or representation of them and their rule over the land.[26] There are Neo-Assyrian royal documents that describe this custom. For instance, the annals of Ashurnasirpal describe his campaigns into foreign lands and how he erected a statue of himself and his "glory": "An image of my likeness I fashioned out of white limestone, my glory, my exceeding great power and my valorous deeds which I had performed in the lands of Nairî, I inscribed thereon, and in the city of Tushha I set it up; and I inscribed a memorial stele and set it in the wall thereof."[27] Another text refers to Ashurnasirpal setting up an image of himself near the images of the kings who came before him: "At the source of the river Subnat, where stand the images of Tiglath-pileser and Tukulti-Urta, kings of Assyria, my fathers, I fashioned an image of my royal person, and I set it up beside them."[28] Similarly, Shalmaneser III, Ashurnasirpal's son, also set up his "royal image": "In my first year of reign I crossed the Euphrates at its flood. To the shore of the sea of the setting sun I advanced. I washed my weapons in the sea; I offered sacrifice to my gods. I climbed Mount Amanus; I cut cedar and cypress timbers. I climbed Mount Lallar, (and) there set up my royal image."[29]

A statue itself may have an inscription stating its purpose. One example comes from Tell Fekheriye in Syria where, in 1979, a Neo-Assyrian (mid-ninth century BCE) basalt statue was found (see fig. 6.2). The statue is of Adad-it'i/Hadd-yith'i (Had-yifi), the ruler of Guzana and Sikan, provinces of the

---

23. Day, "Canaanite Inheritance," 81.
24. Lambert, "Kingship in Ancient Mesopotamia," 58; Levinson, "Reconceptualization of Kingship," 514; Day, "Canaanite Inheritance," 81.
25. For more on the characteristics of the ancient Near Eastern royal ideology, see chapter 7 in this volume.
26. Middleton, *Liberating Image*, 104.
27. Luckenbill, *Ancient Records of Assyria*, #446 on p. 147.
28. Luckenbill, *Ancient Records of Assyria*, #445 on p. 146.
29. Luckenbill, *Ancient Records of Assyria*, #558 on p. 201.

Neo-Assyrian Empire. The statue of the ruler is free-standing, bearded, and wearing a long, Assyrian-type robe, with his hands clasped at his waist.[30] What is significant about this statue is that a bilingual inscription written in Aramaic and Akkadian was inscribed on the front and back of the statue, on the robe's skirt.[31] The inscription describes the statue as a votive offering to the deity Hadad,[32] a god of storms and rain. The inscription used a pairing of Aramaic terms to describe the statue of the ruler Had-yifi as his "likeness" and as his "image."[33] What makes this inscription especially interesting for Hebrew Bible scholars is that these two words in Hebrew are the well-known words "image" and "likeness" found in Yhwh's creation of humanity in Genesis 1:26 ("Then God said, 'Let us make humankind in our image, according to our likeness'") and in Genesis 5:3 (when "Adam . . . became the father of a son in his likeness, according to his image, and named him Seth"). The bilingual inscription on the statue of Had-yifi is the only occurrence of these words as a pair outside the Hebrew Bible.[34] As one can imagine, this possible connection has kept theologians well occupied.[35]

Figure 6.2. The statue from Tell Fekheriye

Summary

As we have seen in this part of the discussion, in the ancient Near East and in Israel/Judah deities were depicted as images, which were then thought to be the representation of that deity.[36] These images were manifestations of the deity, placed where divinity could be encountered.[37] Images of the divine could come in a variety of forms: (1) figurines and other objects and (2) the personhood of the monarch, who was believed to be the image of or adopted son of the divine. Both the Hebrew Bible and material culture loudly attest to these practices. As we shall see in the next part of this chapter, this has the potential to help us better understand ancient Israel's theology of the image of the divine.

30. Garr, "'Image' and 'Likeness.'"
31. Millard and Bordreuil, "Statue from Syria," 137, 139.
32. Also known as "Adad" in Mesopotamia or generally in Canaan/Israel/Judah as "Ba'al."
33. McDowell, *Image of God*, 126.
34. Millard and Bordreuil, "Statue from Syria," 140.
35. For more on this discussion, see McDowell, *Image of God*, 126–31.
36. Cornelius, "Many Faces of God," 21.
37. Sommer, *Bodies of God*, see esp. 221n50.

LOOKING UP

A theology of "image" emerges from the Hebrew Bible that looks both similar to and different from the conception of images in Israel's cultural context. In the surrounding cultures, the deities embodied or were represented by physical images (idols) or kings. Israel's God, on the other hand, was not supposed to be represented with graven images, and his image was not limited to one king but given to all of humanity.[38] In fact, by stating that humanity is created in God's image, the biblical authors show that the idols have been replaced and that all people—men and women, rich and poor, elite and common—represent God within his creation.[39] Worshiping images was a denial not only of their God but also of their core identities as humans.[40] Likewise, mistreating others was a direct affront not only to the God whose image they bore but also to their own identities as divine image bearers.[41]

Genesis 1:26–28 (quoted in part above) is a foundational text for understanding what it means for women and men to be made in God's image and according to God's likeness:

> And God said, "Let us make humankind[42] in our image, according to our likeness. And let him govern over the fish of the sea and over the birds of the skies and over the livestock and over all the earth and over all the creeping things that creep upon the earth."
> So God created humankind in his image,
> In the image of God he created him,
> Male and female he created them.
> And God blessed them, and God said to them, "Be fruitful and multiply and fill the earth and subdue it, and govern over the fish of the sea and over the birds of the skies and over every living thing that creeps upon the earth." (my translation)

---

38. Brueggemann argues that the Hebrew Bible reflection on the image of God is foremost a reflection on "Yahwistic humanness" or "Jewish humanness," and "universal humanness" only by extension (Brueggemann, *Theology of the Old Testament*, 450–51). It is this extended use that can be deduced from passages like Gen. 9:6 and Ps. 8, which I refer to here.

39. Brueggemann, *Theology of the Old Testament*, 452. Phyllis Bird also explains that the creation account in Genesis denies the gods their primary powers: governance and fertility. Man and woman were endowed with the honor to govern creation and the innate ability to "be fruitful and multiply" by divine design, without recourse to the deities who typically claim these roles. Bird, "'Male and Female He Created Them,'" 147.

40. Imes, *Being God's Image*, 74; Lints, *Identity and Idolatry*.

41. I am grateful to Maximus Lucero and Tyler Grimaldo for some of these insights during our class seminar.

42. The Hebrew word here (*'adam*) is gender inclusive, as are the third person masculine pronouns ("him").

Figure 6.3. *Creation of Eve*, marble relief by Lorenzo Maitani on the Orvieto Cathedral in Italy, 1310–30. The second creation account depicted in this relief and recounted in Gen. 2:4–25 provides an up-close perspective of the creation of humanity.

The two terms "image" (*tselem*) and "likeness" (*demut*) overlap in meaning and qualify each other. While the term used for "image" here can refer to idols, there are other words for idols used more frequently and with consistently more negative connotations in the Hebrew Bible (e.g., *pesel*). Using a word that is less common and broader allowed the author of Genesis 1 to fill the term with a positive meaning when applied to humanity.[43] The term translated "likeness" typically has a more abstract sense, denoting that things are similar but not identical. It is possible that both terms are used as a means of lexical variety, as with the use of "to make" (*'asah*) and "to create" (*bara'*) in this account. However, the use of "image" and "likeness" in such close proximity suggests that the author is not just trying to avoid redundancy but to qualify the first term ("image") by making it clear that this new creature is only similar to its Creator.[44]

---

43. As an illustration of the broader semantic range of *tselem*, the term is also used to refer to the mice and tumor replicas that the Philistines made in 1 Sam. 6:5.

44. Recognizing which words the author did not choose helps interpreters home in on the particular meaning of a word in its context (Barr, "Image of God," 24). Barr explains, "It is the choice, rather than the word itself, which signifies" (15).

The three-fold parallelism in Genesis 1:27 invites readers to consider how God's "image" relates to the expression "male and female." There are at least three options: (1) "Male and female" could say something *about God*—that he is communal in nature (so Karl Barth) or that he has both feminine and masculine qualities (so Phyllis Trible).[45] (2) "Male and female" could say something *about humanity*, either that humans reflect God's image most fully when both sexes[46] are together or (3) that both sexes are equally and independently image bearers. Middleton is right to recognize that the parallelism is not entirely synonymous (i.e., the lines are not saying the same exact thing in three different ways). If they were, the third line would be *defining* the previous lines (male and female = image of God). Rather, the third line is progressive, saying something *more* about the image of God—namely, that both sexes embody it individually.[47]

So far, we have learned from Genesis 1:26–28 that the *imago Dei* denotes humanity's similarity to, but not identity with, God, as well as a status that women and men share equally. Ellen Davis describes the *imago Dei* as depicted in this passage as "inherently both powerful and open ended,"[48] and Phyllis Bird calls Genesis 1:27 "at once limited in its content, guarded in its expression, and complex in its structure."[49] How exactly are humans like God? In form (so the rabbinic tradition)?[50] In other attributes, or functions, or by virtue of their relationship to God? As lovely and rich as this foundational text is, theologians must keep reading to see the theology of the *imago Dei* unfold throughout the Hebrew Bible.[51] In what follows, we will look at how the cultural context informs this unfolding portrayal of the image of God with respect to three defining aspects of the image, whether or how the image is affected by sin, and how the New Testament writers understood the image in relationship to Jesus.

Three Models for the Imago Dei

Three key models or perspectives have been proposed for understanding the theology of the *imago Dei*: the ontological, the functional, and the

---

45. J. Richard Middleton describes (and disagrees with) both of these views. Middleton, *Liberating Image*, 49.

46. The terms used for male and female (*zakar* and *neqevah*) are biological terms (denoting sex), not social terms (denoting gender). Middleton, *Liberating Image*, 49.

47. Middleton, *Liberating Image*, 49. Of course, Gen. 2:18 is clear that it is "not good" for humans to be alone but that we were created for community. Even so, that is not the focus of Gen. 1:27.

48. E. Davis, *Scripture, Culture, and Agriculture*, 56.

49. Bird, "'Male and Female He Created Them,'" 130.

50. For a discussion of rabbinic understanding of the *imago Dei*, see Goshen-Gottstein, "Body as Image of God." For a more recent discussion of God's "embodiment," see Stavrakopoulou, *God*.

51. Richard S. Briggs argues that Gen. 1 uses the *imago Dei* language as a "place-holder" to be filled out as the canon unfolds. Briggs, "Humans in the Image of God," 112.

relational.⁵² In all three of these models, humans represent God in some way; the primary contention is one of priority, determining which aspect of the *imago Dei* is the most fundamental to the concept. The ontological model identifies certain qualities (such as rational ability, will, creativity, or moral capacity) that humans uniquely share with God.⁵³ This has been the most popular position throughout most of interpretative history but has fallen out of favor for at least two reasons. First, the more that we learn about the animal world, the more difficult it has become to see a clear-cut distinction between humans and animals in these ontological areas (think of how much we have learned about animal communication and empathy and intelligence!). Second, if a particular quality such as intelligence is the mark of the divine image in humanity, then what would that say of people with cognitive disabilities? Is there some arbitrary level of intelligence (or creativity or empathy, etc.) that marks humanity as image bearers? If so, it threatens to disqualify those who do not reach that mark, or it invites us to evaluate our image bearing on a bell curve, with some far outranking others.

The model most common in biblical scholarship today is the functional model, which sees the vocational role of humanity as the defining mark of the divine image. The cultural context just surveyed strongly supports this view. The fact that kings (like Adad-it'i/Hadd-yith'i) would erect "images" of themselves to represent their rule in their absence, and the fact that kings themselves would be seen as the "image" of the deity to rule on the deity's behalf as their vice-regent, strongly supports the view that the author of Genesis 1 is portraying a democratization of the image of God and its royal function to all of humanity. Whereas ancient Near Eastern creation accounts like Enuma Elish and the Epic of Atrahasis depict the creation of humanity almost as an afterthought to provide slave labor for the gods,⁵⁴ the biblical account depicts humanity as the pinnacle of creation and with the honor and dignity of vice-regents who take part in God's good governance of creation. That language of "ruling" or (probably better) "governing" over all of creation in Genesis 1:26, 28 and other key texts such as Psalm 8, strongly supports the importance of this aspect of the *imago Dei*.

The literary context invites readers to see this "rule" not only (and perhaps not even primarily) in terms of kingship but also in terms of priesthood. As we saw in the previous chapter, Genesis 1–2 describes creation as a cosmic temple, with the first man and woman being the priests who were called to lead all of

---

52. Helpful descriptions of these three models are found in much of the literature on *imago Dei*, but Lucy Peppiatt's handbook is particularly clear. Peppiatt, *Imago Dei*.

53. Some of the intertestamental books (written between 200 BCE and 50 BCE) seem to identify ontological aspects, such as strength or immortality, as the key component of the *imago Dei* (Wisdom 2:23; Sirach 17:1–13; 2 Esdras 8:44).

54. Enuma Elish 6.33–37; Epic of Atrahasis, lines 180–99.

creation in worship and to care for the "temple" of creation.⁵⁵ As elsewhere in the Hebrew Bible, the roles of kingship and priesthood are not mutually exclusive and are probably both at play in this text, and both are functions of the *imago Dei*.⁵⁶ However, the same concern that we had with the ontological model could be raised here: Do those humans who cannot or do not govern or steward creation well bear the image of God to a lesser degree than those with a greater capacity to do so? While these functions are clearly part of what it means to be an image bearer of God, they might not be the primary or most defining part.

A third theological model of the *imago Dei* is the relational model, and it takes two basic forms. The first was popularized by Karl Barth and asserts that God created humanity in community ("male and female," Gen. 1:27) because God as Trinity is communal.⁵⁷ In addition to being an imposition of Christian theology onto an ancient text and probably a misreading of the parallelism of those lines, there are better ways of understanding the relational aspect of the *imago Dei*. Catherine McDowell has argued that the relationship in view is not the communal relationship of humanity reflecting the communal relationship of the Trinity but, rather, the relationship between God and humanity. Specifically, she argues, the image of God pertains first and foremost to a likeness of *kinship* between God and humanity.⁵⁸ Walter Brueggemann, likewise, says that the "central concern of Israel regarding humanity" is "that the human person is *a person in relation to Yahweh*."⁵⁹

A relational model is supported by three key texts in Genesis. First, in the immediate context of Genesis 1, everything from vegetation to animals is said to be created "according to its kind" (CEB). The author uses this expression ten times in Genesis 1:11–25, only to switch course and use "image" and "likeness" terminology for the creation of humanity in Genesis 1:26–27. The

---

55. Levenson, "Temple and the World"; Walton, *Lost World of Genesis One*; Weinfeld, "Sabbath, Temple"; Middleton, *Liberating Image*, 87. Ellen Davis identifies the "dominion" language of Gen. 1:26, 28 as a "silent judgment" to (post)exilic readers of their failure to care for the land they were charged to steward: "The human project on Earth, the macrocosm, may yet fail as dismally as did Israel's project in Canaan, the microcosm." Davis, *Scripture, Culture, and Agriculture*, 63.

56. Melchizedek is the classic example of a priest-king (Gen. 14:18), and David also served in a priestly role while he was king (2 Sam. 6:14–18). Exodus 19:6 also brings together these roles through the description of Israel as a "priestly kingdom," and the similar expression in 1 Pet. 2:9 ("royal priesthood").

57. For a critique of Barth's exegesis, see Bird, "'Male and Female He Created Them,'" 130–33, or Peppiatt, *Imago Dei*, 156–58.

58. McDowell, *Image of God*. For a more concise and accessible discussion, see her essay, "In the Image of God He Created Them."

59. This perspective also supports his view that the *imago Dei* is foremost language of Israelite or Jewish humanness, rather than of a universal humanity (Brueggemann, *Theology of the Old Testament*, 453). Given the relational metaphor, I still find it possible to understand the *imago Dei* as describing the universal human condition because family relations are not dependent on one's knowledge of one's parentage. A son or daughter can be a son or daughter of God, regardless of their recognition of the fact.

effect is to see that humanity is also made after a kind (a species or kin), but they are made according to *God's* kind.[60] Second, in Genesis 5:3, Seth is said to be born in the "likeness" and according to the "image" of his father, Adam, emphasizing the familial relationship between the two. Third, Genesis 9:6 depicts God as the blood avenger of anyone who would kill someone made in his image. According to Israelite law and ancient Near Eastern custom, the blood avenger was the nearest of kin (*go'el*).[61]

The royal function would then be a necessary result[62] of that kinship relationship, as is clear from the deity-king adoption metaphor used throughout the ancient Near East[63] and in Hebrew Bible passages. This is exemplified in Psalm 2:7, in which Yhwh tells the king, "You are my son; today I have begotten you." Reflecting the ontological qualities or characteristics of the one imaged (in this case Yhwh) is also a natural result of kinship. Like father, like son, especially when that Father is the holy God.[64]

Seeing, then, that the three models are not mutually exclusive, figure 6.4 might help us conceptualize the relationship between them.

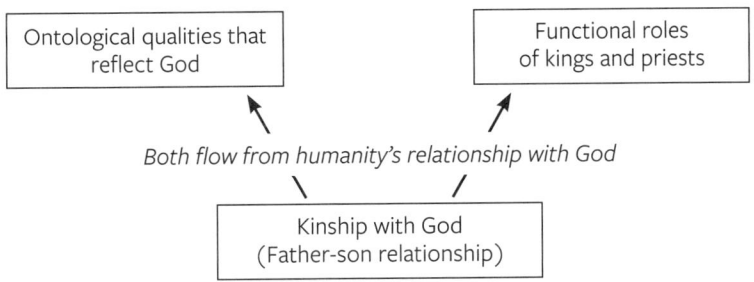

Figure 6.4. Three aspects of the *imago Dei*

60. McDowell, "In the Image of God He Created Them," 38; Drever, "Image, Identity, and Embodiment," 122.

61. Although Gen. 9:6 does not use the word *go'el*, McDowell argues that this role is implied and would have been understood by readers familiar with the law and similar passages describing God as Israel's avenger. McDowell, "In the Image of God He Created Them," 37.

62. Scholars disagree about whether the functional aspect is a purpose or a result of the *imago Dei* (and thus a primary or a secondary aspect). Middleton argues that the function of kingship is the "necessary and inseparable purpose [of the *imago Dei*] and hence virtually constitutive of the image" (*Liberating Image*, 55) whereas McDowell argues that such reasoning is "another case of mistaking implication for meaning" ("In the Image of God He Created Them," 34). The two seem difficult to separate, as a king could not conceive of his firstborn as anything other than his heir to the throne. However, the argument here is that sonship is primary in logic and is more permanent than kingship.

63. For a lengthy discussion on the kinship-kingship connection to the divine image, see McDowell, "In the Image of God He Created Them," 40–41.

64. The language of "son" (rather than the gender-inclusive language of "child") is being maintained in order to preserve the Father/King–son/heir metaphor. Women, of course, are equally in view.

This relationship also conforms to the theological message of grace that permeates Israel's history: God covenants with and saves his people before and in spite of their inability to *be* (ontologically) and *do* (functionally) that which should arise from their identity as God's children. Implicit in humanity's relationship with God (and made explicit in the covenant) is their *capacity* to imitate God's attributes and to practice his rule and care.[65] A fair comparison might be when a parent tells their grown child, "Come on! You're an adult—act like it!" Much of Christian preaching uses the same formula, only with a more nuanced delivery.

The Image and Sin

If the image of God in humanity fundamentally connotes our kinship with him, and our capacity to be and to do what God has called his sons and daughters to be and do, then how does sin fit into the equation? Did we lose or forfeit our identity as image bearers? Or is the image of God something still latent within us, or is it distorted by sin within us? If the deity of an image could be forced out of that image, as noted above, could the image of Yhwh be forced out of his image bearers as well? Psalm 8 seems to suggest that humans still hold that special kinship with Yhwh and have not forfeited or lost their role as royal sons and daughters to govern God's good creation. The psalmist is in awe that such a privileged status and responsibility would still be granted to humanity, and although the words "image" and "likeness" are not explicitly used, the allusions to Genesis 1:26–28 are unmistakable.

> When I look at your heavens, the works of your fingers,
> the moon and the stars, which you made firm,
> What is mankind that you remember him?
> Or the son of man that you care for him?
> You made him a little less than divine,[66]
> and with glory and honor you crown him,
> and you make him reign over the works of your hands;
> everything you have set under his feet. (Ps. 8:3–6, my translation)

---

65. This is not unlike how Israel was charged to reflect God's holiness in Leviticus: "Be holy, for I the LORD your God am holy" (Lev. 19:2; similarly, 20:7, 26, etc.). C. John Collins also discusses the *imago Dei* in terms of capacity in *Reading Genesis Well*, 164.

66. This expression supports the kinship element of the *imago Dei* that is not explicitly stated in this psalm. The verb translated "made him . . . less" denotes a lacking of something (Koehler et al., *Hebrew and Aramaic Lexicon of the Old Testament*, 1:338), and *'elohim* could be referring to God or to the divine. The idea is that the psalmist is like God, but he lacks full deity. The psalmist, like the man and woman of Gen. 1:26–28, was created to be similar to but not identical with God.

Scholars agree that the psalmist is reflecting on the current reality of humanity, as John F. Kilner explains: "The psalmist can find no reasons—no current godly attributes—that warrant humanity's lofty status. Were humanity's status to be rooted in ways that people presently are like God, then those likenesses and humanity's status would indeed be damaged by sin. However, the exalted status continues, even though all the likenesses have not."[67] The continuance of this "exalted status" is also clear in Psalm 144:3–4, which echoes Psalm 8:4 verbatim and then adds this next line: "They are like breath; / their days are like a passing shadow." The psalmists are in awe not of an idealized past reality but of the current reality characterized by mortality. Similarly, when God charges Noah and his family in Genesis 9:6 not to shed the blood of others, it is because those others are made in God's image, a theological reality that must have been retained even after humanity fell into sin and rebellion.

Whereas the relational status of the *imago Dei* was unchanged by the fall, the functional and ontological aspects were diminished and, at some points, even forfeited. Middleton argues that humanity was created to do on earth the same work as the angels do in heaven. When God said, "Let us make humankind in our image" in Genesis 1:26, he was speaking with his heavenly court which, according to Middleton, means that humanity was created not only in God's image but in the collective image of the heavenly beings, including the angels.[68] When Adam and Eve were exiled from the garden of Eden, angels "guarded" (*shamar*) the very place that Adam was first charged to "guard" (*shamar*) in Genesis 2:15 (GNT), thus taking humanity's role of governance.[69] While Psalm 8 seems to maintain that the functional role of humanity was not entirely or permanently revoked, it is true that God maintains the right to occasionally diminish or limit humanity's royal and priestly roles. It is also true that, due to sin, humanity does not execute those roles to their best capacity, which is abundantly clear in our own modern contexts and was also evident in Israel's experience. As we saw in chapter 3, Israel's exile was attributed to their failure to serve Yhwh faithfully and also to their failure to govern creation well by administering justice and caring for their land.

In addition to limiting or distorting the functional aspect of the *imago Dei*, sin also distorts the ontological aspect of the image of God in humanity.

---

67. Kilner, *Dignity and Destiny*, 140–41; cf. Raymond C. Van Leeuwen, who cites Ps. 8 as evidence that the "the image is not lost through sin" ("Form, Image," 4:645). Carmen Imes agrees, stating, "God bestows dignity on humans that does not depend on ability and is not lost due to sin." Imes, *Being God's Image*, 53.

68. Middleton, *Liberating Image*, 59. This is also how the Septuagint understood Ps. 8:5 in its translation of *'elohim* as *angelous* ("angels").

69. Middleton, *Liberating Image*, 59. Carmen Imes adds that the exile of Adam and Eve from the garden did not diminish the image itself or their identity as God's image, but it diminished the glory of that image because "[glory] depends on proximity." Imes, *Being God's Image*, 112.

The law offered to Israel is a reflection of God's character and a guide for reflecting his holiness (Lev. 19:2). Gregory of Nyssa taught how, in a similar way, the Beatitudes cleansed one's image of sin's tarnish in order to uncover the inherent *imago Dei* that lies beneath.[70]

One could say that the effect of sin on the ontological and functional aspects of the *imago Dei* strained the relational aspect of the image, just as a child's behavior or character can strain their relationship with their parents, but the relationship itself is as unfaltering as the grace of God.

The Image and Jesus

The Hebrew Bible conception of the divine image sheds light on several important aspects of the divine image in the New Testament.[71] First, it serves to highlight Jesus's humanity. Passages like Colossians 1:15 and 2 Corinthians 4:4 describe Jesus as "the image of God," a description that would have brought to the mind of any Jewish reader the human identity as described in the Hebrew Bible.[72] Jesus, like every other flesh-and-blood human, bore God's image, and thus he could redeem others who shared that identity. And while the relational aspect of the *imago Dei*, though strained, did not need to be redeemed (God's children would always be his children), the functional and ontological aspects of the image did.

Second, the Hebrew Bible theology of the *imago Dei* corresponds to the sanctification and glorification of the children of God. Seeing the image of God as pertaining first to a relational identity that cannot be altered, even by sin, and secondarily as the capacity to reflect and represent God helps to make sense of New Testament passages that speak to Christ having restored the image of God in humanity (e.g., Rom. 8:29; 1 Cor. 15:49; 2 Cor 3:18; Col. 3:9–10). Upon a close read, these passages are not describing an image that had been totally lost but rather a renewed image *in Christ*.[73] For example,

---

70. For an excellent discussion of Gregory of Nyssa's theology, see Rebekah Eklund's "Blessed are the Image-Bearers."

71. Daniel Treier uses the *imago Dei* to illustrate his methodology of a theological interpretation of Scripture in *Introducing Theological Interpretation*. His insights about how the forward-moving direction of interpretation highlights the anthropology of Christ can be found on pp. 152–256.

72. Unlike humanity, who is made "in" the image of God and "according to" his likeness, Jesus "is the image of the invisible God" with no qualifying prepositions or secondary words (like *demut*, translated "likeness," in Gen. 1:26). However, 1 Cor. 11:7 describes man as the "image" of God with no such qualifications as well. Christopher Kugler argues that these texts would also have brought to mind the preincarnate eternality of the image of Christ (much like Jesus's association with the "Word/Logos" and Wisdom), which was the prototype for the first man and the *telos* of humanity. Kugler, *Paul and the Image of God*.

73. Scholars who see the *imago Dei* as being primarily ontological or functional are more apt to describe the image of God as something that was completely lost due to human failure

Romans 8:29 states, "For those whom he foreknew he also predestined to be conformed to the image of his Son." God's children, already image bearers of God, will be conformed to the image of his Son, who perfectly expresses that image in every way. That is what humanity could not do under the old covenant, and that is what they will finally be able to do under the new covenant through their union with Christ and the indwelling of the Holy Spirit.

Two analogous examples might prove helpful at this point. In the Hebrew Bible, Israel was called God's "servant" regardless of how well they actually executed that role.[74] Most scholars recognize, for example, that the servant in Isaiah 42:1–9 refers to Israel as a nation (especially given the negative assessment of the servant in 42:18–19), but its citation by Matthew in Matthew 12:18–21 shows how Christ, as the perfect servant, has fulfilled the role of God's people without replacing them. Indeed, he exhorts them to follow suit (Matt. 20:26–27; Mark 10:43–44). Another example from Isaiah 5:1–7 is Israel's description as Yhwh's vineyard, which fails to produce good fruit but instead produces the "fruit" of injustice. Even as a failed vineyard, the Israelites maintain the status of vineyard, and when Jesus fulfills their role as the vine, he does not replace them, but he enables them to be what they were always called to be, if they are willing to abide in him (John 15:1–6). In the same way, the image of God was never removed from humanity, but its fruitfulness was restored in Christ.

There also appears to be an aspect of the image of God that remains in the future as part of the glorification of humanity. In 1 Corinthians 15:35–58, Paul contrasts the state of our earthly bodies with the future, glorified state of our bodies, which will be eternal and indestructible. In verse 49, he states, "Just as we have borne the image of the man of dust, we will also bear the image of the man of heaven." Similarly, Paul sees the sonship status of God's people as part of the old covenant (Rom. 9:4), part of the new covenant under Christ (8:15), and also part of the "not yet" realm of the kingdom (8:23). There is continuity and discontinuity between the image bearing of the Hebrew Bible saints, the image bearing of the church age, and the image bearing that awaits us in glory.

---

and rejection. Psalm 8, in such views, describes only the perspective of the first man and woman before sin and those in Christ after his death, resurrection, and ascension, but not those who lived, loved, and trusted Yhwh for the interim thousands of years. Jacobs, *Conformed to the Image of His Son*, 93, 95, 226.

74. The term "servant" develops throughout the book of Isaiah, referring first and most often to the nation of Israel as a whole (e.g., 41:8–9) but also to a prophetic figure (e.g., 49:1–7) and to a prophet-priest who will atone for the sins of Israel and "create a community of servants who are willing to suffer and serve like their master" (52:13–53:12; cf. 1 Pet. 2:20–25). Abernethy, *Book of Isaiah*, 159. Abernethy's entire discussion on the servant theme in Isaiah is excellent (see pp. 137–60).

CONCLUSION

In the ancient Near East, humanity typically encountered the divine in physical images and in the person of the king. Israel's god, however, was not to be represented in physical images or by a select individual because all humans were created to be God's images. The core meaning of this status and identity is that of kinship with God. Sin impedes our ability to carry out the functional and ontological aspects of the *imago Dei*, thus paving the way for kingship and ultimately the coming of Jesus.

LOOKING BACK

1. What objects were viewed as literal images of the divine?
2. What person was viewed as an image of the divine?
3. Do you think that all three models presented in this chapter (ontological, functional, relational) are at work in the *imago Dei*? How would you explain their relationship?
4. How should the *imago Dei* affect the way that we view each other (see James 3:9 for a hint)? How should it affect the way that we view ourselves?
5. How does the image of God connect with other important theological themes discussed so far (for example, household or covenant)?

LOOKING BEYOND

Hundley, Michael B. *Gods in Dwellings: Temples and Divine Presence in the Ancient Near East*. Society of Biblical Literature, 2013.

Imes, Carmen Joy. *Being God's Image: Why Creation Still Matters*. IVP Academic, 2023.

Jones, Beth Felker, and Jeffrey W. Bareau, eds. *The Image of God in an Image Driven Age: Explorations in Theological Anthropology*. Wheaton Theology Conference Series. IVP Academic, 2016.

Middleton, J. Richard. *The Liberating Image: The* Imago Dei *in Genesis 1*. Baker Academic, 2005.

Peppiatt, Lucy. *The Imago Dei: Humanity Made in the Image of God*. Cascade Companions. Cascade Books, 2022.

Treier, Daniel. *Introducing Theological Interpretation of Scripture: Recovering a Christian Practice*. Baker Academic, 2008.

van der Toorn, Karel. *The Image and the Book: Iconic Cults, Aniconism, and the Rise of Book Religion in Israel and the Ancient Near East*. Peeters, 1997.

7

KINGSHIP AND POLITICS
The Sovereignty of God

Traditional monarchies, in which one person is the sole political leader without any checks or balances of power, are an artifact of the past for most of us. We may follow the British royal family with keen interest, and we may binge our historical dramas with their fabulously dressed kings and courtiers, but for most of us, the political structure of a traditional monarchy feels as far removed as King Triton's underwater kingdom. This does put us at a disadvantage for trying to comprehend the ancient Near Eastern world. They had monarchies with a leader who had often inherited that leadership role from his father. The role of a monarch, how that role is understood to function in the ancient Near Eastern world, and even what makes a good leader can be challenging concepts to grasp. In the chapter that follows, we will discuss the royal ideology of kingship in the ancient Near East and how this impacted Israel's view of their human king and their relationship with their divine king.

LOOKING DOWN

In ancient Israel there were various leadership roles, depending on the time period and context in question. For instance, before Israel had a king, leaders were more localized. In this chapter we will introduce the royal ideology of the wider ancient Near East and how this can be observed in the various roles the monarch played in ancient Israel. To set the foundation for this discussion, however, we must first look at pre-monarchic Israel's localized leadership and how the introduction of a monarchy influenced it.

Village Leadership

In chapter 1 we considered the form and function of the household dwelling, its members, and its activities. All members of the household were expected to participate in its survival, but its leadership was found in the patriarch and matriarch, who were ultimately responsible for the protection (patriarch), reproduction (matriarch), and production (both) of the household.[1] While we must recognize that ancient Israelite women probably had more power and authority than we have traditionally given them credit for (especially on a household level), we must also remember that this was not an egalitarian society; women did not have the same rights and privileges as men—even on a household level. Consequently, it was the household patriarch who could serve as part of the village council elders (*ziqneim*), if he was recognized as a notable member of the community.[2] The village elders functioned as an assembly whose public responsibility was to uphold the civil rights of the villagers and to protect the most vulnerable of their community—namely, those without a household of their own to protect them, such as widows, orphans, and foreigners. Those seeking judicial recourse would go to the village gate or courtyard and appeal for a jury of elders to review their case. The assembly would convene at the gate (if they had one) or at the threshing floor (where grain is processed), usually located outside the village—both public places that would keep the trial open.[3] The book of Ruth provides an example of this when Boaz summons ten elders at the village gate to address who will step in as *go'el* (or kinsman-redeemer) to Naomi via Ruth (Ruth 4). Villages that were part of the same clan would meet, with delegates chosen to represent the clan at tribal councils and later at the state level.[4] A judge (*shopet*) was a tribal member to whom the tribal elders could appeal in time of military threat (Judg. 20:1–2; 1 Sam. 11), even if it began as an economic (1 Sam. 13:19–21) or diplomatic crisis (1 Sam. 8:4–5; 11:12–15).[5] Localized government by assembly was an important social institution that remained the ideal even when more centralized political systems, like monarchies and states, developed.[6]

---

1. Meyers, "Procreation, Production, and Protection," 574–76.
2. Matthews and Benjamin, *Social World of Ancient Israel*, 122–23.
3. Matthews and Benjamin, *Social World of Ancient Israel*, 122; King and Stager, *Life in Biblical Israel*, 60.
4. King and Stager, *Life in Biblical Israel*, 60.
5. De Vaux, *Ancient Israel*, 151; Matthews and Benjamin, *Social World of Ancient Israel*, 97.
6. Matthews and Benjamin, *Social World of Ancient Israel*, 122.

Kingship

In the late Iron Age I period (ca. 1020 BCE), the roots of a monarchy were established in Israel (1 Sam. 8). The monarchy was a new practice to Israel and, therefore, in its early days was limited in scope and function; however, it did not take long for the monarchy to evolve with far-reaching socioeconomic effects, including shifting the centralization of leadership from the village level to the state level. This is not to say that village leadership disappeared; rather, it carried on through the monarchic period, but centralization developed and advanced with the advent of the monarchy. The centralization of leadership to a single monarch was reinforced by a royal ideology shared throughout the ancient Near East. As we observed in chapter 6, it was a common practice to view the monarchs as representatives of the divine on earth. This concept of divine or sacral kingship led to a royal ideology that included overarching key functions of the monarch.[7] Bernard Levinson argues that there are six characteristics of ancient Near Eastern royal ideology in which Israel fully participated:

1. The monarch as divine representation;
2. The judicial insight of the monarch;
3. The monarch's ability to administer justice;
4. The evaluation (by the gods and the people) of the monarch's ability to administer justice;
5. The monarch's commitment to the cult of the patron deity;
6. And the monarch's role as the military commander in chief.[8]

Each of these characteristics and how Israel participated in them will be expanded on below.

The first characteristic, as already mentioned above, is the view that the monarch is the adopted son or an appointed representative of the chief deity of the national pantheon. As we observed in chapter 6, viewing the king as the son of a deity or as his divine representative was widely practiced throughout the ancient Near East: Egyptian Pharaohs were simultaneously considered the son of the Sun god, Re.[9] The deification of the king only occurred in Mesopotamia during the Akkadian Period (ca. 2350–2150 BCE); subsequent periods viewed the monarch as divinely appointed by the patron deity to rule.[10]

---

7. Sacred (or sacral) kingship can be defined as the "religious and political concept by which a ruler is seen as an incarnation, manifestation, mediator, or agent of the sacred or holy (the transcendent or supernatural realm)." Westermann, "Sacred Kingship."

8. Levinson, "Reconceptualization of Kingship," 511–12, 518.

9. Day, "Canaanite Inheritance," 81.

10. Lambert, "Kingship in Ancient Mesopotamia," 58; Levinson, "Reconceptualization of Kingship," 514; Day, "Canaanite Inheritance," 81.

In Canaan, Israel, and Judah, the monarch was seen as the adoptive son of the patron deity. Adoption formulas, such as *bekor 'ettenehu* ("I will make him my first-born"), are used to legally bind the monarch to the patron deity, thus appointing the monarch as both the deity's adopted son and earthly counterpart (Ps. 89:26–27; see also 2:7b).[11] Whether the monarch was divine, the adopted son of the divine, or appointed by the divine, the wider ancient Near East shared a royal ideology where the monarch was seen as the image or representative of the divine on earth.

The second, third, and fourth characteristics of the royal ideology are connected and function as a direct result of the monarch's appointment as the adopted son of the patron deity. By virtue of their special status, the monarch is endowed by the deity with judicial insight and wisdom (the second characteristic), which then enables the monarch to administer justice (the third characteristic). Once the monarch ascends to the throne, he proclaims a code of law and/or a special act of "justice" or "equity" (the fourth characteristic).[12] How monarchs carried out their divinely given judicial insights and wisdom was through their policies regarding agriculture, law codes, and acts of justice.

First, one of the more important crises from which the monarchy of Israel emerged was the unpredictable nature of agriculture and how the household survived on the often-inhospitable land.[13] Households and villages were subsistence-level agropastoralists, developing the land as best they could and producing the same products from village to village. The nature of the environment was fragile, which made production and distribution of those products even more challenging, thus putting the survival of the households and villages in jeopardy.[14] The monarchy initiated policies that addressed the agriculture crisis and did so by combining villages and cities that covered a bigger region and had more diverse products[15] and by extracting goods and services in a variety of forms: tithes/offerings and taxes; corvée; interest on debt and rental fees; and the renting, cultivation, or maintenance of estates and/or flocks and herds owned by the palace or temple.[16] Once Israel became a monarchy, their economic context expanded from a simple subsistence-level household economy to a centralized redistributive economy overseen by the monarch.[17]

---

11. Levinson, "Reconceptualization of Kingship," 512–13.
12. Levinson, "Reconceptualization of Kingship," 514–16.
13. Matthews and Benjamin, *Social World of Ancient Israel*, 162.
14. Matthews and Benjamin, *Social World of Ancient Israel*, 162.
15. Matthews and Benjamin, *Social World of Ancient Israel*, 162.
16. Walton, "Economy and Trade," 62; Liverani, *Ancient Near East*, 62–63.
17. As independent kingdoms, Israel and Judah had economies that functioned within a "native tributive mode," meaning that the native, *dominating*, centralized, elite class (primarily the monarchy and the temple complex) extracted tribute from the working, *dominated* class (i.e., households and villages). The tribute was then redistributed, most likely back to the *dominating*,

Kingship and Politics

A second illustration of how an ancient Near Eastern monarch demonstrated their divinely given insight and ability was through the formation of law codes. Upon their coronation, the monarch publicly declared a code of law for the state. These codes were not new; rather, they served as updates to the traditional patterns of taxation and conscription, including outlining the responsibilities of the villages and towns to the state and how the state would reinforce compliance. The most well-known example was initiated by King Hammurabi, who reigned during the Old Babylonian (Amorite) Dynasty from 1728–1686 BCE. At the very beginning of his reign, Hammurabi promulgated his law code, which consisted of a collection of 282 rules. The most well-known copy of this code was written on a diorite stone stela (a monument) with an engraving (or bas-relief) of Shamash, the god of the sun and justice, commissioning Hammurabi to write the lawbook (see fig. 7.1).[18] In Israel, the monarch's legislation of law codes was overseen by a state court that was made up of full-time, monarch-appointed judges (Deut. 17:8–13; 19:15–21; 2 Chron. 19:4–11).[19]

Our third and final illustration of how a monarch demonstrated their divinely given wisdom was through special acts of justice and equity. At the beginning of

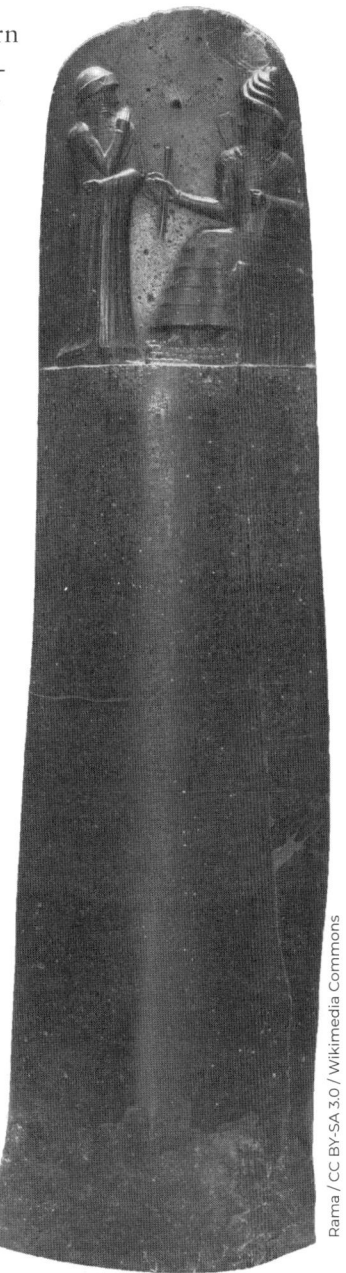

Figure 7.1. The Code of Hammurabi

---

elite class and its dependents. However, once the kingdoms of Israel and Judah were no longer independent but vassals within the Neo-Assyrian Empire (and then Judah within the Neo-Babylonian Empire), the kingdoms were under a *foreign tributary mode*. Israel's and Judah's vassalage treaties required them to send tribute to the Neo-Assyrian Empire (and Judah to the Neo-Babylonian Empire). The tribute was taken from the taxes/tithes that the palace/temple extracted from the households or from draining the central temple or royal treasury, which likely stored the taxes/tithes (see Boer, *Sacred Economy*, 110–45). Roland Boer defines "redistribution" as "goods [that] are appropriated (usually by a central authority) for redistribution to the people" (236). Roger Nam writes that "tribute" as defined in Neo-Assyrian texts is "annual gifting, and its very act affirms and maintains the existing relationship, typically the acknowledgement of vassalhood with all the rights and responsibilities within such an arrangement." Whereas, "'booty' is a one-time gift, after a military decision, that rewards the victor, and establishes the beginning of a relationship" (Nam, *Portrayals of Economic Exchange*, 145n176). See also Shafer-Elliott, "Household Economics."

18. Meek, "Code of Hammurabi," 155.
19. Matthews and Benjamin, *Social World of Ancient Israel*, 167.

their reign, monarchs would proclaim legislation regarding acts of justice and equity—namely, acts that were concerned with the pardon of debts and other obligations, including the return of land to its original owners. In Akkadian this practice was called *Mīšarum*, and the best example of it can be seen in the Edict of Ammisaduqa (see fig. 7.2), the tenth ruler of the Hammurabi Dynasty in Babylon (1646–1626 BCE).[20] Some biblical scholars suggest that the Jubilee year in Leviticus 25 is a *Mīšarum*; however, while there is evidence that *Mīšarum* declared by Mesopotamian kings were actualized, the year of Jubilee, on the other hand, was an ideal law decreed by Yhwh, and there is no evidence that it was actually carried out.[21]

Figure 7.2. Edict of Ammisaduqa

The monarch's appointment by the patron deity and as the adopted son of the patron deity involved the endowment of judicial insight and wisdom, which then enabled the monarch to administer justice, primarily through their policies regarding agriculture, law codes, and acts of justice. The monarch's role as the administrator of justice was considered their primary duty, and as such, a monarch was responsible for ensuring equal access to legal protection for those who were socially marginalized, especially the widows and orphans, for whom the king was their surrogate family patriarch. Furthermore, the monarch was likewise responsible for rooting out injustice (Ps. 72:4).[22] The success of the monarch and their reign was to be evaluated on whether justice for all the people was established and maintained.[23] For example, Hammurabi in Babylon decreed that Marduk (the patron deity) empowered him as king "so that the strong might not oppress the weak, to rise like Šamaš over the

---

20. Finkelstein, "Edict of Ammisaduqa," 183–84.
21. Amit, "Jubilee Law: Ideal Legislation." For a more detailed analysis, see Amit, "Jubilee Law: An Attempt at Instituting Social Justice." For further reading, see Rhodes, *Just Discipleship*.
22. Levinson, "Reconceptualization of Kingship," 515.
23. Levinson, "Reconceptualization of Kingship," 516–17.

black-haired ones, and light up the land."[24] In the Hebrew Bible, the formula "establish justice and equity for all his people" in relation to the role of the monarch is used in three primary ways: (1) This formula is used to describe the ideal of the Davidic dynasty (see 1 Kings 10:9; Ps. 72:1); (2) it is used as the principal expectation of both current and future monarchs (Jer. 22:3, 5, 15; 33:15; Ezek. 45:9); and (3) it is also viewed as the hallmark of the messianic age (Isa. 42:4).[25]

The fifth characteristic in the list above is the monarch's role as the defender and patron of the national cult, which is often best illustrated through their commitment to the house (temple) of the patron deity (2 Sam. 7; 1 Kings 5–8; 2 Kings 18:1–8; 22–23).[26] In the prologue to the Code of Hammurabi, the king references several times his maintaining or rebuilding various temples. Of course, the most well-known example from the Hebrew Bible is King Solomon's building of the temple to Yhwh in Jerusalem (1 Kings 5–8). A less commonly known role of the monarch is their priestly role, which is certainly connected to their role in the national cult. In Israel and Judah, the monarch's unique sacral kingship as the adopted son of Yhwh allowed them an "ex officio priestly status," meaning that their role included being a mediator between the people and the divine, especially within cultic rituals at the divine sanctuary.[27] This does not mean that the monarch performed the daily rituals that were the purview of the priests; however, it does mean that the monarch's involvement was appropriate on certain occasions. Furthermore, the monarch's supreme role in all things, including cultic matters, can be seen in the several instances where a king initiated cultic practice and reform: 1 Kings 12:26–13:1; 2 Kings 16:10–14; 18:1–4; 22:1–23:24.[28]

The final common characteristic of the shared royal ideology is that the monarch was the kingdom's military chief, whose responsibility it was to defend and expand the kingdom. Several examples of this can be seen in Neo-Assyrian texts that describe the royal campaigns of various kings.[29] The Hebrew Bible demonstrates that the monarch was expected to personally lead the military into battle (1 Sam. 10:27b–11:15; 2 Sam. 11:1–2).[30] In 1 Samuel 8:19–20, the Israelites want a king, and even after the prophet Samuel warns them about what a king will do, they still demand one: "But the people refused to listen to the voice of Samuel; they said, 'No! But we are determined

---

24. Levinson, "Reconceptualization of Kingship," 515.
25. Levinson, "Reconceptualization of Kingship," 516–17.
26. Levinson, "Reconceptualization of Kingship," 517.
27. Rooke, "Kingship as Priesthood," 193.
28. Rooke, "Kingship as Priesthood," 195.
29. For examples of Neo-Assyrian royal campaigns, see Oppenheim, "Sargon II (271–705)"; Oppenheim, "Senacherib (704–682)"; Oppenheim, "Esarhaddon (680–669)."
30. Levinson, "Reconceptualization of Kingship," 517.

to have a king over us, so that we also may be like other nations, and that our king may govern us and *go out before us and fight our battles*.'" Israel's first king, Saul, does just this when he initiates a campaign to free the inhabitants of Jabesh-Gilead from the Ammonites (1 Sam. 11); however, Israel's favorite son, King David, gets himself into trouble when he does not do what is expected of a king—accompany his soldiers into battle. "In the spring of the year, the time when kings go out to battle, David sent Joab with his officers and all Israel with him; they ravaged the Ammonites, and besieged Rabbah. But David remained at Jerusalem" (2 Sam. 11:1).

These characteristics summarize the common royal ideology shared throughout the ancient Near East—that the monarch's authority, role, prestige, and power are tied to the understanding that the monarch is the representative or image of the divine on earth.

Summary

Before Israel had a king, leadership was more localized in the form of village elders. Once Israel established a monarchy, local village elders continued in leadership but operated under the authority of the king, and their ideology of the monarchy was typical to that found in the wider ancient Near East, with kings representing the deity and being responsible for matters of law and justice, the cult, and the military.

LOOKING UP

Through the characteristics of kingship discussed above—divine representation, justice, commitment to the cult, and military leadership—we will now explore how the authors of the Hebrew Bible viewed their divine King as well as their human kings. When the latter failed and the Davidic dynasty came to an end, Israel's hopes for kingship were pushed both to the future (toward messianism) and to the past (to the democratization of kingship through the *imago Dei*). Two theological themes surface with regard to each characteristic: (1) Israelite kingship was integrally connected to the relational identity and the functional role of the *imago Dei*, and (2) the human king was always carefully distinguished from the divine King.

Divine Representation

God's kingship is explicitly proclaimed in Exodus 15:18 as the punctuating final line in the Song of the Sea, which celebrates Israel's deliverance from Egypt: "The LORD will reign forever and ever." The exodus from Egypt and the ratification of the covenant at Mount Sinai certainly highlight Yhwh's kingly role over his people, who have now grown to be the "great nation" promised to Abraham and his descendants (Gen. 12:2; 17:20; 35:11). However, God's kingship did not originate with the national status of his people but, rather, is grounded in creation, as the psalmist professes:

> Yet God my King is from old,
>   working salvation in the earth.
> You divided the sea by your might;
>   you broke the heads of the dragons in the waters. . . .
> Yours is the day, yours also the night;
>   you established the luminaries and the sun.
> You have fixed all the bounds of the earth;
>   you made summer and winter. (Ps. 74:12–13, 16–17; cf. 29:10; 93:2–4)

This imagery of bringing order to forces of chaos and taming chaotic waters and sea monsters is a common motif in ancient Near Eastern creation accounts and in the Hebrew Bible, and it serves to highlight Yhwh's role as the true Creator-King. Psalm 104 describes Israel's Creator-King as having full control over the waters, ordering them to cover land, flee to the mountains, or run down the valleys (vv. 6–8). Psalm 89, a psalm that describes the glorious rise and tragic fall of the Davidic monarchy, extends this role to the human king, when God says of his king, "I will set his hand on the sea / and his right hand on the rivers" (v. 25). The human king was to represent the divine King, restraining chaos and the consequences of sin and bringing order to the nation of Israel, just as God brought order to creation.[31]

But what about the rest of humanity, who, as we just saw in the previous chapter, are also made in God's image and charged with governing creation and caring for it (Gen. 1:26–28)? It might seem that Israel's theology of kingship undermines its theology of the *imago Dei*, but the two are integrally connected. The fundamental, *relational* aspect of the *imago Dei* was not destroyed by sin, but the *functional* aspect of the *imago Dei* (what humans are called to do by virtue of their kinship with God) was thwarted. What was originally intended to be the role of all humanity was then particularized in the institution of the monarchy. Theologically, the king's crown was the same crown of humanity in the garden.

Given this link between kingship and the *imago Dei*, it is not surprising that Israel's human king would be called God's "son." Fictive (or adoptive) kinship is a reflection not only of the cultural norms but also of the theology

---

31. Roberts, "Enthronement of Yhwh and David," 679–80.

of the *imago Dei*. If the king is to take the functional role of the *imago Dei*, his kingship must be based on kinship with God. Psalm 2 illustrates this perfectly. In a divine oracle, God says, "I have set my king on Zion, my holy hill," and "you are my son; today I have begotten you" (vv. 6, 7b). Similarly, in 2 Samuel 7:14, God's promises to David regarding his royal heirs involve kinship: "I will be a father to him, and he shall be a son to me." This kinship made the king sacrosanct, so that an offense against the king was also an offense against God.[32] However, unlike the monarchs of some of their contemporaries, the king of Israel was never equated ontologically with God; the Creator-creature distinction was always maintained.[33] In fact, the Deuteronomistic History (Joshua–Kings) goes out of its way to highlight the flaws of Israel's leaders. Gerhard von Rad says of the portrayal of David, "There is no possibility of regarding him as an incarnation of the deity, as, say, the Egyptian mythology of the king does!"[34] Moreover, whereas divine legitimization of a king could lead to the abuse of power, Israel's view of divine legitimization of a king served, at least in theory, to safeguard *against* such abuse.[35]

This raises the question of whether human kingship was viewed positively or negatively. Some streams of Scripture seem to view kingship positively. As noted above, God promised Abraham and his descendants that kings would come from Abraham. The "job description" for a king in Deuteronomy 17:14–20 prescribes in neutral terms what a king should and should not do. Many of the psalms celebrate the king as God's just representative (e.g., Pss. 2; 21; 72; and 110).

Other parts of Scripture seem to view human kingship negatively. In Judges, kings are presented as foolish (like Eglon in Judg. 3) or wicked (like Abimelech in Judg. 9). Gideon's rejection of the people's offer of kingship in Judges 8:23 seems to suggest that the very institution of kingship would be a usurpation of God's kingship (a great irony considering that Gideon nonetheless lived like a king and led Israel into idolatry!). Similarly, when Israel asks Samuel for a king in 1 Samuel 8:6, "the thing displeased Samuel."

One way to understand the relationship between these two portrayals of kingship is to see the positive views of kingship as reflections of earlier views, and the negative views of kingship as reflections of later views from the perspective of the failed monarchy. Another interpretative option sees kingship as a concession to human weakness, a necessary evil in a broken world. However, a closer reading suggests that it was not the institution of kingship that was a problem but, rather, the hearts of the people. Instead of desiring a king who

---

32. Roberts, "Enthronement of Yhwh and David," 682.

33. Schmid, *Historical Theology*, 408. The deification of leaders is by no means restricted to the past. According to Annelle Sabanal, the divine status of the Japanese emperor was ritualized as recently as the 1990s. Sabanal, "Leadership, Power, and Authority," 87.

34. Von Rad, *Old Testament Theology*, 1:309.

35. Sabanal, "Leadership, Power, and Authority," 87.

would represent God, Israel wanted a king who would essentially replace God. This is made explicitly clear when God exposes Israel's motive for wanting a king ("They have rejected me from being king over them," 1 Sam. 8:7), and it is also made implicitly clear through the author's word choices. Jerry Hwang has persuasively shown how the author uses wordplay in 1 Samuel 8–12 to portray God's choice of Saul not as a concession but as poetic justice. God punishes the people by giving them what they ask for.[36] Hwang explains, "The theological coherence of poetic משפט [*mishpat*, "justice"] in structuring the narrative of 1 Samuel 8–12 thus problematizes any characterization of kingship as purely positive or negative, when it is irreducibly both within the divine economy."[37] At least two points of irony emerge: (1) God showcased his own sovereignty by using as the Israelite's punishment the type of human king that Israel requested, and (2) Israel's desire to replace God's kingship was met with the replacement of their requested king.

Administration of Justice

The primary means by which the king would represent God's rule was through his administration of justice. Since justice is a defining mark of divine kingship, as Psalm 82 makes clear, justice was also to be a defining mark of God's royal representatives.[38] What modern people of faith often call the consequences of sin ancients often described in terms of chaos, and just as God gave order to chaos at creation, so also his royal representative was to maintain the order of creation by administering justice.[39] Again, the king's crown was the *imago Dei* crown of the garden. Psalm 72, a psalm associated with Solomon, describes the connection between the king's kinship with God and his administration of God's justice:

> Give the king your justice, O God,
>   and your righteousness to a king's son.
> May he judge your people with righteousness,
>   and your poor with justice. (vv. 1–2)

---

36. Saul's very name means "the one asked for." Hwang, "Yahweh's Poetic *Mishpat* in Israel's Kingship," 351.

37. Hwang, "Yahweh's Poetic *Mishpat* in Israel's Kingship," 361. Robin Routledge also makes a case that the author shows Saul's usurpation of God's kingship by switching from the language of "ruler" to "king" once it is clear that Saul will serve not only as a representation of God's rule but also as a replacement. Routledge, *Old Testament Theology*, 230.

38. In the imaginative divine council scene of Ps. 82, the other so-called deities are demoted for their lack of justice (vv. 2, 7), leaving Israel's God to "judge the earth" and to "possess all the nations" (v. 8 NASB).

39. Roberts, "Enthronement of Yhwh and David," 681.

This ideal vision of the king's administration of justice is showcased in the beginning of Solomon's reign: "Solomon loved the LORD, walking in the statutes of his father David" (1 Kings 3:3). When given the opportunity to ask something from Yhwh, Solomon chose wisdom for the sake of governing his people (v. 9), and God was pleased (v. 10). Solomon proved his skill in justice in the infamous case of the two prostitutes and the living baby (vv. 16–28). However, the further Solomon strayed from Yhwh and his law, the further he also strayed from wisdom and justice, since both find their source in the divine king (see Ps. 72:1a above). By the end of his reign, Solomon's kingship was marked by folly and injustice, with rampant idolatry and forced labor echoing

Figure 7.3. *Josiah Hearing the Book of the Law*, 1873

the slavery that Israel had experienced in Egypt (1 Kings 9:15). The justice that marked the beginning of his reign was all but dissolved by his reign's conclusion.

Like the monarchs of their ancient Near Eastern neighbors, Israel's kings also demonstrated their divinely given justice and wisdom through their attention to the law. The differences, however, are most telling. Whereas kings like Hammurabi had a hand in formulating new law codes (or updating existing ones), God alone was the author of Israelite law. His representative king was to meditate on the law daily (Deut. 17:18–20) so that he would be able to enforce it with wisdom and justice; however, this expectation fell out of practice until Josiah's reforms (see fig. 7.3).

A final point of continuity and discontinuity regarding the king's administration of justice pertains to the special laws canceling debts and returning land to their owners. While the content of the laws—for example, when comparing the Akkadian *Mīšarum* to the Israelite Jubilee year—is similar, the implementation of the laws points to a key theological difference: The Jubilee year was tied not to the beginning of the human king's reign but to a prescribed time every fifty years, which places the credit entirely on the divine King, rather than giving credit to the human king. Again, the Israelite king's Edenic crown reflects the rule of his deity, but it does not replace it.

Service to the Cult

The king's service to the cult is seen in his occasional participation in priestly activities, such as when David wore the priestly ephod and offered sacrifices when bringing the ark of the covenant to Jerusalem (2 Sam. 6:13–14). Psalm 110 also reflects this theology when it ascribes to the Davidic king a priestly role as well. Since the king could not be from both the tribe of Judah (necessary for kingship in the Davidic dynasty) and the tribe of Levi (necessary for the Israelite priesthood), the king's priesthood is analogous to that of the priest-king figure of Melchizedek, who blessed Abram in Genesis 14:18–24.[40]

The prioritization of the temple was also a mark of a faithful king, whereas its desecration was the ultimate mark of apostasy. The high point in Solomon's career was arguably not when he asked for wisdom but when he built and dedicated the temple, whereas the most sinful kings brought idolatry into the house of God (Ezek. 5:11; 8:10).

All of this highlights the spiritual nature of the office of kingship, which Israel considered not a "secular" office but one deeply connected to the other offices of Israel and the spiritual well-being of the covenant people. In fact, the three offices of prophet, priest, and king served as checks and balances in Israelite leadership. When kings strayed from righteousness, the prophets were to call them back, as Nathan called back David after his sin against Bathsheba and Uriah (2 Sam. 12:1–12). Similarly, by meditating on God's law, kings were able to maintain proper worship or reform it when necessary.

The king's connection to the cult is also understandable, since the architecture and rituals of the tabernacle and temple all served to underscore Yhwh's role as the divine King. The sanctuary was constructed as a king's palace, with an inner throne room securely guarded and furnished with lavish settings, including a throne (the ark of the covenant). Those serving the temple dressed in attire that marked them as servants to the King, and the sacrifices offered to Yhwh were gifts—tribute—brought to the king. Even the Hebrew word *hekal* is used for both "palace" and "temple." Everything that Israel knew about the human king was only a shadow in comparison to

---

40. The complications of syntax, semantics, reception history, and interpretation regarding Ps. 110:4 are helpfully outlined in Levine and Brettler, *The Bible With and Without Jesus*, 154–77.

their divine King, and through his service to the sanctuary, the human king was also showing his subservience to the divine King.

Finally, as noted in chapter 5, the sanctuary also recalled the garden of Eden, reminding worshipers that the purpose of humanity was not only to govern creation as royalty but also to care for it as priests and priestesses. The king's responsibility to honor and uphold the cult reflected the royal/priestly vocation of the original image bearers in the garden.

Military Leadership

A king's military leadership might initially appear to be merely a pragmatic or even a negative feature of his office. After all, this role seems to be the primary reason for Israel's initial desire for a king. After watching their divine King fight their enemies with supernatural force for centuries, they still requested a human king to fight their battles. After they initially just asked Samuel for a king to govern them "like other nations" (1 Sam. 8:5), their real motivation surfaces when, after Samuel's warning, they repeat their request: "No! But we are determined to have a king over us, so that we also may be like other nations, and that our king may govern us and go out before us and fight our battles" (8:19b–20). They wanted a king who would not only represent God's military leadership but replace it in human form.

This, of course, is a distortion of the intended relationship between the divine warrior-king and the human warrior-king. Psalm 45 captures well the intended relationship. It is a song celebrating the human king's wedding and praising him for his handsomeness and his grace but especially for his military prowess, which is described entirely in terms of bringing justice and protection to those in need:

> In your majesty ride on victoriously
>> for the cause of truth and to defend the right;
>> let your right hand teach you dread deeds.
> Your arrows are sharp
>> in the heart of the king's enemies;
>> the peoples fall under you. (vv. 4–5)

Then again in verse 7:

> You love righteousness and hate wickedness.
> Therefore God, your God, has anointed you
>> with the oil of gladness beyond your companions.

The military role of the king was thus not for the sake of endless land-grabbing or accumulating wealth or power. Like his wisdom, the king's military power served as a means to uphold justice.

Moreover, in the verse sandwiched between those just cited, the poet highlights the king's representative role:

> Your divine throne is eternal and everlasting;
> The royal scepter is a scepter of justice. (Ps. 45:6 CEB)[41]

This representative role of the military leader helps to unpack the sometimes-uncomfortable description of Yhwh as a divine warrior. This metaphor represents not only ancient Near Eastern expectations of deity but also Israel's theology of warfare. This will be covered much more extensively in the chapter on warfare and peace, but in summary this role entailed the upholding of justice and the protection of the people, particularly the most vulnerable. Just as the original image bearers were to "guard" (*shamar*) the garden (Gen. 2:15 GNT), so also the king is charged to guard his nation, and this work is analogous to, but not to be conflated with, the work of Israel's divine warrior-king.

Democratization and Messianism

As Israel's faith waned and the Davidic dynasty was lost in 586 BCE, the Hebrew Bible writers emphasized Yhwh's kingship.[42] The editorial shape of the book of Psalms also highlights this development. Royal psalms centered on the human king in books I and II (Pss. 1–41; 42–72) make way—after the crisis of the destruction of Jerusalem and the fall of the Davidic dynasty described in book III (Pss. 73–89)—for the celebration of Yhwh as Israel's king, from eternity past to eternity future in books IV–V (Pss. 90–106; 107–50).[43] The

---

41. The NRSV translation of this verse follows the Hebrew syntax more closely, but it implies a shift from an address to the human king to an address to God ("Your throne, O God, is forever and ever"), which is unlikely, given that the entirety of the psalm is addressed to the human king, and elsewhere the human king's throne is identified with God's throne (2 Chron. 9:8) and described as being eternal (2 Sam. 7:13–16). While the reference to *'elohim* could be a direct address to the human king (so Villanueva, *Psalms 1–72*, 235; Kraus, *Psalms 1–59*, 451), it seems more likely that the line is elliptical, a common feature in Hebrew poetry (Longman, *Psalms*, 202; Goldingay, *Psalms*, 2:58; and VanGemeren, *Psalms*, 400). As we will see below, the New Testament writers read passages like this in light of Jesus, who not only *represented* divine rule, but also *incarnated* divine rule (Heb. 1:8).

42. This is ironic because the crisis of 586 BCE was due in no small part to the wayward leadership of Israel's human kings. Eichrodt explains: "Yahweh's title of King provided a shorthand *expression summing up the assurance of the prophetic faith*." Eichrodt, *Theology of the Old Testament*, 1:199.

43. This is the basic thrust of Gerald Wilson's groundbreaking thesis (titled *The Editing of the Hebrew Psalter*), and many Psalms scholars have followed suit. Some have rightfully pointed out a persisting Davidic presence even in the latter part of the book (e.g., Pss. 101; 110; 132; 138–45) that represents a developing messianic hope for a restored Davidic dynasty, but this voice is arguably much quieter than the one highlighting divine kingship. For an excellent survey of contemporary research on the topic, see Howard and Snearly, "Reading the Psalter as a Unified Book."

theology of Psalms essentially responds to the end of the human monarchy with a revived hope in the sufficiency of the divine monarchy.[44]

However, the idea of human kingship was not altogether abandoned. Instead, it was reconceived in two ways, one that looked back at Israel's theological past and one that looked forward into their theological future. When Israel looked back to creation, they once again democratized human kingship and saw that it applied to all humanity. Looking forward, the Israelites pushed their hopes for a representative king into the future in the form of an idealized "messianic" king. Both of these movements deserve attention.

The democratization of kingship has already been seen in Psalm 8, wherein the psalmist is in awe that humanity, even as small and fallen as they are, are still given the honor and responsibility of governing God's creation. Perhaps even more pronounced is the prophet Isaiah's extension of the Davidic covenant in Isaiah 55 to "everyone who thirsts" (v. 1). God will satisfy their thirst and hunger without cost (vv. 1–2), and he even makes this promise: "I will make with you [plural!] an everlasting covenant, / my steadfast, sure love for David" (v. 3). This promise echoes the language of the Davidic covenant in 2 Samuel 7:13–16. Gregory Goswell explains that it is particularly in prophetic texts that focus on the nations' subjugation to God and his people where this democratization features prominently: "In prophetic texts in which rule over the nations is a feature, there is no expectation of a revival of the once-great Davidic Empire. Instead, the memory of the historic imperial rule of the Davidic king is taken up and reapplied to the universal dominion of the Divine King, whose rule over the nations is exercised through nonroyal agents, sometimes by the people of God in general."[45] The functional role of the *imago Dei* and the promises made to David and his descendants were to be extended to all of God's people.[46]

Israel's hopes for the restoration of the Davidic dynasty after the exile were understandably met with disappointment. The prophets had promised a glorious new temple (Ezek. 40–47), but when the new temple's foundation was laid, praise for its completion was mixed with weeping from those who remembered the former temple's superior glory (Ezra 3:12–13). The prophets had also promised peace from their enemies (Isa. 11:6–9), but violent opposition persisted, even from within their own land (Ezra 4; Neh. 4; 6). Furthermore, the

---

44. We see this same theology in Lamentations, which laments the end of the Davidic reign ("The crown has fallen from our head; / woe to us, for we have sinned!," Lam. 5:16) but recognizes the enduring reign of God ("But you, O Lord, reign forever; / your throne endures to all generations," v. 19).

45. Goswell notes Isa. 11:10 as the only exception. Goswell, "What Happened to the Empire of David?," 160.

46. Roberts, "Enthronement of Yhwh and David," 684; Goswell, "What Happened to the Empire of David?," 148–50.

prophets had promised the restoration of the Davidic dynasty (Jer. 33:14–26), but Zerubbabel, though the governor of the postexilic community in Jerusalem and himself a descendent of David[47] (and even dubbed God's "servant," Hag. 2:23), was never independent from Persia's rule. In the words of Sigmund Mowinckel, the postexilic experience of restoration essentially "came to nothing," so that Israel's hopes were then pushed even further into the future and "messianism" developed.[48]

Though messianism grew and developed in the Second Temple period, its seeds were certainly planted in the Hebrew Bible. The term "messiah" referred to anyone "anointed" in some way, which included priests (Lev. 4:16), prophets (1 Kings 19:16), and especially kings—both Israelite (2 Sam. 1:14) and non-Israelite (Isa. 45:1). The term applied to many people who were chosen and set apart by God for a particular purpose. Even the designation "son of God"—used corporally of Israel (Exod. 4:22) but especially used for the adoptive father-son relationship between Yhwh and the king—took on an ontological reality in the New Testament and early church. So Jesus was understood not just relationally as God's son but also metaphysically as God's son.[49] This interpretation (correct on the level of Christian orthodoxy) could potentially miss or overshadow the royal connotations that the term would have communicated to its original hearers. As the Israelites' long-awaited messiah, Jesus was the royal "son" of the divine King, and by redeeming the functional aspect of the *imago Dei*, the final "anointed one" would restore the democratization of kingship.[50] Brothers and sisters, straighten your garden crowns.

---

47. On the historical questions and controversies surrounding Zerubbabel's identity and lineage, see Provan et al., *Biblical History of Israel*, 288–90.

48. Mowinckel, *He That Cometh*, 156.

49. Brueggemann, *Theology of the Old Testament*, 621. A similar move can be seen in the New Testament interpretation of Isa. 7:14 ("Therefore the Lord himself will give you a sign. Look, the young woman is with child and shall bear a son, and shall name him Immanuel"). Isaiah 7:14 uses the Hebrew word *almah* (young woman). This verse was originally understood as referring to the birth of a child to a young woman during the reign of King Ahaz, which would serve as a sign (or proof) that his political enemies would be defeated within a handful of years. When Matthew quoted from Isaiah, he used the Septuagint rendering of this verse, which uses the Greek word *parthenos*, a word that had come to mean "virgin" by the first century CE ("Look, the virgin shall conceive and bear a son, and they shall name him Emmanuel," Matt. 1:23). Mary was then understood to be a literal fulfillment of the "virgin" birth depicted in the Septuagint translation of Isa. 7:14, just as the designation "son of God," which originally had a metaphorical sense in the Hebrew Bible, was taken literally by the early church to refer to Jesus as the ontological son of God.

50. It should not be missed that the "crown" that the Roman soldier used to taunt Jesus was made of thorns—the very word used to describe what the cursed ground would produce after the first humans were deposed of their garden crowns (Matt. 27:29; Mark 15:17; John 19:2; cf. Gen. 3:18).

CONCLUSION

Many of the cultural expectations for kingship were also upheld in ancient Israel. The king was to represent the deity, administer justice to the people, serve the cult, and provide military leadership. The two aspects that distinguish Israelite kingship from Israel's cultural moorings were also integral to the theological developments that emerged after the dissolution of the Davidic dynasty. The link between kingship and the *imago Dei* naturally influenced the re-democratization of kingship, which was always intended to be the role of humanity. Also, the distinction between Israel's divine King and their (failed) human kings pushed expectations of a restored dynasty into the future and ultimately to a figure who could never fail, one who would take the epithet "son of God" to a new level.[51]

LOOKING BACK

1. What are the six characteristics of the ancient Near Eastern royal ideology?
2. What kind of leadership did Israel have before they had a king?
3. What do you consider to be the most significant distinctives of Israel's theology of kingship?
4. In your opinion, which kings of Judah or Israel were the best representatives of kingship? Which were some of the worst?
5. In what ways could Israel's theology of human kingship inform our own political contexts? In what ways should we be cautious *not* to apply Israel's theology of kingship to modern political contexts?

LOOKING BEYOND

Goswell, Gregory. "What Happened to the Empire of David?" *Restoration Quarterly* 63, no. 3 (2021): 148–50.

Hwang, Jerry. "Yahweh's Poetic *Mishpat* in Israel's Kingship: A Reassessment of 1 Samuel 8–12." *Westminster Theological Journal* 73 (2011): 341–61.

Levinson, Bernard. "The Reconceptualization of Kingship in Deuteronomy and the Deuteronomistic History's Transformation of Torah." *Vetus Testamentum* 51, no. 4 (2001): 511–34.

Lewis, C. S. *Mere Christianity*. HarperCollins, 2015.

---

51. N. T. Wright, *Jesus and the Victory of God*, 485–89, 648–51.

Matthews, Victor H., and Don C. Benjamin. *Social World of Ancient Israel: 1250–587 BCE*. Baker Academic, 2005.

Mowinckel, Sigmund. *He That Cometh*. Translated by G. W. Anderson. Abingdon, 1954 (esp. p. 156).

Sabanal, Annelle. "Leadership, Power, and Authority." In *Exploring the Old Testament in Asia: Evangelical Perspectives*, edited by Jerry Hwang and Angukali Rotokha, 81–100. Foundations in Asian Christian Thought. Langham, 2022.

8

LAW AND WISDOM
The Guidance of God

Apparently, people have been enjoying vinaigrettes for thousands of years, and it's no wonder why.[1] The fat of the oil and the acidity of vinegar are a perfect complement. At a molecular level, however, they are utterly incompatible, and no amount of shaking can permanently mix the two (one could use an emulsifier, but that would ruin the illustration). Given the way their layers separate, oil and vinegar are a perfect example of two things that appear to be at odds but actually work together quite effectively (or deliciously, as the case may be!).

Similarly, law and wisdom may not seem to have much in common. They are different types of literature originating and functioning in different arenas of society. But their overall goal is one and the same: living well in community and navigating the complexities of life. In ancient Israel, law and wisdom were seen as complementary, precious divine gifts and deeply formative, helping God's covenant people make the right choices in all aspects of life.

LOOKING DOWN

When engaging with ancient texts, it is important to always keep in mind the concept of genre. "Genre" can be defined as "a category of artistic, musical, or

---

1. "History of Salad Dressings."

literary composition characterized by a particular style, form, or content."[2] To illustrate what genre is, think about your favorite type of movies. Do you like science fiction? Romantic comedy? The list of genres seems limitless because there are many different *types* or *categories* of movies; the type of movie is its genre. Think about what you would expect to see if you were watching a movie whose genre is romantic comedy. There are common elements found in most, if not all, romantic comedy movies. Obviously, there is a meet-cute or "a cute, charming, or amusing first encounter between romantic partners (as in a movie)."[3] The meet-cute is typically followed by some sort of conflict that has the potential to keep the lovers apart. And who could forget the feisty but wise best friend (or parent, or child, etc.) who helps the lovers resolve their conflict? These are just some of the characteristics that make a romantic comedy film part of the romantic comedy genre.

The ancient Near Eastern world also had literary genres. Some of the most popular were narrative (a.k.a. story), poetry, law, wisdom, and prophetic oracles. As we've discussed, ancient Israel was part of the larger ancient Near Eastern world and, as such, had many things in common with their neighbors—including literary genres. The genres that are seen in the Hebrew Bible can also be found in the literature of Israel's neighbors. While there are similarities in form, style, or subject matter, societies adapted the existing genres to fit the circumstances of their own communities. Let's use the romantic comedy illustration again. The books of Jane Austen (the late eighteenth-century to early nineteenth-century British novelist) have been adapted into romantic comedy films. *Emma*, for instance, has been made into seven separate films, including a modern-day adaptation (*Clueless* in 1995). In a similar way, societies in the ancient Near East didn't copy and paste the content within these genres; rather, they adapted them to suit the particular nuances of their culture. An example would be that the hymns of praise (a popular genre) in Israel were sung and written to Yhwh, whereas in Babylon the hymns of praise would have been sung to Marduk (the supreme Babylonian god).

Two of the most popular genres in the ancient Near East are legal material and wisdom literature. This chapter will focus on both genres, summarizing how legal material and wisdom operated within the region, how ancient Israel's versions were similar or different, and how together these two genres aimed (each in their own way) to serve as a guide for living.

2. *Merriam-Webster Dictionary*, "genre," https://www.merriam-webster.com/dictionary/genre. Parts of this introduction are taken from Shafer-Elliott, "Literary Context of the Hebrew Bible" (used with permission of *The Bible for Normal People*).

3. *Merriam-Webster Dictionary*, "meet-cute," https://www.merriam-webster.com/dictionary/meet%20cute.

Legal Material

Tens of thousands of legal documents from all over the ancient Near East have been recovered within the last hundred years.[4] These legal sources can be categorized into two main groups: legal transactions and direct statements of the law. The first category is legal transaction, and most of the legal sources found fall into this group. These finds contain records of various types of legal transactions, including sales, loans, leases, marriages, adoptions, and litigation. Legal transactions are not technically laws themselves but, rather, indirect evidence of the law. In other words, they illustrate how the laws were (ideally) put into practice.[5] It would be like getting a speeding ticket today. The ticket wouldn't normally include the actual law but would indicate how the law was broken.

Direct statements make up the second category of legal sources and are by far the minority of material found. Direct statements include royal decrees and the so-called law codes.[6] The difference between the two statements is their scope: Royal decrees are narrow in scope, targeting limited issues that will immediately affect others—like the cancellation of debts—while law codes are wider in scope, relating to nearly all aspects of law.[7] As we saw in chapter 7, one of the six characteristics of the ancient Near Eastern royal ideology put forward by Bernard Levinson is how the monarch demonstrated their divinely given insight and ability through the formation of legal material. For instance, it was expected that a new monarch would initiate a law code at their coronation. While the monarch was new, the law code itself typically was not; rather, the law code the monarch proposed was more of an update to codes that were already in existence.[8]

Legal material is not only one of the most popular genres found in ancient Near Eastern literature but also one of the more abundant. Like all genres,

---

4. Westbrook and Wells, *Everyday Law in Biblical Israel*, 20.
5. Westbrook and Wells, *Everyday Law in Biblical Israel*, 22.
6. Westbrook and Wells, *Everyday Law in Biblical Israel*, 22. Some argue that the term "law code" is a misapplied name or designation because the legal material in question is neither comprehensive nor prescriptive, as the nature of a law code would designate. They would rather use the term "treatise" because the legal material is more of an instructive and educative model. See Bottéro, *Mesopotamia*, 156–84; Walton, *Ancient Near Eastern Thought*, 269–70.
7. Westbrook and Wells, *Everyday Law in Biblical Israel*, 22. According to Westbrook and Wells, thus far, seven significant law codes have been found in the ancient Near East: (1) the Laws of Ur-Namma, ca. 2100 BCE; (2) the Laws of Lipit-Ishtar, ca. 1900 BCE; (3) the Laws of Eshnunna, ca. 1800 BCE; (4) the Laws of Hammurabi, ca. 1750 BCE; (5) the Middle Assyrian Laws, ca. fourteenth century BCE; (6) the Neo-Babylonian Laws, ca. seventh century BCE; and (7) the Hittite Laws, sixteenth to twelfth centuries BCE (Westbrook and Wells, *Everyday Law in Biblical Israel*, 23). Furthermore, significant law codes have also been found in the Mediterranean basin of the mid-first millennium: (1) the Laws of Drakon, ca. seventh century BCE; (2) the Great Code of Gortyn, ca. fifth century BCE; and (3) the Twelve Tables, ca. 450 BCE (p. 25).
8. Levinson, "Reconceptualization of Kingship," 514–16.

law is adapted to fit the needs of its society and culture; however, the similarities of legal material from different societies throughout the ancient Near East is striking. Westbrook and Wells write that these affinities within legal material attest to "the same underlying principles [that] continued unchanged for millennia and occur all over the region . . . all this evidence points, at the very least, to a common legal tradition that was prevalent throughout the ancient Near East."[9] For instance, a universal legal principle within the region is that taking a sacred oath in the name of one's god (or gods) has a dual legal role: It creates contractual promises, and it can be used as affirming testimony in court. Likewise, the inheritance system of male heirs is universal; all sons inherit equally with a double portion given to the eldest son.[10]

Figure 8.1. Bas-relief on a stele showing Hammurabi receiving the law from the god Shamash

It is the law codes, however, that more fully illustrate the similarities of legal material within the region. Law codes have a common form in that the laws are formulated using a casuistic structure. Casuistry is a case-based method of reasoning that uses general principles from clear-cut cases and applies them to more problematic cases.[11] Casuistic laws (often called "if . . . then" laws) provide a hypothetical situation followed by its legal consequences. Cases like the hypothetical case are treated similarly. One example comes from the Law Code of Hammurabi. As we mentioned in chapter 7, Shamash appointed Hammurabi to initiate a lawbook (see fig. 8.1).[12] The laws cover a range of issues, including economic provisions, family law, criminal law, and civil law, with set fines and punishments that vary depending on the status of the offender and the circumstances of the offenses.[13] Scholars have long pointed

---

9. Westbrook and Wells, *Everyday Law in Biblical Israel*, 23.
10. Westbrook and Wells, *Everyday Law in Biblical Israel*, 23.
11. *Britannica*, "casuistry," https://www.britannica.com/topic/casuistry.
12. Meek, "Code of Hammurabi," 155.
13. *Britannica Academic*, "Code of Hammurabi," https://academic.eb.com/levels/collegiate/article/Code-of-Hammurabi/39076.

to the similarities between the Law Code of Hammurabi and Israel's covenant code in Exodus 20:22–23:19.[14] For instance, the laws regarding assault (21:12–14, 18–32), especially those related to miscarriage and talion (i.e., "eye for eye, tooth for tooth"), demonstrate the similarity between the two codes. One example of a casuistic law in Hammurabi's law code states, "If a son has struck his father, they shall cut off his hand."[15]

Law codes are similar in their casuistic structure but also in the content of the everyday laws contained within them. Cases regarding similar topics are also found in various law codes throughout the region and across time periods. While the facts and outcome may not be identical, the correlations between them concerning similar situations and universal principles are clear.[16]

To further demonstrate this point, we now turn to ancient Israel. The universal principles, analogous situations, and casuistic form found in the various law codes of the region are also found in the Hebrew Bible. The following are but a few examples out of many. First is a case from Exodus, followed by the similar cases found in the Law Code of Hammurabi and the Hittite Laws.

> When individuals quarrel and one strikes the other with a stone or fist so that the injured party, though not dead, is confined to bed, but recovers and walks around outside with the help of a staff, then the assailant shall be free of liability, except to pay for the loss of time, and to arrange for full recovery. (Exod. 21:18–19)

> If a seignior [man] has struck a(nother) seignior [man] in a brawl and has inflicted an injury on him, that seignior shall swear, "I did not strike him deliberately"; and he shall also pay for the physician. (Law Code of Hammurabi 206)[17]

> If anyone injures a person and temporarily incapacitates him, he shall provide medical care for him. In his place he shall provide a person to work on his estate until he recovers. When he recovers, his assailant shall pay him 6 shekels of silver and shall pay the physician's fee as well. (Hittite Law 10)[18]

As we can see in this example, while the details differ, the matter at hand is the same in all three cases—that of a man who has suffered a nonpermanent injury by another man in a fight. The man responsible for the injury is also liable to compensate the injured man for his loss of work and for medical expenses.

One further example comes from a case in Deuteronomy that has parallel cases in the Law Code of Eshnunna and the Law Code of Hammurabi.

---

14. D. Wright, "How Exodus Revises the Laws of Hammurabi."
15. Pritchard, *Ancient Near East*, 174.
16. Westbrook and Wells, *Everyday Law in Biblical Israel*, 24.
17. Quoted in Pritchard, *Ancient Near East*, 175.
18. Quoted in Roth, *Law Collections*, 218.

> If there is a young woman, a virgin already engaged to be married, and a man meets her in the town and lies with her, you shall bring both of them to the gate of that town and stone them to death, the young woman because she did not cry for help in the town and the man because he violated his neighbor's wife. So you shall purge the evil from your midst. But if the man meets the engaged woman in the open country, and the man seizes her and lies with her, then only the man who lay with her shall die. You shall do nothing to the young woman; the young woman has not committed an offense punishable by death, because this case is like that of someone who attacks and murders a neighbor. Since he found her in the open country, the engaged woman may have cried for help, but there was no one to rescue her. (Deut. 22:23–27)

> If a man gives bride-money for another man's daughter, but another man seizes her forcibly without asking permission of her father and her mother and deprives her of her virginity, it is a capital offence and he shall die. (Law Code of Eshnunna 26)[19]

> If a man bound the (betrothed) wife of another man, who had no intercourse with a male and was still living in her father's house, and he has lain in her bosom and they have caught him, that man shall be put to death, while that woman shall go free. (Law Code of Hammurabi 130)[20]

The above cases all deal with the rape of an engaged woman. Again, the overall pattern of the cases is similar with differences in some of the minor details; however, the case in Deuteronomy varies from the others in that it first addresses the issue of the location of the encounter between the man and the engaged woman, disqualifying the sexual encounter as rape if it occurred within the town.[21]

The above examples demonstrate that ancient Israel's law codes were clearly functioning within a larger genre popular throughout the ancient Near East. Universal principles, analogous situations, and the casuistic form were used throughout the region and across time periods. While the facts and outcome may not be identical, the correlations between them concerning similar situations and universal principles are clear.

Wisdom Literature

As we observed above, common principles and concerns can be seen within the various legal materials throughout the ancient Near East. Our next genre,

---

19. Quoted in Pritchard, *Ancient Near East*, 152.
20. Pritchard, *Ancient Near East*, 167.
21. For feminist interpretations of this problematic passage, see Newsom et al., *Women's Bible Commentary*, 52–62.

wisdom literature, similarly offers principles that serve as a guide for good living, but not in a legal sense. Instead, wisdom literature is a compilation reflecting how the pursuit of wisdom provides instructions for maintaining order in society.[22] Wisdom literature in the Hebrew Bible is complex in that it addresses many topics and does so in a variety of ways, but one thing unites them all—they are all composed in a poetic form.[23] Gerhard von Rad writes that "poetic expression was itself rather a specific form of the perception of truth, among ancient peoples one of the most important."[24] The poetic perception that is wisdom literature can be categorized into two basic forms: practical wisdom and philosophical wisdom. While this may be oversimplifying it, these categorizations can help illustrate two of the main functions of wisdom literature.

Practical wisdom is concerned with the practical aspects of life—hence the name. In this sense, wisdom comes in the form of a compilation of wise sayings that are directive for a successful life. A successful life is one where a person is a participating member of their household, clan, tribe, and kingdom. Within the Hebrew Bible, practical wisdom can be found most prominently in the book of Proverbs, which has its closest ancient Near Eastern relation in the Egyptian Instruction of Amen-em-Opet. Proverbs 22:17–24:22 is particularly similar to the Instruction of Amen-em-Opet, as we can see from the example below, which implores the audience to listen to the wise words of the author.

> The words of the wise:
>
> Incline your ear and hear my words,
>   and apply your mind to my teaching;
> for it will be pleasant if you keep them within you,
>   if all of them are ready on your lips.
> So that your trust may be in the Lord,
>   I have made them known to you today—yes, to you. (Prov. 22:17–19)
>
> He Says:
>
> Give thy ears, hear what is said,
> Give thy heart to understand them.
> To put them in thy heart is worth while,
> (But) it is damaging to him who neglects them.
> Let them rest in the casket of thy belly,
> That they may be a key in thy heart.

---

22. Walton, *Ancient Near Eastern Thought*, 279.
23. Von Rad, *Wisdom in Israel*, 24.
24. Von Rad, *Wisdom in Israel*, 24.

> At a time when there is a whirlwind of words,
> They shall be a mooring-stake for thy tongue.
> If thou spendest thy time while this is in thy heart,
> Thou wilt find it a success;
> Thou wilt find my words a treasury of life,
> And thy body will prosper upon earth. (Instruction of Amen-em-Opet, chap. 1).[25]

The appeal to listen to wise words is partnered with how the application of the wisdom provided will result in a prosperous and successful life. Further examples provide more practical words of advice and instruction on a variety of topics, including gossip.

> Sit down at the hands of the god,
> And the silence will cast them down. (Prov. 20:22; 27:1)

> Spread not thy words to the common people,
> Nor associate to thyself one (too) outgoing of heart. (Prov. 20:19; 23:9)

> Better is a man whose talk (remains) in his belly
> Than he who speaks it out injuriously. (Prov. 12:23)[26]

The illustrations of practical wisdom provided by the examples above are but a small sample of those available to us. The sample expands even more when we take into consideration analogous examples from the second category of wisdom literature, that of philosophical wisdom. If practical wisdom is all about pragmatic and sage advice on how to be a successful member of one's community, then philosophical wisdom addresses the bigger picture. Philosophical wisdom is concerned with the big questions, those that are more reflective and deal with the abstruse, such as, Why is there suffering and injustice in the world? Why do bad things happen to good people? It makes sense that philosophical wisdom investigates what is called "theodicy." In general, this term describes any attempt to render suffering and evil intelligible.[27] However, in an ancient world that revolves around appeasing the deities and humanity's relationship to them, theodicy can be refined to what John Walton describes as "questioning the justice of the deity in the context of suffering: the problem of evil."[28] Ancient societies tried to make sense of

---

25. Quoted in Pritchard, *Ancient Near East*, 346.
26. Quoted in Pritchard, *Ancient Near East*, 351.
27. Weber, *Gesammelte Aufsätze*; Laato and de Moor, introduction to *Theodicy in the World of the Bible*.
28. Walton, *Ancient Near Eastern Thought*, 284.

theodicy in several ways: They hypothesized (1) that suffering was a result of a competition between the gods in the divine realm, which makes its way into the human realm; (2) that the deities are not powerful enough to manage the problem of evil; (3) that the divine realm is not just at all; and (4) that a deity has been offended in some way, with the offender having little knowledge of what their offense may have been.[29]

As we discussed in chapter 5, one of the more significant reasons to worship one's deity/deities is to appease them so that they will bring their order, which includes blessings, to the society, household, or person in question. This line of thinking also means that the inverse would be true as well: If the deity/deities were not appeased, then they would bring anger upon the society, household, or person in question. This is what scholars call "retribution"—blessings or suffering caused by the gods as a direct result of a person's action or inaction. If a deity was offended, appeasement could only occur when the offender sought to do so with the appropriate sacrifice; this could be a difficult task, since the offender often had little knowledge of what caused the offense and therefore what the appropriate level of appeasement would be.

The Hittite text of the Plague Prayers of Muršili II reflects such a situation. In it, King Muršili is at a loss for why a severe plague ravaged his kingdom over several decades. The king thinks he has done nothing to deserve this. He states, "When I celebrated festivals, I worshiped all the gods: I never proffered one temple over another."[30] Seeking guidance through divination, King Muršili learns that the gods are angry because of offenses in the heavenly realm and through treaty violations by his father in the earthly realm. Muršili engages in a variety of acts of appeasement (prayers, sacrifices, and confessions) to remedy the situation.[31]

The most well-known example of this kind of philosophical wisdom in the Hebrew Bible is the book of Job. The genre of the book of Job is better known throughout the ancient Near East as "the Righteous Sufferer." This genre reflects on the larger question of theodicy. To frame the question of theodicy in contemporary context, the book of Job asks, Why do bad things happen to good people? One way ancient Israel, like its neighbors, tried to understand its world and its gods was through the idea that obeying/appeasing the deity/deities would lead to blessing, while disobeying/offending the deity/deities would lead to curses or other consequences. Hence, when bad things happened, one assumed it was because one had disobeyed/offended the gods in some way. When Job's world falls apart, he is in shock because it

---

29. Walton, *Ancient Near Eastern Thought*, 284–86.
30. Hoffner, "Theodicy in Hittite Texts," 100.
31. Hoffner, "Theodicy in Hittite Texts," 100–101; Walton, *Ancient Near Eastern Thought*, 287.

doesn't fit within this worldview—he is a righteous man and has done nothing to offend God. Job's friends urge him to put aside his pride and appease God with blanket confessions to restore himself to God's favor—as one does in the ancient Near East. But Job refuses; instead, he maintains his integrity by insisting that his righteousness be taken into consideration. John Walton argues that Job does this for righteousness' sake, not simply to earn a reward.[32]

> If I have walked with falsehood,
>   and my foot has hurried to deceit—
> let me be weighed in a just balance,
>   and let God know my integrity!—
> if my step has turned aside from the way,
>   and my heart has followed my eyes,
>   and if any spot has clung to my hands,
> then let me sow and another eat,
>   and let what grows for me be rooted out. (Job 31:5–8)

If Walton is correct in his interpretation, then we can see how Israel's view of theodicy is slightly modified from that of its neighbors. Walton argues that this modification "seeks to reinterpret the justice of God. . . . The inference to be drawn from this is that if it is determined that God is wise, then it can be accepted that he is just, even if not all the information to evaluate his justice is available."[33] In this instance, then, philosophical wisdom is used to question and equate the justice of the divine with the wisdom of the divine.

Summary

The ancient Near Eastern world was not an individualistic society; a person was viewed as part of their kinship groups: their household, their clan, their tribe, and to some degree their kingdom. For those various kinship groups to survive and perhaps thrive in an often inhospitable environment, the participation of each member was essential. How one became a successful, participating member of society was seen not only in the daily household tasks that needed to be performed but also in the accepted institutional norms that are evident within the legal material and wisdom literature of their culture. As we have seen here, both legal material and wisdom literature provide insight into how ancient Israel functioned as a society within and outside of its neighborly commonalities.

---

32. Walton, *Ancient Near Eastern Thought*, 288.
33. Walton, *Ancient Near Eastern Thought*, 288; see also Walton and Hill, *Old Testament Today*, 306–12.

LOOKING UP

In the second creation account in Genesis, the author provides a close-up description of the natural world God has made, including a river, which flows from Eden and then separates into four headwaters or distributaries that go forth from God's special presence in the garden to water the world (Gen. 2:10). This is an apt image for how we can understand the theological relationship between law and wisdom for ancient Israel.[34] Like the distributaries, which have their source in God's presence and move out to all areas of the world bringing nourishment and flourishing, so also law and wisdom come directly from God in order to nourish all aspects of life.

Like separate rivers from the same source, law and wisdom have similar functions but work (for the most part) within different contexts, so there is naturally overlap and distinction between the two. Since wisdom is the foundational concept, we will look at its theological "currents" first.

Theological Currents of Israelite Wisdom

WISDOM AS A GENRE AND A CONCEPT

Though most modern scholars have not entirely abandoned the identification of a "wisdom" genre, there is increasing recognition that genre is a more fluid category than previously realized, with many genres overlapping and some texts exhibiting features of several genres at once.[35] To use the above example of romantic comedies and science fiction, both are distinct genres, and yet both have important overlaps in theme and even function. (As my husband well knows, I watch action movies for the romance and drama, not for the violent bloodbaths.)

There is little disagreement, however, over the prevalence of the *concept* of wisdom throughout the Hebrew Bible. Let's consider first how the Hebrew Bible describes wisdom, and then how it is exemplified (or not exemplified). Wisdom can be understood as "intelligence and skill in godly living."[36] As is clear from that definition, wisdom is not merely a cerebral exercise, but

---

34. Sirach 24:23–27 also describes the law as overflowing with wisdom like these rivers overflow with water. Joseph Blenkinsopp uses similar imagery of two diverging streams from a single source in his landmark study *Wisdom and Law in the Old Testament*.

35. Will Kynes has written the strongest arguments against identifying wisdom as a genre (see, for example, "Genre as Reception" and *Obituary for "Wisdom Literature"*). Katherine Dell and Michael Fox take more modified positions (Dell, "Deciding the Boundaries of 'Wisdom'"; Fox, "Three Theses on Wisdom"). Andrew Judd's chapter on wisdom in his book *Modern Genre Theory* (pp. 175–201) is the clearest discussion I have read on the topic.

36. Similar definitions include that of Gordon D. Fee and Douglas Stuart, who define wisdom as "the ability to make godly choices in life" (*How to Read the Bible for All Its Worth*, 233), or of William P. Brown, who writes, "Wisdom is the art of living fully, acting justly, and venturing forth reverently." Brown, *Wisdom's Wonder*, 26.

practical, ethical, and theological as well.[37] It is practical because it is lived out in all aspects of life—family, vocation, conflicts, and so on. It is ethical in that it pertains to habits of character formation. And it is theological due to its divine source and purpose.

The theological component is often described using the expression "the fear of the Lord," which describes humanity's response to God, including humble awe and trust. This aspect of wisdom was foundational for the other facets of Israel's wisdom. James Crenshaw observes its import for ethics: "The fear of Yahweh functioned as the compass point from which [the Israelites] took moral readings."[38] Von Rad describes its import for other ways of knowing, explaining that faith, or the theological component of wisdom, "does not—as is popularly believed today—hinder knowledge; on the contrary, it is what liberates knowledge."[39]

Wisdom saturates the pages of Scripture and the lives of God's people. It is found first and foremost in God himself. Job 28 recounts the ways that humanity is skilled in finding all varieties of treasures hidden deep within the earth, but wisdom, the most valuable treasure of all, cannot be found even by the greatest explorer. It is found in the Lord himself and in humanity's "fear of the Lord."[40] Proverbs 8 personifies wisdom as a woman, predating creation itself and delighting in God and his creation.

Adam and Eve had access to this divine wisdom but chose instead a different kind of wisdom. In Genesis 3:1, the serpent is described as "crafty" (*'arum*), a word also used positively of the prudent and wise (e.g., Prov. 12:16, 23; 14:8, 15, 18). The serpent represents what Joseph Blenkinsopp calls "lethal wisdom," which is based solely on "human resources and autonomous reason."[41] It is, for all intents and purposes, folly. Wisdom based solely on one's own resources—especially when gained through deception and disobedience—is a poor substitute for godly wisdom, and the story moves quickly downhill from there.

Solomon is famous for his wisdom, but he also exemplifies folly, and both hinged on his relationship with Yhwh. When he humbled himself before Yhwh as the source of wisdom and the object of his trust and worship, he

---

37. Longman argues that biblical wisdom, particularly its practical aspect, is much more akin to EQ (emotional intelligence) than to IQ (raw intelligence), and it is more concerned with the "knowing how" than just "knowing that." Longman, *Fear of the Lord*, 7.

38. Crenshaw, *Old Testament Wisdom*, 12.

39. Von Rad, *Wisdom in Israel*, 67. Proverbs 1:1–7 serves as the prologue of the book and highlights each of these three facets of wisdom. See Backfish, "Biblical Wisdom as a Model."

40. At a theological level, this is true, but with respect to genre, Longman points out that one difference between law and wisdom is that law comes directly from God, whereas wisdom comes from humanity. Longman, *Fear of the Lord*, 170.

41. Blenkinsopp, *Wisdom and Law in the Old Testament*, 8.

Figure 8.2. *The Judgement of Solomon* by Gustave Doré, 1866. Solomon demonstrated wisdom in 1 Kings 3 when two mothers came to him, both claiming to be the mother of a surviving child.

was blessed with true wisdom; when he turned to other gods, his wisdom quickly turned to folly, causing the dissolution of his kingdom.[42]

Two exemplars of godly wisdom in contexts of alternative wisdom are Joseph and Daniel. Both interpret a king's dreams, and both are clear that

---

42. While Solomon's son, Rehoboam, may have directly caused the split of the northern and southern kingdoms through the harsh treatment of his people, the primary cause was Solomon's apostasy (1 Kings 11:11–13).

their wisdom comes not from their own skills but from God himself. Joseph tells Pharaoh, "It is not I; God will give Pharaoh a favorable answer" (Gen. 41:16). Daniel, likewise, when asked if he can interpret King Nebuchadnezzar's dream, replies, "No wise men, enchanters, magicians, or diviners can show to the king the mystery that the king is asking, but there is a God in heaven who reveals mysteries" (Dan. 2:27–28a). Where Adam and Eve failed to rely on God's wisdom, and where Solomon failed to maintain reliance on God's wisdom, Joseph and Daniel (and many others) exemplify true and resilient wisdom, the foundation of which is trust, or "fear," of the Lord as the source of wisdom.

Since wisdom finds its source in God, it is not limited to the elite or the credentialed. It is offered to the young, the old, the royalty, and the commoner. Just as the *imago Dei* and kingship were meant to be democratized in Israelite theology, so also was wisdom to be sought and fostered by all. The book of Proverbs emphasizes this point, punctuating it with the "valiant woman" in its concluding chapter. Craig Bartholomew and Ryan O'Dowd explain, "The striking image of the valiant woman of wisdom in Proverbs 31 undermines the male and regal associations of wisdom in most ancient cultures. Because wisdom's source is Yahweh, it is freely available to all of his people, male and female, rich and poor."[43] Indeed, we could even say that wisdom is part and parcel of the image of God: By virtue of their kinship with God and vocational calling to govern and care for his creation, all humanity has the responsibility and privilege of attaining wisdom as part of their job description.

Wisdom as Practical and Philosophical

Like that of their ancient Near Eastern neighbors, Israel's wisdom was seen as both practical and philosophical, but in distinction to Israel's contemporaries, both types of wisdom in the Hebrew Bible were expressly theological.

For example, while the pragmatism of the individual proverbs sounds very similar in content and tone to the terse wisdom sayings found elsewhere in ancient Near Eastern literature, for Israel they were contextualized in their covenant relationship with Yhwh. This is why the expression "the fear of the Lord" is used as a refrain throughout Proverbs[44]—to make clear that the wisdom they are to pursue, even in their observation of nature and economics and the seemingly more "secular" corners of life, is to be pursued in a trusting, humble relationship with God. All aspects of life fell within the purview

---

43. Bartholomew and O'Dowd, *Old Testament Wisdom*, 270.
44. Proverbs 1:7, 29; 2:5; 3:7; 8:13; 9:10; 10:27; 14:26, 27; 15:16, 33; 16:6; 19:23; 22:4; 23:17; 29:25.

of God's wisdom, just as all aspects of their lives, from eating to dressing to bathing, fell under the purview of God's holiness.[45]

Practical wisdom—as in the proverbial sayings in Proverbs 10–30 but also in places like Psalm 37—also requires wisdom for sound application. This wisdom is circumstantial and not true in every circumstance, so one must consider how and when to apply each saying. Proverbs 26:4–5 is a classic example:

> Do not answer fools according to their folly,
>   or you will be a fool yourself. (v. 4)
>
> Answer fools according to their folly,
>   or they will be wise in their own eyes. (v. 5)

These two adjacent proverbs are both true in different circumstances, but one must use wisdom to discern when to ignore folly and when to respond to it.[46]

The philosophical wisdom exemplified in books like Job and Ecclesiastes, and also in places such as Psalm 73 and Habakkuk, explores realities outside of the typical paradigms of practical wisdom. How does a person of faith grapple with suffering or death or the purpose of it all? If practical wisdom explores the well-charted trails of Israel's theology, philosophical wisdom bushwhacks through the dense underbrush to explore new territory and ask questions without easy answers. Through this kind of wisdom, readers recognize the limits of human understanding and learn to cope with their current reality, whatever that may be.[47] The experience is at once humbling, maturing, and calming.

This type of wisdom also requires wisdom as much as it offers it. Discernment is particularly required for distinguishing godly wisdom from its alternative. Job's friends, for example, seem to offer orthodox wisdom, but upon closer inspection, they are misinterpreting and misapplying theological truths. Let's just consider Eliphaz's initial charges against Job. Yes, it's true that mortals cannot be more righteous than God (Job 4:17), but Job is not suffering for a lack of righteousness. Yes, it's true that discipline from the Lord should be welcome (5:17), but that is not what is happening in Job's case. And, yes, innocence typically yields blessing and evildoing typically yields suffering (the "retribution principle"), but that does not mean that the inverse is also true, that everyone who suffers does so because of evildoing or that everyone who is blessed must have done something upright (4:7–8). The

---

45. Blenkinsopp, *Wisdom and Law in the Old Testament*, 132.
46. Longman sees this as a major distinction between wisdom and law, that wisdom is circumstantially true whereas law is always true (*Fear of the Lord*, 170–71). As our discussion of law below will make clear, I believe that there are aspects of law that are also circumstantial.
47. Crenshaw, *Old Testament Wisdom*, 184.

book of Job thus juxtaposes two types of wisdom: godly wisdom, which is based on faithfulness and trust even in uncertain, trying circumstances, and anti-wisdom, which is based on a misconstrued theology.

So if Job's friends offer bad wisdom in an attempt to explain his suffering, how does biblical wisdom address the issue of theodicy? We noted above that ancient societies attributed the existence of evil and suffering to conflict between the gods, their lack of power or sense of justice, or retribution for offense. Within biblical wisdom, suffering—like everything else—is tied directly to the covenant. When confronted with suffering and injustice, Israel was encouraged to push in closer to God, closer to his holy presence, the source of wisdom. We see this in Job as he brings his complaints and accusations directly to God. We see this in Psalm 73, when the psalmist is anguished over the prosperity of the wicked (v. 3) and the affliction of the innocent (vv. 13–14), when all along he has been taught that "truly God is good to the upright, to those who are pure in heart" (v. 1). It is not until the psalmist presses in to God's presence and enters his holy space that he is able to see things clearly, with wisdom: "But when I thought how to understand this, it seemed to me a wearisome task *until I went into the sanctuary of God*; then I perceived their end" (vv. 16–17). God is the source of wisdom, and the covenant is the context for gaining wisdom.

Theological Currents of Israelite Law

Covenant is also the context for understanding the law, another "distributary" serving as a guide for living well. Whereas wisdom was primarily within the domain of the household or even the individual, law was the form that godly instruction took at the societal level (clan, tribe, and kingdom).[48] It is no wonder that the prophets, as Israel's covenant enforcers, were particularly concerned with the law, consistently reminding Israel's kings and people of God's expectations for them, their failings, and the ensuing consequences.

Whereas ancient Near Eastern laws were written (or updated) by an ascending monarch in order to demonstrate their divinely given wisdom, the Hebrew Bible illustrates that Israelite law was given directly by the deity to demonstrate Yhwh's inherent wisdom. No Israelite, monarch or otherwise, would be able to claim this level of wisdom or insight. The theological dimension of Old Testament law is also highlighted in the structure and language of the law. As noted in chapter 2, the law served as the stipulations of the covenant, the means by which Israel would enjoy the blessings of the covenant . . . or not. Deuteronomy is particularly clear on this point by punctuating laws with the consequence of breaking them: "So you shall purge the evil from

---

48. Crenshaw, *Old Testament Wisdom*, 3.

your midst."⁴⁹ God is holy, and that which threatened to profane his holiness would be purged from the covenant community.

The law was also contextualized in Israel's historical relationship with Yhwh. Exodus 20:2 introduces the Decalogue by reminding Israel that Yhwh saved them: "I am the LORD your God, who brought you out of the land of Egypt, out of the house of slavery."⁵⁰ Following God's instructions is the right response to liberating grace, and it is the right response specifically for Israel. In other words, these were instructions intended for God's covenant people in order to live within his covenant community and keep them distinct and holy as God's "treasured possession" (Exod. 19:5). Carmen Imes helpfully describes the law as the "house rules" of Yhwh's household, saying, "They are not the main thing, but rather the backdrop for the main thing, the loving relationship."⁵¹ There is no indication in Scripture that those outside of Israel were held to the 613 laws given at Sinai. When the nations are called out, they are never accused of breaking the Sinai laws but, rather, the general, natural law—that of basic decency and justice.⁵²

While the laws given at Sinai were not intended to be binding on other nations, they were intended to be a witness of God's grace and justice to other nations. When the nations heard about the wise and just laws of the Israelites, they would be drawn to the divine Lawgiver (Deut. 4:5–8). Israel's obedience to the law was also an opportunity to express their love for Yhwh, a means to tangibly show their allegiance to their God. It was never enough to love God with their words or with their intellect alone; they were called to love God with all of their heart, soul, and might (6:5).⁵³

So, the law was given to Israel as part of their covenant relationship, to guide them in right living, to provide for Israel a way to show their allegiance to God, and to be a witness to the nations. It is also noteworthy to remember what the law was *not* intended to do for Israel. First, it was *not* intended to serve as a means of salvation. Julius Wellhausen once called the law "a petty scheme of salvation,"⁵⁴ but Israel had already been delivered from Egypt by the time that they received the law, and Moses was emphatic that the next stage in their deliverance (their inheritance of the land) was likewise not due to their own righteousness (Deut. 9:4–6).⁵⁵ Nor was the law to be seen as a burden that was unattainable. Indeed,

---

49. See this and similar expressions in Deut. 13:5; 17:7, 12; 19:13, 19; 21:9, 21; 22:21, 22, 24; 24:7.

50. Carmen Imes even identifies the giving of the law as the literary climax of the Torah. Imes, *Bearing God's Name*, 14–16; cf. Lynch, *Flood and Fury*, 169.

51. Imes, *Bearing God's Name*, 38.

52. Routledge, *Old Testament Theology*, 247–48; Imes, *Bearing God's Name*, 44. This is also probably the law that Paul refers to the nations keeping in Rom. 2:14–15.

53. Levenson, *Love of God*.

54. Wellhausen, *Prolegomena*, 509.

55. In this passage, Moses states three times in as many verses that Israel would not be occupying the land "because of [their] righteousness." Rather, it is because of the wickedness

Moses told the Israelites that the law was "not too hard for [them], nor is it too far away" (30:11). No, the law was intended to be a joy, a delight, and even an expression of freedom, as Psalm 119 proclaims with full force.[56]

Second, the law was *not* intended to function like modern Western legislation. Walton and Walton argue that "prescriptive, codified legislation . . . did not exist in the ancient world."[57] According to Michael LeFebvre, Israel's "law instructions" came to be understood as "law codes" in the Hellenistic era with the law court system of Ptolemy II (284–246 BCE).[58] The term "law" (*torah*) is better understood as "instruction," and the form, language, and function of these instructions are all actually more akin to wisdom than what we consider prescriptive, universal legislation.

The identification of law as wisdom is not a new recognition. The Second Temple book Baruch praises Lady Wisdom and then says this about her: "She [wisdom] is the book of the commandments of God, the law that endures forever" (4:1).[59] The form of casuistic or case laws ("If . . . , then . . .") recalls proverbial sayings, and the apodictic instructions, such as the Decalogue, recall wisdom instruction; thus the two forms of law somewhat parallel the two forms of wisdom.[60] Moreover, the language used to encourage attention to the law is the language of "heeding," "recalling the past," and "meditating," language that evokes wisdom instruction.[61]

Of course, obedience was expected, but learning was primary.[62] Israel was to learn God's will from the law so that they could make wise choices in all aspects of life, even those aspects of life that were not directly mentioned in the law, since the law itself was not exhaustive but, rather, a "representative list."[63] This original function of law instruction also explains why laws seem to be rarely or inconsistently enforced, as well as why laws were continually reapplied in different ways according to Israel's changing circumstances, which brings us to the third misconstrual of the law.

---

of the nations, as God had foretold and promised to Abraham, Isaac, and Jacob (Deut. 9:5; cf. Gen. 15:16).

56. Imes, *Bearing God's Name*, 33.

57. Walton and Walton, *Lost World of the Torah*, 22.

58. This is argued over and against those who place the legislative use of the law back in the time of Ezra or even Josiah. LeFebvre, *Collections, Codes, and Torah*, 259.

59. Blenkinsopp, *Wisdom and Law in the Old Testament*, 168.

60. Blenkinsopp, *Wisdom and Law in the Old Testament*, 102.

61. Blenkinsopp, *Wisdom and Law in the Old Testament*, 118; Walton and Walton, *Lost World of the Torah*, 22, 42.

62. Walton and Walton go so far as to say that "the intention of the Torah is to produce knowledge, not obedience" and that there is no "ought" in biblical law, nor was the law intended to reflect divine character. They understand Paul's statements in 1 Cor. 6:12 and 10:23 as support ("'I have the right to do anything' you say—but not everything is beneficial" [NIV]). Walton and Walton, *Lost World of the Torah*, 162.

63. Walton and Walton, *Lost World of the Torah*, 44.

The law was *not* intended to function as the final word of God's moral revelation. Like a river flowing over a diverse terrain of swift rapids, dramatic waterfalls, or calm eddies, the law was able to change and conform to Israel's changes in circumstances. For the most part, the law given at Sinai was not a radically new instruction but, rather, a recontextualization given to Israel in this new phase of their lives as a nation. They had already been instructed on matters like worship (Gen. 17:1), sanctity of life (9:6), and Sabbath observance (Exod. 16:23), but at Sinai those instructions were elaborated on and recorded. As another example, Exodus 20:24–25 assumes that animal sacrifice could be practiced in various places, whereas Deuteronomy 12:5–14 (representing Israel's situation forty years later) restricts animal sacrifice to the central sanctuary.[64] Wisdom was required to reapply the law to Israel's changing or unique circumstances.[65] The *halakah* (rabbinic legal texts) were one way that devout Jews sought to continually apply the law in all circumstances.[66]

Similarly, many laws were given to address existing cultural norms but certainly not to condone those norms. For example, laws regulating slavery were regulating an existing (and lamentable) reality in the ancient Near East; they were not blanket endorsements.[67] Similarly, Jesus makes this point about divorce when the Pharisees ask him why Moses permitted divorce. Jesus replied, "It was because you were so hard-hearted that Moses allowed you to divorce your wives, but from the beginning it was not so" (Matt. 19:8). The law met Israel where they were but not where they ultimately needed to be. Looking at the redemptive story of the Bible as a whole, we see what William Webb refers to as a "redemptive movement hermeneutic," or a progressive infusion of grace and equality as the redemptive story unfolds, the trajectory of which should be continued in our own day.[68]

Theological Currents of Wisdom and Law Today

If Israelite law was seen primarily as instruction, and if it was given to Israel for a specific time and place, then what is its enduring relevance for Jews and Christians today? Older theological systems within Christianity identified a

---

64. Blenkinsopp, *Wisdom and Law in the Old Testament*, 87.
65. In the case of Zelophehad's daughters, Israel seems to have followed the common practice of passing inheritance down to male heirs (with the firstborn receiving a double portion: Deut. 21:15–17). When Zelophehad dies, leaving behind no sons to inherit his name and land, his daughters appeal to Moses to allow for daughters to also inherit. Moses consults God, who emphatically sides with the women, and the prevailing laws and customs are adapted to new circumstances (see Num. 26:33 for their inclusion in the otherwise male-dominated list of descendants, as well as the fulfillment of their request in Josh. 17:3–4). Wenham, *Numbers*, 192.
66. Blenkinsopp, *Wisdom and Law in the Old Testament*, 168.
67. Esau McCaulley offers a helpful discussion of this topic in *Reading While Black*, 137–63.
68. Webb, *Slaves, Women, and Homosexuals*, 30–31.

threefold division in the law: (1) the ceremonial law, which Christians maintain is now fulfilled in Christ and no longer necessary to keep; (2) the civil law, which was particular to Israel as a theocracy and thus no longer necessary in the church age; and (3) the moral law, summarized in the Decalogue and still applicable today (though Christians disagree over how the Sabbath law is to be applied). However, there is not always such a clear division between these parts, and even the laws that fall outside the category of "moral law" surely have much to teach us. A second interpretative option is to see all of the law as applicable in some way but to look for the spiritual principle of each law and then to apply it in a contextually appropriate way today. For example, the gleaning laws that forbade land owners from fully harvesting their crops so that the poor, widowed, and immigrants could glean (Lev. 19:9–10; Deut. 24:21) should encourage all people to ensure that the poor and marginalized are well cared for.

Viewing law as wisdom instruction at the societal level offers another helpful way of appreciating its modern-day relevance. Just as the person seeking wisdom from wisdom sayings would first reflect on them before determining which to apply in a given circumstance, so also the person (for example, the king) would first reflect on the law to gain wisdom in knowing how to rightly apply it. After all, if the law could be so easily applied apart from wisdom, Solomon would not have needed to ask for wisdom to administer justice (1 Kings 3:9). In Deuteronomy 17, which serves as the "job description" of the king, the king is charged to read the law "all the days of his life" (v. 19). Such reflection would guide his obedience of the law, as manifested in his love for Yhwh ("so that he may learn to fear the Lord his God," v. 19) and his love for neighbor (not "exalting himself above other members of the community," v. 20). The common person was similarly exhorted to "meditate day and night" on the law (Ps. 1:2) so that they could yield the fruit of righteousness (v. 3). Reflection yields informed faithfulness.

CONCLUSION

By examining the cultural and theological currents of these two parallel rivers of wisdom and law, we have seen that, in ancient Israel, both find their origin in Yhwh; both are intended to guide holy, wise, and just living within the covenant community; and both require careful reflection prior to application. While wisdom was primarily located within the realm of the household, law instruction was primarily found in the realm of the tribe, clan, or kingdom. Whereas wisdom, particularly philosophical wisdom, models faithful wrestling with the complexities of life (such as suffering, injustice, and death), law requires a recognition of such complexities for wise application.

LOOKING BACK

1. What are the basic approaches to practical wisdom? Philosophical wisdom?
2. How does Israel adapt the genres of wisdom and law to fit their particular society's needs?
3. What other theological themes covered so far intersect with the themes of wisdom and law?
4. How do modern, popular conceptions of "law" differ from Israel's perceptions of law?
5. Can you think of a story in Scripture (not mentioned in this chapter) that illustrates godly wisdom (or the lack of wisdom)?

LOOKING BEYOND

Blenkinsopp, Joseph. *Wisdom and Law in the Old Testament: The Ordering of Life in Israel and Early Judaism*. Rev. ed. The Oxford Bible Series. Oxford University Press, 1995.

Crenshaw, James. *Old Testament Wisdom: An Introduction*. Rev. ed. Westminster John Knox, 1998.

Imes, Carmen Joy. *Bearing God's Name: Why Sinai Still Matters*. IVP Academic, 2019.

LeFebvre, Michael. *Collections, Codes, and Torah: The Re-characterization of Israel's Written Law*. The Library of Hebrew Bible / Old Testament Studies 451. T&T Clark, 2006.

Walton, John H. *Ancient Near Eastern Thought and the Old Testament: Introducing the Conceptual World of the Hebrew Bible*. 2nd ed. Baker Academic, 2018.

Westbrook, Raymond, and Bruce Wells. *Everyday Law in Biblical Israel: An Introduction*. Westminster John Knox, 2009.

9

WARFARE AND PEACE

The Shalom *of God*

In the US, Indigenous People's Day is set apart as a day to remember and lament the warfare and violence within our own country, which was often justified by the misuse of warfare passages in the Bible.[1] To misuse Scripture to perpetuate violence is obviously problematic. It is also problematic to pretend that violence is no longer an issue for God's people.[2] The prophet Jeremiah's accusations against those unaffected by violence ring true for many of us today:

> They have treated the wound of my people carelessly,
>   saying, "Peace, peace,"
>   when there is no peace. (Jer. 6:14; 8:11)

A call for peace can be an offense to those who are being crushed under the steel boot of oppression. Instead, naming the reality they face gives ear and understanding to their suffering. Just as the psalms of anger (another challenging part of Scripture!) can help those who are traumatized and enraged to feel heard, so also a careful treatment of Israelite warfare and peace can

---

1. For an excellent discussion of this tragic history of misinterpretation and misapplication, see Charles and Rah, *Unsettling Truths*.

2. Millard C. Lind notes how, in addition to misusing Scripture to perpetuate violence, these passages have been used to promote anti-Semitism, blaming Jews for "their" violent texts. Lind, *Yahweh Is a Warrior*, 23.

help those who have experienced the former and long for the latter to feel heard and seen.

LOOKING DOWN

Israel and Judah's geographical location in the ancient Near East as a land bridge between Mesopotamia and Egypt made the area particularly attractive and therefore vulnerable to any rising superpower; consequently, the land of Israel was subjected to or participated in many battles and all-out war. Similar to the other topics covered in this book, warfare throughout the ancient Near East was seen through a spiritual lens and in relationship with the local or national patron deities—this is sometimes referred to as "divine warfare." As part of the wider ancient Near East, Israel also viewed war as the prerogative of Yhwh, as is evidenced in the Hebrew Bible.[3] This chapter will provide a brief look at the concept of divine warfare, followed by preparation for war before the battle commenced, events that took place during the battle, and the aftermath of the battle, with examples from the ancient Near East and the Hebrew Bible.

The Concept of Divine Warfare

The national or local deity/deities were thought to be intimately involved with all aspects of life, including warfare. War was considered to originate from divine command; thus, all war was considered to be divine war and the deity was seen as a divine warrior.[4] As was discussed in chapter 5, ancient Near Eastern religions were intent on appeasing the deities so that the gods would maintain order for their people, including dealing with those who bring disorder, regardless of their status as friend or foe. In this way, divine war was not considered as bringing chaos; rather, divine war was considered as the response of the deity to restore order from the disorder.[5]

One way ancient peoples saw war as creating order out of chaos was to view the concept of divine war as the outcome of judgment from their deity. In Hittite and Mesopotamian sources, war was portrayed as a lawsuit with the deity serving as judge. Treaties were typically ratified in the house of the gods or before a god's symbol or statue, so a judgment by those same gods was necessary if the treaty was broken. If the deity's judgment brought forth

---

3. Niditch, *War in the Hebrew Bible*, 5; Schwartz, "Warfare in the World of the Bible"; Trimm, "Recent Research on Warfare in the Old Testament," 171.
4. Kang, *Divine War*, 108; Walton and Walton, *Lost World of the Israelite Conquest*, 198–99; Schwartz, "Warfare in the World of the Bible," 512–13.
5. Walton and Walton, *Lost World of the Israelite Conquest*, 198.

a conviction that one party did break a treaty, then war was the ultimate corrective (Deut. 4:34; Judg. 11:24, 27).[6]

As the divine warrior, the deity was commonly thought to intervene in battle, which is evidenced in both Egyptian and Mesopotamian sources. However, what is interesting to note is that divine intervention in battle is mostly seen in specific locations during particular periods of time when empires emerged from those locations.[7] It is no coincidence that the divine intervention in battle concept is most clearly seen in the literature of a new empire. Divine intervention in battle is connected to the concept of the divine monarch, which was an essential element in the rise of monarchies and thus empires. As we saw in chapter 7, the monarch was considered the adopted son of or representative of the divine; as a result, it was the divine monarch's duty to be the vessel that carried out the divine warrior's mission. The deity's personal involvement with the commissioned battle carried out by the divine monarch confirmed the monarch's election by the deity as their representation on earth.

The Implementation of Divine Warfare—Pre-Battle

The basic framework for implementing divine war begins with consulting the deities to seek their will regarding whether war should be waged or not. Consultation with the deities was conducted by the priests, who used accepted divination practices, such as omens, oracles, and other methods.[8] Omens, such as liver omens that were popular in Mesopotamia, included sacrificing a sheep by the *bāru*,[9] who then reads its liver to determine if the deity favors war or not. A second popular method included seeking out an oracle. An oracle is a person (or their message) who communicates the divine will. A typical oracle formula includes "god delivers the enemy into the hand of [insert name]." How a priest discerned the divine will using an oracle varied. In the Hittite Empire, three types of divine consultation for an oracle were practiced. The first form is *kin*, which is the use of lots. Second is *musen*, which is the practice of augury—or the observation of the behavior of birds. *Kus*, the third type of divine consultation, is the examination of entrails from a sacrificed animal.[10]

In the Hebrew Bible, Israel seeks omens before battle by inquiring of Yhwh (see Judg. 20:27) and by using divination with the Urim and Thummim—likely

---

6. Such as the New Kingdom, Sargonic, Old Babylonian, and Assyrian Empires. See Kang, *Divine War*, 108; Walton and Walton, *Lost World of the Israelite Conquest*, 207.

7. Kang, *Divine War*, 108.

8. Kang, *Divine War*, 109; Walton and Walton, *Lost World of the Israelite Conquest*, 196–97.

9. The *bāru* is a Mesopotamian "divinatory or astrological priest" who "declared the divine will through signs and omens." *Britannica*, "bāru," https://www.britannica.com/topic/baru-Mesopotamian-priest.

10. Kang, *Divine War*, 109.

the casting of lots by the priest (Exod. 28:30; Num. 27:21; 1 Sam. 28:6). But we also see other types of oracles being consulted, such as the use of a prophet (2 Kings 3:11) or when King Saul seeks out a medium before battle in 1 Samuel 28:8.[11]

Once divine favor has been sought and a favorable answer given, only then could battle plans be made. Who can participate in the battle seems to have been a matter of concern in Deuteronomy. Those men who have built a new, undedicated house, those who have planted a vineyard but not yet enjoyed the fruit, those who were newly engaged, or even those who were afraid or disheartened should not participate in the battle and should return home (Deut. 20:5–8).

Similar to the priests needing to be purified before they can go into the house or presence of the deity, so must the king, the soldiers, and their weapons be consecrated before they can fight on behalf of and alongside their warrior-deity. Purification rituals often included sacrificing to the deity, performing symbolic gestures, and abstaining from certain behaviors, such as sexual intercourse. For example, in Joshua 3:5, the Israelite soldiers are commanded to consecrate themselves before the procession of the ark when they attack Jericho, and in 2 Samuel 11:6–13, Uriah the Hittite refuses to go home and sleep with his wife when David summons him from the battlefield.[12]

Deuteronomy 20:10–11 provides instructions to the Israelites that, prior to laying siege to an enemy town, they were to offer the residents the option of surrender and being reduced to corvée labor.[13] An example of this can be seen in 2 Kings 18, when the army of the Assyrian Empire is about to besiege Jerusalem. The Assyrian Rabshakeh (or military official, v. 28) calls out to the people of Jerusalem to surrender: "Make your peace with me and come out to me; then every one of you will eat from your own vine and your own fig tree, and drink water from your own cistern, until I come and take you away to a land like your own land" (vv. 31–32a). To the city residents surrounded by the enemy, slavery and exile may seem more attractive than death.

The Implementation of Divine Warfare—Battle

The participation of the deity does not end here; as the divine warrior, the deity also participates in the battle and is considered the victor if the enemy is defeated. The deity is represented by their image (a.k.a. their figurine or statue) or symbol and leads the march to battle ahead of the monarch and soldiers.[14] The visibility of the deity's image must have strengthened the soldiers' resolve while at the same time threatening the enemy and their deity.

---

11. Walton and Walton, *Lost World of the Israelite Conquest*, 196–97.
12. Walton and Walton, *Lost World of the Israelite Conquest*, 197–98.
13. Rofé, "Laws of Warfare," 26–28.
14. Kang, *Divine War*, 109; Walton and Walton, *Lost World of the Israelite Conquest*, 199.

In Egypt, the army carried images of the gods and of the Pharaoh's patron deity as battle standards; while in Assyria, symbols of the deities in the form of standards and flags were carried by the armies, along with them came the priests and diviners who served as the ambassadors between the earthly realm and the divine.[15] In Israel, the presence of the divine warrior in battle can be seen in several ways: The divine warrior was symbolically present through the physical presence of the ark of the covenant (Josh. 6:6; 1 Sam. 4:3), through a priest or a prophet being in attendance (Judg. 4:8; 1 Sam. 13:8; 23:6; 2 Kings 3:12), through the king's presence as the divine representative (Isa. 11:10–14), through the raising of Moses's staff (Exod. 17:8–11), and through battle standards (Exod. 17:15).

This leads into another significant concept of divine war. War was seen not just as a battle between enemies but also as a battle between the deities of each group. The outcome of the battle indicates not only which group won or lost but ultimately which deity won and is therefore the highest, mightiest of the gods involved.[16] The loss of the image or symbol of the deity during a battle was a sign of weakness and defeat of the deity (1 Sam. 4:1–11).

The divine warrior's involvement with the divine war culminates in their intervention in the battle itself. Natural phenomena—such as rainstorms, lightning, floods, and earthquakes—during war time were believed to be the divine warrior employing the cosmos as a weapon against the adversary.[17] One example from Mesopotamia comes from the Sargonic Period and is titled "The Exaltation of Inanna," the divine warrior of Sargon's city Akkad. The exaltation states:

> In the van of battle, everything was struck down by you,
> My queen, you are all devouring in your power,
> You kept on attacking like an attacking storm,
> Kept on blowing (louder) than the howling storm,
> Kept on thundering (louder) than Ishkur,
> Kept on moaning (louder) than the evil winds,
> Your feet grew not weary,
> You caused wailing to be uttered on the "lyre of lament."[18]

In the Hebrew Bible, one of the most obvious examples of divine intervention in battle comes from Joshua 10. During a battle between the Israelites and a coalition of Amorite kings, the Lord threw hailstones from heaven. This was followed by the Lord obliging Joshua's request for the sun and the moon

---

15. Craigie, *Problem of War*, 119.
16. Schwartz, "Warfare in the World of the Bible," 513.
17. Kang, *Divine War*, 109; Walton and Walton, *Lost World of the Israelite Conquest*, 200.
18. Kramer, "Hymnal Prayer of Enheduanna," 334.

to stand still, and the scene concluded with the statement, "There has been no day like it before or since, when the LORD heeded a human voice; for the LORD fought for Israel" (Josh. 10:14; see also Exod. 14:19–26; Josh. 10:11; Judg. 5:20–22; 1 Sam. 7:10; Ps. 18:8–14). Likewise, historical events such as the revolt of enemy soldiers were seen as an outcome of their intense fear of the divine warrior. One such example in the Hebrew Bible is found in Judges 7, when the Midianites fled the battle due to their fear of Gideon and his god. Finally, the capture of the statue or symbol of the enemy's deity was the final act that confirmed their defeat (1 Sam. 4:10–11).[19]

The Implementation of Divine Warfare—Post-Battle

Once the enemy is defeated, the victory belongs to the divine warrior. The divine war thus begins and ends with the deity; consequently, the spoils of war were considered sacred and belonged to the divine warrior. The spoil was distributed only after it was dedicated to the deity. In the Hittite kingdom, when they conquered a city it was often destroyed because it was considered sacred to the gods and therefore inaccessible to humanity; total destruction of a city, however, was not always the result, and it seems to have occurred only in the Hittite kingdom in the second millennium BCE. Be that as it may, the idea of total destruction post-battle was not universal in the wider ancient Near East. In fact, the Assyrian annals[20] do not attest to the concept of total destruction.[21]

Regarding whether or not ancient Israel employed the concept of total destruction post-battle has been a matter of some debate. In our English Bibles, the Hebrew word *herem* is often translated as "put under the ban," "devote to destruction," or "utterly destroy," and it frequently occurs in the books of Deuteronomy and Joshua. Two main types of *herem* have been identified in the Hebrew Bible: the first as a sacrifice to Yhwh, the second as an execution of Yhwh's justice.[22] Some scholars argue that the *herem* texts reflect historical events, while others argue that the highly concentrated incidents of *herem* in Deuteronomy and Joshua reflect the theology of the Deuteronomists, who

---

19. Kang, *Divine War*, 46.

20. The Assyrian annals is another name used to describe the annual records inscribed on stone, clay tablets, or other media by Assyrian kings, detailing their military campaigns, building projects, and divine attributions for their successes. These annals were often written in Akkadian cuneiform and served both as historical records and royal propaganda, emphasizing the king's might and the favor of the gods. The annals provide valuable insight into the political, military, and cultural history of the Neo-Assyrian Empire, particularly during the reigns of rulers like Tiglath-Pileser III, Sargon II, and Sennacherib.

21. Kang, *Divine War*, 46–48, 69–70, 143.

22. Schwartz, "Warfare in the World of the Bible," 513; Niditch, *War in the Hebrew Bible*, 150–52.

Figure 9.1. The Lachish Relief, showing prisoners of war being taken into captivity after the Assyrian attack on the Judahite city of Lachish

were more interested in the theological meaning than in the actual practice. For them, the theological meaning of *herem* was symbolic of the necessary outcome of the covenant society of Israel being at odds with the original Canaanite society, necessitating an aggressive and uncompromising break from them.[23]

For example, Deuteronomy 20 lays out specific instructions regarding post-battle conduct as well as pre-battle conduct. If a town was far away and the people refuse to surrender, Israel was to besiege them. Upon conquering them, all the fighting-age males were to be executed, while the women and children became spoils of war along with the livestock and property (vv. 13–14). However, towns that were nearby had a different set of instructions: "But as for the towns of these peoples that the LORD your God is giving you as an inheritance, you must not let anything that breathes remain alive" (v. 16).[24] As we can see, showing Israel to be separate from the original inhabitants of the land is a consistent concern for the Deuteronomists.

Summary

Throughout the ancient Near Eastern world, war was viewed and conducted as "divine warfare" in that it began and ended with the local or national

---

23. Schwartz, "Warfare in the World of the Bible," 513; Kang, *Divine War*, 143.
24. Rofé, "Laws of Warfare," 26–28.

patron deities. War was not considered as creating chaos; rather, it was seen as the deity bringing order out of chaos—especially as a judgment on the breaking of a treaty. Since war was viewed as belonging to the divine, the deity was intimately concerned and thus involved with all aspects of the battle as the divine warrior. The Hebrew Bible illustrates that Yhwh is responsible for winning the war and not the power of the sword, spear, horse (e.g., Josh. 24:12; Ps. 44:3). The deities of the opposing sides had more to lose than just the battle itself; the outcome of the battle was not just about who won but also about whose god was stronger.

LOOKING UP

Warfare was such a near-constant part of life in ancient Israel that its effects would have been felt, in one way or another, by most members of the community. Naturally, warfare intersected with the way the Israelites viewed God; warfare both shaped their theology and was shaped by their theology.[25] Any discussion of the theology of warfare, however, needs to find its beginning, center, and end in another concept: *shalom*.

Beginning with Shalom

Shalom is one of those big Hebrew concepts that embraces more than just one idea, especially depending on the context in which it is used.[26] The sense pertinent to this discussion is represented by the idea of harmony—harmony with God, with others, and with creation. In this way, *shalom* is both the impetus for and the *telos* of divine warfare.

Randy Woodley, Cherokee theologian and activist, uses the analogy of the "Harmony Way," depicted as a circle by many Native Americans, to communicate the communal and interrelated dimensions of *shalom*. Similarly, the biblical conception of *shalom* is a communal concept wherein each member of the covenant community is interdependent on the others; when the *shalom* of some is threatened, the *shalom* of all is threatened.[27] Moreover, through

---

25. For an excellent overview of the similarities and differences between Israel's views of warfare and other ancient Near Eastern ideologies, with particular attention to the mythological and theological components, see Miller, *Divine Warrior in Early Israel*.

26. Philip J. Nel surveys the range of meanings of the root שׁלם, which includes well-being, prosperity, reward, treaty, cessation of war, and harmonious relations. Nel, "שׁלם," 4:130–35.

27. Woodley, *Shalom and the Community of Creation*, 21, 88–89. Specifically, Woodley argues that "*shalom* is always tested on the margins of a society and revealed by how the poor, oppressed, disempowered, and needy are treated" (15). Paul Hanson describes it this way: "*Shalom* was a state of harmony given to the community which acknowledged God's sovereignty and embodied God's righteousness and compassion in its communal life." Hanson, "War and Peace in the Hebrew Bible," 361; see also Wolterstorff, *Until Justice and Peace Embrace*, 69–70.

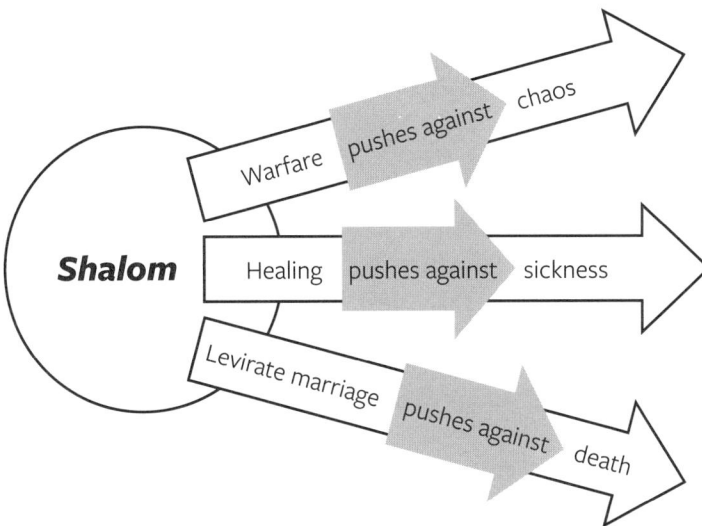

Figure 9.2. The interconnected qualities of the *shalom* circle push against forces of chaos.

the lens of *shalom*, one can see how every other aspect of Israel's theology is interconnected.

Each aspect within this "*shalom* circle" is motivated by a desire for *shalom*, pushing against all evil and chaos that would threaten that harmony (see fig. 9.2). For example, the death of a husband threatens the harmony of the household, particularly the widow. Levirate marriage was a means to restore that harmony. Many other examples could be enumerated: Justice was to push back against injustice, healing would push back against sickness, and warfare should push back against forces of evil that would threaten the safety of the covenant community.[28] Commenting on Psalm 29, Rolf Jacobson describes the peace that results from divine warfare, saying, "The strength of God is given not for the purpose of warfare or conquering power, but paradoxically God's strength quells the warring madness of the children of Adam and Eve."[29] In the new heavens and the new earth, where evil and chaos will be once and for all eradicated, warfare will also be eradicated, and this circle will naturally look different, but at this point in redemptive history, when sin and death are "already" defeated but "not yet" destroyed (from a Christian perspective), the means to keep chaos at bay are still an essential part of the *shalom* circle.

Of course, not all warfare was on the side of order and *shalom*; some warfare was on the side of evil and chaos. The civil war in Judges 20–21 that

---

28. Jerome Creach explains the place of warfare like this: "God engages in warfare to counteract the destructive forces at work in the world." Creach, *Violence in Scripture*, 49.

29. DeClaissé-Walford et al., *Book of Psalms*, 186.

ended in nearly exterminating the tribe of Benjamin and kidnapping hundreds of virgins for the surviving Benjamites is an extreme case in point. Divine warfare, in contrast, was shaped by *shalom*, from beginning to end. We see this in the creation account of Genesis 1, which (especially in v. 2) alludes to the chaos that creator-gods such as Marduk in the Enuma Elish would typically have to fight to bring order to creation. Yhwh, as Israel's divine warrior, defeated the chaos nonviolently.[30] Matthew Lynch remarks on this "glaring omission for its time," saying that "if these introductory stories are trying to teach us to see the world as it ought to be, then *violence has no essential place in God's creation.*"[31] Similarly, in Psalm 104:26, Yhwh has created and tamed the chaos sea serpent, Leviathan, who is depicted as a playful puppy ("Leviathan, which you formed to frolic there," NIV).[32] We see *shalom* breaking through typical warfare in the peaceful resolution of conflict between the northern kingdom of Israel and the Syrian army, which was peacefully spared in 2 Kings 6:21–23 and given a feast instead of death.

There are many other examples of Hebrew Bible warfare that are depicted as extremely violent. This warfare, even if fought to protect or restore *shalom*, can be difficult to stomach, especially when it is portrayed as the work (or command) of a loving God. There are various ways that scholars seek to reconcile the violence of divine warfare with the character of God. Traditionally it was interpreted as a limited, one-time, just punishment of evil. Others see it as an accommodation to the cultural and literary conventions of the time, so that perhaps the extent or nature of the warfare described is hyperbolic or symbolic.[33] Others see it as Israel's perception of God, a "textual God" rather than the "actual God."[34] However one chooses to view the depictions of divine warfare in the Hebrew Bible, we can probably all agree that warfare was both an accommodation to the expectations and reality of the ancient world and also a result of a sinful, broken

---

30. Creach offers an excellent discussion contrasting the combat with chaos in ancient Near Eastern accounts with the nonviolence in Gen. 1 (Creach, *Violence in Scripture*, 18–20). That humanity is created in God's image suggests that we likewise are to combat chaos without violence (25–27).

31. Lynch, *Flood and Fury*, 44.

32. Robert B. Chisholm Jr. colorfully depicts Leviathan as a "big rubber ducky" in this psalm. Chisholm, "Suppressing Myth," 81.

33. I find this position to best accord with the historical and textual data. Matthew Lynch offers one of the most compelling and cogent cases for this position, arguing that much of the violence depicted in the Hebrew Bible is the violence of creation's own self-destruction, and that much of the violence depicted in the "conquest language" of Deuteronomy and Joshua is referring to the destruction of idolatrous practices and the displacement of the Canaanites, who represented their Egyptian overlords. These battles essentially "helped Israel complete the exodus." Lynch, *Flood and Fury*, 175; cf. Copan, *Is God a Moral Monster?*

34. Dallaire, "Taking the Land by Force," 53, 72; cf. Seibert, *Disturbing Divine Behavior*, 170; Boyd, *Crucifixion of the Warrior God*.

world.³⁵ The sources cited in the prior footnotes provide helpful resources for interpretation and modern application (including more comprehensive treatments of the ethical issues of warfare). Given that our focus in this book is the theology espoused by the Hebrew Bible and not the ethical implications of the text, we will focus on the theology of these depictions in this chapter, which should be applicable to various interpretative frameworks.

From this introductory discussion of the relationship between *shalom* and the forces of evil and chaos that oppose it, we can now discuss three primary dimensions of divine warfare, which include God fighting alone for his people, God fighting alongside his people, and God fighting against his people.

God Fighting for Israel

Yhwh's role as warrior is a necessary extension of his role as divine King. Kings represented the principle of order in the ancient world and were understood to be the sovereign protectors of their people.³⁶ This is why prefacing the story of David's sin against Bathsheba and Uriah with the statement, "In the spring of the year, the time when kings go out to battle . . . but David remained at Jerusalem" (2 Sam. 11:1) is ominous. In that culture, kings were expected to fight for their people; by staying in Jerusalem, David was failing his people, both on the battlefield and at home. The image of a divine King who was opposed to evil and who entered into Israel's historical realities, protecting them from enemy attack and injustice, was a great comfort to Israel.³⁷

This type of warfare was also strongly tied to worship. Throughout the exodus narrative, Moses relays God's words to Pharaoh, "Let my people go, so that they may worship me" (Exod. 8:1, 20; 9:1, 13; 10:3). The divine warrior-king is a holy God who desires to live in holy community with his people.

The first explicit description of Yhwh as a warrior is in the victory song of Exodus 15: "The LORD is a warrior; / the LORD is his name" (v. 3). Aside from putting one foot in front of the other, Israel did nothing at all to save themselves from slavery in Egypt or from the army that pursued them. God did it all. In fact, Moses's last words to the Israelites before miraculously crossing through the Red Sea on dry ground were, "The LORD will fight for you, and you have only to keep still" (14:14). There is no missing the central point of this kind of warfare: God is sovereign over all other gods and political powers, and Israel need only trust in him to be saved from their enemies.

---

35. Speaking specifically of warfare as described in Deuteronomy, Goldingay describes this accommodation to the cultural and political norms this way: "Deuteronomy, then, accepts war as a fact. It then controls, circumscribes, directs, and harnesses it to Yahweh's purpose." Goldingay, *Theological Diversity*, 163; cf. Craigie, *Problem of War*, 41.

36. Brueggemann, *Living Toward a Vision*, 104.

37. Creach, *Violence in Scripture*, 71; Craigie, *Problem of War*, 95.

If those for whom God was fighting were encouraged to trust in him through the image of the divine warrior, then those God was fighting against were encouraged to either transform or be destroyed.[38] It is only after numerous requests, warnings, and increasingly catastrophic plagues that Israel was finally freed from Egypt. Speaking centuries later to Israel, who by that time had become their own worst enemy, God makes it clear that both death and transformation are on the table, and God always prefers the latter: "Say to them, as I live, says the Lord God, I have no pleasure in the death of the wicked, but that the wicked turn from their ways and live" (Ezek. 33:11).

This kind of Yhwh-fought warfare is characterized by the use of miracles: waters dividing and then burying the enemy (Exod. 14), walls falling down at the blast of trumpets (Josh. 6), hailstones falling from the sky (Josh. 10), enemies being rendered blind (2 Kings 6). According to Susan Niditch, this kind of Yhwh-only warfare is a subtle critique of traditional warfare, or at least contains "the seeds of an ideology of non-participation," pointing to an ideal of nonviolence.[39] Just as Israel was to leave vengeance to God instead of taking it into their own hands, so also this kind of Yhwh-only warfare allowed Israel to leave warfare to God. It has also been understood as a theological lens through which Israel later viewed their earlier wars. This can be seen in the contrasting presentations of Israel's battle against the Amorite king Sihon in Numbers and Deuteronomy. Numbers 21:21–31 presents the conflict without any mention of Yhwh, but in Deuteronomy 2:24–37 Yhwh instills supernatural fear in the Amorites, hardens Sihon's heart, and delivers them over to Israel.[40]

Even when warfare is left to a just and merciful God, and even when it is a means of salvation from oppression or the impetus for repentance and transformation, it can and should elicit sorrow for the death of the enemies. God himself does not delight in the death of the wicked, inside or outside of Israel (Ezek. 18:23; 33:11). Reception history bears out the tension of reading sorrow in the midst of victory songs. A rabbinic tradition (Babylonian Talmud, Megillah 10b and Sanhedrin 39b) viewed God's judgment of Egypt as fair and right, but also sorrowful, as rejoicing angels are silenced by God himself: "The work of my hands has drowned in the sea and shall you chant songs?"[41] Salvation and judgment, life and death, are two sides of the same

---

38. Brueggemann uses the terms "transform" and "destroy," linking these options directly to Christ's death and resurrection: "In Jesus' decisive action, the kingdom of this world was transformed into the kingdom of God." Brueggemann, *Living Toward a Vision*, 111.

39. Niditch, *War in the Hebrew Bible*, 145.

40. The diachronic history of this "holy war" lens is debated by biblical scholars. Gerhard von Rad's monumental work *Holy War in Ancient Israel* argues that later "enlightened" thinkers during the period of Solomon depicted earlier wars through this spiritual lens (92–93).

41. Cited in Niditch, *War in the Hebrew Bible*, 150.

redemptive coin for biblical theology, as Christians who pass through Good Friday on the way to Easter know well.

God Fighting with Israel

In addition to fighting *for* Israel, Yhwh also fought *with* Israel, highlighting Israel's part in the covenant and their role as Yhwh's representatives. Indeed, while priests would often have special roles in battle (e.g., in the battle of Jericho in Josh. 6), the people as a whole also had a priestly role in battle, "becoming for the duration of the war a holy person."[42] As we saw above, purification, both of the soldiers and of the land, made it clear that such warfare was indeed holy.[43] In addition, this kind of warfare viewed war booty as belonging entirely to Yhwh, and it was either to be completely destroyed as a sacrifice (as in *herem* warfare) or to be put into the sanctuary as an offering to Yhwh.[44] Those who violated these instructions, such as Achan (Josh. 7) or Saul (1 Sam. 13), even out of simple covetousness or ignorance, failed in their priestly roles.

This synergistic kind of warfare was still often characterized by the miraculous, which was a reminder that the credit for victory still went to the divine warrior-king. A prime example is Israel's first battle as a fledgling nation in Exodus 17:8–15. They were waging a defensive war against the Amalekites, and God fought with Israel as long as Moses's hands were raised, but as soon as Moses lowered his hands, the Amalekites would prevail. In this way, God used even Moses's posture of dependence and worship to symbolize Israel's need for Yhwh in battle. Similarly, "anti-military" strategies, such as circumcision on the eve of battle (Josh. 5:3–7)[45] and defining "strength" in terms of Torah obedience (1:7) highlight the miraculous nature of Israel's battles.

Indeed, this kind of warfare was seen as a testing ground for covenant faithfulness, to determine whether or not Israel would continue to fight against sin, or if they would allow it to persist, ultimately transforming them. Judges 2:22–23 describes the testing this way: "In order to test Israel, whether or not they would take care to walk in the way of the Lord as their ancestors did, the Lord had left those nations, not driving them out at once, and had not handed them over to Joshua."[46]

---

42. Liau, "Theology of Warfare in Deuteronomy," 67.

43. Although the term "holy war" is not used in Scripture itself, it communicates an important dimension of Israelite warfare. The term was first coined by Friedrich Schwally in 1901. See Ollenburger, introduction to *Holy War in Ancient Israel*, by von Rad, 5.

44. René Girard made the converse observation, that sacrifice was an outlet for violence, and violence occurred when that sacrificial outlet was unmet (for example, when Cain's sacrifice was deemed unworthy). Girard, *Violence and the Sacred*, 4.

45. Lynch, *Flood and Fury*, 94–96.

46. This passage also notes that God left the nations to serve as a punishment for Israel (Judg. 2:20–21) and so that the new generation could learn warfare (3:2).

Features of this test include multiple aspects. First, would they consult God before battle? Israel could consult God through means typical of their cultural context (such as casting lots, as discussed above), but the simplest means of consulting their God was through prayer. When leaders fail to consult God before battles, they fail the test (Josh 7; 9; 1 Sam. 4; 13).

Second, would Israel willingly fight for Yhwh and his people? The Song of Deborah in Judges 5 celebrates the victory of Israel over the Canaanite army led by Sisera. As the courageous killer of Sisera and the one deemed "most blessed" two times in verse 24, Jael is the (human) star of the poem, and she passes the test of willingness to fight (even as a non-Israelite).[47] Immediately before this stanza, in verse 23, Meroz is cursed two times "because they did not come to the help of the LORD." The blessing for those who help God's people and the cursing for those who do not fulfills the promises of the Abrahamic covenant (Gen. 12:3)[48] and shows that those who sit idly by while others risk their lives fail the test.

Third, would Israel really be on Yhwh's side? In a curious little story tucked away in Joshua 5:13–15, on the eve of the battle of Jericho, Joshua finds himself face to face with the "commander of the army of the LORD" (v. 14, as promised in Exod. 23:20). When Joshua asks him whether he is on the side of Israel or their enemies, he claims to be on "neither" side, the implication being that he is on the side of those who are on *Yhwh's side*, regardless of whether or not they are Israelites. In the context of Jericho, it is once again a non-Israelite woman, Rahab, who proves to be on Yhwh's side, evidenced by her faith and actions (Josh. 2), whereas Achan proves *not* to be on Yhwh's side by stealing some of the plunder that belongs to God (Josh. 7). Those who fight for themselves, rather than for Yhwh, fail the test.

Fourth and finally, would Israel's fighting result in lasting peace and *shalom*, or would it result in more or escalated violence? The book of Judges describes a downward spiral of faithlessness, both spiritually and politically.[49] Each of the six major judge "cycles" or narratives has repeated elements, including a notice of how many years the land was given "rest" or "peace" after God raised a deliverer to rescue Israel from enemy oppression. In each cycle the period of rest grows increasingly shorter, as in each cycle the people grow

---

47. Since most soldiers were men, it would make sense that men would find the metaphor of divine warrior most relatable. However, we do have the occasional woman warrior, such as Jael (or Judith in the Apocrypha) to invite women into this metaphor. Backfish, "Blessed Destroyer," 74.

48. The intentional placement of this line to contrast participation vs. non-participation is helpfully discussed by Lind, *Yahweh Is a Warrior*, 72.

49. This spiral takes a sharp downward turn with respect to the faithfulness of the judges (or saviors as they might better be called) starting in the Gideon narrative. Knight, *Prophet's Anthem*, 91–99.

increasingly less faithful, until there is no mention of peace after Jephthah's defeat of the Ammonites or Samson's defeat of the Philistines. By the end of the book, war against one town escalates to the near-destruction of an entire tribe within Israel, with Israel not only failing the test but even blaming God for their failure (Judg. 21:15).

When Israel became a monarchy, Yhwh continued to fight with his people, but now the Israelite king would also fight as Yhwh's royal representative. It was imperative that the human king fought in alignment with the divine King, or else Israel would be dragged into greater chaos. King Ahaz is a case in point. The prophet Isaiah warned Ahaz against putting his trust in Assyria, hoping to avoid conflict with the northern kingdom of Israel and Syria, but Ahaz would not listen, thus dragging the kingdom of Judah closer and closer to the threatening chaos of Assyria (Isa. 7; 8:5–8).[50]

Subtle critiques of this kind of warfare, or at least hints that such destruction is neither the norm nor the ideal, can be seen in passages like Numbers 31:19–24, where every Israelite soldier who killed a Midianite in battle had to purify themselves for seven days before returning to camp. We have already seen that purification before battle signals that it is a holy affair, but purification after battle also suggests that it does not represent an ethical ideal. Amos 1–2 also critiques the excesses of war, including exiling "entire communities" (1:6) and violating treaty agreements (1:9). Likewise, 1 Chronicles 22:8 recounts how God prohibited David from building the temple because he had "shed much blood" and "waged great wars."[51] Even at its best, warfare was an accommodation to a sinful world and a temporary means of upholding *shalom* for the oppressed; at its worst, warfare was the polar opposite of *shalom*.

God Fighting Against Israel

As we saw in chapter 2, blessings and curses were part of a typical ancient Near Eastern covenant, including Israel's covenant with God (Lev. 26; Deut. 28). The ultimate curse, of course, was the forceful removal from the Promised Land: exile. Just as Israel had been charged to "drive out" the Canaanites before them (Exod. 23:31), so God would use another nation to drive out his own people so that the land could have rest and be cleansed of their sin—in other words, so that the land could once again have *shalom* (Deut. 28:36, 49).[52]

This kind of divine warfare, fought against God's own people, highlights his justice and impartiality. He can judge Israel as he judges other sinful nations. It also highlights God's desire for genuine repentance and transformation.

---

50. Hanson, "War and Peace in the Hebrew Bible," 352.
51. Niditch, *War in the Hebrew Bible*, 139.
52. In the Hebrew Bible, several words are used for "drive out" (*yarash*, *garash*, *halak*, *nahag*), but the idea of removal is the same.

Again and again God forgave and endured his people's sinfulness. He sent prophets to warn, correct, and guide them, but again and again, the people refused to listen. The message that God gives Isaiah to relay to Judah in Isaiah 6:9–10 seems completely counterintuitive until seen in light of God's desire for genuine transformation through judgment:

> And he said, "Go and say to this people:
>
>> 'Keep listening, but do not comprehend;
>> keep looking, but do not understand.'
>> Make the mind of this people dull,
>>> and stop their ears,
>>> and shut their eyes,
>> so that they may not look with their eyes,
>>> and listen with their ears,
>> and comprehend with their minds,
>>> and turn and be healed."

Why does God not want his people to hear Isaiah's message, turn, and be healed? Because God knows that it would only be a temporary, superficial change. Only the full force of the covenant curses, only God fighting against his people, would expose their sin and turn their hearts back to him:

> Then I said, "How long, O Lord?" And he said:
> "Until cities lie waste
>> without inhabitant,
> and houses without people,
>> and the land is utterly desolate;
> until the Lord sends everyone far away,
>> and vast is the emptiness in the midst of the land.
> Even if a tenth part remain in it,
>> it will be burned again,
> like a terebinth or an oak
>> whose stump remains standing
>> when it is felled."
> The holy seed is its stump. (Isa. 6:11–13)

Judah will be cut down to a stump, which might initially sound hopeless. But anyone who has cut down a tree to its stump can anticipate the hope in this imagery, which is picked back up in Isaiah 11:1 to describe a renewed Israel: "A shoot shall come out from the stump of Jesse, and a branch shall grow out of his roots." This new son of Jesse, this new David, will fear Yhwh and will uphold justice for the poor, equity for the meek, and destruction for the wicked, and will finally and fully bring *shalom* to the land (vv. 2–9).

This all sounds redemptive and lovely to those steeped in Israel's unique theology or to those living on the other side of Babylonian captivity. But according to the prevalent theology of warfare at the time, noted in the section above, this was a war between deities, and if Yhwh's people were the ones defeated, then naturally Yhwh himself had been defeated, along with all of his promises and power.[53] Israel's theological crisis is poignantly captured in Psalm 89, which celebrates Yhwh as a victorious creator, king, and warrior (vv. 9–14) and recounts the promises of the Davidic covenant and dynasty enduring "forever" (v. 29). If David's descendants violated the covenant, they would be punished but not deposed (vv. 31–36). "But now," the psalmist cries (v. 38), the Davidic line is cut off and rejected, and the psalmist longs for Yhwh's steadfast love (v. 49). It would take years, prayer, repentance, and meditation on the law and prophets to understand how their divine warrior's aggression against his own people was actually a movement toward transformation and *shalom*.

Ending with Shalom

The prophets had a firm grasp on all these aspects of divine warfare. They had no problem with Yhwh directly fighting for Israel, depicted in graphic terms in passages like Isaiah 34:5:

> When my sword has drunk its fill in the heavens,
>   lo, it will descend upon Edom,
>   upon the people I have doomed to judgment.

The prophets' preference for this kind of Yhwh-only warfare communicated to their audiences a need to patiently wait for God to bring judgment and justice for their enemies.[54] In other contexts, *herem* warfare is echoed in the prophets, with (real or figurative) total destruction of enemies and devotion of the spoil to Yhwh:

> Arise and thresh,
>   O daughter Zion,
> for I will make your horn iron
>   and your hoofs bronze;
> you shall beat in pieces many peoples,
>   and shall devote their gain to the LORD,
>   their wealth to the LORD of the whole earth. (Mic. 4:13)

---

53. Similarly, the Mesha Stele (ca. 840 BCE) explains how the Moabite god Chemosh punished his people by allowing them to be subject to Israel but then helped them to overthrow Israelite control.

54. Lind, *Yahweh Is a Warrior*, 174.

Warfare, for the prophets, is a continued accommodation in a broken world filled with threatening injustices.

Warfare was also seen as an aspect of order pushing back against the chaos of the world in order to bring *shalom*. Isaiah 19 is one of the best illustrations of this. It describes how God will "stir up" warfare in Egypt (vv. 2–4), which will result in humility and fear (v. 16) and ultimately the worship of Yhwh (v. 21) and the honor of being called his "people" (v. 25).

Similarly, Psalm 47 says that Yhwh "subdued" the nations under Israel's feet (v. 3), with the following result: "The princes of the peoples gather as the people of the God of Abraham" (v. 9). Divine warfare, when led by a holy and good God, has its *telos* in *shalom* and in the fulfillment of the Abrahamic covenant: "And in you all the families of the earth shall be blessed" (Gen. 12:3). Paul Hanson describes this extension of blessing to the nations as essential for *shalom* because "for until all nations were brought into the healing orbit of God's peace, wars would continue to rage and chaos would continue to open its ugly maw to devour Israel."[55] This should shape not only our view of God's loving plan for all people but also our view of public policy: Policies that work for the well-being of all people (and not for the profit or enjoyment of a select few) are policies that ensure peace.

The prophetic literature also casts a vision for a time when warfare is no longer a part of the *shalom* circle, no longer a necessary accommodation in a broken world, because the world will be renewed. The prophets look forward to the day in which nations will "beat their swords into plowshares, and their spears into pruning hooks . . . neither shall they learn war any more" (Isa. 2:4; Mic. 4:3).[56] Peace will characterize the new heavens and the new earth, from the political realm to the animal kingdom, and weeping and destruction will be no more (Isa. 65:19, 25; cf. Rev. 21:4).

When Israel was restored from exile in Babylon and returned to their land, their hopes were for this kind of *shalom* and for the "covenant of peace" promised by Ezekiel, who foretold a Davidic king shepherding his restored and unified people living harmoniously in the land, with a rebuilt and glorious temple (37:24–28).[57] However, these hopes were largely met with disappointment. Their temple was subpar (Ezra 3:12–13), enemies continued to oppose God's people (Ezra 4; Neh. 4), and the same sins that characterized the pre-exilic generations resurfaced again, infecting even the Levites and the temple itself (Neh. 13:4–30). Hopes for a restored Davidic dynasty were pushed to

---

55. Hanson, "War and Peace in the Hebrew Bible," 358.

56. This is an exact reversal of the same imagery in Joel 3:10, where the nations are roused and even the weak among them turn their plowshares into swords and their pruning hooks into spears.

57. Nel, "שׁלם," 4:132.

Figure 9.3. *The Peaceable Kingdom* by Edward Hicks, 1834. Isaiah's vision of a peaceable kingdom is juxtaposed with the background scene of colonizers and Native Americans, serving as a sharp contrast between the *shalom* envisioned in the prophets and the human struggle to achieve *shalom*.

the future in the form of an idealized, messianic king, and this instrument of peace would not foremost be a warrior-deity or his representative warrior-king but a suffering servant, who would secure lasting *shalom* by taking the curse of mortality upon himself in order to forever defeat the forces of chaos and death (Isa. 53:4–5) and leave his enduring peace in the world (John 14:27).

CONCLUSION

In this chapter, we have seen that warfare in ancient Israel, like every other aspect of the Israelites' lives, was deeply theological. Whether Yhwh was fighting for them, with them, or against them, it was "divine warfare," intended to save Israel and bring order and *shalom* to the chaos of life. Wars not only affected the political sphere of life but also reflected on the sovereignty of the deities involved, and—in Israel—wars were instrumental in God's redemptive plan of bringing his wayward people to genuine repentance and ultimately blessing all of the families of the earth.

LOOKING BACK

1. What are some of the methods used to determine a deity's wishes regarding war?
2. What is the ancient Near Eastern concept of "divine warfare"?
3. What aspects of the divine warrior image do you consider to be essential to God's character, and what aspects are accommodations to Israel's cultural realities and expectations?
4. Are there any features of divine warfare that encourage you?
5. If warfare is seen as a part of the "*shalom* circle," pushing against injustice and other forms of oppression, how would you conceive of this circle? What elements would be part of ancient Israel's circle, and how would it differ from the *shalom* circle in the new heavens and the new earth?

LOOKING BEYOND

Creach, Jerome. *Violence in Scripture*. Interpretation. Westminster John Knox, 2013.

Hanson, Paul. "War and Peace in the Hebrew Bible." *Interpretation* 38, no. 4 (1984): 341–62.

Lynch, Matthew. *Flood and Fury: Old Testament Violence and the Shalom of God*. IVP Academic, 2023.

Niditch, Susan. *War in the Hebrew Bible: A Study in the Ethics of Violence*. Oxford University Press, 1993.

Schwartz, Mark. "Warfare in the World of the Bible." In *Behind the Scenes of the Old Testament: Cultural, Social, and Historical Contexts*, edited by Jonathan S. Greer, John W. Hilber, and John H. Walton, 506–14. Baker Academic, 2018.

Trimm, Charles. "Recent Research on Warfare in the Old Testament." *Currents in Biblical Research* 10, no. 2 (2012): 171–216.

von Rad, Gerhard. *Holy War in Ancient Israel*. Translated by Marva Dawn. Eerdmans, 1991.

Woodley, Randy. *Shalom and the Community of Creation: An Indigenous Vision*. Eerdmans, 2012.

10

FOOD, FEASTING, AND HOSPITALITY

The Generosity of God

Food and hospitality are in some ways common across cultures, but in other ways they are quite different. What would ancient Israelites make of our modern means of producing and distributing food, to say nothing of frozen food or fast food? And would they be offended at our dinner parties if we failed to greet them with a foot washing? One of my (Libby's) favorite depictions of conflicting hospitality expectations is in Lewis Carroll's *Alice in Wonderland*. Alice is wandering through the woods and comes to a table with far more seats and place settings than attendees, so she makes herself at home with the Mad Hatter and the March Hare as her hosts. Squabbling over whether or not a guest should be offered wine when only tea is available, Alice opines, "Then it wasn't very civil of you to offer it," to which the March Hare rejoins, "It wasn't very civil of you to sit down without being invited." Different views on food and hospitality can lead to confusion, in Wonderland and in reality. This chapter will explore ancient Israel's views and practices on food and hospitality and how these things inform the Israelites' theology.

LOOKING DOWN

Food is something that we all have in common. Food and the meals created from it are more than just sustenance and nourishment; indeed, food and meals function in various social and cultural capacities—or "foodways." Foodways are "the modes of feeling, thinking, and behaving about food that are common to a cultural group; [they] serve to bind individuals in larger social groups through shared understandings of cultural conventions."[1] The study of a group's foodways helps us better understand that group in a myriad of ways, and this chapter will aim to do just that—to explore ancient Israel through its foodways.

This portion of the chapter will feature three types of questions on the subject of foodways in ancient Israel: First, we will explore basic questions about what crops were grown, what animals were raised, and what types of meals were prepared. Second, we will explore questions related to the social aspect of food, such as who typically oversaw the household food and meals. And our final type of question deals with culture. This exploration has the potential to illuminate Israel's attitudes, practices, and rituals around food, and how they inform us about Israel's most basic beliefs about the world and themselves.[2] For our purposes here, we will focus on one particular cultural aspect—how food was used within hospitality norms and practices.

Basic Foodways

As was mentioned in chapter 5, ancient Israelites were agropastoralists—meaning that their primary means of economic activity was through growing crops and raising livestock. This also means that what they ate was dependent on the seasons and environmental and climatic conditions. The three most prominent crops in the Mediterranean diet are grapes, grains, and olives (for the oil) and are often referred to as "the Mediterranean triad." In the Hebrew Bible, essential crops that are often referred to as the so-called "seven species" are specified in Deuteronomy 8:7–8: "For the LORD your God is bringing you into a good land, a land with flowing streams, with springs and underground waters welling up in valleys and hills, a land of wheat and barley, of vines and fig trees and pomegranates, a land of olive trees and honey." These species and others are attested to in both the Hebrew Bible and the archaeological record (like the "Gezer Calendar"; see fig. 10.1), both of which indicate that the types of crops grown in Israel mainly consisted of cereals, legumes, fruits, nuts, and vegetables.

Cereals were the crop that most of the Southern Levant was dependent on, of which barley and wheat (einkorn wheat and emmer wheat) were dominant.[3] Grains could be eaten raw, parched, boiled as porridge or gruel, shaped into

---

1. Simoons, *Eat Not This Flesh*, 3; see also Wood, *Sociology of a Meal*, 40.
2. Harris et al., *Meaning of Food*, viii–ix.
3. Ebeling, "Grains, Bread, and Beer," 99.

dumplings, or baked into bread (both leavened and unleavened) or a variety of cakes.⁴ While bread was indeed part of the daily fare, in times of crisis (such as war, famine, drought, or economic difficulties), food items could be scarce; in these circumstances, porridge was likely eaten as the main meal.

The assortment of baked goods is evident in a number of ancient Near Eastern texts. One such source is an Assyrian "encyclopedia," which has two tablets dedicated to the subject of food and drink. The tablets list two hundred varieties of breads differing based on the flours, kneading, additives, flavors, cooking methods, and presentations.⁵ Furthermore, ancient food historian Robert Curtis notes that throughout the wider ancient Near East there were as many as three hundred varieties of breads, depending on the type of grain used, the grain's quality and color, any additives included (such as ghee, dates, milk, cheese, fruits, and sesame oils), the baking process, the size of the bread, and its geographic origin or use.⁶ The harvest of cereals was so essential to the Israelite diet that two festivals were dedicated to the celebration of it: The Feast of Unleavened Bread was connected to the barley harvest, while Shavuot (or the Festival of Weeks, also known as Pentecost in Greek) was connected to the harvest of wheat that occurred fifty weeks later.⁷

One important staple of the ancient Israelite diet that is often overlooked is the legume plant and its pulse (the pulse is the edible seed within the pod of a legume plant). Broad beans, lentils, chickpeas, bitter vetch, peas, and fenugreek are all types of legumes/pulses that are known from the Hebrew Bible and archaeological samples. Pulses were roasted, used in soups and

Figure 10.1. The Gezer calendar—a tablet from Tel Gezer that describes the agricultural seasons and when to plant what

---

4. Shafer-Elliott, *Food in Ancient Judah*, 119–28.
5. Bottéro, *Oldest Cuisine in the World*, 22; Shafer-Elliott, *Food in Ancient Judah*, 127.
6. Curtis, *Ancient Food Technology*, 205; Shafer-Elliott, *Food in Ancient Judah*, 127.
7. Ebeling, "Grains, Bread, and Beer," 103.

stews, cooked and eaten whole, and ground into flour and used for cakes.⁸ Culinary tablets from Babylonia include many recipes for stews made from lentils, vegetables, and various types of fresh and not so fresh meats. Stews were likely the main meal that average Israelites ate on a regular basis. The Hebrew word for stew, *nazid*, is used to describe stews of vegetables or legumes (Gen. 25:29, 34; 2 Kings 4:38–40; Hag. 2:12).⁹

Ancient Israel had several different types of fruit trees, which contributed significantly to their diet and economy. The main type of fruit trees were grape (vine), fig, pomegranate, olive, date, sycamore, and possibly mulberry, carob, and apricot.¹⁰ Fruit was eaten fresh and dried, was added to other foods (such as bread and cakes), and was made into other products such as wine, oil, juice, and syrup. Throughout the Hebrew Bible, fruit trees and vines, such as the olive tree, grapevine, and fig tree, are used as symbols of Israel's economic prosperity, destruction, and restoration (Deut. 28:40; Neh. 5:11; Jer. 31:12; Hos. 2:8, 22; Amos 4:9; Mic. 6:15; Hag. 2:19). The pomegranate is a symbol of fertility (likely because of its many seeds) and was used in ancient Israelite art and religious ritual (Exod. 28:31–34; 39:22–26; 1 Kings 7:18–20, 42; Jer. 52:22) (see fig. 10.2).¹¹

Nuts have a high caloric value and are rich in protein, fat, vitamins, and minerals; thus, they were an essential part of the ancient diet. Nut trees grown in ancient Israel include almond, pistachio, and walnut; nuts were eaten raw or roasted, and some, like the pistachio, were even pressed for their oil and used for medicinal purposes.¹²

Since vegetables are highly perishable, very few archaeological remains have been found, with some exceptions in arid environments (such as Egypt and the Great Rift Valley). Consequently, the main source for our knowledge of vegetables in ancient Israel is the Hebrew Bible, which has only a few references to vegetables and even fewer mentions of

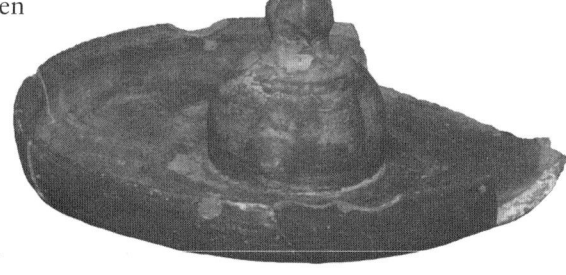

Figure 10.2. Pomegranate-shaped vessel from ancient Israel, eighth to seventh centuries BCE. It was discovered in Tomb 6 at the Tel Halif Iron Age II cemetery.

Photo by Patty O'Connor-Seger, courtesy of the Lahav Research Project

---

8. Zohary, *Plants of the Bible*, 82–84; Shafer-Elliott, "Fruits, Nuts, Vegetables, and Legumes," 150.

9. Bottéro, *Textes Culinaires Mesopotamiens*, 48; Shafer-Elliott, *Food in Ancient Judah*, 132.

10. Borowski, *Agriculture in Iron Age Israel*, 101–2; MacDonald, *What Did the Ancient Israelites Eat?*, 28–30; Shafer-Elliott, "Fruits, Nuts, Vegetables, and Legumes," 140.

11. Shafer-Elliott, "Fruits, Nuts, Vegetables, and Legumes," 143–45.

12. Mahjoub et al. "Pistacia Atlantica Desf"; Tufts University, "Nuts for You"; Shafer-Elliott, "Fruits, Nuts, Vegetables, and Legumes," 146.

specific vegetables. This could be due to the challenging environment and climate, which made horticulture (or garden cultivation and management) difficult to develop. A more likely reason is that vegetables were not highly valued as a product, especially compared to meat, which is portrayed favorably within the Hebrew Bible. Regardless of how vegetables are presented in the biblical text, they were cultivated in ancient Israel. The few that the Hebrew Bible does mention include garden rocket (or arugula), cucumbers, leeks, onions, and garlic. Most vegetables could only be eaten when in season; however, some (like garlic) were dried and stored for future use.[13]

Ancient Israel, like the rest of the ancient Near East, was dependent on its herds. Sheep, goats, and cattle were the main types of domesticated animals raised in the land of Israel and were important sources of meat as well as being essential for their secondary products,[14] such as their hair (sheep and goats), hides and labor (cattle), and various dairy products (such as butter, cheese, curds, and yogurt). These bovids[15] were also the primary acceptable animals for religious sacrifice.[16] It must be noted, however, that societies in ancient Israel did not eat meat as regularly as many of us do today.[17] Israel's dependency on their animals for their secondary products was so great that meat was generally reserved for special occasions, such as religious rituals, weddings, and hospitality feasts. Ethnographic studies of traditional societies in the Middle East have noted that people ate meat on special occasions but made exceptions if meat was obtained through the hunting of wild game, if the herd needed to be culled, if an animal was sick or injured, or if the household needed immediate income. Once butchered, the entire animal was utilized—nothing went to waste. If a household was unable to consume an entire animal before it started to spoil, they offered the meat for purchase or as a gift to members of the village, allowing the household an opportunity to recoup some of their losses or participate in reciprocal exchange.[18] When meat was eaten in ancient Israel, it was usually roasted (usually associated with religious ritual, Exod. 12:4–9) or boiled (Ezek. 24:5; Mic. 3:3). Throughout

---

13. Borowski, *Agriculture in Iron Age Israel*, 135–36; Shafer-Elliott, "Fruits, Nuts, Vegetables, and Legumes," 148.

14. Justin Lev Tov defines "secondary products" as "those things not requiring animals' deaths." Lev Tov, "Animal Husbandry," 77.

15. A bovid is "any of a family (Bovidae) of ruminants that have hollow unbranched permanently attached horns present in usually both sexes and that include antelopes, oxen, sheep, and goats." *Merriam-Webster Dictionary*, "bovid," https://www.merriam-webster.com/dictionary/bovid.

16. Lev Tov, "Animal Husbandry," 81.

17. This doesn't mean that the Israelites never ate meat. The archaeological evidence clearly points to meat being consumed—how much depends on a variety of factors including the geopolitical situation and the economy of the household.

18. Watson, *Archaeological Ethnography in Western Iran*, 108–9; Shafer-Elliott, *Food in Ancient Judah*, 130.

the ancient Near East, stews were common daily fare, which often included meat when it was available.[19]

Social Foodways

Subsistence-level societies could be seen as an "all-hands-on-deck" type of culture. Ancient Israel was no different, with all members of the household, regardless of sex, age, or any other differential, participating in and imperative to the survival of the household. The needs of which were dependent on several factors, including the seasons and other environmental and climatic conditions, the geopolitical environment, as well as the life cycle of the members of the household. The maintenance of the household was supported through various tasks related to production,[20] with food preparation being of significant importance. Sociologist Jack Goody defines the category of food preparation as "the art of cooking and cuisine," with a major factor being who is the food preparation group and who is the food consumption group (they are not always the same).[21] Archaeologist Christine Hastorf studies the social life of food, utilizing ethnographic and archaeological case studies from 185 societies, all of which indicate that women were/are responsible for the majority of food preparation, "performing more than 80 percent of these tasks in any one group.... The only [food related] tasks that men tended to dominate in were hunting, butchering, generating fire, and farming (plowing)."[22] Hastorf writes that it is "through these acts [of food preparation] women acquire their own place and enablement, with their productive contributions being linked especially to familial prestige and position as well as training the next generations in these useful skills."[23]

Evidence suggests that ancient Israelite households fall into this pattern of food preparation. Women of the household oversaw and performed the tasks associated with food preparation, which required significant skill as well as power and authority within the household (see fig. 10.3). Carol Meyers contends that ancient Israelite women's daily activities were just

---

19. Bottéro, "Cuisine of Ancient Mesopotamia," 42.
20. Wilk and Rathje note that there are four categories of domestic tasks that households perform that demonstrate their social and economic roles. These categories are production, distribution, transmission, and reproduction. Production is defined as "human activity that procures resources or increases their value." Distribution is "the process of moving resources from producers to consumers and could include the consumption of resources," which differs from transmission as "a special form of distribution that involves transferring rights, roles, land, and property between generations." The last category is reproduction, or "the rearing and socializing of children." Wilk and Rathje, "Household Archaeology," 622, 624, 627, 630.
21. Goody, *Cooking, Cuisine, and Class*, 47 (see also 44–49).
22. Hastorf, *Social Archaeology of Food*, 183.
23. Hastorf, *Social Archaeology of Food*, 183.

Food, Feasting, and Hospitality

Figure 10.3. Statue from ancient Egypt of a woman grinding grain (Old Kingdom: 2474–2444 BCE)

Marcus Cyron / CC BY 3.0 / Wikimedia Commons

as time-consuming and energy demanding as men's, arguing that women's tasks required more technical skill then men's.[24] Transforming inedible, raw products into edible food required skills that were essential to the household. As the senior woman of the household, the matriarch operated as the "manager" of the household's food, including organizing it into various foodstuffs and deciding how much of it would be stored, distributed, or prepared into meals, which would have included overseeing who ate, when, and how much.

The Hebrew Bible provides several examples that illuminate this point. Our most detailed example of the matriarch of the household and her authority over its foodways is found in Proverbs 31:10–31. This passage lists the many things the matriarch does on a daily basis to care for her household. Although the text portrays a woman of means, she still exemplifies the type of role the matriarch in ancient Israel had, especially over the household foodways.[25] For example, Proverbs 31:14–15 states,

> She is like the ships of a merchant,
>   she brings her food from far away.
> She rises while it is still night
>   and provides food for her household
>   and tasks for her servant-girls.

Additionally, verse 27 affirms,

> She looks well to the ways of her household,
>   and does not eat the bread of idleness.

---

24. Meyers, *Rediscovering Eve*, 184.
25. Proverbs 31:10–31 is likely from the Persian Period but could still be helpful in illustrating the power of the matriarch in pre-exilic Israel.

As manager of the household, the matriarch in Proverbs 31 strengthens her household.

A second example that intends to portray a woman from the Iron Age is found in 1 Samuel 25, when Abigail defuses a potentially dangerous situation that her husband, the foolish Nabal, initiates by insulting the soon to be king, David. Abigail neutralizes the situation by sending David enough food for a (royal?) feast: "two hundred loaves, two skins of wine, five sheep ready dressed, five measures of parched grain, one hundred clusters of raisins, and two hundred cakes of figs" (v. 18). Abigail's authority over the household food is demonstrated here in that she does not request permission to send enough provisions for a festive meal—she simply does it.

A third and final example is found in 2 Kings 4:8–10 when the Shunammite woman steps outside the cultural conventions of hospitality and invites the prophet Elisha to stop in for a meal whenever he was in the region, followed by having an upper room built on the roof of the house for him.[26] Like the woman of strength in Proverbs 31 and Abigail in 1 Samuel 25, the woman of Shuman exhibits her role of authority within the household through food and housing. These examples portray women, in particular the matriarch, having control over the household provisions, thus demonstrating a woman's authority and influence on the household foodways and economy.[27]

Cultural Foodways

The final category deals with the cultural element of ancient Israelite foodways. If the social element focuses on the people and food, the cultural aspect emphasizes that particular society's attitudes, practices, and rituals around food, and how they inform us about that society's most basic beliefs about the world and themselves.[28] Food and meals are innately full of meaning. From everyday meals to special occasion meals, something is always being communicated—whether we are aware of it or not; hence, food and meals are also innately political. The meaning behind a meal is as diverse as the meal itself and as powerful as any political event. As a cultural-political tool, meals can be used in establishing, maintaining, legitimating, reinforcing, and even deconstructing household manners, customs, and traditions, including various issues related to authority, identity, power, and gender.[29] The cultural element of food is a sizable component of any society and is well beyond the scope of this chapter; consequently, for our purposes here, we will focus on

26. See more on hospitality norms below.
27. Shafer-Elliott, "Heroines of Every Day Life," 9; Shafer-Elliott, "Anthropology of Food," 443–44.
28. Harris et al., *Meaning of Food*, viii–ix.
29. Hamilakis, "Food Technologies," 40; Shafer-Elliott, "Women and Economics," 119.

one particular cultural aspect: how food is used within hospitality norms and practices.

Sharing a meal has the capacity to connect those at the table. As a political strategy, meals function as a means to both break down barriers and build boundaries—and none more so than the meal served as a measure of hospitality. Hospitality was a fairly significant responsibility because through it a household determined if a stranger was friend or foe; if the stranger was going to improve or compete with the household for resources, labor, and goods; or if the stranger's goal was war or peace.[30] In a society based on kinship, strangers posed a threat, which hospitality attempted to neutralize by temporarily adopting the stranger into the household as a guest.

As a result of the major responsibility hospitality had, there were clear cultural norms[31] that each party—namely, the host and the guest—was expected to abide by. The patriarch of the household was the host and only he (or someone with the patriarch's permission) was allowed to extend the invitation of hospitality to the stranger. The host would offer the first verbal invitation, which the stranger would refuse; it was not until the second invitation was extended that the guest would accept. The stranger's refusal of the first invitation may have been a signal to the host that the stranger did not intend to impose or threaten the household. Part of the invitation included offering water for washing their feet, preparing a modest meal of bread and water, and offering rest. Foot washing was a symbolic act in that it signified that the stranger was now a guest (Gen. 18:4; 19:2; 24:32; 43:24) and part of the household for the duration of their stay, which was predetermined for an exact amount of time in the invitation (in biblical examples, visits are no longer than four days). Since the guest was considered part of the household, even for a limited time, the patriarch now had the responsibility to protect the guest for the duration of their stay. While the original meal offered was a modest one (bread), in reality the meal presented was a generous feast. A feast of abundance was a political tactic that was used to decipher whether a stranger posed a potential threat or could be a potential ally.[32] During a guest's stay, proper hospitality practices dictated that the host could not ask questions into the affairs of the guest, including their destination. Similarly, the guest could not ask for anything or show any interest in the host's household.

---

30. Matthews and Benjamin, *Social World of Ancient Israel*, 82; Herzfeld, "As in Your Own House," 77.

31. Cultural norms are the *unwritten rules* of a specific culture that "can take the form of a practice, belief, diet, ritual, or set of expectations"; furthermore, cultural norms are often unquestioningly followed and "come to govern all aspects of life" (Wright and Novotny, "Bodies: A Digital Companion"). Food and the meals created from them are significant carriers of cultural norms in any society.

32. Gudme de Hemmer, "Invitation to Murder," 91.

It was expected that the guest would not impoverish their host during their stay and would bless the household upon their departure, illustrating that they are indeed allies.[33]

One of several examples of hospitality in the Hebrew Bible is found in Genesis 19:1–11. In this narrative, two divine messengers arrive in Sodom one evening. Lot, who lives in Sodom and is the nephew of Abraham, sees the two strangers and offers them hospitality for the night, including offering them water to wash their feet and offering rest. The strangers refuse Lot's first invitation, but when he insists with a second invitation, the strangers accept. Lot presents the strangers with a feast that includes unleavened bread. Before they went to bed, the men of Sodom surrounded the house, demanding Lot to cast out the strangers he was hosting so that they may sexually assault / rape them. Lot refuses and offers his virgin daughters to the men instead. When the men of the city are about to break down the door, the strangers pull Lot back inside and strike the men with blindness. This narrative is often used in discussions about homosexuality; however, the leading cultural aspect of this passage is hospitality, not sexuality. Per hospitality norms, the (divine) strangers were just inducted as members of the household for the night; consequently, also per hospitality norms, it is Lot's responsibility as the patriarch and host to protect his guests at all costs—apparently even at the expense of his daughters.[34]

Hospitality was a cultural practice that was imperative to the survival of the household. As noted above, the meal initially offered was a modest one, but then a feast was served. Ideally, by this generous act, both the host and the guest were honored with the meal breaking down whatever boundaries were there.[35] Furthermore, offering hospitality was mutually beneficial in that everyone would need hospitality at some point. As the Bedouin in the land of Israel still say, "Today's host is tomorrow's guest."[36]

Summary

This portion of the chapter explored ancient Israel through its foodways. This was undertaken by featuring three types of questions on the subject of foodways in ancient Israel: Our first set of questions were basic ones that

---

33. Matthews and Benjamin, *Social World of Ancient Israel*, 83–86; Bailey, *Bedouin Culture in the Bible*, 63–68.

34. In chapter 1, we noted that it was the patriarch's responsibility to protect the women in his household. Hospitality narratives, such as the one in Gen. 19:1–11, rightly bring up questions regarding Lot's responsibility as the patriarch versus his responsibility as a host. Was he forced to choose between the two?

35. Matthews and Benjamin, *Social World of Ancient Israel*, 85.

36. Bailey, *Bedouin Culture in the Bible*, 64.

answered what types of crops and animals were grown and raised, and what types of meals were prepared from them. Questions related to the social aspect of food made up our second category, and we asked questions about who typically oversaw the household food and meals. The third set of questions focused on those related to food and ancient Israelite culture, which has the potential to illuminate Israel's attitudes, practices, and rituals around food, and how those inform us about Israel's most basic beliefs about the world and themselves.[37] By highlighting the cultural norms of hospitality and the role food plays within it, we were able to catch a glimpse of the political and yet imperative nature of hospitality for the ancient Israelite household. Food is about much more than what we grow and eat; rather, food is a significant carrier of a society's cultural norms. Food and the meals prepared from foodstuffs are social and political events rich with meaning.

LOOKING UP

In order to explore the theology of food, eating, and hospitality in ancient Israel, we will build on the three questions addressed above, looking at the theology of food itself, the social aspects of food and its production and distribution, and finally hospitality as it pertains to God as the divine host.

A Theology of Food and Eating

We saw in chapter 4 that food was a marker of holiness, as seen in the dietary laws in the Hebrew Bible. Israel's daily eating habits were constant reminders of their covenant identity as God's holy people, set apart from the world to be his instrument of grace to the nations. It follows, then, that Israel's food production and preparation were seen as spiritual tasks.

Food was first and foremost a gift from God. God provides food for the animal world, and he provides the "Mediterranean triad" (italicized below) for his people:

> You cause the grass to grow for the cattle,
> > and plants for people to use,
> to bring forth food from the earth,
> > and *wine* to gladden the human heart,
> *oil* to make the face shine,
> > and *bread* to strengthen the human heart. (Ps. 104:14–15)[38]

---

37. Harris et al., *Meaning of Food*, viii–ix.
38. Brueggemann notes how these three main crops were also taken up as sacramental elements in the church. Brueggemann, "Food Fight," 332.

Notice that food is not merely necessary to survive but also enjoyable. As C. S. Lewis famously argued, material goods are a gift from God and should be enjoyed as such: "He invented eating. He likes matter. He invented it."[39] Of course, good gifts can become idols that turn our attention away from God, but they can just as easily be what Cameron H. J. Jorgenson calls "an icon of the divine," pointing us to their divine source with gratitude and worship.[40]

Food was also a reminder for Israel to depend daily on God as the source of their sustenance. His provision of manna in their wilderness wanderings is a beautiful illustration of this. Not only were they only permitted to collect enough bread for that one day (except for the day before Sabbath, when they could collect for both days), but regardless of how much they were able to collect, everyone had just enough, and no one had more than they needed (Exod. 16:4–18).

As their provider of food, God is described with imagery that ancient readers would have associated with the feminine, since it was the matriarch of the household who was responsible for food preparation and distribution. In addition to providing Israel with their natural food (as we saw in Ps. 104) and with supernatural food of manna and quail (as in Exod. 16), God is depicted with the intimate language of a nursing mother:

> He set him atop the heights of the land,
>   and fed him with produce of the field;
> *he nursed him* with honey from the crags,
>   with oil from flinty rock;
> curds from the herd, and milk from the flock,
>   with fat of lambs and rams;
> Bashan bulls and goats,
>   together with the choicest wheat—
> you drank fine wine from the blood of grapes. (Deut. 32:13–14)

This maternal metaphor not only speaks to God's attentive nature, presence, and provision[41] but also invites women to identify with this "feminine" side of the divine, and it reminds us that God is above gender, neither male nor female.[42]

Food was also a means of remembrance, most notably on feast days. Nathan MacDonald explains, "Memories are formed within communities, and food is one of the ways in which communities structure the past."[43] We have

---

39. Lewis, *Mere Christianity*, 64.
40. Jorgenson, "Pleasures of Food," 484.
41. Claassens, *The God Who Provides*, 10.
42. See Amy Peeler's excellent book on this topic, *Women and the Gender of God*.
43. MacDonald, *Not Bread Alone*, 71.

already seen how several of Israel's festivals commemorating important salvific events were also harvest festivals (Passover, Weeks, and Booths), bringing together God's provision of Israel in the present with his acts of salvation in the past. These shared festival meals were arguably even more than acts of remembrance. The Mishnah (Pesahim 10.5) describes the Passover meal this way: "In every generation a man must so regard himself as if he came forth himself out of Egypt." Brant Pitre explains, "In some mysterious way, they saw each Passover, 'in every generation,' as a way of sharing in the original act of redemption."[44] In the same way, many Christian traditions see the Lord's Supper, or Eucharist, as a remembrance that "in some mysterious way" brings the worshiper into union (spiritually or physically) with the body and blood of Jesus.

A Theology of Food Economics

The sociological and ecological implications of Israel's foodways are deeply theological because Israel's covenant obligations included their care for others and for the land. Since every member of the household contributed to the production, preparation, storage, or distribution of food, each member was seen as valuable. Even those who did not or could not contribute were to be provided for through the gleaning laws. Deuteronomy 24:19–22 commands Israelites to leave portions of their wheat, olive, and grape harvests for the widows, orphans, and foreigners, thus providing all three of the "Mediterranean triad" foods to everyone in need. Even their hospitality laws far exceed our modern expectations, which are typically restricted to family and friends we already know.[45] In ancient Israel, the stranger and the foreigner were to be the recipients of Israel's generosity, which is echoed in Jesus's reminder to extend hospitality first and foremost to those who cannot repay (Luke 14:13–14).

Figure 10.4. *Ruth Gleaning* by Lucien Pissarro, 1896

---

44. Pitre, *Jesus and the Jewish Roots of the Eucharist*, 65–66.
45. Melton, "Invitation to a New Era," 117.

Israel's laws represented a "covenant economy" of how Israel was to think about food and others. Walter Brueggemann describes the distortion of these values through the Bible's depiction of Pharaoh, who functions as a metaphor for greed, accumulation, and exploitation. Pharaoh preys on people's anxiety over food scarcity, gaining power over his people by controlling all of the food sources. Instead of leading with a "covenant economy" in which every person had equal access and agency over their foodways, Pharaoh's economy was an "economy of accumulation in which the strong could take from the weak in the service of uncurbed appetite for more."[46]

The Joseph story is an interesting illustration of this point. In one sense, we can see in this story God's provision for his people and even the initial fulfillment of his promise to Abraham that through his family "all the families of the earth [would] be blessed" (Gen. 12:3), but we also see how Joseph's economic policies of accumulation led (ironically!) to slavery. When the Egyptians came to Joseph for food (the food that they themselves had produced during the seven years of plenty) during the famine, they pled for Joseph to take their land and their very lives in slavery to Pharaoh in exchange for food (47:19, 25). The narrator describes it like this: "So Joseph bought all the land of Egypt for Pharaoh. All the Egyptians sold their fields, because the famine was severe upon them; and the land became Pharaoh's. As for the people, he made slaves of them from one end of Egypt to the other" (47:20–21). Of course, God's providence was also at work in the "saving of many lives" (50:20 NIV), but the means by which that saving was carried out resulted in slavery. Surely such a thing would never happen in Israel, right? Right? Wrong.

Even though the Torah prohibited future Israelite kings from this kind of accumulation (Deut. 17:16–17), Samuel warned the people that the king they so desperately wanted would accumulate their food, land, and even enslave their sons and daughters (1 Sam. 8:11–17). Solomon fulfills this warning to a tee. And whereas the Israelites seldomly ate meat, Solomon's household ate enough meat for an army every day (1 Kings 4:22–23). God delivered his people from Pharaoh, but they re-created another Pharaoh for themselves![47]

The prophets also spoke out against such accumulation at the expense of the poor and apathy in the midst of the suffering of others (Isa. 3:14–15; Ezek. 16:49–50; Amos 6:4–6; 8:4–8). In the New Testament, Jesus warns against accumulation driven by food anxiety (Luke 12:16–21) and assures his disciples that God feeds his people as he feeds the ravens (12:24). Even in anticipation

---

46. Brueggemann, "Food Fight," 323.
47. Brueggemann, "Food Fight," 324. Brueggemann notes how Ps. 72 seems to be a counterbalance to royal accumulation. Though this psalm is associated with Solomon (at least in the heading of the psalm), the psalmist paints a picture of what kingship *should* have looked like: caring for the needy and assuring that justice was granted to all.

of Jesus's birth, Mary, his mother, foresaw the overturning of the standard food economy where the haves accumulate more and the have-nots lose what little they have.[48] She sang:

> [God] has brought down the powerful from their thrones,
>   and lifted up the lowly;
> he has filled the hungry with good things,
>   and sent the rich away empty. (1:52–53)

The "covenant economy" that God outlines in the covenant laws, and that Mary reaffirms and Jesus fulfills through the inbreaking of his kingdom, is an economy where the have-nots are given their fill—of justice and of food.

In addition to the sociological aspects of Israel's foodways, the ecological aspects are also deeply theological. As we saw in chapter 3, the Israelites (like Adam before them, Gen. 2:15) had a responsibility to care for the land they were given, for it ultimately belonged to God and could be taken from them should they fail to give it the rest needed for healthy rejuvenation (2 Chron. 36:21). Although many of us are sheltered from the disastrous effects of poor land management, harmful agricultural processes, and inhumane treatment of livestock and migrant farm workers, it is our responsibility as God's people to work toward and vote for policies that uphold the value of the land that grows our food and feeds our livestock. As consumers, we have a responsibility to look beyond the food packaging to ensure that we are supporting companies and growers that care for God's good land. As agriculturalist and author Wendell Berry argues, "To live, we must daily break the body and shed the blood of Creation. When we do this knowingly, lovingly, skillfully, reverently, it is a sacrament. When we do it ignorantly, greedily, clumsily, destructively, it is a desecration. In such desecration we condemn ourselves to spiritual and moral loneliness, and others to want."[49] Just as food can serve as an "idol" or an "icon," so also our treatment of the land and those who work it and depend on it can draw us away from God or closer to him.

A Theology of the Hospitality of God

What does it mean for God to extend hospitality to his people? In what ways is God's hospitality similar to ancient Israelite cultural norms, and in what ways is it different from those norms? Ancient Israelite hospitality built bridges and boundaries between the host and guest, and we can see how God's covenant relationship with Israel did the same. The covenant was filled with images of hospitality: ceremonial washings, shared meals, promises of

---

48. Brueggemann, "Food Fight," 328–29.
49. Berry, "Gift of the Good Land," 281. Also cited in Wirzba, *Food and Faith*, 1.

protection, and a desire for worshipers to dwell in the Lord's "house," or sanctuary.[50]

As a host, God offered protection, deliverance, and flourishing to the "guests" who would dwell with him in the Promised Land. In return, Israel was to remain loyal to Yhwh and to the laws of the covenant. The boundaries of this host-guest relationship are seen perhaps most clearly in Israel's worship and holiness laws, which carefully detailed how, when, and where Israel could approach their holy God.

Another aspect of ancient Israelite hospitality that corresponds to divine hospitality is the concept of testing. Just as a host was able to use a shared meal to determine the intentions of his guests, so also God "tests" his people with food. Of course, when an omniscient God tests his people, he is not trying to determine something that he does not already know but, rather, trying to teach his people something that *they* need to know. Starting in the garden, God gave his people a choice between obedience and disobedience: "And the LORD God commanded the man, 'You may freely eat of every tree of the garden; but of the tree of the knowledge of good and evil you shall not eat, for in the day that you eat of it you shall die'" (Gen. 2:16–17). Spoiler alert: Adam and Eve failed the test.[51] Later, immediately after Israel is delivered from slavery in Egypt, they grumble in the wilderness of Sin for food. God sent them manna, but he tested them with this heavenly food, permitting them to collect only enough for each day (Exod. 16:4). Many failed that test as well (16:20, 27). At Sinai they received the dietary laws (Lev. 11; Deut. 14). We saw in chapter 4 that God may have had various motives for giving these laws, but one rationale is that the daily choice between permitted and prohibited food was a way for God to test his people and for them to show their love for God, as his covenant people. When God sets before his people the choice of "life" and "death" (Deut. 30:15, 19), he does so, in part, as a host offering food to his guests.

We also see in divine hospitality the generosity that was not expected of a host but that was often lavished on guests. Whereas human motives may have been about power or politics, the generous hospitality of Israel's God flows from his love and grace, core attributes of his being. From the abundance of the garden of Eden to the God who "spread a table in the wilderness" (Ps. 78:19), God's generosity is boundless. Indeed, the psalmist paints a picture of

---

50. Some of these are noted in Brittany Melton's excellent article "Invitation to a New Era," 136.

51. L. Juliana M. Claassens notes how even the punishment for eating the prohibited food "impacts God's provision of food." Instead of freely eating of any tree in the garden, Adam and Eve will be exiled from the garden, and the ground that they were charged to work and protect (Gen. 2:15) is now cursed and will produce food only through "painful toil" (3:17 NIV). Claassens, *The God Who Provides*, 29–30.

a table prepared for the worshiper, whose "cup overflows" (23:5). The eschatological feast described in Isaiah 25 comes complete with Michelin Star cuisine:

> On this mountain the Lord of hosts will make for all peoples
>   a feast of rich food, a feast of well-aged wines,
>   of rich food filled with marrow, of well-aged wines strained clear.
>   (v. 6)

In one sense, this is a typical "diacritical feast," the kind that is hosted by the rich and powerful and whose guest list is restricted to the same, but in another sense, this feast is entirely atypical. Andrew Abernethy explains, "What breaks the mold is that this feast is offered to everyone, regardless of social or economic or nationalistic status."[52] L. Juliana M. Claassens makes a similar point, noting that in verses 6–8 alone the expression "all people" is used no less than five times, emphasizing the cosmic scope of God's covenant love.[53]

Not only is the guest list limitless, but the length of stay is likewise limitless. Whereas traditional hospitality maintained a reasonable limit of stay, four or so days, Yhwh's guests desire to "dwell in the house of the Lord" forever (Pss. 23:6; 27:4). And if the Israelites are faithful to God and faithful to extend hospitality to others, especially the vulnerable and marginalized, then God's hospitality will indeed be limitless, as Jeremiah promised: "If you do not oppress the alien, the orphan, and the widow, or shed innocent blood in this place, and if you do not go after other gods to your own hurt, then I will dwell with you in this place, in the land that I gave of old to your ancestors forever and ever" (Jer. 7:6–7).

In the New Testament, God's generous hospitality is echoed in Jesus's first miracle of keeping the wine flowing at a wedding (John 2), feeding of the multitudes (Matt. 14–15; Mark 6; 8; Luke 9; John 6), and washing the feet of his disciples (John 13). Jesus's most generous offering of food was given to his disciples hours before his betrayal and death (Luke 22:19–20; 1 Cor. 11:24–25). It included bread and wine, representing Jesus's body and blood—his very life. Unlike the manna from heaven that sustained Israel on a daily basis, Jesus explains that his body is the heavenly manna that provides eternal life (John 6:50, 54). And whereas blood consumption was prohibited under the old covenant, "for the life of every creature is its blood" (Lev. 17:14; cf. Deut. 12:23), for this very reason, it was given as the life-giving seal of the new covenant (Luke 22:20).[54]

---

52. Abernethy, "Feast and Taboo Eating in Isaiah," 401.
53. Claassens, *The God Who Provides*, 72.
54. The New Testament also concludes with the image of the consummation as a wedding feast of the Lamb and the church (Rev. 19).

CONCLUSION

Foodways and hospitality in ancient Israel are at once relatable and also (in the infamous words of Alice) "curiouser and curiouser!" Food was essential for life, provided means of forging and testing alliances, and enabled Israel to remember and relive the greatest moments of their history, thus forming them to extend God's generosity to the land, its workers, and those in need of its produce. A theology of food and hospitality should likewise challenge us today to be thoughtful stewards of the land and its resources, and to consider how our policies as community members and our choices as individual consumers affect all people involved. A biblical theology of food and hospitality should also strengthen our trust and fill us with gratitude for the God who provides generously.

LOOKING BACK

1. What types of crops and animals were grown and raised in ancient Israel? What types of products and meals were made from them?
2. Who typically oversaw the household food and meals?
3. How was food used within hospitality norms?
4. What has been your experience with food? Have you seen it as an idol, distracting you from God, or as an icon, pointing you to God and his generosity?
5. In what ways can we foster a "covenant economy" instead of an "economy of accumulation" when it comes to food production and distribution? What other theological themes discussed so far come into play?
6. What aspects of God's hospitality did you find most encouraging? How might that shape your life and faith?

LOOKING BEYOND

Borowski, Oded. *Agriculture in Iron Age Israel*. Eisenbrauns, 1987. Reprint, American Schools of Oriental Research, 2002.

Brueggemann, Walter. "Food Fight." *Word & World* 33, no. 4 (2013): 319–40.

Claassens, L. Juliana M. *The God Who Provides: Biblical Images of Divine Nourishment*. Abingdon, 2004.

Fu, Janling, Cynthia Shafer-Elliott, and Carol Meyers, eds. *The T&T Clark Handbook of Food in the Hebrew Bible and Ancient Israel*. T&T Clark, 2022.

Jorgenson, Cameron H. J. "The Pleasures of Food and the Good Life." *Review and Expositor* 117, no. 4 (2020): 483–96.

MacDonald, Nathan. *What Did the Ancient Israelites Eat? Diet in Biblical Times.* Eerdmans, 2008.

Melton, Brittany. "An Invitation to a New Era of Biblical Theology: Towards an Old Testament Theology of Hospitality." *Tyndale Bulletin* 74 (2023): 113–41.

Wirzba, Norman. *Food and Faith: A Theology of Eating.* Cambridge University Press, 2011.

CONCLUSION
Sifting the Data

We have attempted to demonstrate how an understanding of Israel's cultural contexts enriches our understanding of Israel's theologies. It is not easy work. It involves study, interpretation, and humility. It would, of course, be much simpler to ignore the real world of ancient Israel all together and to assume that their ways of life and conceptions of the world were more or less identical to our own. It would be like if an archaeologist wanted to say something about an ancient site, but instead of doing the hard work of excavating the site and meticulously cataloging and analyzing her findings, she just looked at the surface of the ground and guessed at its contents. If theology is deduced from one's own limited assumptions, it will remain limited and most likely wrong. A grounded theology is a theology that is based on the deepest strata of a culture. While this book could admittedly dig much deeper, we hope that it has inspired and equipped readers to continue exploring the theologies of the Hebrew Bible in light of the world of its origin.

SYNTHESIZING THE DATA: What Have We Found, and What Does It Mean?

Now that we have "excavated" our site, cataloged our findings, and analyzed the data, a summary report might help to synthesize the information.

Households: The Relationship of God

Most people may not have considered "household" as a prominent theological theme within the Hebrew Bible; hopefully, you've reconsidered this after reading chapter 1. In this chapter we first learned that the ancient Israelite household was a multigenerational community that lived and worked together for the survival of the household. We focused on three important aspects within the ancient Israelite household (material, social, and behavioral), its everyday functions, and special occasions. We delved into the structure and layout of these households, highlighting various aspects such as roles and responsibilities within the household.

The way that ancient Israelites thought about their own households sheds invaluable light on how they thought about their relationship to God and to each other. They viewed God through household metaphors. God was their life-giving midwife, their nurturing mother, their protective father, their loving husband, and their redeeming relative. Even when our own family members fall short of their responsibilities, God fulfills each role perfectly. This use of household metaphor helps us know God more deeply and relate to him more meaningfully.

The communal focus of the Israelite household also encourages us to view our lives in connection with others, within our own households, in our communities, and globally. Just as every person within the Israelite household was essential for survival, we need to view members of God's household as valuable, and just as Israelite law contained "structures of grace" to protect the most vulnerable, we need to recognize how our actions (or inaction) affect the larger family of God.

Covenant: The Loyalty of God

If household was the most unexpected theological theme, then covenant is the most predictable. Then again, we hope that placing the theme of covenant within its wider contextual world will help us gain a greater awareness and appreciation of the substantial role it plays in the Hebrew Bible. We began by discussing the terminology of covenant and its shades of meaning, including the custom of cutting or dividing animals as a symbol of ratifying the covenant. We highlighted the similarities between biblical covenants and treaty forms found in the ancient Near East, particularly in the book of Deuteronomy. We also discussed other types of covenants mentioned in the Hebrew Bible, such as those made between individuals or groups. We delved further into specific covenants, such as the Sinai/Horeb covenant in Deuteronomy, which emphasizes Israel's obligation to obey God's laws and remain loyal to him alone. Additionally, we touched on how biblical covenants can be seen as both conditional and unconditional, depending on different contexts within each covenant.

The use of this well-known form of contractual agreement to describe the promises made between God and his people highlights the grace and loyalty of God. The consistent reminder of their historical relationship—that Israel's covenant partner rescued them from slavery, even before expecting any loyalty in return—highlights the gracious nature of Israel's suzerain. That grace is met with radical loyalty when Israel consistently fails to obey the covenant stipulations, and the suzerain, who has every right to abrogate the covenant, chooses instead to forgive his vassal people.

We also saw how covenant is tied to both election and mission, which are by no means contradictory but actually integrally connected. God chose (elected) Israel as his covenant people to bring God's blessing to all of creation. From the opening pages of Scripture to its close, God consistently reaches out to his people, with promises and expectations, establishing relationships based on covenantal loyalty.

Land: The Presence of God

Most of us are not tied to the land the way our ancestors were, let alone the ancient Israelites. In this chapter we began by considering the symbiotic relationship between the land and ancient Israel. More specifically, we investigated several land-related relationships including geography and topography, economy, fertility, inheritance, how the development of the monarchy changed land ownership, and the restoration of land in the stipulations of the sabbatical and Jubilee years.

Israel's experience in the land impacted their views of God, creation, and their communities. The land was a gift from God and a sign of God's covenant faithfulness, but it also presented challenges that would test the Israelites' faithfulness to Yhwh. The challenges of a subsistence economy, coupled with Israel's location along major trade routes and the influence of many competing religions, made it very difficult for Israel to remain wholly devoted to Yhwh. The land also required care and rest. It was not theirs to exploit but theirs to steward, as the sabbatical and Jubilee years were to remind them. Finally, the land offered Israel a means by which to love their neighbors, to care for those who were landless and without means of support. Failure to live faithfully before God, the land, and their neighbors would result in expulsion from the land.

Holiness and Purity: The Sanctity of God

The concept of purity and holiness in the ancient Near Eastern and Israelite world is one that is challenging for us to fully comprehend in the twenty-first century. In this chapter, we first tried to alleviate some of the mystification by looking broadly at the ancient beliefs and practices surrounding holiness and purity as found in both ancient Near Eastern texts and the Hebrew Bible.

These texts illustrate that following the laws of physical and moral purity (as seen in Leviticus) served more than one purpose.

On one hand, these laws helped to keep the deity's dwelling place sacred and free from pollution, which then satisfied the sense of order both in the cosmological realm and in the earthly realm. On the other hand, many of these laws in the Hebrew Bible are set within a domestic context using the framework of Israel's kinship groups, which illustrates that the laws weren't just for the priests, sacrifices, or the sanctuary—rather, holiness was for all of Israel. The various laws pertaining to holiness and purity (such as the dietary laws) served as daily reminders of this fact: Israel was to reflect the holiness of God in all aspects of their lives, from their work to their treatment of others to their daily meals and, not least of all, to their worship. Just imagine if everything we ate or wore reminded us of the holiness of God and of our responsibility to reflect that holiness!

Holiness also emphasizes the aspect of mutuality that we saw in the concept of covenant between the suzerain and the vassal. Holiness originates in God and may be reflected by God's people insofar as they remain close to God and maintain the physical and moral expectations of the covenant. This can seem like an impossible expectation, unless we remember that our holiness is dependent on God. We can be holy because God makes us holy (Lev. 22:32) and offers his Spirit to sanctify us (Rom. 15:16).

Worship: The Grace of God

Chapter 5 first investigated the debate about "official" and "unofficial" religious rituals. This was followed by a discussion of the public service rituals ancient Israel used in their worship of their national deity, Yhwh, including where those rituals took place, when they occurred, in what manner were they conducted, and who conducted them.

The place of worship, centering around one sanctuary, highlighted the oneness of Yhwh as the only deity Israel was to worship. It also served as a microcosm of creation, and thus a reminder of God's original charge for humanity to serve all of creation as priests and priestesses. The sacrificial rituals themselves, though similar to many ancient Near Eastern practices, were not meant to appease a disgruntled deity but to cleanse the sacred space and make communion with God possible. These rituals were serious, but they were also full of joy and gratitude, as modern worship should likewise be reverent and joyous. Moreover, the sacrificial rituals did not stand on their own as a means of forgiveness but followed heartfelt repentance, as David's prayer powerfully illustrated (Ps. 51:16–19). We also saw how the Levitical priests who mediated in the sanctuary rituals were representative of Israel as a whole, who was called to be a priestly kingdom, a descriptor of God's people that extends into the New Testament as well (1 Pet. 2:5, 9; Rev. 1:6; 5:10).

Images of God: The Reflection of God in Humanity

In the ancient Near East, the "image" of the divine typically took one of two forms. A deity could take up residence in a figurine or a statue, its presence often activated through a ceremony that would "open the mouth" of the deity. These images are found in Israelite houses and in sanctuaries. The deity could also choose to associate his or her image with the king, either as a representative of the deity or as the deity incarnate. The kings could erect images to represent themselves in distant parts of their reign, instilling loyalty. These statues then served as an image (the statue) of the image (the king) of the divine.

The biblical concept of the *imago Dei* builds on these historical precedents and transforms them. Yhwh's images are in fact embodied representations of his rule, but that representation is extended to all of humanity (Gen. 1:26–28). The images do not belong in a sanctuary; instead, the cosmic temple of creation was meant to remind humanity not only of their royal purpose but also of their priestly purpose of caring for the creation they govern. Finally, the Hebrew Bible emphasizes perhaps most fundamentally the relational aspect of the *imago Dei*: Humanity is God's image by virtue of their status as sons and daughters, a status that cannot be revoked, even when their actions do not conform to their identity. Thus, the purpose and identity of what it means to be human (that universal, existential question!) is directly tied to our relationship to God. We fulfill our purpose in life, and we are *most human*, when we live as children of God, representing his care for the world and for the people around us.

Kingship and Politics: The Sovereignty of God

In chapter 7, we first looked at pre-monarchic Israel's localized leadership. With the advent of Israel's monarchy, it was essential that we look more broadly at the ideology of kingship found in the ancient Near East, of which Bernard Levinson argues there are six common characteristics: the monarch as divine representation; the judicial insight of the monarch; their ability to administer justice; the evaluation (by the gods and the people) of the monarch's ability to administer justice; their commitment to the cult of the patron deity; and their role as the military commander in chief. Four of these characteristics received further attention (divine representation, justice, commitment to the cult, and military leadership), highlighting how the authors of the Hebrew Bible viewed both their divine king and their human king.

While Israel's pragmatics of kingship shared commonality with their ancient Near Eastern neighbors, their theology of kingship held important distinctions. One distinction was due to their belief that all of humanity, and not only the kings, were made in God's image. As sin thwarted the functional role of humanity to govern creation with justice, kings took that representative role, just as priests took the representative role of caring for the sacred spaces. The king's role in the cult was a reminder that Israel's political sphere was holy and that by serving Yhwh in his sanctuary, they were serving a divine King in his earthly palace. The king's role as a military leader was likewise to reflect the divine King's concern for justice (Ps. 45:4). The end of the monarchy marked a turning point in Israel's theology, inviting God's people to remember back to when kingship was democratized among all of humanity and also inviting them to look forward in hopes of a new, messianic king.

Law and Wisdom: The Guidance of God

In chapter 8, we saw that ancient Near Eastern legal material was abundant and served to fit the needs of the society. Since societies have similar needs, many laws are similar across societal borders. Whereas the law codes of Israel's neighbors were often attributed to the reigning or ascending king, Israel's law was attributed to Yhwh, and the king was charged with the proper application of the law, which required wisdom and justice.

We also saw how law functioned as more than legal code. It was also (and perhaps even primarily) legal instruction and guidance on how to live well and harmoniously. This is why the Hebrew Bible emphasizes the importance of meditating on the law (e.g., Josh. 1:8; Ps. 1:2), not so much for the sake of memorizing isolated rules as for the sake of being formed by the will of God to make good choices, even in areas not addressed in the "playbook."

Wisdom, though a different type of literature, served a similar purpose of helping God's people function well in relationship to their deity and with each other. It focused on the practical aspects of daily life, as well as the existential questions of meaning and suffering. Like law, discerning and applying wisdom requires a certain amount of wisdom, thus driving God's people back to the source of wisdom, the very presence and guidance of God, for their own flourishing and for God's glory.

Understanding biblical law and wisdom as two streams with the same goals of justice and flourishing should encourage modern people of faith not to abandon biblical law as irrelevant but to cherish it as a reflection of a good God who desires to guide his people. When we view them through the lenses of their cultural landscape and of wisdom, we can discern how these ancient laws reflect both the broken world in which they were made and the brighter hope to which they point.

Warfare and Peace: The Shalom of God

Warfare was an inescapable reality in the ancient Near East, as it continues to be in many corners of the world today. It was also a theological reality, as it was believed that deities fought for, with, and sometimes even against their people. Consequently, people would need to prepare for battle by inquiring of their deity and going through the necessary ritual steps to purify the soldiers before and after battle, as well as consecrating the war booty to the deity.

Theologically, however, warfare was not perceived as an endgame, but as one of many means of eradicating chaos and preserving order. This kind of harmony is an essential aspect of *shalom*, which was the original ideal in creation and the future hope of full redemption for which God's covenant people longed.

We saw that when God fights *for* his people, both his sovereignty and his mercy are highlighted, with forgiveness and nonviolence piercing the narratives in countercultural ways (e.g., 2 Kings 6:22). When God fights *with* his people, it is a test of faithfulness, whether they will consult and trust him, whether they will fight willingly alongside their fellow Israelites, whether they will fight for Yhwh's agenda and not their own, and whether their efforts will lead to lasting *shalom*. When God fights *against* his own people, we see his impartiality and desire for true repentance. Viewing all three of these modes of warfare against the standards of ancient Near Eastern warfare helps readers to see the hints of nonviolence throughout, and the movement toward a kingdom of *shalom*, where "nation shall not lift up sword against nation, neither shall they learn war any more" (Isa. 2:4; cf. Mic. 4:3).

Food, Feasting, and Hospitality: The Generosity of God

The famous American chef James Beard once wrote that "food is our common ground, a universal experience."[1] Food is one often overlooked way that we can learn about and come to understand other people and groups, including ancient ones. Hopefully chapter 10 expanded our knowledge of and appreciation for ancient Israel (we also hope it made you a little hungry, too). The first course featured three categories of questions on the subject of ancient Israelite foodways. We began by looking at the various cereals, legumes, fruit trees, and vegetables that were grown, along with which animals were most commonly raised and what secondary products were made from them. This led us to discuss what types of meals were prepared. Second, we investigated the social aspect of food, including the women who typically

---

1. Beard, *Delights and Prejudices*, 11.

oversaw the household food and meals and the power and authority they had within the household as a result of it. And finally we dealt with the cultural element, which has the potential to illuminate Israel's attitudes, practices, and rituals around food, and how they inform us about Israel's most basic beliefs about the world and themselves. The second course focused on one particular cultural aspect—how food was used within hospitality norms and practices.

For our third and final course, we explored the theology of food, its social and ecological aspects, and divine hospitality. As a gift from God, food was a tangible reminder of God's goodness and Israel's dependence on him for their survival. This was true for their "daily bread," and especially for their special meals, which were opportunities for people to remember God's provision and deliverance. Israel's theology of food also had a sociological and ecological impact, as the Israelites were to ensure the well-being of those who produced the food, those who had no access to food, and the land on which the food was produced, creating an economy of covenant equity rather than one of accumulation and greed. Finally, we saw how Yhwh's hospitality mirrored and exceeded the cultural expectations of hospitality at every turn. As the divine Host, he offered protection for his people, tested their loyalty, and extended unexpected generosity. His guest list extended to anyone who would accept his hospitality, and the stay was limitless. Shouldn't we all desire such perfect hospitality, to "dwell in the house of the LORD [our] whole life long" (Ps. 23:6)?

FUTURE EXCAVATIONS: Suggestions for Further Study

It is our hope that this book has helped you to see how the theologies of God's people in the Hebrew Bible are intrinsically tied to the various contexts in which they lived, ate, married, fought, worshiped, and more. Of course, much more remains to be explored. This is just one attempt at connecting the dots between Israel's cultural context and theologies. Just as archaeologists intentionally leave a certain percentage of their sites unexcavated, so too have we left room for further research.

Other aspects of Israel's life that might deserve further attention include education, health and healing, economics, or traditions of grieving and views of death. While we occasionally extended our view of theology from Israel's purview to that of our own faith contexts, a more systematic comparison of Israel's theological "afterlives" in the various Jewish and Christian traditions would be fruitful. Finally, while we chose to organize our study thematically and with more emphasis on the final form of the Hebrew text than on its development, a diachronic approach that seeks to trace Israel's cultural world and flowering theology would provide a different perspective and perhaps help readers to see the bigger picture of Israel's history and theology unfold.

However you choose to approach Israel's grounded theology, and wherever your studies take you from here, we hope that your study of the Bible will always draw you deeper into its history and closer to its God.

BIBLIOGRAPHY

Abernethy, Andrew. *The Book of Isaiah and God's Kingdom: A Thematic-Theological Approach*. New Studies in Biblical Theology 40. Apollos, 2016.

———. "Feast and Taboo Eating in Isaiah: Anthropology as a Stimulant for the Exegete's Imagination." *Catholic Biblical Quarterly* 80, no. 3 (2018): 393–408.

———, ed. *Interpreting the Old Testament Theologically: Essays in Honor of Willem VanGemeren*. Zondervan, 2018.

Ackerman, Susan. "Asherah." In *The Oxford Companion to the Bible*, edited by Bruce M. Metzger and Michael D. Coogan, 62. Oxford University Press, 1993.

Albertz, Rainer, and Rüdiger Schmitt. *Family and Household Religion in Ancient Israel and the Levant*. Eisenbrauns, 2012.

Allen, Paula Gunn. "The Psychological Landscape of Ceremony." *American Indian Quarterly* 5, no. 1 (1979): 7–12.

Alpert Nakhai, Beth. "When Considering Infants and Jar Burials in the Middle Bronze Age Southern Levant." In *Tell It in Gath: Studies in the History and Archaeology of Israel; Essays in Honor of A. M. Maier on the Occasion of His Sixtieth Birthday*, edited by Itzhaq Shai, Jeffrey R. Chadwick, Louise Hitchcock, Amit Dagan, Chris McKinny, and Joe Uziel, 100–128. Ägypten und Altes Testament 90. Zaphon, 2018.

Altmann, Peter. "Festive Meals and Identity in Deuteronomy." *The Bible and Interpretation* (blog), February 2012. https://bibleinterp.arizona.edu/articles/alt368020.

Amit, Yairah. "The Jubilee Law: An Attempt at Instituting Social Justice." In *Justice and Righteousness: Biblical Themes and Their Influence*, edited by Henning G. Reventlow and Yair Hoffman, 47–59. Journal for the Study of the Old Testament Supplement Series 137. JSOT Press, 1992.

———. "The Jubilee Law: Ideal Legislation." TheTorah.com, 2015. https://thetorah.com/article/the-jubilee-law-ideal-legislation.

Archaeological Institute of America. "Tell or Tel." Accessed March 6, 2019. https://www.archaeological.org/education/glossary#t.

Arnold, Bill T., and Brent A. Strawn, eds. *The World Around the Old Testament: The People and Places of the Ancient Near East*. Baker Academic, 2016.

Averbeck, Richard. "Clean and Unclean." In VanGemeren, *New International Dictionary of Old Testament Theology and Exegesis*, 4:477–86.

———. "כפר." In VanGemeren, *New International Dictionary of Old Testament Theology and Exegesis*, 2:691–709.

———. "Reading the Ritual Law in Leviticus Theologically." In Abernethy, *Interpreting the Old Testament Theologically*, 135–49.

Backfish, Elizabeth H. P. "Biblical Wisdom as a Model for Christian Liberal Arts Education." *Christian Higher Education* 18, no. 5 (2019): 382–96.

———. "Blessed Destroyer: The Characterization of Jael as a Warrior in Command and an Instrument of YHWH." In *Characters and Characterization in the Book of Judges*, edited by Keith Bodner and Benjamin J. M. Johnson, 55–74. T&T Clark, 2023.

Bailey, Clinton. *Bedouin Culture in the Bible*. Yale University Press, 2018.

Baker, Heather D. "Urban Craftsmen and Other Specialists, Their Land Holdings, and the Neo-Assyrian State." In *Dynamics of Production in the Ancient Near East*, edited by Juan Carlos Moreno García. Oxbow Books, 2016 (consulted online).

Balberg, Mira. "The Animalistic Gullet and the Godlike Soul: Reframing Sacrifice in Midrash Leviticus Rabbah." *Association for Jewish Studies Review* 38, no. 2 (2014): 221–47.

Balentine, Samuel E., ed. *The Oxford Handbook of Ritual and Worship in the Hebrew Bible*. Oxford University Press, 2020.

Barcelona Field Studies Center. "Over-Cultivation." https://geographyfieldwork.com/GeographyVocabularyGCSEFarming.htm.

Barr, James. "The Image of God in the Book of Genesis: A Study of Terminology." *Bulletin of the John Rylands Library* 51, no. 1 (1968): 11–26.

Bartholomew, Craig G. *Where Mortals Dwell: A Christian View of Place for Today*. Baker Academic, 2011.

Bartholomew, Craig, and Ryan O'Dowd. *Old Testament Wisdom: A Theological Introduction*. IVP Academic, 2011.

Beard, James. *Delights and Prejudices*. Running Press, 2002.

Becking, Bob. *The Fall of Samaria: An Historical and Archaeological Study*. Brill, 1992.

Beckwith, Roger T., and Martin J. Selman, eds. *Sacrifice in the Bible*. Wipf & Stock, 1995.

Berlejung, Angelika. "Washing the Mouth: Consecration of Divine Images in Mesopotamia." In van der Toorn, *The Image and the Book*, 45–72.

Berry, Wendell. "The Gift of the Good Land (1979)." In *The Gift of the Good Land: Further Essays Cultural and Agricultural*, 267–81. Counterpoint, 1981.

Bidmead, Julye, and F. Rachel Magdalene. "Legal Status." In *The Oxford Encyclopedia of the Bible and Gender Studies*, edited by Julia M. O'Brien (consulted online).

Bird, Phyllis. "'Male and Female He Created Them': Gen 1:27b in the Context of the Priestly Account of Creation." *Harvard Theological Review* 74, no. 2 (1981): 129–59.

Blenkinsopp, Joseph. *Wisdom and Law in the Old Testament: The Ordering of Life in Israel and Early Judaism*. Rev. ed. The Oxford Bible Series. Oxford University Press, 1995.

Block, Daniel I. *Covenant: The Framework of God's Grand Plan of Redemption*. Baker Academic, 2021.

Boer, Roland. *The Sacred Economy of Ancient Israel*. Library of Ancient Israel Series. Westminster John Knox, 2015.

Borowski, Oded. *Agriculture in Iron Age Israel*. Eisenbrauns, 1987. Reprint, American Schools of Oriental Research, 2002.

Bottéro, Jean. "The Cuisine of Ancient Mesopotamia." *The Biblical Archaeologist* 48, no. 1 (March 1985): 36–47.

———. *Mesopotamia: Writing, Reasoning, and the Gods*. Translated by Zainab Bahrani and Marc Van De Mieroop. University of Chicago Press, 1992.

———. *The Oldest Cuisine in the World*. Translated by Teresa Lavender Fagan. The University of Chicago Press, 2004.

———. "The Oldest Cuisine in the World." In *Everyday Life in Ancient Mesopotamia*, edited by Jean Bottéro, 43–64. Johns Hopkins University Press, 2001.

———. *Textes Culinaires Mesopotamiens*. Eisenbrauns, 1995.

Boyd, Gregory A. *Crucifixion of the Warrior God: Interpreting the Old Testament's Violent Portraits of God in Light of the Cross*. 2 vols. Fortress, 2017.

Brenner, Laurie. "What Is a Symbiotic Relationship?" Sciencing, updated March 24, 2022. https://sciencing.com/symbiotic-relationship-8794702.html.

Briggs, Richard S. "Humans in the Image of God and Other Things Genesis Does Not Make Clear." *Journal of Theological Interpretation* 4, no. 1 (2010): 111–26.

Britannica. "Bāru." Last accessed November 19, 2024. https://www.britannica.com/topic/baru-Mesopotamian-priest.

———. "Casuistry." Last accessed May 16, 2023. https://www.britannica.com/topic/casuistry.

Britannica Academic. "Code of Hammurabi." Last accessed March 2, 2023. https://academic.eb.com/levels/collegiate/article/Code-of-Hammurabi/39076.

Broshi, Magen, and Israel Finkelstein. "The Population of Palestine in Iron Age II." *Bulletin of the American Schools of Oriental Research* 287 (1992): 47–60.

Brown, F., S. Driver, and C. Briggs. "בְּרִית." In *Brown-Driver-Briggs Hebrew and English Lexicon*. Hendrickson Publishers, 1999.

Brown, William E. "Inheritance." In *Baker's Evangelical Dictionary of Biblical Theology*, edited by Walter E. Elwell. Baker, 1996 (consulted online at https://www.biblestudytools.com/dictionaries/bakers-evangelical-dictionary/inheritance.html).

Brown, William P. *Wisdom's Wonder: Character, Creation, and Crisis in the Bible's Wisdom Literature*. Eerdmans, 2014.

Browning, W. R. F. "Asherah." In *A Dictionary of the Bible*. Oxford University Press, 2009 (consulted online).

———. "Baal." In *A Dictionary of the Bible*. Oxford University Press, 2009 (consulted online).

Brueggemann, Walter. *Divine Presence amid Violence: Contextualizing the Book of Joshua*. Cascade Books, 2009.

———. "Food Fight." *Word & World* 33, no. 4 (2013): 319–40.

———. Foreword to *Holiness in Israel*, by John G. Gammie. Wipf & Stock, 1989.

———. *The Land: Place as Gift, Promise, and Challenge in Biblical Faith*. 2nd ed. Overtures to Biblical Theology. Fortress, 2002.

———. *Living Toward a Vision: Biblical Reflections on Shalom*. Pilgrim Press, 1982.

———. *Reverberations of Faith: A Theological Handbook of Old Testament Themes*. Westminster John Knox, 2002.

———. *Theology of the Old Testament: Testimony, Dispute, Advocacy*. Fortress, 1997.

———. *Worship in Israel: An Essential Guide*. Abingdon, 2005.

Bullinger, Henrich. "A Brief Exposition of the One and Eternal Testament or Covenant of God." In *Fountainhead of Federalism: Heinrich Bullinger and the Covenantal Tradition*, edited by Charles McCoy, 99–139. Westminster John Knox, 1991.

Burke, David G. "Baal." In *The Oxford Companion to the Bible*, edited by Bruce M. Metzger and Michael D. Coogan. Oxford University Press, 1993 (consulted online).

Calvin, John. *Institutes of the Christian Religion*. 2 vols. Edited by John T. McNeill. Translated by Ford Lewis Battles. Westminster, 1960.

Cambridge Dictionary. "Bas-relief." https://dictionary.cambridge.org/us/dictionary/english/bas-relief.

Cargill, Robert R. "Why Christians Should Adopt the BCE/CE Dating System." The Bible and Interpretation, September 2009. https://bibleinterp.arizona.edu/opeds/why_3530.

Carter, Charles E. "A Discipline in Transition: The Contributions of the Social Sciences to the Study of the Hebrew Bible." In *Community, Identity, and Ideology: Social Science Approaches to the Hebrew Bible*, edited by Charles E. Carter and Carol Meyers, 3–36. Sources for Biblical and Theological Study 6. Eisenbrauns, 1996.

Charles, Mark, and Soong-Chan Rah. *Unsettling Truths: The Ongoing, Dehumanizing Legacy of the Doctrine of Discovery*. InterVarsity, 2019.

Chisholm, Robert B., Jr. "Suppressing Myth: Yahweh and the Sea in the Praise Psalms." In *The Psalms: Language for All Seasons*, edited by Andrew J. Schmutzer and David M. Howard Jr., 75–84. Moody, 2013.

Claassens, L. Juliana M. *The God Who Provides: Biblical Images of Divine Nourishment*. Abingdon, 2004.

Collins, C. John. *Reading Genesis Well: Navigating History, Poetry, Science, and Truth in Genesis 1–11*. Zondervan, 2018.

Cook, Sarah. "BCE and CE versus BC and AD." Bible Odyssey. https://www.bibleodyssey.org/articles/bce-and-ce-versus-bc-and-ad/.

Copan, Paul. *Is God a Moral Monster? Making Sense of the Old Testament God*. Baker Books, 2011.

Cornelius, Izak. "The Many Faces of God: Divine Images and Symbols in Ancient Near Eastern Religions." In van der Toorn, *The Image and the Book*, 21–43.

———. "The Visual Representation of the World in the Ancient Near East and the Hebrew Bible." *Journal of Northwest Semitic Languages* 20, no. 2 (1994): 193–218.

Cornell, Collin. "Israel's Priority in Old Testament Missiology." *Missiology: An International Review* 51, no. 4 (2023): 347–60.

Craigie, Peter C. *The Problem of War in the Old Testament*. Eerdmans, 1978.

Creach, Jerome. *Violence in Scripture*. Interpretation. Westminster John Knox, 2013.

Crenshaw, James. *Old Testament Wisdom: An Introduction*. Rev. ed. Westminster John Knox, 1998.

Cross, Frank Moore. *From Epic to Canon: History and Literature in Ancient Israel*. Johns Hopkins University Press, 1998.

Curtis, Robert I. *Ancient Food Technology*. Technology and Change in History Series 5. Brill, 2001.

Dallaire, Hélène M. "Taking the Land by Force: Divine Violence in Joshua." In *Wrestling with the Violence of God: Soundings in the Old Testament*, edited by M. Daniel Carroll R. and J. Blair Wilgus, 51–74. Eisenbrauns, 2015.

Darby, Erin. *Interpreting Judean Pillar Figurines*. Forschung zum Alten Testament 2/69. Mohr Siebeck, 2014.

Darby, Erin, and Izaak J. de Hulster. *Iron Age Terracotta Figurines from the Southern Levant in Context*. Brill, 2021.

Daviau, P. M. Michele. *Houses and Their Furnishings in Bronze Age Palestine: Domestic Activity Areas and Artefact Distribution in the Middle and Late Bronze Ages*. JSOT/ASOR Monograph Series 8. Sheffield Academic Press, 1993.

Davis, Ellen F. *Scripture, Culture, and Agriculture: An Agrarian Reading of the Bible*. Cambridge University Press, 2009.

Davis, Katherine. "The Metaphor of Sexual and Physical Violence as a Speech Act in Ezekiel 16." *Journal for the Study of Bible and Violence* 2 (2023): 21–33.

Day, John. "The Canaanite Inheritance of the Israelite Monarchy." In *King and Messiah in Israel and the Ancient Near East: Proceedings of the Oxford Old Testament*

Seminar, edited by John Day, 72–90. Journal for the Study of the Old Testament Supplement Series 270. Sheffield Academic Press, 1998.

deClaissé-Walford, Nancy, Rolf A. Jacobson, and Beth LaNeel Tanner. *The Book of Psalms*. New International Commentary on the Old Testament. Eerdmans, 2014.

de Hulster, Izaak J. "Iron Age Terracotta Figurines from the Levant: A Comparative and Iconographic Perspective." In *Iron Age Terracotta Figurines from the Southern Levant in Context*, edited by Erin D. Darby and Izaak J. de Hulster, 10–49. Culture and History of the Ancient Near East 125. Brill, 2021.

Dell, Katherine. "Deciding the Boundaries of 'Wisdom': Applying the Concept of Family Resemblance." In *Was There a Wisdom Tradition? New Prospects in Israelite Wisdom Studies*, edited by Mark Sneed, 145–60. SBL, 2015.

Dempster, Stephen G. *Dominion and Dynasty: A Theology of the Hebrew Bible*. New Studies in Biblical Theology 15. IVP Academic, 2003.

de Vaux, Roland. *Ancient Israel: Its Life and Institutions*. Translated by John McHugh. Eerdmans, 1997.

Dever, William G. *Did God Have a Wife? Archaeology and Folk Religion in Ancient Israel*. Eerdmans, 2005.

Dietler, Michael, and Brian Hayden. "Digesting the Feast: Good to Eat, Good to Drink, Good to Think: An Introduction." In *Feasts: Archaeological and Ethnographical Perspectives on Food, Politics, and Power*, edited by M. Dietler and B. Hayden, 1–20. Smithsonian Series in Archaeological Inquiry. Smithsonian, 2001.

Dospěl, Marek. "A Rival to Solomon's Temple: The Place of Worship at Tel Moẓa Explained." Biblical Archaeology Society, September 14, 2021. https://www.biblicalarchaeology.org/daily/biblical-sites-places/temple-at-jerusalem/a-rival-to-solomons-temple/.

Douglas, Mary. "Deciphering a Meal." *Daedalus* 101 (1972): 61–81.

———. *Leviticus as Literature*. Oxford University Press, 2001.

———. *Purity and Danger: An Analysis of Concepts of Pollution and Taboo*. Routledge & Kegan Paul, 1966.

Drever, Matthew. "Image, Identity, and Embodiment: Augustine's Interpretation of the Human Person in Genesis 1–2." In *Genesis and Christian Theology*, edited by Nathan MacDonald, Mark W. Elliott, and Grant Macaskill, 117–28. Eerdmans, 2012.

Dumbrell, William. *Covenant and Creation: An Old Testament Covenant Theology*. Rev. ed. Paternoster, 2013.

Ebeling, Jennie R. "Ethnoarchaeology." In Shafer-Elliott, *Five-Minute Archaeologist*, 154–56.

———. "Grains, Bread, and Beer." In Fu et al., *T&T Clark Handbook of Food*, 99–112.

———. *Women's Lives in Biblical Times*. T&T Clark, 2010.

Eichrodt, Walther. *Theology of the Old Testament*. 2 vols. Translated by John A. Baker. SCM, 1961; Westminster 1967.

Eklund, Rebekah. "Blessed are the Image-Bearers: Gregory of Nyssa and the Beatitudes." *Anglican Theological Review* 99, no. 4 (2017): 729–40.

Faust, Avraham. *The Archaeology of Israelite Society in Iron Age II*. Translated by Ruth Ludlum. Eisenbrauns, 2012.

Fee, Gordon D. and Douglas Stuart. *How to Read the Bible for All Its Worth*. 4th ed. Zondervan, 2014.

Finkelstein, J. J., trans. "The Edict of Ammisaduqa." In Pritchard, *Ancient Near East*, 183–87.

Foster, Richard J. *Celebration of Discipline: The Path to Spiritual Growth*. Hodder & Stoughton, 2008.

Fox, Michael. "Three Theses on Wisdom." In *Was There a Wisdom Tradition? New Prospects in Israelite Wisdom Studies*, edited by Mark Sneed, 69–86. SBL, 2015.

Frankel, David. "Integrating the Exodus Story into the Festivals." TheTorah.com. Accessed January 4, 2022. https://thetorah.com/article/integrating-the-exodus-story-into-the-festivals.

Frayne, Douglas R., and Johanna H. Stuckey. *A Handbook of Gods and Goddesses of the Ancient Near East: Three Thousand Deities of Anatolia, Syria, Israel, Sumer, Babylonia, Assyria, and Elam*. Eisenbrauns, 2021.

Frevel, Christian, and Christophe Nihan, eds. *Purity and the Forming of Religious Traditions in the Ancient Mediterranean World and Ancient Judaism*. Dynamics in the History of Religions 3. Brill, 2012.

Frymer-Kensky, Tikva. "Pollution, Purification, and Purgation in Biblical Israel." In *The Word of the Lord Shall Go Forth: Essays in Honor of David Noel Freedman in Celebration of His Sixtieth Birthday*, edited by Carol L. Meyers and M. O'Connor, 399–414. American Schools of Oriental Research, 1983.

Fu, Janling, Cynthia Shafer-Elliott, and Carol Meyers, eds. *The T&T Clark Handbook of Food in the Hebrew Bible and Ancient Israel*. T&T Clark, 2022.

Gammie, John G. *Holiness in Israel*. Fortress, 1989.

Gane, Roy E. "Ritual and Religious Practices." In Balentine, *Oxford Handbook of Ritual and Worship*, 223–39.

———. "Worship, Sacrifice, and Festivals in the Ancient Near East." In Greer, Hilber, and Walton, *Behind the Scenes of the Old Testament*, 361–67.

Garr, W. Randall. "'Image' and 'Likeness' in the Inscription from Tell Fakhariyeh." *Israel Exploration Journal* 50, nos. 3–4 (2000): 227–34.

Ginsburskaya, Mila. "Purity and Impurity in the Hebrew Bible." In *Purity: Essays in Bible and Theology*, edited by Andrew Brower Latz and Arseny Ermakov, 3–29. Pickwick, 2014.

Girard, René. *Violence and the Sacred*. Translated by Patrick Gregory. The Johns Hopkins University Press, 1972.

Goetze, Albrecht. "An Old Babylonian Prayer of the Divination Priest." *Journal of Cuneiform Studies* 22, no. 2 (1968): 25–29.

Goldingay, John. *Israel's Gospel*. Vol. 1 of *Old Testament Theology*. IVP Academic, 2003.

———. *Israel's Faith*. Vol. 2 of *Old Testament Theology*. IVP Academic, 2006.

———. *Israel's Life*. Vol. 3 of *Old Testament Theology*. IVP Academic, 2009.

———. *Psalms*. Vol. 2, *Psalms 42–89*. Baker Commentary on the Old Testament Wisdom and Psalms. Baker Academic, 2007.

———. *Theological Diversity and the Authority of the Old Testament*. Eerdmans, 1987.

Goody, Jack. *Cooking, Cuisine, and Class: A Study in Comparative Sociology*. Cambridge University Press, 1982.

Goshen-Gottstein, Alon. "The Body as Image of God in Rabbinic Literature." *Harvard Theological Review* 87, no. 2 (1994): 171–95.

Goswell, Gregory. "What Happened to the Empire of David?" *Restoration Quarterly* 63, no. 3 (2021): 140–60.

Gottwald, Norman K. "Sociology of Ancient Israel." In *The Anchor Yale Bible Dictionary*, edited by David N. Freedman, 79–89. Yale University Press, 1992.

Greer, Jonathan S. *Dinner at Dan: Biblical and Archaeological Evidence for Sacred Feasts at Iron Age II Tel Dan and Their Significance*. Culture and History of the Ancient Near East 66. Brill, 2013.

Greer, Jonathan S., John W. Hilber, and John H. Walton, eds. *Behind the Scenes of the Old Testament: Cultural, Social, and Historical Contexts*. Baker Academic, 2018.

Gudme de Hemmer, Anne Katrine. "Invitation to Murder: Hospitality and Violence in the Hebrew Bible." *Studia Theologica* 73, no. 1 (2019): 89–108.

Guichard, Michaël, and Lionel Marti. "Purity in Ancient Mesopotamia: The Paleo-Babylonian and Neo-Assyrian Periods." In Frevel and Nihan, *Purity and the Forming of Religious Traditions*, 47–114.

Hall, Mark G. "A Hymn to the Moon-God, Nanna." *Journal of Cuneiform Studies* 38, no. 2 (1986): 152–66.

Hamilakis, Yannis. "Food Technologies/Technologies of the Body: The Social Context of Wine and Oil Production and Consumption in Bronze Age Crete." *World Archaeology* 31, no. 1 (1999): 38–54.

Hanson, Paul. "War and Peace in the Hebrew Bible." *Interpretation* 38, no. 4 (1984): 341–62.

Hardin, James W. *Lahav II—Households and the Use of Domestic Space at Iron II Tell Halif: An Archaeology of Destruction*. Reports of the Lahav Research Project at Tell Halif, Israel Series 2. Edited by J. D. Seger. Eisenbrauns, 2010.

Harmanşah, Ömür. "Beyond Aššur: New Cities and the Assyrian Politics of Landscape." *Bulletin of the American Schools of Oriental Research* 365 (2012): 53–77.

Harris, Patricia, David Lyon, and Sue McLaughlin. *The Meaning of Food*. Globe Pequot Press, 2005.

Hartenstein, Friedhelm. "God, Gods, and Humankind (Worldview)." In Balentine, *Oxford Handbook of Ritual and Worship*, 146–59.

Hastorf, Christine A. *The Social Archaeology of Food: Thinking About Eating from Prehistory to the Present*. Cambridge University Press, 2017.

Hays, Christopher B. *Hidden Riches: A Sourcebook for the Comparative Study of the Hebrew Bible and Ancient Near East*. Westminster John Knox, 2014.

Herzfeld, Michael. "As in Your Own House: Hospitality, Ethnography, and the Stereotype of Mediterranean Society." In *Honor and Shame and the Unity of the Mediterranean*, edited by David D. Gilmore, 75–89. American Anthropological Association, 1987.

Hess, Richard S. "The Family in the Old Testament as a Theological Model for Covenant Community." In Abernethy, *Interpreting the Old Testament Theologically*, 270–79.

———. *Israelite Religions: An Archaeological and Biblical Survey*. Baker Academic, 2007.

Hieke, Thomas. "Ritual Experts and Participants in the Ancient Near East and the Hebrew Bible." In Balentine, *Oxford Handbook of Ritual and Worship*, 179–93.

Hiers, Richard H. "Transfer of Property by Inheritance and Bequest in Biblical Law and Tradition." *Journal of Law and Religion* 10, no. 1 (1993): 121–55.

"History of Salad Dressings." The Association for Dressings and Sauces. Accessed November 13, 2024. https://dressings-sauces.org/history-of-salad-dressings/.

Hitchcock, Louise A. "Cult Corners in the Aegean and the Levant." In *Household Archaeology in Ancient Israel and Beyond*, edited by Assaf Yasur-Landau, Jennie R. Ebeling, and Laura B. Mazow, 321–45. Culture and History of the Ancient Near East 50. Brill, 2011.

Hoffner, Harry A., Jr. "Theodicy in Hittite Texts." In *Theodicy in the World of the Bible*, edited by Antti Laato and Johannes C. de Moor, 90–107. Brill, 2003.

Hopkins, David C. *The Highlands of Canaan*. The Social World of Biblical Antiquity Series 3. Almond Press, 1985.

Howard, David M., Jr., and Michael K. Snearly. "Reading the Psalter as a Unified Book: Recent Trends." In *Reading the Psalms Theologically*, edited by David M. Howard Jr. and Andrew J. Schmutzer, 1–35. Lexham Academic, 2023.

Hugenberger, Gordon P. *Marriage as a Covenant: Biblical Law and Ethics as Developed from Malachi*. Baker, 1998.

Hundley, Michael B. *Gods in Dwellings: Temples and Divine Presence in the Ancient Near East*. Society of Biblical Literature, 2013.

———. "Sacred Space and Common Space." In Balentine, *Oxford Handbook of Ritual and Worship*, 161–78.

Hunt, Robert C. *Beyond Relativism: Rethinking the Concepts of Property and Land Tenure*. Cambridge University Press, 2010.

Hurowitz, Victor. "Solomon's Temple in Context." *Biblical Archaeology Review* 37, no. 2 (2011): 46–57, 77–78. https://library.biblicalarchaeology.org/article/solomons-temple-in-context/.

Hwang, Jerry. "Yahweh's Poetic *Mishpat* in Israel's Kingship: A Reassessment of 1 Samuel 8–12." *Westminster Theological Journal* 73 (2011): 341–61.

Imes, Carmen Joy. *Bearing God's Name: Why Sinai Still Matters*. IVP Academic, 2019.

———. *Being God's Image: Why Creation Still Matters*. IVP Academic, 2023.

Jacobs, Haley Gorganson. *Conformed to the Image of His Son: Reconsidering Paul's Theology of Glory in Romans*. IVP Academic, 2018.

Jasanoff, Maya. "Ancestor Worship." *The New Yorker*, May 2, 2022, 69–73.

Jennings, Willie James. *Acts*. Belief: A Theological Commentary on the Bible. Westminster John Knox, 2017.

Jenson, Philip P. *Graded Holiness: A Key to the Priestly Conception of the World*. Journal for the Study of the Old Testament Supplement Series 106. Sheffield Academic Press, 1992.

———. "Holiness in the Priestly Writings of the Old Testament." In *Holiness: Past and Present*, edited by Stephen Barton, 93–121. T&T Clark, 2002.

Johnson, Dru. *Knowledge by Ritual: A Biblical Prolegomenon to Sacramental Theology*. Eisenbrauns, 2016.

Johnston, Philip. *Shades of Sheol: Death and Afterlife in the Old Testament*. InterVarsity, 2002.

Jones, Beth Felker. *Practicing Christian Doctrine: An Introduction to Thinking and Living Theologically*. Baker Academic, 2014.

Jones, Beth Felker, and Jeffrey W. Bareau, eds. *The Image of God in an Image Driven Age: Explorations in Theological Anthropology*. Wheaton Theology Conference Series. IVP Academic, 2016.

Jorgenson, Cameron H. J. "The Pleasures of Food and the Good Life." *Review and Expositor* 117, no. 4 (2020): 483–96.

Judd, Andrew. *Modern Genre Theory: An Introduction for Biblical Studies*. Studies in Method. Zondervan Academic, 2024.

Kang, Sa-Moon. *Divine War in the Old Testament and in the Ancient Near East*. De Gruyter, 1989.

Kataja, Laura, and Robert Whiting. *Grants, Decrees and Gifts of the Neo-Assyrian Period*. State Archives of Assyria 12. Helsinki University Press, 1995.

Keel, Othmar. *The Symbolism of the Biblical World: Ancient Near Eastern Iconography and the Book of Psalms*. Translated by Timothy J. Hallett. Eisenbrauns, 1997.

Keel, Othmar, and Christoph Uehlinger. *Gods, Goddesses, and Images of God in Ancient Israel*. Translated by Thomas H. Trapp. Fortress, 1998.

Kilchör, Benjamin. "Levirate Obligation in the Hebrew Bible." In *Oxford Bibliographies*. Accessed August 9, 2024. https://www.oxfordbibliographies.com/view/document/obo-9780195393361/obo-9780195393361-0296.xml.

Kilner, John F. *Dignity and Destiny: Humanity in the Image of God*. Eerdmans, 2015.

King, Philip J., and Lawrence E. Stager. *Life in Biblical Israel*. Westminster John Knox, 2001.

Kitchen, Kenneth A., and Paul J. N. Lawrence. *Treaty, Law and Covenant in the Ancient Near East*. 3 vols. Harrassowitz Verlag, 2012.

Klawans, Jonathan. *Purity, Sacrifice, and the Temple: Symbolism and Supersessionism in the Study of Ancient Judaism*. Oxford University Press, 2006.

Kletter, Raz. *Judean Pillar-Figurines and the Archaeology of Asherah*. British Archaeological Reports 636. Tempus Reparatum, 1996.

Knight, Michelle. *The Prophet's Anthem: The Song of Deborah and Barak in the Narrative of Judges*. Baylor University Press, 2024.

Koehler, Ludwig, Walter Baumgartner, M. E. J. Richardson, and J. J. Stamm. *Hebrew and Aramaic Lexicon of the Old Testament*. 5 vols. Brill, 1999–2001.

Kramer, S. N., trans. "The Hymnal Prayer of Enheduanna: The Adoration of Inanna of Ur." In Pritchard, *Ancient Near East*, 332–37.

Kraus, Hans Joachim. *Psalms 1–59: A Commentary*. Translated by Hilton C. Oswald. Augsburg, 1988.

Kugler, Christopher. *Paul and the Image of God*. Lexington Books / Fortress Academic, 2020.

Kutsko, John. *Between Heaven and Earth: Divine Presence and Absence in the Book of Ezekiel*. Eisenbrauns, 2000.

Kynes, Will. "Genre as Reception: A Multidimensional Network Approach." *Journal of the Bible and Its Reception* (2023): 1–29.

———. *An Obituary for "Wisdom Literature": The Birth, Death, and Intertextual Reintegration of a Biblical Corpus*. Oxford University Press, 2019.

Laato, Antti, and Johannes C. de Moor. Introduction to *Theodicy in the World of the Bible*, edited by Antti Laato and Johannes C. de Moor, vii–liv. Brill, 2003.

Lambert, W. G. "Kingship in Ancient Mesopotamia." In *King and Messiah in Israel and the Ancient Near East: Proceedings of the Oxford Old Testament Seminar*, edited by John Day, 55–70. Journal for the Study of the Old Testament Supplement Series 270. Sheffield Academic Press, 1998.

Lauinger, Jacob. "The Neo-Assyrian *adê*: Treaty, Oath, or Something Else?" *Journal for Ancient Near Eastern and Biblical Law* 19 (2013): 99–115.

———. "Neo-Assyrian Scribes, 'Esarhaddon's Succession Treaty,' and the Dynamics of Textual Mass Production." In *Texts and Contexts: The Circulation and Transmission of Cuneiform Texts in Social Space*, edited by Paul Delnero and Jacob Lauinger, 285–314. De Gruyter, 2015.

Lawrence, Jonathan D. "Clean/Unclean, Pure/Impure, Holy/Profane." In Balentine, *Oxford Handbook of Ritual and Worship*, 301–10.

LeFebvre, Michael. *Collections, Codes, and Torah: The Re-characterization of Israel's Written Law*. The Library of Hebrew Bible / Old Testament Studies 451. T&T Clark, 2006.

Levenson, Jon D. *The Love of God: Divine Gift, Human Gratitude, and Mutual Faithfulness in Judaism*. Princeton University Press, 2016.

———. *Sinai and Zion: An Entry into the Jewish Bible*. Harper & Row, 1985.

———. "The Temple and the World." *Journal of Religion* 64 (1984): 275–98.

Levine, Amy-Jill, and Marc Zvi Brettler. *The Bible With and Without Jesus: How Jews and Christians Read the Same Stories Differently*. HarperCollins, 2020.

Levine, Baruch A. *Leviticus*. The JPS Torah Commentary. Jewish Publication Society, 1989.

Levinson, Bernard. "The Reconceptualization of Kingship in Deuteronomy and the Deuteronomistic History's Transformation of Torah." *Vetus Testamentum* 51, no. 4 (2001): 511–34.

Lev Tov, Justin. "Animal Husbandry: Meat, Milk, and More." In Fu et al., *T&T Clark Handbook of Food*, 77–98.

Lewis, C. S. *Mere Christianity*. HarperCollins, 2015.

Liau, Timothy. "Theology of Warfare in Deuteronomy." *Taiwan Journal of Theology* 15 (1993): 61–81.

Lind, Millard C. *Yahweh Is a Warrior: The Theology of Warfare in Ancient Israel*. Herald, 1980.

Lints, Richard. *Identity and Idolatry: The Image of God and Its Inversion*. New Studies in Biblical Theology 36. Apollos / IVP Academic, 2015.

Liverani, Mario. *The Ancient Near East: History, Society, and Economy*. Routledge, 2014.

Longman, Tremper III. *The Fear of the Lord Is Wisdom: A Theological Introduction to Wisdom in Israel*. Baker Academic, 2017.

———. *Genesis*. The Story of God Bible Commentary. Zondervan, 2016.

———. "Kinsman-Redeemer and Levirate." In *Dictionary of the Old Testament: Wisdom, Poetry & Writings*, edited by Tremper Longman III and Peter Enns, 378–83. IVP Academic, 2008.

———. *Psalms: An Introduction and Commentary*. Tyndale Old Testament Commentary. IVP Academic, 2014.

Longman, Tremper III, and Peter Enns, eds. *Dictionary of the Old Testament: Wisdom, Poetry & Writings*. IVP Academic, 2008.

Lucas, Ernest C. "Sacrifice in the Prophets." In *Sacrifice and the Bible*, edited by Roger T. Beckwith and Martin J. Selman, 59–74. Wipf & Stock, 1995.

Luckenbill, Daniel David. *Ancient Records of Assyria and Babylonia*. Vol. 1, *Historical Records of Assyria from the Earliest Time to Sargon*. Greenwood Press, 1968.

Lynch, Matthew. *Flood and Fury: Old Testament Violence and the Shalom of God*. IVP Academic, 2023.

MacDonald, Nathan. *Not Bread Alone: The Uses of Food in the Old Testament*. Oxford University Press, 2008.

———. "The Spirit of YHWH: An Overlooked Conceptualization of Divine Presence in the Persian Period." In *Divine Presence and Absence in Exilic and Post-Exilic Judaism*, edited by Nathan MacDonald and Izaak J. de Hulster, 95–120. Forschungen zum Alten Testament 2. Reihe 61. Mohr Siebeck, 2013.

———. *What Did the Ancient Israelites Eat? Diet in Biblical Times.* Eerdmans, 2008.

Maeir, Aren M. "Gath." In *Encyclopedia of the Bible and Its Reception*, edited by Constance M. Furey et al. De Gruyter, 2010 (consulted online).

Mahjoub, F., K. A. Rezayat, M. Yousefi, M. Mohebbi, and R. Salari. "*Pistacia atlantica* Desf: A Review of Its Traditional Uses, Phytochemicals and Pharmacology." *Journal of Medicine and Life* 11 (2018): 180–86.

Maimonides. *The Code of Maimonides, Book 10: The Book of Cleanness.* Edited by Julian Obermann. Translated by Herbert Danby. Yale University Press, 1954.

Martin, Oren R. *Bound for the Promised Land: The Land Promise in God's Redemptive Plan.* New Studies in Biblical Theology 34. InterVarsity, 2015.

Master, Daniel M. "Chronology of the Southern Levant." In *The Oxford Encyclopedia of the Bible and Archaeology*, edited by Daniel M. Master, 455–61. Oxford University Press, 2013.

Matthews, Victor H. *The Cultural World of the Bible: An Illustrated Guide to Manners and Customs.* 4th ed. Baker Academic, 2015.

———. "Family, Children, and Inheritance in the Biblical World." In Greer, Hilber, and Walton, *Behind the Scenes of the Old Testament*, 403–8.

Matthews, Victor H., and Don C. Benjamin. *Social World of Ancient Israel: 1250–587 BCE.* Baker Academic, 2005.

Mazar, Amihai. "Temples of the Middle and Late Bronze Ages and Iron Age." In *The Architecture of Ancient Israel: From the Prehistoric to the Persian Periods*, edited by Aaron Kempinski and Ronny Reich, 161–87. Israel Exploration Society, 1992.

Mazar, Amihai, and Nava Panitz-Cohen. "To What God? Altars and a House Shrine from Tel Rehov Puzzle Archaeologists." *Biblical Archaeology Review* 34, no. 4 (2008): 40–47, 76.

McCaulley, Esau. *Reading While Black: African American Biblical Interpretation as an Exercise in Hope.* IVP Academic, 2020.

McClellan, Daniel O. *YHWH's Divine Images: A Cognitive Approach.* Ancient Near East Monographs 29. SBL, 2022.

McConville, Gordan. "בְּרִית." In VanGemeren, *New International Dictionary of Old Testament Theology and Exegesis*, 1:747–55.

McDowell, Catherine L. "In the Image of God He Created Them: How Genesis 1:26–27 Defines the Divine-Human Relationship and Why It Matters." In *The Image of God in an Image Driven Age: Explorations in Theological Anthropology*, edited by Beth Felker Jones and Jeffrey W. Barbeau, 29–46. IVP Academic, 2016.

———. *The Image of God in the Garden of Eden: The Creation of Humankind in Genesis 2:5–3:24 in Light of the* mīs pî pīt pî *and* wpt-r *Rituals of Mesopotamia and Ancient Egypt.* Pennsylvania State University Press, 2015.

McGeough, Kevin M. "Cosmology, Near East." In *Oxford Bibliographies*. Accessed October 26, 2023. https://www.oxfordbibliographies.com/display/document/obo-9780195393361/obo-9780195393361-0201.xml.

Meek, Theophile J., trans. "The Code of Hammurabi." In Pritchard, *Ancient Near East*, 155–79.

Melton, Brittany. "An Invitation to a New Era of Biblical Theology: Towards an Old Testament Theology of Hospitality." *Tyndale Bulletin* 74 (2023): 113–41.

Mendenhall, George. "Covenant Forms in Israelite Tradition." *The Biblical Archaeologist* 17, no. 3 (1954): 50–76.

———. *Law and Covenant in Israel and the Ancient Near East*. The Biblical Colloquium, 1955.

Merriam-Webster Dictionary. "Bovid." https://www.merriam-webster.com/dictionary/bovid.

———. "Dowry." https://www.merriam-webster.com/dictionary/dowry.

———. "Genre." https://www.merriam-webster.com/dictionary/genre.

———. "Gleaning." https://www.merriam-webster.com/dictionary/gleaning.

———. "Meet-cute." https://www.merriam-webster.com/dictionary/meet%20cute.

———. "Strongman." https://www.merriam-webster.com/dictionary/strongman.

Meshel, Ze'ev. "Kuntillet 'Ajrud." In *The Oxford Encyclopedia of Archaeology in the Near East*, edited by Eric M. Meyers. Oxford Biblical Studies Online. Accessed January 20, 2020.

Meyers, Carol. "Archaeology—A Window to the Lives of Israelite Women." In *Torah*, edited by Irmtraud Fischer, Mercedes Navarro Puerto, Andrea Taschl-Erber, and Jorunn Økland, 61–108. SBL—The Bible and Women Series 1.1. Brill, 2012.

———. "The Family in Early Israel." In Perdue et al., *Families in Ancient Israel*, 1–47.

———. "Having Their Space and Eating There Too: Bread Production and Female Power in Ancient Israelite Households." *Nashim: A Journal of Jewish Women's Studies & Gender Issues* 5 (2002): 14–44.

———. "Procreation, Production, and Protection: Male-Female Balance in Early Israel." *Journal of the American Academy of Religion* 51, no. 4 (1983): 569–93.

———. *Rediscovering Eve: Ancient Israelite Women in Context*. Oxford University Press, 2013.

Middleton, J. Richard. *The Liberating Image: The* Imago Dei *in Genesis 1*. Baker Academic, 2005.

Milgrom, Jacob. *Leviticus 1–16: A New Translation with Introduction and Commentary*. Anchor Bible 3. Doubleday, 1991.

———. *Leviticus 17–22: A New Translation with Introduction and Commentary*. Anchor Bible 3a. Doubleday, 2000.

———. *Leviticus 23–27: A New Translation with Introduction and Commentary*. Anchor Bible 3b. Doubleday, 2001.

Millard, A. R., and P. Bordreuil. "A Statue from Syria with Assyrian and Aramaic Inscriptions." *The Biblical Archaeologist* 45, no. 3 (1982): 135–41.

Miller, Patrick D. *The Divine Warrior in Early Israel*. Harvard University Press, 1973.

———. *The Religion of Ancient Israel*. Library of Ancient Israel. Westminster John Knox, 2000.

Moberly, R. W. L. *Old Testament Theology: Reading the Hebrew Bible as Christian Scripture*. Baker Academic, 2013.

Monson, John. "The New 'Ain Dara Temple: Closest Solomonic Parallel." *Biblical Archaeology Review* 26, no. 3 (2000): 20–35, 67.

———. "Original Context and Canon." In Abernethy, *Interpreting the Old Testament Theologically*, 25–42.

Mowinckel, Sigmund. *He That Cometh*. Translated by G. W. Anderson. Abingdon, 1954.

Mtshiselwa, Ndikho. *To Whom Belongs the Land? Leviticus 25 in an African Liberationist Reading*. Bible and Theology in Africa 23. Peter Lang, 2018.

Nam, Roger S. *Portrayals of Economic Exchange in the Book of Kings*. Brill, 2012.

National Geographic. "Rain Shadow." Updated October 19, 2023. https://education.nationalgeographic.org/resource/rain-shadow/.

Naudé, Jackie A. "קדש" In VanGemeren, *New International Dictionary of Old Testament Theology and Exegesis*, 3:877–87.

Nel, Philip J. "שלם" In VanGemeren, *New International Dictionary of Old Testament Theology and Exegesis*, 4:130–35.

Newsom, Carol A., Sharon H. Ringe, and Jacqueline E. Lapsley, eds. *Women's Bible Commentary*. 3rd ed. Westminster John Knox, 2012.

Niditch, Susan. *War in the Hebrew Bible: A Study in the Ethics of Violence*. Oxford University Press, 1993.

Niehr, Herbert. "In Search of YHWH's Cult Statue in the First Temple." In van der Toorn, *The Image and the Book*, 73–95.

Nihan, Christophe. "Forms and Functions of Purity in Leviticus." In Frevel and Nihan, *Purity and the Forming of Religious Traditions*, 311–67.

Ollenburger, Ben C. Introduction to *Holy War in Ancient Israel*, by Gerhard von Rad, 1–34.

Oppenheim, A. Leo, trans. "Esarhaddon (680–669): The Syro-Palestine Campaign." In Pritchard, *Ancient Near East*, 271.

———, trans. "Sargon II (271–705): The Fall of Samaria." In Pritchard, *Ancient Near East*, 266–69.

———, trans. "Senacherib (704–682): The Siege of Jerusalem." In Pritchard, *Ancient Near East*, 269–71.

Oxford English Dictionary. "Endogamy." Accessed August 9, 2024. https://www.oed.com/dictionary/endogamy_n.

Park, Sung Jin. "The Cultic Identity of Asherah in Deuteronomistic Ideology of Israel." *Zeitschrift für die alttestamentliche Wissenschaft* 123, no. 4 (2011): 553–64.

Parpola, Simo, and Kazuko Watanabe. *Neo-Assyrian Treaties and Loyalty Oaths*. State Archives of Assyria 2. Eisenbrauns, 2014.

Peeler, Amy. *Women and the Gender of God*. Eerdmans, 2022.

Peppiatt, Lucy. *The Imago Dei: Humanity Made in the Image of God*. Cascade Companions. Cascade Books, 2022.

Perdue, Leo G. "The Household, Old Testament Theology, and Contemporary Hermeneutics." In Perdue et al., *Families in Ancient Israel*, 223–58.

Perdue, Leo G., Joseph Blenkinsopp, John J. Collins, and Carol Meyers, eds. *Families in Ancient Israel*. The Family, Religion, and Culture Series. Westminster John Knox, 1997.

Pitre, Brant. *Jesus and the Jewish Roots of the Eucharist: Unlocking the Secrets of the Last Supper*. Image, 2016.

Plum, Karin Friis. "Genealogy as Theology." *Scandinavian Journal of the Old Testament* 3, no. 1 (1989): 66–92.

Pritchard, James B., ed. *The Ancient Near East: An Anthology of Texts and Pictures*. Princeton University Press, 2011.

Provan, Iain. *Seriously Dangerous Religion: What the Old Testament Really Says and Why It Matters*. Baylor University Press, 2014.

Provan, Iain, V. Philips Long, and Tremper Longman III. *A Biblical History of Israel*. Westminster John Knox, 2003.

Rasmussen, Carl G. *Essential Atlas of the Bible*. Zondervan, 2013.

Rhodes, Michael J. *Just Discipleship: Biblical Justice in an Unjust World*. IVP Academic, 2023.

Richter, Sandra L. *The Epic of Eden: A Christian Entry into the Old Testament*. IVP Academic, 2008.

———. *Stewards of Eden: What Scripture Says About the Environment and Why It Matters*. IVP Academic, 2020.

Roberts, J. J. M. "The Enthronement of Yhwh and David: The Abiding Theological Significance of the Kingship Language of the Psalms." *Catholic Biblical Quarterly* 64, no. 4 (2002): 675–86.

Rofé, Alexander. "The Laws of Warfare in the Book of Deuteronomy: Their Origins, Intent and Positivity." *Journal for the Study of the Old Testament* 32 (1985): 23–44.

Rogerson, John. "The Family and Structures of Grace in the Old Testament." In *The Family in Theological Perspective*, edited by Stephen Barton, 25–42. T&T Clark, 1996.

Rooke, Deborah W. "Kingship as Priesthood: The Relationship Between the High Priesthood and the Monarchy." In *King and Messiah in Israel and the Ancient Near East: Proceedings of the Oxford Old Testament Seminar*, edited by John Day, 185–208. Journal for the Study of the Old Testament Supplement Series 270. Sheffield Academic Press, 1998.

Roth, Martha T. *Law Collections from Mesopotamia and Asia Minor*. Edited by Piotr Michalowski. Scholars Press, 1995.

Routledge, Robin. *Old Testament Theology: A Thematic Approach*. Apollos, 2008.

Ryczkowski, Angela. "Five Types of Ecological Relationships." Sciencing. Updated March 24, 2022. https://sciencing.com/five-types-ecological-relationships-7786.html.

Sabanal, Annelle. "Leadership, Power, and Authority." In *Exploring the Old Testament in Asia: Evangelical Perspectives*, edited by Jerry Hwang and Angukali Rotokha, 81–100. Foundations in Asian Christian Thought. Langham, 2022.

Sailhamer, John. *Introduction to Old Testament Theology: A Canonical Approach*. Zondervan, 1995.

Schachter, Lifsa. "The Garden of Eden as God's First Sanctuary." *Jewish Bible Quarterly* 41, no. 2 (2013): 73–77.

Schloen, J. David. *The House of the Father as Fact and Symbol: Patrimonialism in Ugarit and the Ancient Near East*. Studies in the Archaeology and History of the Levant 2. Eisenbrauns, 2001.

Schmid, Konrad. *A Historical Theology of the Hebrew Bible*. Eerdmans, 2018.

Schwartz, Mark. "Warfare in the World of the Bible." In Greer, Hilber, and Walton, *Behind the Scenes of the Old Testament*, 506–14.

Seibert, Eric A. *Disturbing Divine Behavior: Troubling Old Testament Images of God*. Fortress, 2009.

Shafer-Elliott, Cynthia. "All in the Family: Ancient Israelite Families in Context." In *Mishpachah: The Jewish Family in Tradition and in Transition*, edited by Leonard Greenspoon, 33–43. Studies in Jewish Civilization. Purdue University Press, 2016.

———. "The Anthropology of Food in the Hebrew Bible." In *The T&T Clark Handbook of Anthropology and the Hebrew Bible*, edited by Emanuel Pfoh, 433–54. T&T Clark, 2023.

———. "Economics—Hebrew Bible." In *The Oxford Encyclopedia of the Bible and Gender Studies*, edited by Julia M. O'Brien (consulted online).

———, ed. *The Five-Minute Archaeologist in the Southern Levant*. Equinox, 2016.

———. *Food in Ancient Judah: Domestic Cooking in the Time of the Hebrew Bible*. Equinox, 2013.

———. "Fruits, Nuts, Vegetables, and Legumes." In Fu et al., *T&T Clark Handbook of Food*, 139–55.

———. "Gender Archaeology." In Shafer-Elliott, *Five-Minute Archaeologist*, 165–69.

———. "The Heroines of Every Day Life: Ancient Israelite Women in Context." In *Jews and Gender*, edited by L. J. Greenspoon, 1–13. Studies in Jewish Civilization. Purdue University Press, 2021.

———. "Household Archaeology." In Shafer-Elliott, *Five-Minute Archaeologist*, 161–64.

———. "Household Economics." In *The Oxford Handbook for Wealth and Poverty in the Biblical World*, edited by Roger Nam and Samuel Adams. Oxford University Press, forthcoming.

———. "The Literary Context of the Hebrew Bible." *The Bible for Normal People* (blog), October 21, 2022. https://thebiblefornormalpeople.com/literary-context-of-hebrew-bible/.

———. "The Role of the Household in the Religious Feasting of Ancient Israel and Judah." In *Feasting in the Archaeology and Texts of the Hebrew Bible and the Ancient Near East*, edited by Peter Altmann and Janling Fu, 199–221. Eisenbrauns, 2014.

———. "Women and Economics in Ancient Israel and Judah." In *Economics and Empire in the Ancient Near East*, edited by Matthew J. M. Coomber, 108–27. Guides to the Bible and Economics 1. Cascade Books, 2023.

Simoons, Frederick J. *Eat Not This Flesh: Food Avoidances in the Old World*. University of Wisconsin Press, 1967.

Sklar, Jay. *Leviticus: An Introduction and Commentary*. Tyndale Old Testament Commentary 3. IVP Academic, 2014.

———. *Sin, Impurity, Sacrifice, Atonement: The Priestly Conceptions*. Hebrew Bible Monographs 2. Sheffield Phoenix, 2015.

Smith, Mark. *The Early History of God: Yahweh and the Other Deities in Ancient Israel*. 2nd ed. Eerdmans, 2002.

———. "'Your People Shall Be My People': Family and Covenant in Ruth 1:16–17." *Catholic Biblical Quarterly* 69, no. 2 (2007): 242–58.

Snell, Daniel C. *Religions of the Ancient Near East*. Cambridge University Press, 2011.

Sommer, Benjamin. *The Bodies of God and the World of Ancient Israel*. Cambridge University Press, 2009.

———. "Dialogical Biblical Theology: A Jewish Approach to Reading Scripture Theologically." In *Biblical Theology: Introducing the Conversation*, edited by Leo Perdue, Robert Morgan, and Benjamin D. Sommer, 1–54. Library of Biblical Theology. Abingdon, 2009.

Soulen, R. Kendall. *The God of Israel and Christian Theology*. Fortress, 1996.

Stark, David J. "To Your Seed I Will Give . . . : The Land(s) Promised to Abraham in Genesis and Second Temple Judaism." *Bulletin for Biblical Research* 30, no. 1 (2020): 1–21.

Stavrakopoulou, Francesca. *God: An Anatomy*. Knopf, 2023.

———. "'Popular' Religion and 'Official' Religion: Practice, Perception, Portrayal." In *Religious Diversity in Ancient Israel and Judah*, edited by Francesca Stavrakopoulou and John Barton, 37–58. T&T Clark, 2010.

Strawn, Brent, ed. *The Oxford Encyclopedia of the Bible and Law*. Oxford University Press, 2015.

Terrien, Samuel. *The Elusive Presence: The Heart of Biblical Theology*. Religious Perspectives 26. Harper & Row, 1978.

Tomasino, Anthony. "עוֹלָם." In VanGemeren, *New International Dictionary of Old Testament Theology and Exegesis*, 3:345–51.

Torrance, T. F. "The Israel of God: Israel and the Incarnation." *Interpretation* 10, no. 3 (1956): 305–20.

Treier, Daniel. *Introducing Theological Interpretation of Scripture: Recovering a Christian Practice*. Baker Academic, 2008.

Trimm, Charles. *The Destruction of the Canaanites: God, Genocide, and Biblical Interpretation*. Eerdmans, 2022.

———. "Recent Research on Warfare in the Old Testament." *Currents in Biblical Research* 10, no. 2 (2012): 171–216.

Tufts University. "Nuts for You." Tufts University Health & Nutrition Letter. December 18, 2013. https://www.nutritionletter.tufts.edu/general-nutrition/nuts-for-you/.

Uehlinger, Christoph. "Anthropomorphic Cult Statuary in Iron Age Palestine and the Search for Yahweh's Cult Images." In van der Toorn, *The Image and the Book*, 97–155.

van der Toorn, Karel, ed. *The Image and the Book: Iconic Cults, Aniconism, and the Rise of Book Religion in Israel and the Ancient Near East*. Peeters, 1997.

———. "The Nature of the Biblical Teraphim in the Light of the Cuneiform Evidence." *Catholic Biblical Quarterly* 52, no. 2 (1990): 203–22.

———. *Sin and Sanction in Israel and Mesopotamia: A Comparative Study*. Van Gorcum, 1985.

VanGemeren, Willem A., ed. *The New International Dictionary of Old Testament Theology and Exegesis*. 5 vols. Zondervan, 1997.

———. *Psalms*. The Expositor's Bible Commentary 5. Rev. ed. Zondervan, 2008.

Van Leeuwen, Raymond C. "Form, Image." In VanGemeren, *New International Dictionary of Old Testament Theology and Exegesis*, 4:643–48.

Villanueva, Federico. *Psalms 1–72: A Pastoral and Contextual Commentary*. Asia Bible Commentary. Langham, 2016.

Vitalis Hoffman, Mark, and Robert A. Mullins. *Atlas of the Biblical World*. Fortress, 2019.

Viviano, Pauline A. "Covenant." In *The Oxford Encyclopedia of the Bible and Law*, edited by Brent A. Strawn. Oxford University Press, 2015 (consulted online).

von Rad, Gerhard. *Holy War in Ancient Israel*. Translated by Marva Dawn. Eerdmans, 1991.

———. *Old Testament Theology*. 2 vols. Translated by D. M. G. Stalker. Harper & Row, 1957–60.

———. "The Promised Land and Yahweh's Land in the Hexateuch." In *The Problem of the Hexateuch and Other Essays*. Translated by E. W. Trueman Dicken, 79–93. SCM, 1984.

———. *Wisdom in Israel*. Translated by James D. Martin. Abingdon, 1974.

Waltke, Bruce K., with Charles Yu. *An Old Testament Theology: An Exegetical, Canonical, and Thematic Approach*. Zondervan Academic, 2007.

Walton, John H. *Ancient Near Eastern Thought and the Old Testament: Introducing the Conceptual World of the Hebrew Bible*. 2nd ed. Baker Academic, 2018.

———. *Covenant: God's Purpose, God's Plan*. Zondervan, 1994.

———. *The Lost World of Genesis One: Ancient Cosmology and the Origins Debate*. IVP Academic, 2009.

———. *Old Testament Theology for Christians: From Ancient Context to Enduring Belief*. IVP Academic, 2017.

Walton, John H., and Andrew E. Hill. *Old Testament Today: A Journey from Original Meaning to Contemporary Significance*. Zondervan, 2004.

Walton, John H., and J. Harvey Walton. *The Lost World of the Israelite Conquest: Covenant, Retribution, and the Fate of the Canaanites*. The Lost World Series 4. IVP Academic, 2017.

———. *The Lost World of the Torah: Law as Covenant and Wisdom in Ancient Context*. Lost World Series 6. IVP Academic, 2019.

Walton, Joshua. "Economy and Trade." In Fu et al., *T&T Clark Handbook of Food*, 57–74.

Watson, Patty Jo. *Archaeological Ethnography in Western Iran*. Viking Fund Publications in Anthropology 57. University of Arizona Press, 1979.

Webb, William. *Slaves, Women, and Homosexuals: Exploring the Hermeneutics of Cultural Analysis*. IVP Academic, 2001.

Weber, Max. *Gesammelte Aufsätze zur Religionssoziologie*. Vol. 1. Mohr, 1920.

Weinfeld, Moshe. "Sabbath, Temple and the Enthronement of the Lord—The Problem of the *Sitz im Leben* of Genesis 1.1–2.3." In *Mélanges bibliques et orientaux en l'honneur de M. Henri Cazelles*, edited by A. Caquot and M. Delcor, 502–12. Alter Orient und Altes Testament 212. Neukirchener / Butzon & Bercker, 1981.

Wellhausen, Julius. *Prolegomena to the History of Ancient Israel, with a Reprint of the Article "Israel" from the "Encyclopedia Britannica."* Translated by J. Sutherland Black and Allan Menzies. Cambridge University Press, 2013 [1885].

Wenham, Gordon J. "Deuteronomy and the Central Sanctuary." *Tyndale Bulletin* 22 (1971): 103–18.

———. *Numbers: An Introduction and Commentary*. Tyndale Old Testament Commentary 4. IVP Academic, 1981.

———. "The Theology of Old Testament Sacrifice." In *Sacrifice and the Bible*, edited by Roger T. Beckwith and Martin J. Selman, 75–87. Baker, 1995.

Westbrook, Raymond, and Bruce Wells. *Everyday Law in Biblical Israel: An Introduction*. Westminster John Knox, 2009.

Westermann, Claus. "Sacred Kingship." In *Encyclopedia Britannica*. https://www.britannica.com/topic/sacred-kingship.

White, Ellen. "High Places, Altars and the Bamah." Biblical Archaeology Society, updated June 16, 2024. https://www.biblicalarchaeology.org/daily/ancient-cultures/ancient-israel/high-places-altars-and-the-bamah/.

Wilk, Richard R., and William L. Rathje. "Household Archaeology." *American Behavioral Scientist* 25, no. 6 (1982): 617–39.

Willett, Elizabeth A. R. "Infant Mortality and Women's Religion in the Biblical Periods." In *The World of Women in the Ancient and Classical Near East*, edited by Beth Alpert Nakhai, 77–96. Cambridge Scholars Publishing, 2008.

———. "Women and Household Shrines in Ancient Israel." PhD diss. The University of Arizona, 1999. https://repository.arizona.edu/handle/10150/288986.

Williams, Michael D. *Far as the Curse Is Found: The Covenant Story of Redemption*. P&R, 2005.

Wilson, Gerald Henry. *The Editing of the Hebrew Psalter*. SBLDS 76. Scholars Press, 1985.

Wilson, Jan. *"Holiness" and "Purity" in Mesopotamia*. Alter Orient und Altes Testament. Butzon & Bercker, 1994.

Wirzba, Norman. *Food and Faith: A Theology of Eating*. Cambridge University Press, 2011.

Wolterstorff, Nicholas. *Until Justice and Peace Embrace: The Kuyper Lectures for 1981 Delivered at the Free University of Amsterdam*. Eerdmans, 1983.

Wood, R. C. *The Sociology of a Meal*. Edinburgh University Press, 1995.

Woodley, Randy. *Shalom and the Community of Creation: An Indigenous Vision*. Eerdmans, 2012.

Wright, Christopher J. H. "אב." In VanGemeren, *New International Dictionary of Old Testament Theology and Exegesis*, 1:219–23.

———. "Biblical Reflections on Land." *Evangelical Review of Theology* 17, no. 2 (1993): 153–67.

———. "Leviticus." In *New Bible Commentary: 21st Century Edition*, edited by Gordon J. Wenham, J. Alex Motyer, Donald A. Carson, and R. T. France, 121–57. InterVarsity, 1994.

———. *The Mission of God: Unlocking the Bible's Grand Narrative*. IVP Academic, 2006.

———. *Old Testament Ethics for the People of God*. InterVarsity, 2004.

Wright, David P. "How Exodus Revises the Laws of Hammurabi." TheTorah.com, 2019. https://thetorah.com/article/how-exodus-revises-the-laws-of-hammurabi.

Wright, Katheryn, and Kristin Novotny. "Bodies: A Digital Companion." Champlain College Center for Publishing, 2018. https://scalar.usc.edu/works/bodies/index.

Wright, N. T. *Jesus and the Victory of God*. Christian Origins and the Question of God 2. Fortress, 1996.

———. *Surprised by Hope: Rethinking Heaven, the Resurrection, and the Mission of the Church*. HarperOne, 2008.

Yasur-Landau, Assaf, Jennie R. Ebeling, and Laura B. Mazow, eds. *Household Archaeology in Ancient Israel and Beyond*. Culture and History of the Ancient Near East 50. Brill, 2011.

Yee, Gale A. "'He Will Take the Best of Your Fields': Royal Feasts and Rural Extraction." *Journal of Biblical Literature* 136, no. 4 (2017): 821–38.

———. "Ideological Criticism: Judges 17–21 and the Dismembered Body." In *Judges and Method: New Approaches in Biblical Studies*, 2nd ed., edited by Gale A. Yee, 146–70. Augsburg Fortress, 2007.

Zevit, Ziony. "A Phoenician Inscription and Biblical Covenant Theology." *Israel Exploration Journal* 27 (1977): 110–18.

———. *The Religions of Ancient Israel: A Synthesis of Parallactic Approaches*. Continuum, 2001.

Zohary, Daniel, Maria Hopf, and Ehud Weiss. *Domestication of Plants in the Old World: The Origin and Spread of Domesticated Plants in Southwest Asia, Europe, and the Mediterranean Basin*. 4th ed. Oxford University Press, 2012.

Zohary, Michael. *Plants of the Bible*. Cambridge University Press, 1982.

SCRIPTURE INDEX

Old Testament

Genesis

1 188n30
1–2 34, 40, 60, 62, 106, 129
1:2 106, 188
1:4 62n42
1:6–7 73
1:10 62n42
1:11–25 130
1:12 62n42
1:18 62n42
1:21 62n42
1:22 62n43
1:25 62n42
1:26 125, 129, 130n55, 133, 134n72
1:26–27 130
1:26–28 82, 87, 126, 128, 132, 132n66, 145, 223
1:27 123, 128, 128n47, 130
1:28 18, 62, 62n43, 129, 130n55
1:31 62n42, 106
2:1–2 106
2:3 106
2:4–25 127
2:7 49
2:10–14 107
2:15 61, 64, 68, 107, 133, 151, 213, 214n51
2:16–17 214
2:18 128n47
2:22–24 14
3:8 61
3:15 18
3:17 214n51
3:18 153n50
3:23–24 61
5:3 125
6:14 44
6:22 44
7:10–11 73
8:2 73
8:20–21 98
9 40
9:1 18
9:4 32
9:6 126n38, 131n61, 133, 175
9:9–17 34
9:12 31n22
9:16 31n22
12 34
12:1 34, 44
12:1–3 37n36
12:2 34, 145
12:2–3 34
12:3 18, 34, 40, 67, 112, 192, 196, 212
12:7 34, 54, 61n39
13:15 61n39
13:17 61n39
14:12–16 8
14:13 30
14:18 130n56
14:18–24 149
15 24, 34
15:7 36n30, 61n39
15:18 61n39
15:10 37n36
15:12–21 44
15:16 173–74n55
17:1 34, 35, 44, 175
17:5–6 32
17:6 41
17:7 31n22, 32
17:13, 19 31n22
17:8 32, 59n8
17:10 34, 44
17:11 32
17:13 31n22
17:19 31n22
17:20 145
18:4 207
19:1–11 208, 208n34
19:2 207
21:23 30
21:25–34 30
22:16 45
22:18 45
24:28 4
24:32 207
25:29 202
25:34 202
26:26–33 30
26:29 30
27:49 54
28:4 61n39
28:10–22 96
28:13 61n39
31:19 121
31:34–35 121
31:44–50 30
32:28 12
35:11 18, 41, 145
35:14 122
38 19n44
41:16 170
43:24 207
46:31 4
47:19, 25 212
47:20–21 212
48:4 61n39
49:28 5
50:20 212

Exodus

3:5 96
4:22 153
4:22–23 13
6:4 61n39
6:6 16n32
6:7 41, 59n8
6:8 61n39
6:14 5
6:25 5
8:1 189
8:20 189
9:1 189
9:13 189
10:3 189
12:1–13 100n24
12:3–4a 11
12:4–9 203
12:7–9 11
12:14–20 100n25
12:21–27 100n24
12:26–27 19
13:3–10 100n25
13:8 19
14 190
14:14 189
14:19–26 184
15:3 189
15:13 16n32
15:18 144
16:4 214
16:4–18 210
16:20 214
16:23 175
16:27 214
17:8–11 183
17:8–15 191
17:15 183
19:4 35
19:4–6 33, 35
19:5 35, 38, 39, 44, 173
19:5–6 112
19:6 35, 40, 130n56

251

19:8 38
20:2 36, 173
20:3 53
20:3–4 114
20:4–5 122
20:11 106
20:12 6
20:22–23:19 161
20–24 30, 31
20:24–25 175
21:12–14 161
21:18–19 161
21:18–32 161
23:10–11 56
23:11 57
23:15 100n25
23:16 100n26, 100n27
23:20 192
23:31 193
23:34 100n26
24:3 38
24:8 37n36, 43
24:10 122
25:29 122
25:30 122
28:30 182
28:31–34 202
29:38–42 98
29:40–41 122
30:6 24
30:10 100n28
31:16 31
32 112
32–34 38
32:4–5 115
32:26 112
32:29 112
34:6–7 38
34:18 100n25
35:13 122
37:16 122
39–40 106
39:22–26 202
39:32 106
39:36 122
39:43 106
40:9 106
40:23 100
40:25 100
40:27 100
40:29 100

Leviticus

2 98
2:1 99
2:1–2 99
2:4 99
2:4–5 99
2:7 99
2:8–10 99
2:13 99
2:14 99
2:15 99
3:3–4 99
3:9–10 99
3:14–15 99
4:1–5:13 99
4:6–7 108
4:16 153
5:14–6:7 99
7:12–15 99
7:15 10
11 214
11:44 90
11:44–45 82
11:45 90
12 78, 79
12:4 79
12–15 79
13:2–8 77
13:9–17 77
13:18–23 77
13:24–28 77
13:29–37 77
13:38–39 77
13:40–44 77
13:47–59 77
14:33–53 77
14:34 61n39
15:2–15 78
15:2–17 78
15:4–5 78
15:6 78
15:9 78
15:12 78
15:13–15 78
15:16–17 78
15:18 78
15:19–24 78
15:19–30 78
15:25–30 78
16 100n28
16:24 98
17:11 108
17:14–20 215

18:2–5 80
18:6–16 81
18:6–18 80
18:17–18 81
18:19 80
18:19–23 81
18:20 80
18:21 80
18:22 80
18:23 80
18:24–30 80
18:25 68
18:28 64, 68, 81
19 87
19:2 82, 90, 91, 132n65, 134
19:9–10 57, 63, 176
19:34 17
20:2 82
20:7 82, 132n65
20:22 68
20:24 81
20:26 81, 90, 132n65
21:8 82
22:18 98
22:32 222
23:5 100n24
23:6–8 100n25
23:13 122
23:15–21 100n26
23:18 122
23:22 57
23:26–32 100n28
23:34–36 100n27
23:37 122
23:39–43 100n27
24:1–4 100
24:5–9 100
25 58
25:1–7 56n25
25:3–5 64
25:4 57
25:6–7 57
25:8 58
25:9 100n28
25:10–12 58
25:23 58, 61
25:25–33 15
25:48–49 15, 57
26 13, 42, 193
26:3–6 64
26:12 59n8

26:26 10
26:31–33 64
27:9–25 57
27:28 83
27:30 63

Numbers

1:2 5
1:16 5
3:7–8 107
4:7 122
6:15 122
6:17 122
6:22–27 99
7:1 83
10:10 99
11:12 61n39
14:7 62n42
15:24 122
21:21–31 190
25:3 53
25:10–13 32
25:13 31n22
26:33 175n65
27:21 182
28–29 122
28:16 100n24
28:17–25 100n25
28:26–31 100n26
29:12–34 100n27
31:19–24 193
32:22 62
32:29 62
35:9–30 57
35:19–27 15
35:34 63, 64

Deuteronomy

1–4 36
1:1–4:14 29
1:8 61n39
1:25 62n42
1:35 62n42
1:35–36 61n39
2:24–37 190
3:25 62n42
4:5–8 173
4:6–8 82, 112
4:21–22 62n42
4:26 29
4:31 41
4:34 181

4:37 39
4:40 31
4:44–27:8 29
5:2–3 31, 41
5:6 29
5:6b 29
5:8–9 122
5:29 31
6:3 62n43
6:3 31
6:4–5 31
6:5 173
6:10 62n42
6:13–14 53
6:14 31
6:18 31, 62n42
6:24 31
7:7–8 61
7:7–10 31
7:13 62n43
8:1 62n43
8:7 62n42
8:7–8 200
8:10 62n42
9:3 62
9:4–6 61, 173
9:5 173–74n55
9:6 62n42
9:8–9 66n49
10:1–2 29
10:8 99
10:13–14 31
10:19 17
11:17 62n42
12:5–14 175
12:11 105n50
12:23 215
13:4 31
13:5 173n49
13:17 62n43
14 214
14:26 11
14:28–29 63
15–18 53
15:1 56n25, 58
15:7–9 16
15:12 58
16:1–2 100n24
16:3–4 100n25
16:5–7 100n24
16:8 100n25
16:9–12 100n26
16:13–15 100n27

17:7 173n49
17:8 105n50
17:8–13 141
17:12 173n49
17:14–20 41, 146
17:16–17 212
17:18–20 148
17:19 176
17:20 176
18:6–8 105n50
19:13 173n49
19:15–21 141
19:19 173n49
20:5–8 182
20:10–11 182
20:13–14 185
20:16 185
21:9 173n49
21:15–17 175n65
21:21 173n49
22:21 173n49
22:22 173n49
22:23–27 162
22:24 173n49
24:7 173n49
24:17–22 17n36
24:19–21 57
24:19–22 211
24:21 63, 176
24–29 29
25:5–6 17, 57
25:5–10 8
26:14 10
27:9–26 29
28 13, 42, 193
28:1–5 53
28:1–11 31
28:1–14 29
28:14 31
28:15–68 29
28:20 31
28:25 31
28:36 193
28:36–37 31
28:40 202
28:49 193
28:65–67 31
29:10–12 31
29:18 31
29:26–28 31
30:1 31
30:1–8 31
30:6 43

30:9 31
30:11 174
30:15 214
30:16 62n43
30:19 214
31:7 61n39
31:10–13 29
31:20–21 61n39
31:23 61n39
32:6 13
32:11–13 13n24
32:13 14
32:13–14 210
33:10 111

Joshua

1:6 61n39
1:7 191
1:8 224
1:13 61n39
2 192
2:6 4
3:5 182
5:3–7 191
5:13–15 192
6 190
6:6 183
6:19 83
7 191, 192
9 30, 192
10 183, 190
10:11 184
10:14 184
11:23 61
17:3–4 175n65
18:1 62
21:43–45 61
22 105n51
23:13 62n42
23:15–16 62n42
24:2–13 36
24:12 186
24:25 30

Judges

2:17 53
2:20–21 191n46
2:22–23 191
3:2 191n46
3:7 103
4:8 183
5:20–22 184

6:25 53
7 184
8:23 146
11:11 97
11:24 181
11:27 181
11:29–31 97
11:34 97
11:39 97
17:5 121
18:14–20 121
19:18 97
20–21 187
20:1–2 138
20:1–3 97
20:8–10 97
20:27 181
21:1 97
21:5 97
21:8 97
21:15 193

Ruth

1:16 17
2:2–9 57
4:5 17
4:13–22 17
4:18–22 19

1 Samuel

1:9 97
1:21 99
1:24–28 98
3:3 97
4 192
4:1–11 183
4:3 183
4:10–11 184
7:5–11 97
7:6 122
7:9 98
7:10 184
8 139
8–12 147
8:4–5 138
8:5 150
8:6 146
8:7 147
8:11–17 212
8:19b–20 150
10:17–24 97
10:27b–11:15 143

11 138, 144
11:12–15 138
12:10 53
13 191, 192
13:8 183
13:19–21 138
15:12–21 97
15:33 97
19:13 121
19:16 121
20:8 30
21 122
21:1–10 97
22:16–19 97
23:6 183
23:18 30
24:20 5
25 206
25:18 206
28:6 182
28:8 182

2 Samuel

1:14 153
3:12–13 30
5:3 97
6 98
6:13–14 149
6:14–18 130n56
7 32, 45, 143
7:6 36n30
7:9 35, 36n30
7:10 32, 35
7:12 35
7:13–16 32, 35, 151n41, 152
7:14 13, 146
7:16 43
11:1 144, 189
11:1–2 143
11:6–13 182
12:1–12 149
13 xvii
15:7 97
21:6 97
23:5 32
23:16 122

1 Kings

2:4 45
3:3 148
3:6 32

3:9 176
3:10 148
3:16–28 148
4:22–23 212
5–8 97, 143
5:12 30
6:38 106
7:18–20 202
7:23–26 106
7:42 202
7:48 122
8 98
8:24 32
8:27 95
9:4–5 32
9:9 53
9:15 148
10:9 143
11:11 32
11:11–13 169n42
12:25–33 97
12:26–13:1 123, 143
15:18–19 30
16:32 103
18 53, 104
18:19 53
19:16 153
20:34 30
21:7 62
22:19 122n16

2 Kings

3:11 182
3:12 183
4:8–10 206
4:10 4
4:38–40 202
6 190
6:21–23 188
6:22 225
7:2 73
7:19 73
10:29 97
11:4 30
11:12 30
16:10–14 143
17:35–36 53
18:1–4 143
18:1–8 143
18:4 101
18:28 182
18:31–32a 182
21:1–7 101

21:2–4 103
21:7 53, 103
21:19–22 101
22–23 143
22:1–23:24 143
22:32 101
22:37 101
23:19 97
23:24 121
24:9 101
24:19–20 101

1 Chronicles

22:8 193
28 97

2 Chronicles

2–7:11 97
4:19 122
9:8 151n41
19:4–11 141
21:7 32
33:3 103
36:21 68, 213

Ezra

3:12–13 152, 196
4 152, 196

Nehemiah

4 152, 196
5:11 202
6 152
8:14 100n27
13:4–30 196

Job

1:4 11
4:7–8 171
4:17 171
5:17 171
10:9 49
10:18 14
31:1 89
31:5–6 89
31:5–8 166
31:13 89
31:16 89
31:33 89

Psalms

1–41 151
1:2 176, 224
1:3 176
2 146
2:6 146
2:7 13, 131
2:7b 140, 146
8 126n38, 129, 133
8:3–6 132
8:4 133
8:5 133n68
9:14 12n20
11:7 122
17:15 122
18:8–14 184
21 146
22:9–10 14
22:27 113
23:5 215
23:6 215, 226
24:2 106
24:7 122n16
24:9 122n16
27:4 122, 215
27:7–8 122
29 104, 187
29:10 106, 145
37 171
39:12 61
40:8 43
42–72 151
42:2 122
44:3 186
45:4 224
45:4–5 150
45:6 151
46:3 106
46:4 106
46:6 106
47 122n16
47:1 113
47:3 96
47:9 196
51:16–19 222
60:10 122
63:2 122
67:1–3 113
68:4 53, 104
68:5–6 18
68:9 53, 104
68:24–35 122n16
72 146, 212n47

72:1 143
72:1a 148
72:1–2 147
72:4 142
73 171
73–89 151
73:1 172
73:3 172
73:13–14 172
73:16–17 172
74:12–13 145
74:16–17 145
78:19 214
82:2 147n38
82:7 147n38
82:8 147n38
84:2 113
84:7 122
84:9 122
84:10 113
87 66
89:3–4 32
89:9–14 195
89:25 145
89:26–27 140
89:29 32, 195
89:31–36 195
89:35–36 32
89:38 195
89:38–51 35
89:39 32
89:49 195
90–106 151
90:3 49
91:14 13
93 122n16
93:2–4 145
96–99 122n16
98 66
101 151n43
104 60
104:3 53, 104
104:6–8 145
104:14–15 209
104:26 188
106:28 10
107–50 151
108:10 122
110 146, 149, 151n43
119 174
119:19 61
132 151n43

132:5 32
132:11–12 45
132:12 32
132:13–14 106
132:13–18 32
138–45 151n43
138:4–5 113
144:3–4 133
146:9 18

Proverbs

1:1–7 168n39
1:7 170n44
1:29 170n44
2:5 170n44
2:17 30
3:7 170n44
7:14 99
8:13 170n44
8:24–29 73
9:10 170n44
10:27 170n44
12:16 168
12:23 164, 168
14:8 168
14:15 168
14:18 168
14:26 170n44
14:27 170n44
15:1–2 89
15:16 170n44
15:33 170n44
16:2 89
16:6 170n44
19:23 170n44
20:9 89
20:19 164
20:22 164
22:4 170n44
22:17–19 163
22:17–24:22 163
23:9 164
23:17 170n44
26:4–5 171
27:1 164
29:25 170n44
31 170, 206
31:10–31 205, 205n25
31:14–15 6, 205
31:27 6, 205

Isaiah

1:8 12n20, 67
1:16–17 88
2:4 196, 225
3:14–15 212
5:1–7 135
6 122n16
6:1 122
6:9–10 194
6:11–13 194
6:13 42n47
7 193
7:14 153n49
8:5–8 193
11:1 42n47, 194
11:2–9 194
11:6–9 152
11:10–14 183
19:2–4 196
19:16 196
19:16–25 40
19:18–22 67
19:21 196
19:24–25 113
19:25 67, 196
24:18 73
34:5 195
40:10–11 39n39
41:8–9 135n74
42:1–9 135
42:4 143
42:6 18
42:18–19 135
43:15 63
43:16–21 39n39
45:1 153
49:1–26 39n39
49:15 13
51:7 43
52:13–53:12 135n74
53:4–5 197
55:1 152
55:1–2 152
55:3 32, 152
56:3–8 67
60:10–14 66
62:4 49
62:4–5 15
63:1–3 122
64:8 13
65–66 60
65:17 68
65:19 196

Scripture Index

65:25 196
66:9 14
66:21 113
66:22 68

Jeremiah

1:10 42
2:2 14
3:1–2 64
3:18 54
6:14 179
7:1–15 111
7:4–6 65
7:6–7 215
8:11 179
11:10 53
11:17 53
16:5–9 10, 10n16
16:13 54
16:15 54
22:3 143
22:5 143
22:15 143
24:1–10 66
24:6 42
24:6–7 66
24:7 15n30, 59n8
24:8 66
30:1–3 39n39
31:12 202
31:31 43
31:33 35, 41, 43
31:33–34 43
31:34 15n30
32:36–41 39n39
32:38 59n8
33:12–26 32
34:8–9 30
34:18 24
34:19 24
52:22 202

Lamentations

2:1 12n20
5:16 152n44
5:19 152n44
5:20–22 35

Ezekiel

1:22 122
1:26 122
1:26–28 115
5:11 149
8:10 149
10:1 122
10:3–4 115
10:18–19 64
11:16 36n30
11:19 35
11:20 59n8
14:11 59n8
16:8 122
16:49–50 212
18:23 190
24:5 203
33:11 190
34:11–24 39n39
36:24 39n39
36:26 35, 43
37:1–14 42
37:11–14 39n39
37:16–22 43
37:23 41
37:23 59n8
37:24–28 196
37:27 59n8
40–47 152
43:2–5 115
45:9 143
47:1–12 106

Daniel

2:27–28a 170
7:9 122

Hosea

1:9–10 42n47
2:2 15
2:5 15
2:6–13 15
2:8 202
2:14–15 15
2:16 15
2:20 15
2:22 202
2:23 42n47
6:6 111n70
11:1–4 13
11:8–9 39

Joel

3:10 196n56

Amos

1–2 193
1:6 193
1:9 193
4:4 97
4:9 202
5:5 97
5:25 111n70
6:4–6 212
7:13 97
8:4–8 212

Micah

3:3 203
4:3 196, 225
4:13 195
6:15 202

Haggai

2:12 202
2:19 202
2:23 153

Zechariah

8:8 59n8
14:8 106

Malachi

1:2 33
1:6 13, 33
2:14 30, 45n57
3:10 73

Old Testament Apocrypha

Baruch

4:1 174

1 Maccabees

12:9 89

2 Esdras

8:44 129n53

Sirach

17:1–13 129n53
24:23–27 167n34

Wisdom

2:23 129n53

New Testament

Matthew

1:23 153n49
3:17 16
12:18–21 135
14–15 215
19:8 175
20:26–27 135
26:28 43
27:29 153n50

Mark

6 215
8 215
10:43–44 135
15:17 153n50

Luke

1:52–53 213
2:41–51 19
5:33–35 16
9 215
9:35 16
12:16–21 212
12:24 212
14:13–14 211
22:19–20 215
22:20 215

John

2 215
6 215
6:50 215
6:54 215
13 215
14:27 197
15:1–6 135
19:2 153n50

Romans

1:16 xix
2:9–10 xix
2:14–15 173n52
5:14–19 43
8:15 135
8:23 135
8:29 134, 135
9:4 135
15:16 222

1 Corinthians

6:12 174n62
10:23 174n62
11:7 134n72
11:24–25 215
15 68
15:12–22 43
15:35–58 135
15:49 134

2 Corinthians

3:18 134
4:4 134

Colossians

1:15 134
3:9–10 134

Hebrews

1:8 151n41
3–4 43
9:13–14 117
10:4 116

1 Peter

1:16 90
2:5 223
2:9 223, 130n56
2:20–25 135n74

Revelation

1:6 223
5:10 223
11:15 43
19 215n54
19:7–9 16
21 68
21:4 196
22:1–2 106

SUBJECT INDEX

Aaron, 99
Abernethy, Andrew, 215
Abigail, 206
Abimelech, 30
Abner, 30
Abraham, 30, 32, 34–35, 37n36, 39n39, 40, 44–45, 112, 145, 146
Abrahamic covenant, 36n30, 41, 44, 192, 196
Achan, 191–92
Adadit'i/Hadd-yith'i, 124–25, 129
Adad-nerari III, 28
Adam, 19, 43, 61, 62, 65, 68, 107, 131, 133, 133n69, 214n51
adê (loyalty oath), 26
adultery, spiritual, 14
agricultural practices
   crops grown, 200–201, 209n38
   domesticated animals, 203–4
   economic policies and, 140
   food production, 7–8, 9, 52
   gleaning, 57, 63, 211
   land cultivation and rest, 55–56
   tributary surplus extraction, 55, 140–41n17
Ahab, 30, 62
Ahaz, 193
Ain Dara temple, 96, 97
Akkad, 183
Akkadian Period, 124, 139
Alice in Wonderland (Carroll), 199
Allen, Paula Gunn, 49
altars, 120
Amalekites, 191
Amen-em-Opet, 163–64
Ammon, 52
Ammonites, 144, 193

Amorites, 30
ancestors, sacrifices offered to, 10, 10n16
anthropomorphic figurines, 103–4, 120
anti-Semitism, 179n2
archaeology, defined, xvi
Asa, 30
'asham (guilt offering), 99
Asherah, 53, 103, 103n45
Ashurnasirpal, 124
Assurbanipal, 27–28, 75, 75n18
Assyria, 67, 183, 193
Assyrian annals, 184n20
Assyrians, 26–28, 36, 182
atonement, 99, 108–11, 116–17
authority, 6
Averbeck, Richard, 84, 108

Baal, 53, 103
Babylon, 142
Balberg, Mira, 109n65
Barth, Karl, 128, 130
Bartholomew, Craig, 170
Bathsheba, 149, 189
BCE, use of term, xix–xx
Beard, James, 225
Beatitudes, 134
bene Yisrael (sons/children of Israel), 12
Ben-hadad, 30
Benjamites, 188
berit (covenant), 23–24, 34. *See also* covenant(s)
Berry, Wendell, 63, 68, 213
bet 'ab (father's household), 4–5
bet 'em (mother's household), 4–5
Bethel, 97, 123
Bethlehem, 97

betselem 'elohim (in the image of the deity), 123
bet Yisrael (household of Israel), 12
Bible. *See* Hebrew Bible
Bible With and Without Jesus, The (Levine and Brettler), xviii
biblical theology, xvii
biennial fallowing, 56
Bird, Phyllis, 126n39, 128
Blenkinsopp, Joseph, 168
blessing, 39–41, 54, 63–64, 72, 90, 95, 111, 165, 171, 192, 196, 198, 221
Block, Daniel, 34
blood purification, 79
Boaz, 17, 138
Boer, Roland, 140–41n17
booty, war, 140–41n17, 191, 225
Brettler, Marc Zvi, xviii
Bronze Age, xx, 24
Brueggemann, Walter, 18, 44n51, 59, 62, 64, 66, 88, 112n73, 116, 126n38, 130, 190n38, 209n38, 212
Bullinger, Henrich, 45

Calvin, John, xiv
Canaan, 52, 59, 60, 73, 124
Canaanites, 53, 64, 103, 192
Carter, Charles E., 54–55
casuistic laws, 160–61
CE, use of term, xix–xx
ceremonial law, 176
Chalcolithic, xx
chaos, 59, 75, 79, 81, 87, 95, 101, 106, 145, 147, 180, 186–89, 188n30, 193, 196–97, 225
Chemosh, 195n53
childbirth impurities, 79
chronological periods, xx
Cis-Jordan hill country, 50, 52
civil law, 176
Claassens, L. Juliana M., 214n51, 215
Coastal Plain, 50
Code of Eshnunna, 159n7, 161–62
Code of Hammurabi, 141, 143, 159n7, 160–62
common, vs. holy, 83–84
communal solidarity, 16–20
community
 of family, 4–5
 humanity created in, 130
 multigenerational households, 1, 4
 solidarity within, 16–20
 worship in, xiv
consecration, pre-battle, 182
context-canonical theology, xviii

corpse-related pollution, 77
corvée labor, 55, 140, 182
cosmogony, 73
cosmology, 73, 81, 105
covenant(s)
 Abrahamic, 36n30, 41, 44, 192, 196
 based on obligation and commitment, 36n32
 conditional elements, 44–45, 44nn51–52, 45n57
 Davidic, 36n30, 41, 44, 45, 195
 economy, 212–13
 God's with Israel, xiv–xv, 30–31, 34–41, 104–5
 as grounded in a historical relationship, 35–37
 in household ideology, xv, 11
 kinship/secular, 29–30, 33
 land as a gift of, xv, 31–32, 59
 law as part of relationship with God, 172–75
 new covenant, 43, 116
 Noahic, 44
 promises, 18–19, 104
 relationships between biblical, 41–43
 royal grant, 31–32
 similarities to treaties, 28–29
 Sinai/Horeb, 30–31, 36, 41, 44n51, 45, 105, 116, 145, 175
 summary, 220–21
 terminology, 23–24
 unconditional elements, 44–45, 44nn51–52, 45n57
 as uniquely gracious, 38–39
 as universal in scope, 39–41
Creach, Jerome, 187n28, 188n30
creation, 60, 60n38, 68, 85, 87, 145, 167, 188
Crenshaw, James, 168
crop rotation, 55–56
crown of thorns, 153n50
cult centers, 96–97, 96n12
cult complexes, 96–97, 96n12
cult corners, 102
cult places, 95–96, 96n10
cult sites, 96n10
cult stands, 120
cultural norms, xiii–xiv, 207n31
curses, 193
Curtis, Robert, 201
customs, 80

daily household functions, 7–10, 204–6, 204n20
Dan, 97, 123
Daniel, 65, 168–69

Subject Index

David, 17, 19, 30, 32, 35, 43, 44n51, 45, 110–11, 130n56, 144, 146, 149, 151n43, 152–53, 152n44, 189, 193, 194, 206
Davidic covenant, 36n30, 41, 44, 45, 195
Davis, Ellen, 57–58, 128, 130n55
Day of Atonement, 100, 108, 109
death
    corpse-related pollution, 77
    sorrow for enemies', 190–91
deities
    appeasement of, 165–66
    as divine warriors, 180–81
    enraged by impurity, 76
    houses of, 73–74, 120, 121–22
    images of, 103–4, 120–23, 125
    kings as adoptive sons of, 140
    kings as images of, 123–25, 139–40
    moral pollution as punishment from, 80
    retribution, 165–66
    sacrifices and offerings to, 98–99
    service rituals to, 74–76, 94–95, 121–22
    worship of, 53, 103, 114–15
Dempster, Stephen G., 19
demut (likeness), 127
Deuteronomy, 29, 30–31, 182, 184–85, 189n35
dialogical biblical theology, xviii
dietary staples, 200–203
distribution, household, 7–8, 204n20, 210
divination practices, 181
divine accommodation, xiv
divine warfare
    battle, 182–84
    concept of, 180–81
    God fighting against Israel, 193–95
    God fighting for Israel, 189–91
    God fighting with Israel, 191–93
    post-battle, 184–85
    pre-battle, 181–82
    shalom and, 195–97
    violence of, 187–89
Douglas, Mary, 84, 107
Dumbrell, William, 34, 43n48

Ebeling, Jennie R., 14
economy
    agrarian, 55
    covenant, 212–13
    food, 211–13
    foreign tributary mode, 140–41n17
    household, 7, 52
    land-based, 52–53
    native tributary mode, 55, 140n17
    redistributive, 140
    subsistence, 7, 8, 10, 52, 54, 99, 101, 140, 204, 221
Eden, 49, 59, 60, 61, 62, 63–64, 65, 68, 106–7, 133, 150, 167, 214
Edict of Ammisaduqa, 142
Edom, 52
'edut (testimony), 24. *See also* covenant(s)
Egypt, 52, 67, 120n4, 123–24, 145, 181, 183, 190, 212, 214
Eichrodt, Walther, 151n42
elders, 138
election, 40, 40nn41–42
Eliphaz, 171
Elisha, 206
endogamy, 5–6
Enuma Elish, 129, 188
environmental stewardship, 68, 130n55, 213
Ephraim, 50
Epic of Atrahasis, 129
epistemology, 113
equity, 142–43
Esarhaddon, 27–28
Esther, 65
ethics, 168
ethnoarchaeology, xvii n5
ethnography, xvii n5
Eve, 61, 62, 65, 107, 133, 133n69, 214n51
evil, problem of, 164–65, 171–72
"Exaltation of Inanna, The," 183
exile, 64–67, 68, 133, 193, 196, 214n51
Ezekiel, 35, 43, 64, 115, 196

fallowing systems, 55–56
family, defined, 4
feasting
    food as means of remembrance, 210–11
    generosity of God and, xv, 214–15
    in households, 10–11, 102
    sacrifices, 10, 10n16
    summary, 226
Feast of Unleavened Bread, 201
fertility rituals, 103–4
festivals, 18–19, 113–14, 201, 211
fictive kinships, 33, 145–46
figurines, 103–4, 120–23
food and foodways
    basics, 200–203
    cultural, 206–8
    defined, 200
    dietary staples, 200–203
    distribution of, 7, 210
    generosity of God and, xv

in hospitality norms and practices, 207–8
meat eating, 203–4, 203n17
Mediterranean triad, 200, 209, 211
preparation, 7–8, 9–10, 10n13, 204–6, 204n20, 210
production, 7–8, 9, 52
purity laws, 84–85, 85n62, 107–8, 214
social structures, 204–6
summary, 225–26
theology of, 209–13
used for sacrifices and offerings, 98–99
foreign tributary mode, 140–41n17
functional model of *imago Dei*, 129–30, 131–32, 131n62, 133–34, 134n73, 145

Galilee, 50
Gammie, John G., 88–89
genealogies, 19
generosity, xv, 16–17, 214
genital pollution, 78, 78n36
genres, 157–58
Gezer Calendar, 200, 201
Gibeah of Saul, 97
Gibeonites, 30
Gideon, 146, 184
Gilead, 52, 97
Gilgal, 97
Ginsburskaya, Mila, 87
Girard, René, 191n44
gleaning, 57, 63, 211
God
  covenant with Israel, xiv–xv, 30–31, 34–41, 104–5
  divine name of, xix
  as father, 13–14
  fighting against Israel, 193–95
  fighting for Israel, 189–91
  fighting with Israel, 191–93
  generosity of, xv, 214
  grace of, 38–39, 132
  holiness of, xv, 82–83, 90
  hospitality of, 213–15
  imago Dei, 119, 126–32, 130n59, 134–35, 145–46, 170, 223
  incapability of describing, 115
  Israelites relationship to, 11–12
  as Israel's *go'el*, 15–16
  Jesus as Son of, 153, 153n49
  kings as images of, xv
  kingship of, 145
  kinship relationship between Israel and, 12, 33
  knowing, 15n30
  "lisping" of, xiv
  as married to Israel, 14–15
  as a midwife, 14
  as a nursing mother, 13–14, 14n26, 210
  presence of, 60, 83, 115–16
  promises of, 18–19
  redemption, 39–41
  revelation, 39–41
  testing by, 214
  use of gendered pronouns in reference to, xix
  worship of. *See* worship
  See also Yhwh
Godfather, The (film), 33
gods. *See* deities
go'el (kinsman-redeemer), 8–9, 15–16, 17n37, 19n44, 57, 131, 138
gold, 82, 85, 90
Goldingay, John, 12–13, 37, 41n46, 44n52, 109, 114n79, 115n83, 189n35
Goody, Jack, 204
Goswell, Gregory, 152
government, 138. *See also* monarchy
grace
  God's, 38–39, 132
  receiving purification as, 109
  structures of, 16–17, 57
gratitude, 109–10
Gregory of Nyssa, 134
grounded theology, meaning of, xiv
guilt offerings, 99, 109

Hammurabi, 141, 142–43, 148, 160
Hanson, Paul, 186n27
Hastorf, Christine, 204
hatta'ah (sin offering), 99
Hattusili III, 25
Hebrew Bible
  covenants, 35–43
  cultural contexts of, xiii–xv, xx
  genealogies, 19
  genres in, 158
  kinship, 4–5
  "monumental vs. the mundane" issue, xvi–xvii
  treaties in, 28–29
  use of term, xix
  worship in, 18–19
Hebron, 97
Hellenistic Period, xx, 24, 174
herem (destroy), 184–85, 191, 195
hesed (steadfast love), 109–10
Hezekiah, 100
Hicks, Edward, 197

Hiram, 30
Hittite Laws, 159n7, 161
Hittites, 24–26, 180, 184
holiness
    vs. commonness, 83–84
    in creation accounts, 87
    cultural contexts of, 72
    dual nature of, 72–73
    God's, xv, 82–83, 90
    graded, 85–86
    moral, 86
    in the New Testament, 90
    performance of service rituals and, 74–76
    of the prophets, 87–88
    ritual, 86
    in Second Temple Judaism, 89
    separation as a consequence of, 83, 90
    summary, 221–22
    theology of, 82–85
    in wisdom literature, 88–89
    See also purity
Holy Spirit, 43
holy war, 190n40, 191n43
Horus, 124
Hosea, 15, 42n47
hospitality, xv, 207–8, 211, 213–15, 226
households
    behavioral aspect, 7
    communal focus, xiv, 16–17
    contemporary examples, 4
    covenant concept in, xv, 11, 37
    cultural contexts of, 20
    daily functions, 7–10
    defined, 4
    economy of, 7, 52
    house functions, 3–4
    house size, 2–3
    influence on theology of Israel, 11–12
    living arrangements, xiv
    living rooms, 10
    material aspect, 2–4
    matriarch's roles, 6, 205–6, 210
    multigenerational communities, 1, 4
    patriarch's roles, 6, 8–9, 138
    religious rituals, 8, 11, 18–19, 101–4
    social aspect, 4–6
    special occasions and feasting, 10–11
    structures of grace, 16–17, 57
    summary, 219–20
    theology of communal solidarity, 16–20
    theology of roles and metaphors of, 12–16

humanity, created as image of God, 119, 126–32, 126n39, 133
Hwang, Jerry, 147

iconography, xvii n5
iconolatry, 121n8
idolatry, 115, 115n83, 149
image(s)
    ancient concepts of, 119
    cultural contexts of, 123
    deities depicted as, 103–4, 120–23, 125
    Jesus and, 134–35
    of kings, xv, 123–25, 129
    modern concepts of, 119
    sin and, 132–34
    summary, 223
    theology of, 126–28
    use of in battle, 182–83
    worship of forbidden, 114–15, 122, 126
    of Yhwh, 122–23, 126n38
imago Dei (image of God), 119, 128–32, 130n59, 134–35, 145–46, 170, 223
Imes, Carmen, 133n67, 133n69, 173
impurity
    moral pollution, 79–81
    physical pollution, 76–79, 84
    vs. purity, 83–84
    removal of via sacrifice, 109
    risks of, 76
    sin, 84
    See also purity
Indigenous People's Day, 179
individuals and individualism, 4, 5
infant mortality rates, 14, 101
inheritance
    land as, 8–9, 53–54, 57, 61–62
    laws, 54, 63, 160
    transmission of, 8–9
International Trunk Road, 52
Iron Age, xx, 2–3, 8, 11, 97, 102–3, 139, 206
Isaac, 30, 44–45
Isaiah, 42n47, 49, 88, 135n74, 194
Israel and Israelites
    as children of God, 13–14
    collectivism, 19
    cultural contexts of, xiii–xv, xx
    deliverance from Egypt, 144–45, 190
    divine kingship in, 124
    exile of, 64–67, 68, 133, 196
    geography and topography, 50–52
    God as *go'el*, 15–16
    God fighting against, 193–95
    God fighting for, 189–91
    God fighting with, 191–93
    as God's child, 13–14

God's covenant with, xiv–xv, 30–31, 34–41, 104–5
as God's servant, 135, 135n74
household influence on theology of, 11–12
humanness, 130n59
kinship relationship between God and, 12, 33
laws, 172–75
as married to God, 14–15
place of in redemption story, xix
as a priestly kingdom, 112
relationship to God, 11–12
relationship to land, 49–50
rest in the land, 62n44
settlements, xvi
social ethics, 17
study of ancient, xvi
supersessionism view of, xviii–xix
tells, xvi
temple complexes, 97
worship of deities other than Yhwh, 53, 103, 114–15
Israelite Four-Room House, 3
It's a Wonderful Life (film), 12, 16

Jabesh-Gilead, 144
Jacob, 30
Jacobson, Rolf, 187
Jael, 192
Jehoiada, 30
Jennings, Willie James, 67
Jenson, Philip, 85
Jephthah, 193
Jeremiah, 15n30, 35, 42, 43, 64–65, 66, 111, 179, 215
Jericho, 192
Jerusalem, 97, 103, 123n18, 182
Jesse, 194
Jesus, 16, 43, 116–17, 134–35, 134n72, 151n41, 153, 153nn49–50, 175, 190n38, 212–14, 215
Jezreel/Esdraelon Valley, 52
Joab, 144
Job, 165–66, 171–72
Johnson, Dru, 113
Jonathan, 30
Jordan-Rift Valley, 52
Jorgenson, Cameron H. J., 210
Joseph, 168–69, 212
Joshua, 30, 61, 62, 184
Josiah, 100, 148
Jubilee years, 58, 67, 142, 148–49
Judah, 14–15, 39, 43, 50, 68, 88, 97, 124, 193, 194
justice, 142–43, 147–49

kabod theology, 115, 123
Kilner, John F., 133
King's Highway, 52
kingship
  administration of justice, 142–43, 147–49
  as adoptive sons of patron deities, 140
  as caring for the needy, 212n47
  characteristics of, 139–44
  democratization of, 151–53
  divine representation, 144–47, 151n43, 181
  function of, 131n62
  human, 151n41
  images of, xv, 123–25, 129, 139–40
  and *imago Dei*, 145–46
  military leadership, 143–44, 150–51, 193
  negative views of, 146–47
  positive views of, 146–47
  priestly role of, 130n56, 143, 149–50
  sacred, 123n22, 139, 139n7
  summary, 223–24
  Yhwh's, 145, 151–52, 151n42
  See also monarchy
kinship
  covenants, 29–30, 33
  fictive, 33, 145–46
  between God and humanity, 130, 132n66
  go'el (kinsman-redeemer), 8–9, 15–16
  between Israel and God, 12
  marriage and, 5–6
  social structures, 4–5
kipper (atonement), 108
Klawans, Jonathan, 108n64, 110
Kugler, Christopher, 134n72
Kuntillet 'Ajrud, 97, 103

Laban, 30
land
  as a covenant gift, xv, 31–32, 59
  cultivation and rest, 55–56
  economy and, 52–53
  fertility of, 53, 104
  geography and topography of Israel, 50–52
  as inheritance, 8–9, 53–54, 57, 61–62
  Israel's relationship to, 49–50
  monarchy and influence on, 54–55
  possession of Promised Land, 62–64
  promised by God, 61–62, 104
  purging of, 64–67
  royal land grants, 28
  social welfare and, 56–59
  spiritualizing of, 66, 67–68
  stewardship of, 68, 130n55, 213
  summary, 221

Subject Index

symbiotic relationships with, 50, 56–57, 59, 61
theology of, 59–60, 63, 66–68
universalizing of, 66–67, 67n53
water and, 50
Yhwh as true owner of, 67
Lauinger, J., 26
law(s)
  addressing cultural norms, 175, 175n65
  casuistic, 160–61
  ceremonial, 176
  civil, 176
  codes, xv, 141, 148, 159, 159nn6–7, 174
  food purity, 84–85, 85n62, 107–8, 214
  genital pollution, 78
  gleaning, 57, 63, 211
  God as author of Israelite, 148
  inheritance, 54, 63, 160
  Jubilee years, 58, 67, 142, 148–49
  legal material, 159–62
  moral, 176
  moral pollution, 79–81
  physical pollution, 76–79
  sabbatical year, 57–58
  summary, 224
  theology of Israelite, 172–75
  theology of modern, 175–76
  tithing, 63
  wisdom and, 157, 168n40, 171n46, 174, 176
leaders
  deification of, 146n33
  village elders, 138
  See also kingship; monarchy
LeFebvre, Michael, 174
legal material, 159–62
legal transactions, 159
lethal wisdom, 168
Levenson, Jon, 36, 37, 105–6, 114n78
Levi, 40
Leviathan, 188
Levine, Amy-Jill, xviii, 149n40
Levinson, Bernard, 139, 159, 223
levirate marriage, 8–9, 17–18, 17n37, 19n44, 187
Levites, 66n49, 99n20, 111–13, 114n78, 196
Lewis, C. S., 210
Lind, Millard C., 179n2
living arrangements, xiv
living rooms, 10
Longman, Tremper, III, 171n46
Lot, 208
Lynch, Matthew, 188, 188n33

MacDonald, Nathan, 210
Maimonides, 85n62
Malachi, 33
mamlakah (kingdom), 5
Marduk, 142, 188
marriage
  as a contract, 6
  covenant, 29–30, 45n57
  God's relationship to Israel as, 14–15
  kinship and, 5–6
  levirate, 8–9, 17–18, 17n37, 19n44, 187
  Ruth's proposal to Boaz, xiii
Mary, 153n49, 213
material culture
  defined, xvi
  households, 2–4
maternal mortality rates, 14, 101
matriarchs
  household roles, 6, 205–6, 210
  leadership roles, 138
matteh (tribe), 5
Matthews, Victor, 16, 53
McDowell, Catherine, 130, 131n62
meals, role of, xviii, 206
mediation, 111–13, 112n73
Melchizedek, 130n56, 149
men
  authority of, 138
  bet 'ab (father's household), 4–5
  domestic labor activities, 204
  genital pollution, 78, 78n36
  inheritance transmission, 9
  lifespan, 101
  made in God's image, 126–28, 126n39
  marriage contracts, 6
  patriarch's household roles, 6, 8–9, 138
  protection role, 8–9
Mendenhall, George, 37n34
menstrual impurities, 78
Meroz, 192
Mesha Stele, 195n53
Mesopotamia, 52, 73–74, 82n49, 124, 139, 180–81, 183
messianism, 152–53
methodology
  cultural contexts, xv–xvii
  suggestions for further study, 226–27
  theology, xvii–xix
Meyers, Carol, xvi, 204–5
Middleton, J. Richard, 128, 131n62, 133
Midianites, 184, 193
military leadership, 143–44, 150–51, 193
Miller, Patrick, 98

minḥah (offering), 98–99
Mīšarum (acts of justice and equity), 142, 149
Mishnah, 211
mishpaḥah (clan), 5
Mizpah, 97
Moab, 52
Moabites, 195n53
model shrines, 102
monarchy
    ancient concepts of, 137–38
    characteristics of, 139–44
    extractions from subjects, 55
    influence of on land, 54–55
    representation of divine kingship, 123–25, 123n22
    traditional, 137
    See also kingship
monolatry, 114
Monson, John, xviii
"monumental vs. the mundane" issue, xvi–xvii
moral law, 176
moral pollution, 79–81
mortality rates, 14, 101, 101n35
Moses, 38, 43, 62, 111, 112, 173, 173n55, 175, 175n65, 189, 191
mouth-washing/mouth-opening rituals, 121–22
Mowinckel, Sigmund, 153
Muršili II, 24–26, 165

Nabal, 206
Naboth, 62
Nam, Roger, 140–41n17
name theology, 115
Naomi, 17, 63, 138
Nathan, 149
native tributary mode, 55, 140n17
Negev of Judah, 52
Neo-Assyrian Empire, 26, 125, 140–41n17, 184n20
Neo-Babylonian Period, xx
Neolithic, xx
new covenant, 43, 116
New Testament, xviii, 16, 43, 60, 90, 134–35, 153, 215
Niditch, Susan, 190
Nihan, Christopher, 76, 79
Nimrud Prism, 123
Noah, 19, 32, 34, 44, 133
Noahic covenant, 44
Nob, 97

O'Dowd, Ryan, 170
offerings, 98–99, 107–11

ʻolah (burnt offering), 98–99
Old Babylonian (Amorite) Dynasty, 141
omens, 181
ontological model of *imago Dei*, 129, 131–32, 133–34, 134n73
oracles, 181–82
Osiris, 124

parity treaties, 25–26
Passover, 18–19, 211
patriarchs
    hospitality roles, 207
    household roles, 6
    leadership roles, 138
    protection roles, 8–9, 208n34
peace
    offerings, 109
    summary, 225
    warfare and, xv, 186–89, 187n28
Peaceable Kingdom, The (Hicks), 197
Perdue, Leo G., 11, 19
Perez, 19
Persian Period, xx, 205n25
Pharaoh, 123–24, 139, 183, 189, 212
philosophical wisdom, 164–66, 170–72
Phinehas, 32
Philistia, 97
Philistines, 193
physical pollution, 76–79
pilgrimages, 19
pillar houses, 3
Pissarro, Lucien, 211
Pitre, Brant, 211
Plague Prayers of Muršili II, 165
politics, xv
pollution
    moral, 79–81
    physical/ritual, 76–79
practical wisdom, 163–64, 170–72
preparation, food, 7–8, 9–10, 10n13, 210
priesthood, 99–100, 111–13, 112n73, 114n78, 129–30, 130n56, 143, 149–50
primogeniture, 54
production, household, 7–8, 9, 52, 204n20
Promised Land, 49, 59, 60, 61–64, 66, 104
prophets
    on accumulation of food, 212
    holiness of, 87–88
    on importance of repentance, 111
    on warfare, 195–97
    warnings of, 194
protection, household, 8–9, 208n34
Provan, Iain, 115

Ptolemy II, 174
purity
  AI standards of, 71
  cultural contexts of, 72
  dual nature of, 72–73, 72n4
  food, 84–85, 85n62, 107–8
  graded, 85–86
  vs. impurity, 83–84
  outside the sanctuary, 76
  performance of service rituals and, 74–76
  pre-battle purification rituals, 182, 191
  receiving purification, 108–9
  the sanctuary and, 73–74
  summary, 221–22
  See also holiness; impurity

Rahab, 192
Ramses II, 25
Rathje, William L., 204n20
Re, 123, 139
redemption
  Bible as a redemptive movement hermeneutic, 175
  Israel's place in story of, xix
  as a socioeconomic institution, 59
  universal scope of, 39–41, 113
Rehoboam, 169n42
relational model of *imago Dei*, 131–32, 133–34, 145
relationships, between parents and children, 18n40
religious rituals
  figurines, 103–4
  graded holiness and, 85–86
  in households, 8, 11, 18–19, 101–4
  the "how" of, 107–11
  official vs. unofficial, 93–94
  pre-battle purification and consecration, 182, 191
  priests, 99–100
  public, state, 94–101
  sacrifices and offerings, 98–99, 107–11
  service rituals to deities, 74–76, 94–95, 121–22
  the "when" of, 113–14
  the "where" of, 105–7
  the "who" of, 111–13
repentance, 109–11
reproduction, 8, 9, 101, 204n20
retribution, 165–66
revelation, xvii, 39–41
Richter, Sandra, 36n31, 68
ritual pollution, 76–79

river imagery, 167, 167n34, 175
Rogerson, John, 16–17
Roman Period, xx
Routledge, Robin, 34n27, 110
royal decrees, 159
royal grant covenants, 31–32
royal land grants, 28
Ruth, 17, 57, 63, 138
Ruth Gleaning (Pissarro), 211

Sabanal, Annelle, 146n33
sabbatical years, 56, 57–58, 67
sacrifices
  animals for, 203
  in divination practices, 181
  laws about, 175
  under the new covenant, 116
  as opposite of eating, 109n65
  as an outlet for violence, 191n44
  as part of feasting, 10, 10n16
  in public rituals, 98–99
  theology of, 107–11
Sailhamer, John H., xvii
salvation
  communal focus, xiv
  judgment and, 190–91
  law not intended as means of, 173
  order of, 110
Samaria, 50, 103, 123
Samson, 193
Samuel, 143–44, 146, 150, 212
sanctuaries
  king's service to, 149–50
  locations in Hebrew Bible, 97
  performance of service rituals in, 74–76
  purity and, 73–74
  purity outside of, 76
  as the "where" of worship, 105–7
Sargonic Period, 183
Sargon II, 123
Saul, 144, 147, 147nn36–37
Schachter, Lifsa, 107
Schwally, Friedrich, 191n43
Second Temple literature, 89
secular, vs. spiritual, 83n57
secular covenants, 29–30, 33
Sekhmet, 120n4
Seleucid Empire, 89
service rituals, 74–76, 94–95, 121–22
Seth, 131
settlements, xvi
Shalmaneser III, 124

shalom (peace), 40, 186–89, 186n27, 192–93, 195–97, 225
Shamash, 141, 160
Shavuot, 100, 201
shebet (tribe), 5
Shechem, 30
Shephelah, 50, 52
Shiloh, 97
short-term fallowing, 56
shrines, 96–97, 96n12, 102, 120n1
Shunammite woman, 206
Sihon, 190
sin
 defeat of, 187
 the image and, 132–34
 offerings, 99, 108, 109
Sinai/Horeb, 214
Sinai/Horeb covenant, 30–31, 36, 41, 44n51, 45, 105, 116, 145, 175
Sisera, 192
Sklar, Jay, 108
social structures, 4–5
social welfare, land and, 56–59
Sodom, 208
Solomon, 30, 45, 148, 149, 168–69, 169n42, 212
Solomon's temple, 96, 106, 143
Sommer, Benjamin, xviii
Song of Deborah, 192
Song of the Sea, 144–45
Soulen, R. Kendall, xviii–xix
Southern Levant, xvi, 50–52
spiritual, vs. secular, 83n57
spiritual adultery, 14
Stark, J. David, 67n53
statutes, 80
stewardship, 68, 130n55, 213
subsistence economy, 7, 8, 10, 52, 54, 140, 204, 221
succession narratives, xviii
suffering, 164–66, 171–72
supersessionism, xviii–xix
Sutter's Mill, 81–82
suzerain treaties, 24–26, 38
Symmetric Syrian Temple Type, 95
systematic theology, xvii

tabernacles, 105–7
Tamar, xviii
Tel Halif, 102
Tell Fekheriye, 124–25
tells, xvi
temple complexes, 95–96, 95n7, 97

temples, 73–74, 95–96, 97, 105–6, 115–17, 120n1, 149
temptation, 63–64
Ten Commandments, 38, 114, 114n80
teraphim (household gods), 121
terminology, xix–xx
tetragrammaton, xix
theodicy, 164–65
theology
 of communal solidarity, 16–20
 defined, xvii
 of food and eating, 209–11
 of food economics, 211–13
 of holiness, 82–85
 of hospitality of God, 213–15
 of household roles and metaphors, 12–16
 of the "how" of worship, 107–11
 of image, 126–28
 of *imago Dei*, 128–32, 145–46
 influence of household on, 11–12
 of Israelite law, 172–75
 kabod, 115, 123
 kingship, 144–53
 of kinship/secular covenants, 33
 of land, 59–60, 63, 66–68
 of modern law and wisdom, 175–76
 name, 115
 practitioners of, xvii–xviii
 of *shalom*, 186–89
 of the "when" of worship, 113–14
 of the "where" of worship, 105–7
 of the "to whom" of worship, 114–15
 of the "who" of worship, 111–13
 of wisdom, 167–72
 Zion, 66–67
theriomorphic figurines, 120, 120n4
Thummim, 181–82
tithing, 63
Torrance, T. F., 40
trade routes, 52
Trans-Jordan, 52
transmission, household, 8, 204n20
treaties and loyalty oaths
 Assyrian treaty-oaths, 26–28, 36
 form of in Deuteronomy, 29
 Hittite, 24–26
 parity, 25–26
 ratification of in house of gods, 180–81
 similarities to covenants, 28–29
 suzerain, 24–26, 38
 Vassal Treaties of Esarhaddon (VTE), 27–28
Trible, Phyllis, 128
tribute, defined, 140–41n17

Trinity, communal relationship of, 130
tsara'at (major pollution), 77
tselem (image), 127, 127n43

Uriah, 149, 182, 189
Urim, 181–82

van der Toorn, Karel, 72
vassals, 24, 27–28
Vassal Treaties of Esarhaddon (VTE), 27–28
village leadership, 138
violence
  of divine warfare, 187–89, 188n33
  misusing Scripture to perpetuate, 179
  sacrifice as an outlet for, 191n44
von Rad, Gerhard, 37n36, 146, 163, 168, 190n40

Walton, J. Harvey, 174
Walton, John H., 46, 87, 164, 166, 174
warfare
  as battle between deities, 183
  divine, 180–86, 187–97
  divine warrior participation, 182–84
  God fighting against Israel, 193–95
  God fighting for Israel, 189–91
  God fighting with Israel, 191–93
  herem (destruction), 184–85, 191, 195
  holy war, 190n40, 191n43
  natural phenomena as divine intervention, 183–84
  post-battle activities, 184–85
  pre-battle activities, 181–82
  royal leadership, xv, 143–44, 150–51, 193
  shalom and, xv, 186–89, 187n28, 192–93, 195–97
  summary, 225
  violence of divine, 187–89, 188n33
Webb, William, 175
well-being offerings, 109, 109n66
Wellhausen, Julius, 173
Wells, Bruce, 160
Wenham, Gordon, 107
Westbrook, Raymond, 160–62
Wilk, Richard R., 204n20
Willett, Elizabeth, 101
Wilson, Gerald, 151n43
Wilson, Jan, 82n49
wisdom
  anti-wisdom, 172
  defining, 167–68, 167n36, 168–70
  divine, of kings, xv, 141–42
  as a genre, 167

godly, 172
law and, 157, 168n40, 171n46, 174, 176
lethal, 168
literature, 88–89, 162–66
philosophical, 164–66, 170–72
practical, 163–64, 170–72
summary, 224
theology of, 167–72
Yhwh as source of, 170
women
  authority of, 138
  bet 'em (mother's household), 4–5
  domestic labor activities, 9–10, 204–6
  female anthropomorphic figurines, 103–4
  genital pollution, 78–79
  identification of with feminine side of God, 210
  lifespan, 14, 101
  made in God's image, 126–28, 126n39
  marriage contracts, 5–6
  maternal mortality rates, 14, 101
  matriarch's household roles, 6, 138, 205–6, 210
  reproductive role, 9, 101
  warriors, 192n47
Woodley, Randy, 186n27
worship
  as appeasement, 165–66
  aspects of, 105–15
  in community, xiv
  of God, xv
  God-focused vs. human focuses models of, 114n79
  in Hebrew Bible, 18–19
  the "how" of, 107–11
  non-dualistic sense of, 114
  repentance as prerequisite for, 111
  as service ritual, 94–95
  summary, 222–23
  the "when" of, 113–14
  the "where" of, 105–7
  the "to whom" of, 114–15
  the "who" of, 111–13
  without the temple, 115–17
Wright, Christopher, 13, 61, 67, 85, 112

Yhwh
  Asherah and, 103–4, 103n45
  Creator-King, 145
  divine image of, 122–23
  glory of, 123
  humanity created as image of, 123
  Israelite law from, 172–75

as Israel's divine warrior, 188–93
kingship, 145, 151–52, 151n42
as source of wisdom, 170
temples to, 123
as true owner of land, 67
use of oracles to discern will of, 181–82
use of term, xix
worship of as an image forbidden, 115, 122
worship of deities other than, 53, 103, 114–15
See also God

zebah (offering), 98–99
Zedekiah, 30
Zelophehad, 175n65
Zerubbabel, 153
ziggurats, 73–74
Zion theology, 66–67
zoomorphic figurines, 103, 120, 123